The Importance of Elgar

Elgar in Gloucester, 1922. Photograph by Richard Hall.

The Importance of Elgar

An Anthology

Compiled by
Andrew Dalton, Kevin Mitchell, David Morris & Andrew Neill

Edited by David Morris and Andrew Neill

THE BOYDELL PRESS

First published 2026
The Boydell Press, Woodbridge

ISBN 978-1-83765-349-2 hardback
ISBN 978-1-83765-352-2 paperback

The Boydell Press is an imprint of Boydell & Brewer Ltd
and of Boydell & Brewer Inc.
website: www.boydellandbrewer.com

Our Authorised Representative for product safety in the EU is
Easy Access System Europe - Mustamäe tee 50, 10621 Tallinn, Estonia,
gpsr.requests@easproject.com

A CIP catalogue record for this book is available
from the British Library

In Memoriam

Diana McVeagh
(1926–2025)

Sir Andrew Davis, CBE
(1943–2024)

Dr Jerrold Northrop Moore
(1934–2024)

Published in celebration of the 75th anniversary
of the formation of The Elgar Society
29 January 1951

Contents

Illustrations

With the exception of that from The Illustrated London News, *all the photographs included in this volume have been generously provided by Arthur Reynolds from his unique collection. One of the most photographed composers of his time, Elgar was both a good self-publicist and, as these photographs show, something of a dandy. This selection of images covers aspects of his life from a young man to a time when he could display the awards his musical career had brought him.*

Foreword

Sir Mark Elder, CH, CBE
President of The Elgar Society

The seventy-fifth birthday of the society dedicated to the memory of Edward Elgar is certainly something to celebrate. The number and sheer variety of contributors to this new book is testament to the power that his music still holds. But he will always need champions and championing. Some of his most ambitious pieces demand repeated listening – both for performers and audience. The two symphonies or the violin concerto, for example, will not immediately reveal all their secrets.

As I have rehearsed and performed these wonderful scores, I have so often been struck by the tremendously detailed instructions Elgar gives us. He was so concerned to make his vision clear, so apprehensive we would not easily 'get' him. But 'get' him we must; he has so much to say to us.

His emotional range is so wide and deep. At one end, there is the charm and lightness of the *Wand of Youth* music, at the other, the turbulent joy and dark shadows of each movement of the Second Symphony. Sometimes, the public face – the patina of 'hope and glory' – gets in the way. But it is in the private worlds that his true essence is to be found. The search for that quality has been at the heart of my own relationship with Elgar over these last twenty-five years in Manchester with the Hallé. To spend time on these works is so rewarding – finding more drama and lyricism in the three main oratorios and *The Music Makers* or digging down into the subtleties and intense longing of the Violin Concerto. What a journey it has been!

With this extraordinary collection of essays, I hope that more and more people will realise the enormous place Elgar can have in our lives. Let us hope that, translated into many other languages, it will excite the curiosity and passion of countless other people. Gradually, perhaps, more performances will be given all over the world. That many of these writers are from countries other than Britain is surely a very good sign; it is only through live performance that we can hope to extend Elgar's reputation and success.

I remember vividly conducting in Atlanta, Georgia, the first ever performance there of the Second Symphony. The audience responded very warmly to making that journey with us. In the intermission of the second concert, the orchestra invited me downstairs to share a surprise. They had organised a huge cake to be made and everyone had a slice. On the top, there was a lovely message from the composer: 'Thank you all so very much! Best wishes EDWARD ELGAR'. I felt we had made real headway that night.

Or the time in the Philharmonie in Berlin, with the marvellous Deutsches Symphonie-Orchester, when we also played the Second Symphony for the first time for that orchestra. The public was very concentrated, I remember, and gave us a tremendous ovation. Of course, many of my colleagues have given terrific performances in a great many countries, but there are still several works of Elgar that remain unknown...

This important anthology deserves to be read by anyone and everyone who is a music lover in the hope that we can all share our passion and belief in THE IMPORTANCE OF ELGAR.

Preface

Stuart Freed
Chairman of The Elgar Society

As we approach the middle years of the twenty-first century, it hardly seems credible that for the twenty years following Elgar's death his reputation as a great composer declined to such an extent that his music was barely considered internationally and apart from a few notable exceptions (the Cello Concerto, *Pomp and Circumstance* March No.1 and *The Dream of Gerontius*), fared little better in the land of his birth.

It was into this climate of relative neglect and at the suggestion of Sir Adrian Boult, that the Elgar Society was founded in 1951, emerging, as it did, from the Elgar Festival held in Malvern in 1950. A committee was formed initially under the chairmanship of John Tompkins, who was succeeded by A.T. (Bertie) Shaw, who went on to serve as Chairman into the mid 1970s. In many ways Albert Thompson Shaw was the guiding light during the Society's formative years and his influence can be felt into the present day. He was a great supporter of music in and around Worcester, having taught art and music at the Royal Grammar School, served as organist of St Leonard's, Newland and sung in the Three Choirs Festival Chorus. In addition, he wrote extensively about music, editing the Three Choirs Festival programme book and writing programme notes for other local music groups. It is estimated that he wrote in excess of 5000 articles for the Berrow's Newspaper Group, for which he acted as music critic for over fifty years. Shaw set the pattern for the Society, which was developed and built upon by his successors as Chairman. Consequently, throughout its existence the Society has maintained its focus upon bringing the life, times and, above all, the music of Edward Elgar to the public, through its diverse range of activities that include support for performers, recordings and, of course, the publications that it has produced, to which this volume can be added.

A glance at the list of contributors to this book will indicate the esteem in which the music of Elgar and the Society which bears his name is held.

Articles by some of the finest contemporary performers, composers, academics and musicologists, both within the UK and from overseas, is a testament to the progress that has been made by the Society and others over the last seventy-five years in raising the profile of Sir Edward Elgar and his music. Each contributor has, either willingly or accidentally, addressed what Elgar means to them and the basis for their admiration. For some it is the sheer beauty of his music and the genius that he brought to its composition. For others it is the endless fascination with a man whose often mercurial character led him to enjoy the enduring friendship of loyal supporters, whilst maintaining the ability to alienate others whom he believed, rightly or wrongly, to have offended him in some way.

The Importance of Elgar is a dual celebration. On the one hand it is a salute to the life and works of arguably England's finest composer, whose music encompasses the concert hall, the stage, chamber music, the world of choral music and lighter fare. However, it is also a celebration of the continued existence of a Society whose sole purpose is to perpetuate the reputation of Elgar and to continue to promote an interest in his life and an appreciation of his music. We, the readers of this book, owe a debt of gratitude to all of those who have contributed articles, to those who have worked tirelessly to ensure that the project has been brought to a successful conclusion, but above all to all of the Society's volunteers, who over seventy-five years have continued to ensure that it thrives.

Acknowledgements

Naturally the compilers of this volume thank all those who contributed to this collection of essays, their reward being no more than knowing that their words will be respected and translated to a wider world as sympathetically as possible. Inevitably, when considering the names of those who have contributed some rather obvious ones are absent. Inevitably, not all those approached felt able to write and others, who promised to do so found that time proved to be an unrelenting enemy. Of those who wrote, many are extremely busy musicians and others have achieved eminence in their respective fields. Nevertheless, they found the time to complete an essay at our request. Without them this book would not exist.

Many individuals afforded assistance in arranging introductions to potential authors and by giving wider advice. We wish to thank Relf Clark, John Francis, Elgar's great-nephew Paul Grafton, Marie Kedroff of IMG Artists, Andrew Keener, Tia Ling of Askonas Holt, Nigel Simeone, Richard Strivens, Christopher Wentworth-Stanley, the Development and Concerts Teams at the London Philharmonic Orchestra and their Development Director Laura Willis. Arthur Reynolds was, as usual, generous in allowing photographs from his collection to be used and David Lemon in Vancouver made many helpful suggestions. Richard Smith kindly agreed to undertake the oncrous work of producing an index. The production of a book such as this relies on the goodwill and advice of many individuals, notably Stuart Freed, the Chairman of The Elgar Society and the other members of the committee established to consider ways of celebrating the Society's semisesquicentennial anniversary: Ruth Hellen, Jonathan Hope, Martyn Marsh, David Morris, Geoff Scargill, Peter Smith, Michael Trott and Chris Warsaw, who joined us electronically from her home in Arizona. Furthermore, both editors are grateful to their friends and families (notably Victoria Neill) for their patience whilst this book was coaxed into existence.

Dr Michael Middeke, the Editorial Director, Modern History and Music of Boydell & Brewer responded immediately to the idea of this book and working with him, Nick Bingham, Head of Production and Crispin Peet, Editorial Assistant, has been a pleasure. We are most grateful to them for their advice, guidance and wider assistance.

The Elgar Society's *Journal* is produced thrice yearly by an editorial team, of which we are both members, the others being Andrew Dalton and Kevin Mitchell. Without their advice and support production of this book would not have been possible.

David Morris and Andrew Neill

Introduction

This book is dedicated to the memory of the conductor Sir Andrew Davis and Elgar's biographers Diana McVeagh and Dr Jerrold Northrop Moore. Although Sir Andrew and Dr Moore indicated a willingness to do so, neither was able to contribute an essay for this book before their deaths in 2024. However, through their recordings, broadcasts and writing their contribution to our understanding and appreciation of Elgar's music places us all in their debt. Diana McVeagh died as this book commenced the production process, and it is entirely appropriate that she should share this dedication.

Is Elgar, or rather is Elgar's music, important? That he was important to many is obvious from the numerous books and pamphlets devoted to his life and art published during his lifetime and, of course, since his death. All the same the question requires an answer. From the sole evidence of performances of his music around the world the answer is possibly at best 'yes, but for only one or two works' or 'not really' and at worst 'no'. Nevertheless, more and more performances of Elgar's music are now taking place in Germany, throwing into relief the response of some of the Viennese critics on first hearing Elgar's music, as Dr Wilhem Sinkovich shows in his invaluable commentary. Furthermore, the response to the request to contribute essays under the title 'The Importance of Elgar' confirms that his music remains important to those who wrote for this book: the musicians, composers, and those listeners who are Elgar's audience. However, as Benjamin Britten said: 'Music does not exist in a vacuum, it does not exist until it is performed'.[1] So, if this book encourages performances of Elgar's music, it has itself become important.

To commemorate the 90th anniversary of Elgar's death in 2024, the editors of the Elgar Society's *Journal* wrote to a wide range of eminent musicians and commentators asking them if they would consider writing an

[1] From a speech by Benjamin Britten, given in the Aspen Amphitheatre, Aspen, Colorado on 31 July 1964. Benjamin Britten, *On Receiving the First Aspen Award* (London: Faber and Faber, 1978), 13.

1. 'The Makers of British Music: Famous Living British Composers of the Old School and the New'. After Samuel Begg (1854–1919): relief halftone, published in *The Illustrated London News* 24 October 1908. (Reproduced by kind permission of The National Portrait Gallery, reference: D4228).

Sir Granville Bantock, Mr Josef Holbrooke, Mr Coleridge Taylor, Mr Percy Pitt, Mr Cyril Scott, Mr Hamilton Harty, Sir George Clement Martin, Miss Ethel Smyth, Dr Ebenezer Prout, Mr Henry Walford Davies, Dr William Hayman Cummings, Mr Edward German, Sir Walter Parratt, Sir Charles Villiers Stanford, Sir Edward Elgar, Dr Frederic Hymen Cowen, Sir Alexander Campbell Mackenzie, Sir Hubert Hastings Parry, Sir Frederick Bridge.

essay under the general title 'The Importance of Elgar'. It was hoped that the response would be sufficient to fill the pages of the *Journal* during 2024. It is clear from this collection that the response was exceptional and would have overwhelmed the limited space available in the three editions of the *Journal* published annually. Presenting these essays in the form of a book is a suitable and permanent alternative, with the prospect of a wider readership too, as well as a means of celebrating the Society's 75th anniversary in 2026.

If we begin with the music Elgar the man soon emerges, and the man and the music become indivisible. Much the same, of course, can be said about most great artists, and the more we understand them, the more we understand their art. Some artists, such as Brunelleschi, Leonardo, Shakespeare, Picasso, Beethoven and Wagner, changed their world. Elgar did not change anything musically, but he changed much else as his friend and supporter Frank Schuster made clear. Schuster died in 1927 and bequeathed £7,000 to Elgar: 'because he had saved England from the reproach of having produced no composer "worthy to rank with the great masters"'.[2]

Following an earlier bereavement, Schuster attended a performance of Elgar's First Symphony during World War I, after which he wrote to the composer:

> As long as I have *it* I can bear my losses, although I thought when I went into the hall today that I *couldn't*. I felt then as I never have but as you, I fear, sometimes do – that life was not worth the living & you would not be sorry to lose it. Then came your symphony – and in a moment I knew I was wrong. In it is *all love* – and love makes life possible. I wonder if you realise when you feel despondent & embittered what your music is to me – and therefore to countless others? You may not care to be of use to those who live after you – but surely it must be *something* to you to know you are giving happiness & hope & consolation to your fellow creatures? Bless you for it anyway.[3]

Elgar, born in 1857, lived through the development of the 'Second Viennese School' led by Arnold Schoenberg and his disciples, Berg and Webern, but he also grew up as the chromatic and at times tonally challenging music of Wagner permeated many aspects of European music-making. Much has been written about the influence of Wagner on Elgar's music but, as an essentially melodic composer who never had a composition lesson in his life, it is hardly surprising that he showed little interest in 'twelve-note composition', although by emphasising this we are in danger of ignoring what

2 Michael Kennedy, *Portrait of Elgar* 3rd edn. (Oxford: Clarendon Paperbacks, 1993), 307.

3 Ibid., 272.

might be described as his modernism. Robert Saxton puts this into context and stresses how brilliant Elgar was at keeping his various audiences satisfied through, say, the complexities of his symphonies and the subtle artlessness of *Salut d'Amour*.

It is easy to compartmentalise Elgar's life, particularly when considering the relatively barren years after his wife Alice's death in 1920. Then he settled into a comfortable old age: conducting, broadcasting and recording. Hints of a more radical musical direction that he might have taken are shown in his Symphonic Study *Falstaff* of 1913, and the first movement of his Piano Quintet composed as World War 1 came to its end. Even earlier, two Part-Songs from his Op.52 set composed in 1907: *There is Sweet Music* and *Owls (an Epitaph)* showed a surprising originality which could have led anywhere. John Bridcut, in his essay *Elgar the Modernist,* asks 'what does he [Elgar] signify in the Second Symphony when the percussion's violent hammering tries to destroy the music for a while? (This was five years earlier than Carl Nielsen's destruction by timpani in his Fourth Symphony)'. The critic, Paul Driver, in a 2016 review, goes some way to answering this question when he compared Stravinsky's *The Rite of Spring* and Elgar's Symphony and considered what they had in common: 'notably a rhythmic power and effectiveness hardly to be matched. ... The drumming-up [in the Symphony] of what now seems prophetic terror ... because it still has a shock-value arguably transcending *The Rite of Spring*'s, for it intimates an all too actual, rather than anthropological horror'. Driver ended his piece reflecting on the kinship of the two works but concluded that 'it is the Elgar that is the more modern'.[4] This claim will astonish many, notably those who consider Stravinsky one of the greatest, seminal and original of 20th-century composers and who may have given Elgar's music little thought, or at best allowed themselves to subscribe to pre-conceived opinions about his music. However, a careful listen to the Symphony's *presto* which follows the self-absorbed crisis at the climax of the *larghetto* may well encourage a re-consideration of a work that preceded Stravinsky's *Rite* by exactly two years.

At the head of this Introduction an illustration from *The Illustrated London News* is reproduced. At the centre of a group of British composers sits Edward Elgar, his head tilted slightly to his right. It is an assured pose, that of a man at the peak of his musical powers and confident of his place in his country's musical life. The date is 24 October 1908 and in under two months his First Symphony will have received its premiere in Manchester, the first symphony by an Englishman to travel around the world. Elgar is

4 *The Sunday Times*, 1 June 2016.

surrounded by his peers, most of whom he has eclipsed as a composer and many whose modest reputations will die with them, and in its way, this picture is a commentary on British music generally at a critical point in its musical development. For the next twenty years it is the individuality of his style which will dominate British music: its grandiloquence and contrasting intimacy, his melodic skill and brilliant and original orchestration. Of those illustrated above, except for Elgar, only Stanford and Parry and possibly Ethel Smyth and Samuel Coleridge-Taylor have a chance of their music being performed, and then only through a few of their better-known compositions.

Nevertheless, some notable names are missing; those of a younger and significant generation. Vaughan Williams had yet to make a substantial mark on Britain's cultural life: his *Tallis Fantasia* and *Sea Symphony* were two years away. Walton was only six years old and Tippett three. Britten would be born five years later. However, 1908 was the year Gustav Holst competed his opera *Savitri*, a miniature masterpiece which, sadly, would take years to be recognised as such.

In 1950 one of Britain's greatest and most versatile conductors, Sir Adrian Boult, sowed the seeds that led to the formation of The Elgar Society the following year. Boult became the fledgling Society's first President, to be succeeded by Sir Yehudi (later Lord) Menuhin following Boult's death in 1983. Their links to Elgar proved invaluable but not essential for the Society to grow and fulfil its aims. Boult was, of course, a leading promoter of Elgar's music and that of many of his contemporaries. Seventy-five years later this Society faces many challenges that could not have been anticipated in 1951, not least the increasing pressure on funding for 'classical' music and the ability of any person to seek musical gratification at the touch of their telephone. No doubt even this technological marvel will seem out of date one day.

Except for the general title 'The Importance of Elgar' given to each essayist, we laid down no prescription, but a few patterns emerged as we received their essays, and we have divided them loosely into the sections that follow. There are writers who feel his music is not generally important but, nevertheless, it is important to them, while the American conductor Leonard Slatkin bemoans the paucity of performances of Elgar's music on the concert platforms of his country. Others write about the joy of discovery as they explored his music. Every writer has something to say and what, in most cases, Elgar's music means to them. Two significant interpreters of his music make important but differing points. Martyn Brabbins writes: 'Elgar's music teaches me so much about life, and rather mundanely perhaps, about conducting.' And Edward Gardner emphasises Elgar's contemporary international significance: 'His love of Italy and his position as a pan-European composer is much more interesting for me than as an emblem of a certain period of British history.'

In some ways this book signifies a break with the past generation of Elgar biographers. Apart from McVeagh, whose pioneering biography from 1955[5] had a great influence on her successors such as Michael Kennedy and Jerrold Northrop Moore, some of the essays within reflect new thought from a younger generation that came to Elgar's music after these authors published their books. Of course, Miss McVeagh remained as clear and to the point as always (as demonstrated by her essay), but happily there is nowadays some newer thinking applied to Elgar's music by a younger generation. If Elgar's music suddenly disappeared, most of those who contributed to this volume would be the poorer, and many would feel bereft. Frank Schuster, the son of German émigrés, understood instinctively the various emotional aspects of Elgar's music and for those who love Elgar's music like Schuster it occupies a special place in their hearts. He, like many others, would have found the reaction of Viennese critics and audience to Elgar's music, as described by Dr Sinkovich, very disappointing. It is almost as if they resent an outsider trespassing on their world. Those who perform or just listen to Elgar's music may well be justified in expressing their astonishment that such distinguished commentators could apparently not see beyond the notes; or is it they misunderstood the music of an emotional Englishman who '...had the faith to commit himself, to assert his convictions, to be fired by his aspirations, and to share his dreams'?[6]

In 1957 Bernard Herrmann, the American composer and conductor, concluded a centenary tribute by writing: 'For Elgar's music is, in the end, an affirmation of the miracle of life and never a negation of it. This accomplishment certainly places him with the very greatest of the masters of music.'[7] It is unlikely that any of those who contributed to this book would disagree with the German conductor Florian Csizmadia: 'I hope the time has come to see him as a composer of universal importance whose music has so much to offer people today and, I am convinced, in the future.'

Andrew Neill
London, 2025

5 Diana McVeagh, *Edward Elgar: His Life and Music* (London: J.M. Dent & Sons Ltd, 1955). In 1955 Dr Percy Young's invaluable *Elgar O. M.* was also published, by Collins.

6 Ibid., 216.

7 H.A. Chambers (Ed.), *Edward Elgar Centenary Sketches* (London: Novello and Company, 1957), 21.

1

Composers and the Importance of Elgar

2. Elgar aged eleven in 1868 from the George Evans Studio in Worcester.

~ James Macmillan

I first heard Elgar's *The Dream of Gerontius* when I was about sixteen years old. I was a schoolboy at a comprehensive secondary school in Ayrshire and it was one of the prescribed works in the music class. In Scotland all the state Catholic schools are controlled by the local council authorities just like the non-denominational schools, and when I was fourteen I had to change schools. There were issues about curriculum clashes at my local Catholic secondary – Music and German were in the same list so I couldn't study both, or something. So, my parents moved me to the local non-denominational school. And this being Scotland, that meant that it was culturally a very Protestant school.

In the 1970s kids didn't swap around like this and my move raised eyebrows. I became the only Catholic at the new school, and the local Catholic community regarded the decision as controversial. My parents even got a letter from the local bishop complaining about their decision and berating them for letting the side down.

Consequently, when it came to studying *The Dream of Gerontius* there was a low-level puzzlement and bewilderment as to what it was all about from others in the room, whereas for me it felt like an encounter with the soundtrack of my life up until that point. I had lived with the concept of Purgatory, and the preparatory cleansing of souls before going to God, since I was a little boy. I believed it was the most natural thing that would happen to most of us. I probably still do.

And when I had been an altar boy a few years earlier I had encountered the death of elders regularly. We had to serve the priest at every Requiem Mass and so I would very often be up close to grieving relatives, helping the clergy distribute Holy Communion to very distraught people, young and old. I don't think most children experience that kind of thing, especially nowadays – being up close to grief, sometimes on a weekly basis. There was also the Catholic practice of bringing the body into the church the night before the Requiem Mass where it would lie close to the Blessed Sacrament as a vigil before the soul's final journey. Sometimes I had to serve Mass on those mornings at 7:30am and would arrive early, before the priest, and had to turn on all the lights myself. For a little boy, being alone in a totally dark church with a dead body was terrifying. But it had to be done.

So, when I saw and heard Elgar's masterpiece for the first time it felt like a re-encounter with all these things set to music. Newman's poem and Elgar's powerful music took me again to those early memories which came flooding back. It is a work which revealed the purgatorial journey which has always been a reality for me but did so clothed in a unique and emotionally powerful beauty.

A few years before this I had fallen in love with the music of Richard Wagner. I was totally bewitched by it – taken over and prematurely enraptured, as so many others have experienced. When *The Dream* began to unfold for me I could pick up the resonances and echoes and recognised that Elgar had been through the same bewitchment before me. I could hear the Wagnerian influence, but this time it was with an English accent and a Catholic intent. I don't think I have ever recovered from the shock and delight of that first teenage encounter!

The musicologist, conductor and professor of music at Glasgow University, John Butt wrote: 'Elgar's Catholic upbringing tends to be underplayed in most writings on the composer, but it may nevertheless be one of the most significant sources of his compositional character'.[1] Since the composition of *The Dream of Gerontius* commentators have fallen over themselves in an attempt to paint Elgar's Catholic faith as weak or insignificant. Even his biographer Jerrold Northrop Moore wrote this: 'It is therefore perhaps inevitable that, when he produced *The Dream of Gerontius*, a setting of a poem by a Roman Catholic Cardinal which explores various tenets of the Catholic faith, people should jump to the conclusion that his Catholicism underlay his whole life. But his faith was never that strong'.[2]

This anxiety on the part of some has nevertheless been explained recently by the Princeton scholar Charles Edward McGuire: 'The popular negating of Elgar's Catholicism both at his death and today serves an obvious end: it makes Elgar's music safer, more palatable for a British audience. In essence, it creates an avatar for Elgar as the "essentially English composer" beyond the reach of any of the complicating factors of partisan religion'.[3]

1 John Butt, 'Roman Catholicism and being musically English: Elgar's Church and Organ Music', from *The Cambridge Companion to Elgar*, ed. Daniel M. Grimley and Julian Rushton (Cambridge: Cambridge University Press, 2004), 107.

2 Dr Moore's comments derive from a piece published on the Website of The Elgar Society.

3 Charles Edward McGuire, 'Measure of a Man: Catechizing Elgar's Catholic Avatars', from *Edward Elgar and His World*, ed. Byron Adams (Princeton, NJ: Princeton University Press, 2007), 7.

In a Radio 3 Essay on 'Elgar and Religion' the pianist Stephen Hough said:

> When he decided in 1899 to set Cardinal Newman's *The Dream of Gerontius* to music, he was taking an enormous risk. It was his first major commission, and his career was all set to take off. So to choose this deeply Catholic text in a country where 'Papists' were a suspicious, despised and even ridiculed minority was to court disaster. Yet he went ahead, with total disregard for any possible censure or disfavour. So it's hard to believe that the words had no religious meaning for him at the time, especially as he was aware that his faith was an impediment to his career.[4]

If it is true that *The Dream of Gerontius* is the composer's masterwork, and a work of extraordinary vision, then it was a vision burnished with courage, foolhardiness even, and gained singularly through a particularly defined religious tradition and sensibility. This was the kind of framework regarded as vital and necessary by T.S. Eliot when he outlined the conditions required for outstanding visionary art. When an artist is truly focused 'on the narrow way' he or she can channel their creativity and imagination with a direct and laser-like energy. When Elgar let loose this energy in this work, shaped, informed and profoundly inspired by the specific spiritual context in which he had been raised, in considering humanity's *raison d'être* on its journey from life, through death and into the afterlife, there was an extraordinary explosion in the composer's musical soul. Some cultural commentators maintain that religion nowadays could only hinder and diminish the artistic imagination. Conversely for Elgar though, religion was not a restriction in *The Dream*. It turned out to be an imaginative liberation.

Elgar's dogged determination to see this project through even amid his fears of the profound scepticism and potential hostility that such a work might attract is inspiring. It is a great lesson from musical history to be learned by any composer living today, and not just Catholic ones. One learns that sometimes those deep initial instincts, absorbed from one's own experiences and upbringing, learned at the feet of family elders and the wider communities who gave shape and direction in one's life, can be the right ones. And those subliminal memories, personal and communal can be encouraged to bubble up anew and take flight in fresh and unexpected ways in one's own work.

I think this is why, in surveying the history of art music since *The Dream of Gerontius*, there have been an extraordinary number of composers who,

4 BBC Radio 3, from *The Essay*, a 2007 broadcast by Sir Stephen Hough titled *Elgar and Religion*.

in their very different ways have been involved in a search for the sacred in their music. To the surprise of many secular observers and musicologists, there have been a large number of composers in the last 100 years or so who have been very religious or have allowed spiritual instincts and tendencies free range to flourish in their music. Stravinsky was as conservative in his theology as he was revolutionary in his music making. He set the psalms, he set the Mass, he was a believer. Schoenberg, that other great polar figure of early modernism re-converted to a practising Judaism after he left Germany in the 1930s. His later work is infused with a Jewish character and motivation. He was a mystic and interested in the relationship that music had with silence. Perhaps that's why John Cage studied with him, seeing a similar mystical tendency in the older figure.

And then there was Olivier Messiaen who was famously Catholic, whose every note seemed to have been inspired by his theological curiosity and liturgical experience. He wrote one opera, *St Francis of Assisi* but the most popular French Catholic opera of the twentieth century was by Francis Poulenc, *Dialogues of the Carmelites,* which explores Catholic martyrdom and religious courage in the face of murderous persecution.

And after Shostakovich there came a whole group of post-war composers from behind the old Iron Curtain whose work has been shaped by religious influences – Arvo Pärt from Estonia, Górecki from Poland, Kancheli from Georgia and various Russians, Schnittke, Gubaidulina and Ustvolskaya – who all showed immense courage in rejecting the dead-hand, politically imposed orthodoxy of the day in Soviet times: state atheism. Some of them suffered for this, and Pärt was exiled for many years before returning to Estonia where he now lives and works in his 90th year.

Elgar was to suffer for his courageous vision as performances of *The Dream* were banned as 'inappropriate' in Gloucester Cathedral for a decade after the premiere, and performances in places like Hereford and Worcester were only permitted with large sections bowdlerised, with much of the objectionable Catholic dimension removed. It is thought by some that the vehemence of the reaction impacted greatly on the composer, even to the extent of him gradually losing his faith over the rest of his life. He may also have been seduced by the fame and praise which came his way in the wake of his more secular instrumental works which turned him into a national treasure. Indeed, he was to become Britain's official composer, being made a baronet, awarded the Order of Merit and appointed as Master of the King's Music. Proclaimed as 'quintessentially English' he became a totem of nationalism. Enjoying all that, why go back to the depredations of Catholic martyrdom?

But it was from this religion of martyrs and saints that Elgar drew his most unfettered freedom to visualise a work of greatness. And as a teenage boy in 1970s Ayrshire, I began to realise this. I fell in love with *Gerontius*, and its power and beauty have lived with me ever since. I could even claim that it has been a significant factor in the way my musical life has developed in the years since, pointing me in the directions I have taken and the works I have chosen to write.

At the time I started studying the work at school the local parish priest asked me to start playing the organ for Mass. Apart from accompanying the hymns and other liturgical bits and pieces I had no idea of what else to play. I hadn't learned any real organ repertoire and so relied on my fledgling improvisational abilities. But I had just acquired the vocal score of *The Dream of Gerontius*, which I still have. So, one day after I had received the Blessed Sacrament I returned to the organ console and opened the piano score at the opening page of the Prelude. I found an appropriate registration and started playing it gently as my family, relatives, friends and parishioners filed in line to receive Communion. Elgar would have done something similar in his early life, and those early experiences of liturgy, community and the numinous then led directly to the composition of *The Dream of Gerontius*.

~ Colin Matthews

Elgar regarded as the quintessential English composer has always seemed to me the wrong way round of looking at his achievement. His roots are scarcely English: after all there was little or no tradition subsequent to Purcell (whom Elgar greatly admired) and it was the extraordinary accomplishment of his work which marked the establishment of something completely new for English music. Initially his music did follow the English predilection for oratorio in the tradition of Handel and Mendelssohn, but the most potent influences on him were probably Schumann, Brahms, Dvořák and Wagner. This is far from anything that he might have learned from his compatriots – apart perhaps from Parry – and the closest parallels to him are not his English contemporaries but Strauss and Mahler.

While he knew Strauss both personally and musically (Strauss described him as 'the first English progressivist') it seems unlikely that he knew any of Mahler's music. He may have heard Mahler conduct Wagner in London in 1892 and must have been aware of the performances of *Sea Pictures* and *Enigma Variations* which he gave in New York in 1910, but that is the extent of their connection, even if as symphonists they have a great deal in common. As a composer of exceptional individuality, he might be compared to Sibelius, but although *The Music Makers* shared its premiere with Sibelius's Fourth Symphony in 1912 there is no record of the two composers speaking to each other on that occasion. Sibelius paid a fulsome tribute to him after his death, but we have no idea of what Elgar made of Sibelius.

Although he was in his forties by the time of *Enigma,* he had established a personal style relatively early on. But unlike many of the younger generation coming of age around 1900 the music of his maturity reflected none of the advances that prevailed in the early years of the century. Holst for instance, a much more eclectic figure, was well aware of the music of Debussy, Schoenberg and Stravinsky, even if those influences are sublimated in his music. We know that in later years Elgar increasingly felt that his music was unfashionable, but it is unthinkable that he might have adjusted his style to accommodate changing tastes.

This element of consistency is one of the things that marks Elgar out as exceptional: 'important', the theme of these essays, goes without saying. He matched a structural complexity only paralleled by Mahler with the orchestral skills of Strauss, all of this against a background of thorough absorption in Central European music. This is overlaid by a remarkable inventiveness arrived at in an almost improvisatory manner. He was capable of composing at great speed but then would proceed to shake his ideas up almost as if in a kaleidoscope before arriving at a definitive form. This approach is like no other composer.

Although I have placed some emphasis on Mahler here, it has to be admitted that, in terms of their methods of composing, the connection is rather distant. Comparing their two great unfinished works, Mahler's Tenth Symphony is – in one respect at least – complete: there is not a missing bar in the work as Mahler drafted it. It would have been subject to very extensive revision, but its incompleteness doesn't stand in the way of our perception of it as a powerful five movement structure. It fell to Deryck Cooke to unravel what at first sight looks like a chaotic manuscript; and Tony Payne was the first to grasp the implications of Elgar's sketches for the Third Symphony, which, because they follow his usual working methods, give so little indication of how they were to be assembled.[1]

Yet it is clear that the symphony was complete in Elgar's mind, and it is tragic that illness prevented him from continuing just as he was beginning to put the work into full score. He was full of ideas, but at the end of his life not advancing into a new world. Nevertheless, the visionary aspect of so much of his music pervades the sketches, and it is a vital part of the exceptional legacy he left. Perhaps one of the most significant aspects of that legacy is that he had few if any followers. The sheer power of invention in his music inspires nothing but admiration and respect, and who would want a pallid imitation of such a major composer?

1 A 1905 letter from Jaeger suggests a concert at a German music festival which he would have shared with Mahler's Third Symphony, but it came to nothing.

~ David Matthews

When I think about Elgar there are immediately two ways I feel particularly close to him. One is that, like him, I am essentially self-taught in composition. I cannot compare myself with Elgar in instrumental skills, or in conducting, but when I began to compose at the age of sixteen (my first piece, rather pretentiously, was a large-scale symphony) I had no one to help me learn how to write for the orchestra, except my brother Colin, who also became a composer. Much later I did have lessons from several other composers. Elgar had violin and piano lessons, and became especially proficient on the violin, but no teacher of composition. Every skill he had as a composer came, almost miraculously, from his inner genius. Among the great composers – and Elgar is certainly one of them – he seems to have been unique.

The other way I feel close to Elgar is that like his, my own music is deeply affected by the English landscape. Many of my initial ideas come from walking in the countryside, when I often feel as if the landscape is speaking to me. In a famous letter he wrote to his friend Sidney Colvin in 1921, Elgar wrote: 'I am still at heart the dreamy child who used to be found by Severn side with a sheet of paper trying to fix the sounds and longing for something very great.' I know exactly what he meant. For most of his life Elgar chose to live close to his childhood landscape – in Worcester, Hereford and Malvern – and his music drew strength from being composed in proximity to the source of its inspiration.

Elgar's music has two voices. One is energetic, extrovert, confident, urban: we associate it with his own time (what more appropriate music to accompany the images of Edwardian England could there be than the *Pomp and Circumstance* marches, or the opening of the First Symphony?). The other voice is reflective, nostalgic, sometimes heartbreakingly poignant: it is a rural voice, the voice of his native landscape, where he grew up. The special quality of Elgar's pastoral music was well expressed by Vaughan Williams when he wrote that it 'has that peculiar kind of beauty which gives us, his fellow countrymen, a sense of something familiar – the intimate and personal beauty of our own fields and lanes.' Vaughan Williams emphasised that this quality was not found in Elgar's *popular* style, 'but at those moments when he seems to have retired into the solitude of his own sanctuary'.[1]

I love both sides of Elgar, the symphonies and the overtures and particularly the tone poem *In the South,* with its fabulous opening culminating with the great horn theme at figure 7 which makes my hair stand on end just thinking about it. But I want to mention two pieces in particular, in the first of which his rural voice is predominant, and is also important in the second. The first piece is the *Introduction and Allegro,* which I think is probably the best piece ever written for strings (though Vaughan Williams's *Fantasia on a theme of Thomas Tallis,* which shows its influence, is almost its equal). The *Introduction and Allegro* demonstrates to the full Elgar's brilliant understanding of what string instruments can do. He writes for solo quartet and string orchestra, as Vaughan Williams later did in his *Tallis Fantasia,* and the richness of sound he obtains from juxtaposing the quartet with the (mostly divided) strings is continually thrilling. In contrast, there is the superb two-part writing for the whole string body, *fortissimo, nobilmente,* at figure 12. And then the fugue, written at Jaeger's suggestion – what a fugue! And the 'Welsh' tune that comes into full prominence near the end shows how close Elgar could come to folk music without making it central to his language, as Vaughan Williams and Holst were later to do.

Secondly, *Falstaff,* which has claim to be the greatest of all Elgar's works. In *Falstaff* we hear the urban and rural voices in clear juxtaposition. The whole score shows Elgar at his most eloquent and also his most adventurous, so it's hardly surprising that early audiences were somewhat bewildered by it. Elgar was not at all as conservative as many commentators continue to say. For much of the first 500 bars the tonality is remarkably fluid: the music rarely stays in one key for more than a few bars without change. Only in the second half of the work does it settle down. Its opening demonstrates what I mean. The work, which Elgar subtitled 'Symphonic Study in C minor', begins with the main Falstaff theme, unaccompanied: it rollicks along in typically Elgarian long/short note values, pivoted on the note G with which it begins, ends and rests at its mid-point, but its tonal stability is undermined by the series of descending augmented fourths by which it progresses. The first three bars (plus the upbeat) contain ten of the twelve notes of the chromatic scale. What key is it in? It could be G major or minor, or G could be felt as the dominant of C minor, as would be appropriate. In fact, G turns out to be the mediant of E flat major, the key in which the next theme appears, though this too is chromatically inflected

1 Ralph Vaughan Williams, 'What Have We Learnt from Elgar?' in *National Music and Other Essays,* 2nd edn. (Oxford: Oxford University Press, 1987), 251–2.

to a degree that make its tonality hard to pin down. This theme evokes Falstaff's wit, and its melodic shape is highly adventurous with spectacular upward leaps of a 13th and downward cascades that imitate Falstaff's laughter and are very similar to those at the opening of Verdi's *Falstaff*, surely not coincidentally. The opening theme returns, with trilling descending harmony above it which sounds like a preparation for C minor, but instead the music cadences again into E flat and Prince Hal's main theme, one of Elgar's great swaggering tunes and placed so that it appears the culmination of everything that's happened so far. This theme and the opening theme are linked: the first four notes of Hal's theme are notes 1, 3, 2 and 5 of Falstaff's, so it is as if Hal is Falstaff's idealisation of his younger self.

In complete contrast there are the two rural interludes. In the first Falstaff is asleep, and in his dream he remembers nostalgically the time when he was page to the Duke of Norfolk. This beautiful music is scored mostly for strings in a straightforward A minor in strong contrast to all the chromaticism of the previous music. In the second, evoking a Gloucestershire orchard, a folk dance on wind, tabor and tambourine alternates with wistful strings: Elgar at his most nostalgic.

I have arranged two of Elgar's works, one an augmentation and the other a reduction. It is perhaps surprising that Elgar the accomplished violinist wrote no mature string chamber music until in 1918, towards the end of his creative life, he started work on three major works: the Violin Sonata, Piano Quintet and String Quartet. The String Quartet is of course superbly written, though I feel it sometimes almost bursts at the seams. It is another of Elgar's most 'modern' works; some of it sounds like early Schoenberg. After listening to a performance in 2002 I wondered if it could work as a string orchestra piece, and that year I arranged the slow movement, and George Vass conducted it that year at the Deal Festival. In 2010 I arranged the other two movements and the complete piece was played at the Presteigne Festival that year, not far away from Elgar country, again conducted by George Vass. The substantial part of the arrangement is, of course, the addition of a double bass part, but I also thickened the upper parts in a number of places. At two points in the first movement and at the end of the Andante I preserved the original writing for solo strings. Since the first performance there have been two CD recordings. I hope that Elgar would have approved of this arrangement, which like Schoenberg's arrangement of *Verklärte Nacht*, transforms the piece into something quite different.

My other arrangement is of *Sospiri*, that 'wounded heart-cry'[2] as Michael Kennedy called it, written immediately before the First World War

[2] Michael Kennedy, *Portrait of Elgar*, 2nd edn. (Oxford: Oxford University Press, 1982), 260.

and premiered at the opening Promenade Concert ten days after war had been declared. How much more appropriate it was than the banal patriotic music that surrounded it, though the audience would not have realised this. I was able to reduce Elgar's unusual scoring for string orchestra, harp and harmonium to a string quartet, and the arrangement was premiered at the Elgar Festival in Worcester in 2018. It has since been recorded for CD by the Kreutzer Quartet.

I often wonder if my own music has been influenced by Elgar. Not in an obvious way I think, which is hardly surprising. But when a few years ago I was writing my *Shiva Dances* for the English String Orchestra (which was premiered at the 2018 Elgar Festival) I chose to write it for string quartet and string orchestra, and I constantly had the *Introduction and Allegro* in mind. And I like to think that I belong to the English tradition that began with Elgar and continued through Vaughan Williams, Holst, Walton, Tippett and Britten. I'm much concerned with tradition, more so I think than most of my contemporaries. I can still feel I have a link – as Elgar did – to the Classical symphonic tradition, especially to Beethoven. I don't feel that Elgar's music is irrelevant to the present day, even though it might seem so rooted in its own time. Where I feel closest to Elgar is in his expression of deep feelings about life, and in his use of expressive melody to convey these feelings. In every note of the music he wrote, you can hear Elgar's voice speaking directly to us with passionate intensity. In contrast, I find most of the music of our own day to be inhibited in its capacity to express feeling, and when it does so these feelings are often negative.

Sigmund Freud was almost Elgar's exact contemporary (though I doubt if Elgar knew much about him; I've found no mention of Freud in his correspondence, nor in any of the Elgar literature). Freud was much concerned with polarities, and one of the most important for him was the opposition of the life instinct and the death instinct. On the one hand, some people aim at happiness and fulfilment, attempting to transcend the state of ordinary unhappiness that Freud thought was our natural condition; on the other hand, some give in to despair and negation of life – the death instinct. Elgar's music is never simply optimistic. In writing about the Second Symphony, James Hepokoski noted, with superb insight, that 'it is touched throughout by a melancholy awareness of the dreamlike quality and transitoriness of things: ghosts of unsustainability, regret, and loss of innocence lurk everywhere. In this valedictory world the magnificent *fortissimo* moments of attainment and affirmation seem simultaneously to be melting away; and Elgar often shores up such moments with rises and underswells in unexpected places, as if he were trying to sustain an illusion forever slipping away from his grasp.'[3] Yet even in the Cello Concerto, which has more moments of uncertainty and regret than any of his other major works, Elgar never gives in to despair. At the end, after the most searching and anguished passage he ever wrote, Elgar returns to his opening heroic solo gesture, as if to say, here I am, Edward Elgar, not to be defeated. He is always on the side of the life instinct, in opposition to much of the music of today which seems crippled by the death instinct. We live in terrible times, to be sure, but in Elgar's lifetime the worst war in human history took place. Yet throughout his creative life Elgar gives us a model of what I think art ideally should be, an affirmation of life without ever being unaware of, or ignoring, its opposite. Elgar's underlying affirmativeness is something we composers today can still connect with and learn from. I certainly have.

[3] James Hepokoski, 'Elgar' in D. Kern Holoman (ed.), *The Nineteenth-Century Symphony* (New York: Schirmer Books, 1997), 329.

~ Robert Saxton

To consider the importance of Elgar begs the question as to what is meant by 'importance'. This, of course, applies to anyone who has, in the estimation of others in a particular field or the eyes of the 'establishment', achieved something of note. In mathematics and the sciences, technical progress is evident and unarguable. One example from many is the fact that mathematics could only advance in the West by means of the use of Arabic numerals and associated concepts (algebra being an Arabic term). In other words, neither opinion nor value judgement forms part of the equation.

In the humanities, the matter is less clear-cut in a number of ways so, in order to avoid what would necessarily involve an entire volume addressing aesthetics and value across various cultures and epochs, let us assume that what is being considered for our purposes is the estimation of an artist by his/her professional contemporaries and successors. How this relates to society at large is yet another issue to ponder. In brief: scientists do not have to concern themselves with 'instant' communication and understanding. The disciplines making up the body of the humanities are expected to communicate to an increasingly broad range of recipients. There are, of course, exceptions to any generalised statement, but let us accept the definition given for the purposes of our discussion.

What the question of Elgar's importance asks is this: in the history of Western (European) Music what is Elgar's ranking? This leads us to ask how his place in the pantheon is arrived at. The topic has been considered by many writers and performers, ranging from Paul Harper-Scott's path-breaking and thought-provoking book[1] which places Elgar as a Modernist alongside Richard Strauss, Mahler, Nielsen and Sibelius to Daniel Barenboim, subjectively, saying that, great though Elgar is, he is not 'important' in the sense that Mahler is. This brings us back to where we began; besides being unsupportable in any meaningful sense, it is unsubstantiated relativism, a mere opinion.

1 *Edward Elgar, Modernist* (Cambridge and New York: Cambridge University Press, 2006).

Composers are often divided by musicologists into two camps: those who accept the status quo and, in the case of the so-called outstanding ones, are subtly original. Byrd, Purcell and Mozart come to mind for a number of reasons which we won't go into here. Then there are those who 'cause trouble'; one thinks of Monteverdi's innovations resulting in his well-known conflict with the theorist Giovanni Artusi. Haydn was daringly innovative in his isolation at Esterhazy (as he said himself) and Stravinsky, coming from the then relatively recent Russian 'orbit' is an obvious case of upsetting the proverbial apple cart. I cite the latter, because it is worth recalling that Elgar's Symphony No. 2 and Stravinsky's *Petrushka* were both premiered in 1911 and neither is run-of-the-mill fare. We might, with justification, accept Elgar's work as superficially conservative (small 'c') and Stravinsky's ballet as innovatory, which it undoubtedly was. Elgar's work, while conserving and facing the challenge of the symphonic heritage (for example, we might hear the gesture at the beginning and the quiet ending as reminiscent of Brahms's Symphony No. 3, which Elgar conducted several times) is definitely and subversively, I would argue, not music which operates in anything approaching orthodoxy concerning fundamental structural principles vital to the Austro-German sonata. Indeed, these principles are frequently 'shadows' or ghosts even in the music of a composer working within the Great Tradition, such as Mahler. It is this tangential relationship to underlying principles which can lead us to consider Elgar as a European Modernist, as Strauss indeed claimed was the case. In its own way, his music arguably confronts the symphonic heritage with an originality similar to that which Stravinsky displayed in relation to the then (relatively new) Russian Ballet tradition.

Schoenberg's 1906 Chamber Symphony No. 1, with its tonal background of, and conclusion in, E major in conjunction with its Liszt-influenced compression of four 'orthodox' movements into a continuous musical argument towards an organically conceived and achieved structural goal is, without question, conservative (in the literal sense) and embedded within a specific tradition, its radical departure from convention by means of dense contrapuntal thought resulting in its originality as a chamber symphony. Both Elgar's symphonies, despite their apparently more traditional full orchestral surfaces, unsurprisingly bear less relation to the Austro-German heritage than does Schoenberg's. This turns certain common assumptions upside down. Indeed, we can go further: Stravinsky's Modernism was not, in fact, iconoclastic, but emanated from a world of theatre music and the Classical (although new) Russian ballet, the extraordinary originality of *Petrushka* being in its 'natural' innovations regarding musical time and structure fashioned in accordance with the stage action/dance. Its cross-cutting technique and orchestral sonorities indeed seem 'new' even today and were, as we know, taken a stage further in 1913, in *The Rite of Spring.*

I am fascinated by the fact that both Elgar (primarily a concert composer) and Stravinsky (a theatre-inspired composer) worked in a non-linear fashion, sketching scraps and fragments to be assembled. Of course, both had a pre-conceived idea of what each work was doing and where it was going, but neither drafted music in a 'narrative' or sequential manner.

We know that Elgar genuinely loved composers we might not consider 'important' now, such as Chabrier (whom Ravel admired almost above everyone except Mozart) and whose flair for orchestration and the writing of high quality 'light' music had a considerable effect on Elgar. This is another feature of Elgar's broad-based and open attitude to many types and genres of music.

In the late chamber music, I sense qualities which I also find in later Fauré; I am not speaking analytically, so much as in terms of atmosphere, gesture and a slightly intangible quality. Elgar's 1918 Piano Quintet, for all its occasional Brahmsian surface features, seems to me to share a singular vision as does Fauré's Op. 115 work for the same medium. Both seem to embrace and sense a new world of musical/psychological questing, in conjunction with new methods of achieving this. It is something which both Debussy and Fauré expressed in their late works (like Elgar, they, too, were 'accused' of failing powers when, with hindsight, the opposite appears to be the case) and is a feature of much early twentieth-century art, literature and music. Indeed, Elgar and Fauré, besides both sporting large moustaches, were both friends of Frank Schuster and met at his house.

Little of Elgar's 'important' music has anything to do with the (so-called) English choral church tradition (the lineage of the great choral works belonging to the concert/symphonic heritage) and, as for the 'English' sound of the string orchestra repertoire, he more-or-less invented it. The *Serenade* and the *Introduction and Allegro* surely form the bedrock on which Vaughan Williams, Holst, Warlock, Tippett, Lutyens, Britten and others built and this is evidently an aspect of importance, let alone remarkable originality. As a mature composer, Elgar always seemed to forge music from his own crucible. Of course, there are influences (the opening of *Alassio* is clearly a tribute to Strauss's *Don Juan*, but artists have played such games for centuries) and there had to be.

We are back where we began. We live in an epoch when many seemingly established values regarding technical and aesthetic standards are in question across the board, from the media to university campuses. This is hardly unique to the first quarter of the twenty-first century; the entire seventeenth century in Europe witnessed an unparalleled clash of ideas and developments with the advent of scientific method, experiment and theory, and the arts moving fairly swiftly from the late Renaissance to what we now term the Early Baroque. All this against the background of the English Civil War and the Thirty Years War on the continent.

Context is vital to our assessment of Elgar. Elgar was born one year after Robert Schumann's death and died when Pierre Boulez was nine years old, his life span ranging from the early railways and the predominance of sail to international air travel and transatlantic liners. It is easy to overlook his interest in, and enthusiasm for, the up-to-date, manifest not only in his absorption with chemistry experiments but also in his having a chauffeur and a car and enjoying the latest 1920s cocktails from the USA, such as the Manhattan. From that period, the opening of the Third Symphony with its consecutive fifths and harmonic character is as much part of its time as Puccini's *Turandot* or Sibelius' Seventh Symphony, both the latter considered (particularly with hindsight) as Modernist in specific ways.

Elgar's range as a communicator is out of the ordinary: few composers have crossed barriers as he did. At one end of the spectrum there are salon (Palm Court) pieces such as *Salut d'Amour* and public music as in the *Pomp and Circumstance* Marches (not all of them 'popular', as we know); at the other end, contemplative, private music as we hear in the late chamber works as mentioned; and, in between, serious, visionary and profound works such *The Dream of Gerontius*, amongst others. Every one of the latter displays, as do the symphonies and the violin and cello concertos, an unforcedly original mind combined with a wholly fresh and personal harmonic sense. The movement of the sounding bass in relation to possible harmonic roots (a matter which I addressed with regard to 'Nimrod' in a talk to the Elgar Society) makes even a piece such as *Salut d'Amour* unusual (it is far from being a 'standard' salon music offering). Elgar's writing for the orchestra (rather than 'orchestration') works hand-in-glove with his large-scale formal and rhythmic sense; witness, for example, the last few pages of the First Symphony, where the motto theme and its accompanying/secondary layer seem unsynchronised and, then, all comes together in a moment unique in music, combining virtuosic layered polyphonic orchestral writing, musical meaning and sheer visceral immediacy at a stroke.

Elgar's importance is surely not in doubt. His range of expression, range of genres, technical accomplishment 'across the board' and quality of ideas as well as his tangential position with regard to any one tradition (however deceptive the surface may be) cohere to ensure that he is viewed and heard as an artist of the first rank. The fact that his music continues to speak to a broader range of people than, say, Mahler or Strauss (who, by and large, communicate far less with listeners outside the concert and opera realms) makes Elgar a figure who communicates profoundly nearly a century after his death in both public and private realms. His musical development not only charted and created the transition from late Romanticism to early Modernism, but also displayed (and continues to do so) a unique and profound expressivity. I rest my case.

∾ Ian Venables

My earliest memory of discovering Elgar's music was when I bought a vinyl LP of the *Enigma Variations*, recorded on the Decca *World of the Great Classics* label and conducted by Pierre Monteux. Hearing this orchestral masterpiece for the first time was a revelation, and it marked the beginning of my life-long love of Elgar's music. I was, of course, fortunate to have stumbled upon his most famous work and even today Monteux's historic 1958 recording holds up well against some of the more recent ones.

In 1973, I was appointed as the organist and choirmaster of St Thomas' Church in Liverpool, where I found choosing repertoire for a small amateur choir quite a challenge. However, I remember introducing them to Elgar's exquisite anthem, *Ave Verum Corpus*, and I would often play an arrangement of the *Imperial March* as an organ voluntary after the services. By the mid 1970s I regularly attended the 'Industrial Concerts' given by The Royal Liverpool Philharmonic Orchestra under their principal conductor, Sir Charles Groves. He was especially fond of Elgar's music and each season there was usually one of the composer's works on the programme and during the 1976 concert series I was lucky to be invited to an open rehearsal for a recording of Elgar's oratorio *Caractacus*. Groves's EMI recording is still, in my opinion, the finest on record.

My deepening love of Elgar's music inevitably drew me to the city of Worcester, where I would come on a Saturday afternoon to hear Choral Evensong in the Cathedral. It was here that I first heard Elgar's anthem *Great is the Lord*, conducted by Donald Hunt. Of course, while I was growing up in Liverpool, I had no idea that I would eventually make my home in Worcester, arriving there in the Autumn of 1986 to take up a teaching post at The Royal Grammar School. In the Spring following my arrival, I set off to explore the surrounding countryside, beginning with a walk on the Malvern Hills and a visit to Elgar's grave at the nearby St Wulstan's Church at Little Malvern, ending up at his birthplace in Broadheath. In those days, the cottage was accessed through the front garden via a latch gate that had the amusing sign – 'please Boult the gate'! I was warmly welcomed by the curator, James Bennett, who gave me a tour of the house and its collection of Elgar memorabilia; I was particularly impressed by being shown the original manuscript of the Second Symphony.

During that first summer, I composed a short work, entitled *Pastorale* for violin and piano. It is my tribute to Elgar and its opening melody came to me on one of my walks. If Elgar is correct when he said 'My idea is that there is music in the air, music all around us, the world is full of it and you simply take as much as you require', then, perhaps, in the *Pastorale* I too may have tapped into this shared musical well-spring, if only for a brief moment. Of all my compositions, it is my *Piano Quintet* that is most indebted to Elgar. The work was commissioned by the Malvern Festival and premiered at the Malvern Theatres in 1996. I recollect studying the score of Elgar's Quintet, as well as quintets by others, but ultimately decided that Elgar's would best serve as my model. I was especially struck by his cyclical approach and by its tripartite structure, with its first movement that opens with a slow introduction, followed by an *allegro*. However, while Elgar's first movement develops several contrasting themes, mine is in strict Classical Sonata form. Like Elgar, the second movement of my quintet is a melancholy *Adagio* that begins in a similar vein to his, with a wistful melody played by the viola. Throughout this movement I adopt Elgar's episodic approach, alternating passionate outbursts with slower and more reflective passages; I also reprise melodic fragments from the first movement, that give the music its cyclical feel. As with Elgar, the last movement is an energetic finale. It is fascinating to note that over the years concert performances of my *Piano Quintet* have often been coupled with that of the Elgar.

In the early 1990s I was introduced to Lady Trudy Bliss by Gerald Towell, former chairman of the Arthur Bliss Society. We became good friends, and it was on her prompting that I composed the song 'Flying Crooked' – a setting of a humorous poem by Robert Graves. Lady Bliss also suggested that I join the Elgar Society. She even paid for my first year's subscription! It was at an event held by the Worcestershire Branch that I first met the Elgar scholar, Jerrold Northrop Moore. We too, became friends and whenever we met, our conversations about music would naturally turn to his work on Elgar. Sometimes, I would act as a sounding board, listening to him read through a draft of a new chapter he was writing, occasionally stopping to ask what I thought or to consult me about a technical matter. As far as my own music was concerned, Jerry gave me tremendous encouragement. After hearing my *String Quartet*, he wrote: 'first and foremost, I like it best (except one certain song) of all your music. For the Quartet takes up a central matter of music, the contrast of urgent rhythm with lyric melody: set out with utmost attraction at the beginning, and never lost sound of through the whole work'. The song he refers to is my setting of A.E. Housman's poem 'Because I liked you better,' which I dedicated to him.

Elgar's influence upon my creative life came full circle in 2013, when I was commissioned by the Malvern Concert Club to compose a song cycle for the baritone, Roderick Williams. The Concert Club was founded by Elgar in 1903, and his close friend, Arthur Troyte Griffith (whom Elgar immortalised in Variation No. VII of his *Enigma Variations*) was its first Secretary. In *The Song of the Severn*, I wanted to consider how poets and musicians had been inspired by the Worcestershire landscape. I was reminded of the Welsh poet Owen Sheers's eloquent description of landscape poetry: it can 'speak about us – the people who live in, look at and remember the places ... which have, in turn, remembered us; as individuals, as communities, as history'. In this way, landscape can reflect so much of ourselves, our memories and our collective past. It is simply waiting for the poet to discover and so 'illuminate that which we thought we already knew and make us see that which we thought we'd already seen'. These sentiments could equally be applied to Elgar, who felt that music resonated in everything around us and who was intimately connected with the Worcestershire countryside.

The Song of the Severn opens with a setting of John Masefield's dramatic poem *On Malvern Hill.* The poet narrates the same mythical story that had inspired Elgar's *Caractacus* but now refashioned into verse. Whether I found the poem, or it found me, knowing Elgar's oratorio was certainly a significant reason for me to set these words. Elgar has cast a long (benign?) shadow over Worcestershire and, in this cycle, I wanted to acknowledge this as well as expressing my own appreciation of him. My initial thoughts centred upon the idea of incorporating within the cycle, a quotation from one of Elgar's works, which I intended as a kind of 'homage'; I later dismissed this idea as being too clichéd. Fortunately, I found a poem by John Drinkwater, entitled 'Elgar's Music' written in 1935 the year after the composer's death. However, the second half of this 'Petrarchian' sonnet was not, in my opinion, inspired poetry, and so unusually for me I decided to set only the first part:

How quietly he sleeps upon the hill
That sees the seasons go by Severnside
He who by music manifested still
Across the earth the ancient English pride –
This Worcester man who out of little lanes
Of whitethorn bud, and Evesham orchards bright
In harvest, made a magic that disdains
That easy summons of the lesser light

As I began to set the opening lines a sudden rush of musical ideas came. Later, once I had written them down, I realised that there was a something familiar resonating in the music but could not grasp what it was and so I showed it to my partner, the pianist Graham J. Lloyd. He immediately recognised that there was an echo of the 'Sea Slumber-Song' – the first of Elgar's *Sea Pictures* – concealed within it. This allusion had been an entirely unconscious one, but once it had been revealed, I decided to integrate it within the song's evolving structure. So, strange as it may appear, Elgar made his presence known, and perhaps it is not too fanciful to suggest that *his* music is indeed 'in the air'.

One of the most exciting musical developments in Worcester in recent years was the founding of the Elgar Festival in 2018 under its artistic director, Kenneth Woods. Held during the week closest to Elgar's birthday on 2 June, this annual festival presents a wide range of events, talks and concerts performed by its orchestra-in-residence, the English Symphony Orchestra. In the 2022 Festival Gala concert there was a performance of *The Song of the Severn* in a new arrangement for orchestra by the Dutch musician, Vincent Onken. The concert also included a performance of Elgar's overture *In the South*. Over the past five years it has grown into one of the most important British music festivals and whilst Elgar's music remains the festival's primary focus, Kenneth Woods's innovative programming blends familiar works with music by a featured contemporary composer. I am delighted to say that I was asked to be its Composer-in-Residence in 2025 in celebration of my 70th birthday.

As a coda to this brief tribute, I find it fascinating to note that Elgar and I share the same publisher, Novello and Co. When I contacted them, I was often asked 'how is our other Worcester composer doing'! Amused by this, I have now come to realise that it is a compliment of the highest order to be associated with Elgar in any way. He is Britain's greatest composer and one I have admired and revered throughout my life. I hope that, perhaps in some small way, I have been able to play a part in continuing the tradition that was so vital to his own creative journey.

~ Debbie Wiseman

The first piece of Elgar that I listened to from beginning to end was the Cello Concerto – his final substantial orchestral work - in a recording by Jacqueline du Pré that was, for me, transformative. The emotion, melancholy, lyricism, melodic invention – I found it utterly addictive and would listen to it over and over again. After that it was the *Enigma Variations*; and hearing 'Nimrod' for the first time had the same effect. I was compelled to listen to it innumerable times, marvelling at its beauty, introspection, nobility. Then came his second symphony – bursting with inventiveness. I was hooked.

When I was at music college and made the pilgrimage to the Proms each year, Elgar's *Pomp and Circumstance* Marches – the climax of the Last Night – were to me the musical personification of pageantry and would always stir the audience into a raucous display of flag-waving patriotism; but it has been suggested in certain quarters that Elgar's greatness is undermined by the characterisation of his contribution to music as jingoistic. In fact Elgar himself was never happy with the idea of putting words to the melody from his first *Pomp and Circumstance* march, and this militaristic use of his music upset him.

Elgar's greatness lies in the depth of his musical language, his dazzling orchestrations, the emotion and expression that reaches out directly to the listener. Like the best radio broadcasters who give you the impression that they're in the room with you and sharing their thoughts and music, I feel, when I'm listening to Elgar, that he's speaking directly to me. It's not only about the pomp and pageantry, or the genius in his orchestration and colours – in the final analysis, it comes down to his simple directness which touches me more than anything complex or studied. His melodies soar and you soar with them, without question. He creates a deeply personal creative world, and evokes a vast range of emotions – beauty, loneliness, romance, splendour – in a way that is completely natural. Here is a composer who can conjure up music that is at once profound, gentle, and dazzling. The communication he has with the listener is slightly different each time his music is played, as the melodies dig deeper into your soul. Elgar's music can be played many, many times without ever losing its appeal – with each repeat it is possible for the listener to find something new, something different; discovering another gem of a counter-theme, or another orchestral colour that might have eluded the ear the first time around. Marvelling at his brilliant orchestration can, on occasions, be as rewarding as marvelling at his expressive thematic writing.

Elgar's music somehow managed to navigate around the modernism that was bubbling up in European music from the 1890s, and he also avoided the inspiration of English folk songs that the next generation of British composers would embrace, led by Vaughan Williams. He is the most internationally renowned British composer since Henry Purcell, and I find it hard to disagree with the many who regard him as our 'National' composer.

3. Elgar aged fourteen in 1871 from the Bennett Studio in Foregate Street, Worcester.

2

The View From the Podium

Martyn Brabbins

Fortunately for me the music of Edward Elgar has featured heavily throughout my conducting life, and for this I am of course immensely grateful. Elgar's music teaches me so much about life, and rather mundanely perhaps, about conducting. It is no surprise to me that there are books dedicated to the topic of conducting Elgar's music. His scores are so clear, with so many detailed instructions and guides – to tempo, to dynamic nuances, to articulation and accentuation, to balance – and yet, or perhaps because of this plethora of detail, once all of this information is absorbed and implemented, the music flies off the page in a totally natural and expressive way.

As for the life lessons the music gives us, that is for each individual listener to experience. Surely one of the essential features of great music is that each of us takes from it something entirely individual and personally fulfilling.

As a British conductor, and having studied composition before I took up the baton, I have long felt compelled to be an advocate for living composers. Thus, there is a healthy list of world premiere performances to my name. Having spent time – a lot of time actually! – in my early twenties composing, I have a profound empathy for composers. I know just how difficult, nigh on impossible at times, it is to put one's ideas down on paper! In addition, there is this simple truth: every composition begins as a new piece, and without having a premiere, there is no chance of a second performance or indeed of it establishing itself as a repertoire piece.

The compulsion I have as a British conductor is to take music written by British composers, both old and new, with me as I travel overseas to conduct. It is often said that our music does not 'travel well'. I am not so sure I agree. I had three memorable experiences of conducting Elgar's music during 2024, in Finland, Sweden and Japan, that have had a big impact on audiences and musicians are alike.

In March 2024 I was in Lahti with the Symphony Orchestra conducting *The Dream of Gerontius* with the Dominante choir from Helsinki, Christine Rice, David Butt Philip and Christopher Maltman. This was the first time the piece had been performed in the wonderful Sibelius Hall, and the concert attracted a full house. From the first moment to the last of Elgar's profoundly moving score one sensed the audience was totally engrossed in the journey, and the exultant and enthusiastic reception we received at the conclusion of *Gerontius* was striking in its energy. As I prefer, there was no interval in the performance, and the cumulative effect of Gerontius's journey from life to death and thence to heaven, even for a non-believer can touch listeners in most unexpected ways. (As a footnote – also memorable was a unique post-concert moment. David, Christopher and I were invited by a couple of female choristers to join them and fifteen or so of their colleagues in an anteroom, where the ladies serenaded us with a most exquisite rendition of a Finnish folk song: a totally spellbinding conclusion to the evening.)

April found me unexpectedly in Malmö conducting the First Symphony, replacing our dear friend Sir Andrew Davis. This was not the first time the Malmö Symphony Orchestra had played the symphony but in no way was it a repertoire piece for them. Elgar was a masterful orchestrator, but his remarkable skill demands of an orchestra to realise every detail and nuance imagined by the composer. The Malmö musicians relished the challenge and really rose to the occasion, delivering a heartfelt performance which I certainly experienced as a wonderful tribute to Sir Andrew.

The Tokyo Metropolitan Symphony Orchestra is one of several brilliant orchestras to be found in Japan's capital city. I took a thoroughly English programme to them in October opening with *In the South* followed by Finzi's marvellous clarinet concerto with Annelien Van Wauwe as the eloquent soloist, and concluding with Vaughan Williams's enigmatic Ninth Symphony. All the pieces were new to the orchestra. It was truly a privilege and a pleasure to introduce these marvellous musicians to this programme and to sense their enthusiasm and genuine pleasure as we explored these masterly scores together. *In the South* was a real knockout with them, and their surprise and joy at getting to know this music more than a century after its composition was wonderful to witness. They performed the score with total command and exactly the right amount of both panache and pathos. The packed audience in the Suntory Hall was as delighted as the orchestra, and a throng of autograph hunters – a Japanese speciality – was to hand after the concert to show their appreciation.

Three of Elgar's finest compositions, many miles from home, and yet communicating very directly with large and hugely appreciative audiences. Well-travelled Elgar to say the least!

~ Adrian Brown

When reflecting on all the musical aspects of Elgar, what it means to me, its effect on so very many listeners and the country in general, I believe one factor is the sheer emotional impact of his music.

That he touched the hearts of the Nation with *Pomp and Circumstance* and 'Nimrod' is more than enough to demonstrate his importance, for he gave us a release for deep feeling and emotion; a sense of occasion and security. 'Nimrod' is about a deep friendship that can only be expressed in crafted notes. I often say to players to play his *pp* for your own ear and your own emotion, for it is not only a public expression but a personal connection with your inner self.

Elgar, like Berlioz, was largely self-taught. This, it seems to me, gave him a freedom away from the Victorian academic 'straight-jacket' that is frankly rather obvious in his predecessors. He was not taught to uphold the principles of composition or even more importantly orchestration. He soaked up all he could by himself, over years of experience in the 'galley', learning a craft unique to him; informed, playable and totally practical, which in itself gives joy to orchestral members and conductors. I feel that in all music there has never been anyone so good at setting down what to actually play and conduct. He was a genius. That is enough for me to extol his importance! I might add also that he gave a kick-start in technique to all the composers who followed him in this country: Bax, Vaughan Williams, Holst, etc. It gave them bravery in the use of voices and the orchestra.

We might, perhaps, overlook the importance of his climb from the background into which he was born, not least with a great lady's support – Alice. Struggling 1898; knighthood 1904! – having produced music the public loved and the establishment admired. The social and financial restrictions in his musical apprenticeship are an example now to *all*, proving that you can come from nowhere, with God-given gifts, and achieve the heights of inspiration. He composed music with a love for the orchestra and the players, and gave the lowest of the low, the second violins, something far superior to play and enjoy compared to most of what had been composed during the previous 50 years. As a conductor, rarely do I depart from a marking or a dynamic; the violins never have to 'cheat'!

I believe a certain Austrian conductor called Elgar 'third-rate Brahms'. Contempt prior to investigation! For Elgar's use of form is important and trail-blazing even if the works of 1900–1910 do not have the discord or growing rhythmic complexity of some of his contemporaries' compositions. However, from 1912 onwards there is a melodic chromaticism that pervades the scores, as if Debussy had crossed the Channel in a boat with Schoenberg. Yes, the sound is rich and grand in the symphonies but in the Second he is expressing the passing of a golden age, never to return after the cruel sparsity of the war to come. The works composed during and after the conflict see the texture paired down to the barest minimum, for instance in the Cello Concerto. Perhaps we have come to realise, unlike those critics in the 1940s to the 60s, that this 'old-fashioned' form and deep feeling is something much more important for us to nurture and love.

But it is important to recognise that the form of the music is, for all that it is a symphony or a concerto, original. I have insufficient space to celebrate this but the form of the A-flat symphony, with the use of its motto, carefully crafted and not contrived, is astonishing. The two middle movements, linked as they are in material where the quickest quixotic notes become the most eloquent *Adagio*, is totally beautiful and original. Also consider that the cadenza in the Violin Concerto is not a 'display cabinet' in the first movement but becomes a most moving rumination of all the themes, emotionally 'sorting himself out' as the quiet climax to the work.

The Second Symphony has four movements, each in different metres. The first movement's swinging energy is like a finale; a four-square march; a triple-time double scherzo with pastoral interludes and a natural transition to the foreboding first heard in movement one; and a finale that with its pace and grandeur in steady triple-time can augment so easily the fast triplets of the first movement, portraying the golden sunset of an era. So, the journey from the energy and delight of movement one to the disintegration of delight of movement four, becomes the actual narration of the work.

The Cello Concerto is unusually in four movements, giving time for display, an elegy and a chromatic, searching finale.

I have mentioned just a few masterpieces, but there are many more. Elgar's inspiration proves the important point that we weren't 'The Land without Music'!

Finally, the importance of his recordings. Was there a better conductor of his own and others' compositions? Strauss, yes, orchestrally but we have little idea of his operatic interpretations. Elgar, often in pre-electric recordings too, recorded so much of his music and so well! Many works were recorded but not, sadly, the *Introduction and Allegro*. Under a very 'knowing baton' he gave us 'his way' with the music. Nervous, quick, balanced and structured and for us, a foil to an expansionist Barbirolli and a perhaps steadier Boult. An encyclopaedic insight into the standards and improvement of orchestral playing over those years. Compare the LSO of 1929 to the then new LPO in *Froissart* in 1933.

Elgar is a part of my life I could not be without. He makes me feel with his scores that I can know him and share his sadness, frustrations of acceptance and the spiritual triumph that I hear so deeply at the end of *The Apostles.* For me, that ending is so well composed, building up overwhelmingly in its passion and grandeur. Every note I conduct of his music gives me an evangelistic belief in the importance of this great man.

~ Florian Csizmadia

It is hard to define what makes a composer 'important', and depending on the categories that one chooses, Elgar might not be considered important at all. He left no work that changed world-wide music history like Beethoven's symphonies or Wagner's *Tristan*, his influence on younger composers was exclusively restricted to the British Isles, and he was not a revolutionary who put musical grammar upside-down like some twentieth century ultra-modernists (although he was far more modern than some people believe…). It goes without saying that these are not the only parameters that make a composer 'important', and all I can do within the limited space of this contribution is to answer the question from a purely personal viewpoint.

I well remember how I first came across Elgar's music. When I was a teenager, I tuned into a radio broadcast without knowing what music was being played and was totally bowled over by the emotional power and technical mastery of the piece in question. Here was a composer who definitely had something to say and did that in a highly individual and masterly way – and I didn't know him! Afterwards, it turned out that it had been Elgar's Piano Quintet. Perhaps this has influenced my understanding of Elgar's music to this day: to look at his music without any prejudices, national background or stylistic orientation and to just appreciate it as 'music'.

Growing up as a German musician in Germany in the 1980s and 90s meant that I literally didn't come into touch with Elgar's music, either in the conservatory or in the concert hall. (Luckily, times have changed in this respect…) Nonetheless, Elgar remained a constant fixpoint in my musical thinking, although this was at that time, I fear, a rather unsophisticated love for a composer and his music that I happened to like but that I had certainly not yet fully understood. It was only much later in my life that I had the possibility to study Elgar's music in greater detail and from the dual perspective of musicologist and performing musician.

Work on my doctoral dissertation on Elgar's complete choral works involved hours of studying Elgar's sketches and manuscripts in the British Library and (at that time) at the Birthplace Museum. Everyone who has ever studied composers' handwriting will know how closely this brings one in touch with the personality behind the works, and tracing the path from the first sketches to the finished masterwork opened my eyes to the sheer incredible technical mastery of Elgar's works.

Turning to orchestral conducting in the mid-2010s and becoming Music Director of a fine German provincial orchestra allowed me to perform for the first time in my life nearly all of Elgar's major and a host of his smaller orchestral works – and it was not only a first time for me, but also for the orchestra which hadn't played any Elgar besides the occasional *P&C No. 1* in some New Year's Concert. Working on Elgar's music with an orchestra that doesn't have any Elgarian tradition was an incredible experience for me: you can't play the music just through and fix a few difficult spots. Instead, you must carefully work on all aspects of the score: articulation, balance, and above all phrasing (and many difficult passages, especially for the strings). When it came to the actual performances it almost felt like premieres, and it was both, the rehearsal process and the concerts, that opened my eyes to what I may call in the context of this contribution the 'importance of Elgar'. For the first time I became aware of Elgar's incredible technical mastery in all musical parameters: his handling of the orchestra that is comparable to the one of the best composers of his time (from the Austro-German tradition Mahler, Strauss and Reger come instantly to my mind) and with examples of which one could fill a handbook on orchestration; his sovereign thinking in terms of musical form which is never used as a form filled with music but as a form developed from the musical ideas (in this respect, he is, in my opinion, far more successful than Mahler and can be compared to Sibelius); and his unique ability to sweep the audience off their feet (I particularly remember a performance of *In the South* after which our traditionally slightly reserved Northeast German audience proverbially went mad). I suspect that the latter quality became somewhat out of fashion in the course of the twentieth century, but I think nowadays we see these things differently and no composer should be ashamed of uplifting his audience and giving them a good time. Elgar certainly knew how to achieve this and, in this respect, also his *P&C No. 1* is far better music than is sometimes assumed.

What makes Elgar a unique and unquestionably important composer is the fact that he relies on tradition but found his own individual musical language, one that is instantly recognized and not derivate of other composers. He amalgamated a lot of influences in an eclectic manner, but it is virtually impossible to trace back individual traits of his music to concrete models. Instead, he welded the influences into his personal musical language and created his own distinct sound world.

In his works he runs the complete gamut from elevated exultation to black despair, from triumphal peroration to intimate idyllic and pastoral feelings, from humour to wistfulness. Therefore, his music encompasses in quite a Mahlerian sense 'the whole world', or, as Elgar himself would have said, 'the whole of human life' (*Falstaff*) or 'a wide experience of human life' (First Symphony). In this respect, Elgar's music has a timeless quality which makes it mandatory that, as with the music of other great composers of the past, every generation must think about it anew.

I never understood why Elgar's symphonies were classified in the *New Grove* as ranking 'high [...] in English musical history'. In my opinion, one would do Elgar more justice by just omitting the word 'English'. I notice a growing interest in Elgar's music outside of Great Britain, but I still feel that his works are often seen as something exotic, coming from a foreign country whose immense musical heritage we don't know much about. That's why I always try to avoid programming Elgar's works in concerts dedicated exclusively to British music. Instead, I find it important to put Elgar into an international perspective and I hope that the time has come to see him as a composer of universal importance whose music has so much to offer people today and, I am convinced, in the future.

❧ Hilary Davan Wetton

Elgar and The English Choral Tradition

Elgar's contribution to the English oratorio tradition is very fully documented. It is entirely possible to argue that, in their own way, the three greatest works: *The Dream of Gerontius, The Kingdom* and *The Apostles,* have a similar significance in his life to that of *The Ring* in Wagner's. Aside from mentioning that both Elgar and my great teacher, Sir Adrian Boult, believed that *The Kingdom* was his greatest achievement, I intend to focus this brief article on Elgar's 'Choral Songs' which constitute an extraordinary group of pieces in the repertoire for large choirs.

These remarkable works have very little in common with the Renaissance Madrigal, except in their intense response to text. *Go, Song of Mine,* an exceptional achievement by any standard, is richly polyphonic without making the words indecipherable. Indeed, Elgar's capacity to use short-lived doublings to reinforce brief moments of textural or musical intensity is notable in this piece, as are his wide range of expression markings. Moreover, his phrasing marks, which include traditional staccato dots, staccato with accents, vertical staccatissimo lines and marcato horizontal lines, are extraordinarily detailed. In the case of the last note of the piece, the word 'Go!', there are dots with lines over them for the only time in the work; how we convey that unequivocally to an audience is a major challenge for any conductor.

The interpretation of these markings could easily occupy half of a choir rehearsal by themselves. Very few composers have left such specific instructions for the conductor and we should surely seek to be unusually meticulous in transmitting these to our performers. The obvious question arises: will the audience be aware of any of these fine details? The answer surely is that in some exceptional way, the projection of the words to the listeners is intensified by these very precise directions as to attack, release and duration. I think we can be pretty sure that Elgar could hear the exact sounds he was writing in his mind's ear; that alone places the interpreter under a major obligation to take care of them.

Of course, there is much more to Elgar than note length. The opening of *Owls*, for example: a rising third for the tenors and basses in time and a semitonal downward response by the altos and sopranos with an *ad lib* pause on the first note, followed immediately with an *a tempo* on the second note, again presents us with a level of detail most composers would not attempt. Those two downward notes also provide the last sounds in the piece. This time, the dynamic has changed from *pp* to *pppp*; the first note is in time but marked *rit.* and the last note, a staccato quaver, rather than the original, full-length crotchet. It is an almost obsessive approach to composition and yet, the sense of something inexorable proceeding from the beginning to the end and carrying throughout a sense of doom and portent is palpable. It is worth remembering that the rather elusive text is by the composer himself. How much he sought or received Alice's help is uncertain, but it is impossible to mistake the white heat of his inspiration which emerges from it.

The Opus 71/72/73 songs are a particularly fine collection and work well as a sequence, both in sentiment and stylistic variety. The key shift from *The Shower* to *The Fountain* is a little abrupt but I have never felt it unreasonably jarring. *The Shower* needs altos and tenors who can sing articulated semiquavers *leggiero* with complete rhythmic stability and the conductor needs to be very clear which part needs to be to the fore from bar to bar. The final climax, a bar of *allargando* followed by two bars of *molto largamente,* needs careful handling; Elgar's *largamenti* are easily exaggerated, but the *molto* gives us a clear direction to be genuinely broad. As so often with Elgar, the mood changes swiftly and there are only two bars between *ff* and *p*, which can challenge the singers if they are not on top of the music. Closing the 'n' of 'rain' at the end will add to the wonderful effect of the beautifully voiced final chord with its optional low E flat – surely not really optional if the true effect is to be projected.

Each of the succeeding songs has equivalent detail to which the conductor must attend. These are works that really need preparation and certainty. The harmonic language is almost Straussian in its richness, yet in an instant, Elgar can switch to a very simple texture in which one part is unequivocally melodic. Every detail of Henry Vaughan's text provokes some new imaginative stroke from the composer and almost every bar has some fresh marking from the composer which requires detailed attention from the conductor. To balance this detail with a broad sweep in the performance is genuinely challenging, but when the pieces work they give the audience an intense experience of how words can be brought to life by a great composer. Each song of this set is a miniature tone poem and the evident care that Elgar has taken over the smallest detail surely tells us that he thought the pieces significant. Even the very last note is written with meticulous care: *Love's Tempest* ends with a minim tied to a quaver with an arrow on it. *Serenade* ends with a crotchet tied over the bar line to a minim, tied to a quaver with no marking of any kind though the whole chord has a *diminuendo* to *pp* over the top of it. I always encourage a choir to think the *dim.* in quaver pulsations so that it is truly progressive and even. That last bar alone could reasonably occupy 5 or 6 minutes of a rehearsal!

The conclusion of this brief survey seems clear: Elgar clearly invested enormous care and attention in these 'Choral Songs' and the result is a whole collection of masterpieces for *a cappella* choir. They should be in the repertoire of any good choir; just as with Holst, in their way they show the quality of the composer as clearly as the largest orchestral works do. They deserve to be much better known and we would surely be clamouring for Radio 3 to broadcast them more often!

~ Edward Gardner

Conducting the Symphonies

I grew up with Edward Elgar's music, singing as a chorister in Gloucester Cathedral. Elgar's music was a major part of my life, guided by Cathedral organist John Sanders. John had played the organ in *Gerontius* for Herbert Sumsion, who in turn had played for Elgar. I often think how privileged I was to be connected to this tradition. John Sanders was a particular help to me when I started conducting.

Elgar's scores are saturated with markings – a post-Mahler addiction to prescribe obsessively how the notes should be played. I found it overwhelming, and, as a conductor, it's easy to be bogged down in these markings at the expense of the bigger span. John really helped me to understand this. 'It is' (and I remember his exact words) 'Elgar just saying "take care of my music"'.

I think about this often: both the intention, and Elgar's precious vulnerability. An example is in the opening of the First Symphony; for the second phrase Elgar writes accents on all the bass notes in the *forte* repeat – if you play this literally, the music can sound dull and four-square. This cannot be what the hypersensitive musician Elgar intended. We need to shape and phrase the music, take the essence of the instruction, and then form it as you would with Schumann or Brahms. This applies to the opening of both symphonies, and much more besides. People talk of the Edwardian bombast in Elgar's music, but for me this comes from a misreading of his intentions.

Symphony No. 1

So much of Elgar's music paints the lonely voice against the world. The opening of the First Symphony has this human fragility, sharing with the opening of *The Dream of Gerontius* the essence of the soulful theme from Wagner's *Parsifal*, a melody signifying a wounded world.

The tread underneath the melody tells us we are going on a journey. Rehearsing this opening, that's in the forefront of my mind – it can't be static, but at the same time it should feel world-weary; I find there's a tiny bandwidth for this to work. The sudden change to the *allegro* is arresting after this melancholic opening statement. The tempo change is not easy: you are confronted with *appassionato* in the first bar, accents on the second beat, very specific strings to use in the first violin melody, moving from *piano* to *forte* in four bars with hairpin swells, and many more indications. The music needs direction, but if it is too quick all the detail is lost. For me, this passage contains something intrinsic to Elgar and his music: passionate, yet insecure and troubled.

Michael Kennedy described the end of the first movement as having 'miraculous scoring'. He is absolutely right, and I find it incredibly touching if the pulse can remain, without releasing the tempo too much – then the disintegration to the most chamber-like privacy in the music can truly feel like a wistful, resigned shrug of the shoulders.

I imagine the second and the third movements as a span, almost like photographic negatives of each other, bound by that wondrously transformative bridge passage. The texture Elgar asks us to produce at the beginning is fascinating: scurrying violins, at a speed that is on the edge of possibility - but *pianissimo*! The stress of playing this, even with one of the greatest orchestras like the London Philharmonic, generates volume, and you have to fight it. The raised heart-beat accompaniment is marked *piano*, so louder than the violins, and once you achieve this contrast the texture reveals itself – a veiled intensity, burning from inside with turmoil.

In the connecting passage between the two movements, I have to be careful not to drop below the speed of the *Adagio* for, magically, the third movement is a result of the dark *scherzo* we have just heard, and the dramatic thread stays taut. This is a moment of such fragility it is difficult to comprehend that the fury has abated to such a tiny point for the tenderness of the new melody to flower. I find it very moving every time I conduct it.

So much of the *Adagio* is chamber music on an orchestral scale; rehearsals are for the musicians to listen to each other, find the same language for the gestures, how to pass melodies across the orchestra, how much space to take to allow maximum expression. My role is to keep the flow and flexibility through it, never letting the music drop: the tempo marking is slow, but not funereal – this music is alive!

Although Elgar's texture is denser than Brahms, one is often dealing with the same issue: keeping melodic flow, allowing it to sing, without sacrificing the structure of the music, the harmonies and articulation. The *Allegro* in the last movement is a prime example of this. The tendency of orchestras is to sit in the verticality of the music, but I need to push to unlock the passion in the melody – it takes time to find the sweet spot, where that all exists together. I love to hear this passage flying, with space for the accompaniment to sound. Not easy!

Like one of his heroes, Brahms, Elgar waited before composing his First Symphony, and the result was a musical journey on an even larger scale. It is quite overwhelming to reach the end where the 'keening' opening melody we heard almost an hour ago is transformed in richness and triumph, and virtuosity.

I am conflicted by Elgar's own conducting. I used to take his performances as a bible for how the music should sound. Now I am not so sure. There are certainly humbling things to be learnt from listening to him, but I also think you hear almost too clearly Elgar's personality on the podium; a little insecure, passion burning underneath, but still not sure if everyone respected his music. For me, this sometimes results in strikingly quick tempi and his slow movements not really given space to sound. Here I am talking about tiny margins, but I think Elgar's inherent modesty and shyness take his conducting in a certain direction. Learning this helped me trust my own instincts for pacing in his music.

Symphony No. 2

Elgar gave us three windows into the world of the Second Symphony: the dedication 'in memoriam' to Edward VII, the Shelley quote at the beginning of the score, 'Rarely, rarely, comest thou, Spirit of Delight', and something Elgar wrote in a letter to his beloved Alice Stuart Wortley: 'in these three works I have *shewn* myself'.[1] The symphony certainly seems to mark the end of an era, and also pours out emotion in an almost shockingly unguarded way.

At the beginning of the piece I am lost in a forest of instructions – *largamente, accelerando, in tempo, con anima, piu sostenuto, accelerando, sempre animato* and multiple tempo changes, all within the first minute of music. Played without the push and pull of these markings, the opening explosion can sound like a *Pomp and Circumstance* March – with the flexibility Elgar demands of us, something completely different emerges – music that feels heroic, but passionately restless, searching and dangerous; both player and listener should not feel safe. I am not sure I know another symphonic passage that requires such a combination of *bravura*, flexibility and virtuosity from an orchestra. Throughout the movement we are

[1] Jerrold Northrop Moore, *Edward Elgar: The Windflower Letters* (Oxford: Clarendon Press, 1989), 107. From a letter dated 29 August 1912 to Alice Stuart Wortley. The three works to which Elgar refers, are his Violin Concerto, Second Symphony and the setting of Arthur O'Shaughnessy's Ode, *The Music Makers*.

managing huge contrasts; tenderness, music that feels it could almost stop, and within a few bars a furious racing *allegro*.

The ending of the movement caps this all: the opening theme played as nobly as ever, then a wild *accelerando* at the end to the finishing line. So much of this piece seems to be Elgar at his most emotionally released.

When I think of the dedication to King Edward, I think of the slow movement. But the funeral march of the opening is deceptive; the music develops magically into Mahlerian passion; it seems to be more than just a dedication to his revered King - more a loss of an era, love and identity. It is this unbridled emotion that I find intoxicating throughout this symphony.

After the final note of the score Elgar writes where he composed the symphony: 'Tintagel and Venice'. He considered himself a composer in the German tradition, but he looked to Italy for hot-blooded freedom. His love of Italy and his position as a pan-European composer is much more interesting for me than as an emblem of a certain period of British history.

The third movement has to feel risky, and I relish the challenge of pushing the tempo to its edge – and even with the more ruminative second theme, Elgar fills the score with rubato markings (echoing the restlessness of the opening of the symphony). Interestingly many of these markings are not in the original orchestral parts, just in the score. Part of me likes to think this was intentional, to keep the feeling of spontaneity, but it certainly makes it difficult! There is nothing quite like the reprise, the two melodies of the movement played together, with a bass drum and timpani heartbeat growing to overwhelm the rest of the orchestra for an instant. It is utterly thrilling. I think it is a description of a panic attack: Elgar acknowledging some emotional over-indulgence, the shame of a love affair perhaps, leading to his heart thudding deafeningly in his temples.

Rehearsing the finale, I often start with slow play-throughs of the central furioso development – it's one of the hardest things Elgar ever wrote; even just for players to understand how they relate to each other's phrases is demanding. This is a complexity seen rarely in his other works. I talked about flow at the beginning of the First Symphony; the challenge at the beginning of the Second's last movement is finding the right feeling for all three contrasting melodies, without obviously manipulating the tempo too much. Whenever I have performed the Second I have always found this is a difficult but ultimately rewarding challenge.

As I wrote before, the great German composers were icons for Elgar; the serene beauty of Beethoven's slow movements, or the perfection of form and melody of Schumann. The final *stanza* of this symphony is intrinsically related to the end of Brahms's Third Symphony; the music seems to slip through my fingers as we approach the final resolution. Honestly, standing in front of it, you get to share the most intimate feeling of Elgar's own vulnerability. It is a feeling I do not get from any other work I conduct.

I have been asked which of the two Symphonies is my favourite to conduct. I am not sure I can answer, as I oscillate between the two. Sometimes I'm drawn to the Brahmsian form of the First, at other times to the deeper, more explicit emotion of the Second. Certainly, the Second takes us on a more enveloping journey, both in rehearsals and performance, but both symphonies reward conductor and orchestra immensely and show us the genius of this great symphonic composer.

~ Tom Higgins

One afternoon, when a student, I listened to the violinist Paul Beard reminisce about Elgar. Beard (1901–1989) was among the last of a long line of players who had the privilege of working with Elgar. It was a glimpse into an earlier world where orchestral players got to know the composer as both man and artist. Beard's encounter with Elgar stretched a long way back, but there had been a lasting effect on him. It showed in the way he spoke about Elgar – movingly, fondly even.

In time I came to realise that what I had heard formed a large part of what makes Elgar important. His maturing as a composer at the turn of the twentieth century marked a new era in British music. He expressed grandeur and lyricism on a symphonic scale and proved finally that Britain was, after long-held doubts, a great musical nation. The pivotal point came when his contemporaries understood this and had the confidence to say so. Indigenous yet international, British symphonic music could now be programmed unashamedly alongside the continental masters – Elgar gave his country the assurance it had lacked for so long.

But for all the public acclaim, Elgar's importance went deeper amongst orchestral musicians. Many experienced a feeling of direct communication with him. Part of his significance was his brilliant handling of the orchestra – at the time it was quite new. Contemporary composers marvelled at his skills, but what gave his reputation its fascination was his consideration for orchestral players. His instrumentation set higher standards in playing, yet was joyous to perform, beyond which players were thrilled by the sounds going on around them. They were the first to hear his innovative scoring and recognise his genius. For them it was a matter of satisfaction that a work such as *In the South* (*Alassio*) could rank alongside any of Richard Strauss's tone poems.

Elgar enjoyed many stunning premieres and perhaps endured his fair share of dubious first performances, but there are good grounds for believing that he never lost the support of British orchestras. The long-term success of a composer has more to do with the understanding of performers than with what critics may say. In early middle age, Elgar stood on the brink of national recognition. The 'Edwardian Era' or the close of the Belle

Époque – whatever you call those years – belonged to him. Many of the large works by which he is best remembered were composed during this period and, as his fame spread, so his relationship with orchestral players deepened. His great friend and biographer, the violinist W.H. (Billy) Reed (1875–1942) first met him in 1898, when playing in rehearsals for *Caractacus.* Elgar was conducting and Reed recalled how the orchestra 'adored him'. It was to be a life-long affection.

A few years later, Elgar dedicated his *Cockaigne* Overture 'To my many friends, the members of British orchestras'. It was an outward sign, powerfully made, that players had got to know him as man and artist. To all the instrumentalists Elgar worked with, his sometime 'prickly' personality didn't seem to have been on show. For this piece of intelligence, we have Reed again to thank. His famous story of asking Elgar for harmony and counterpoint lessons and being gently rebuffed is revealing. Reed, then a member of the Queen's Hall Orchestra, was prompted to approach Elgar immediately after rehearsing the funeral march from *Grania and Diarmid.* He was 'thrilled by the music' and 'newness of the orchestral sound'. After Elgar's refusal, he worried that the composer would be annoyed with him, but discovered that with Elgar's subsequent appearances with the orchestra the composer always found an opportunity to say something personal to him.

Early in 1905 Elgar completed his *Introduction and Allegro for Strings,* a work premiered by the newly formed London Symphony Orchestra and intended to show off the orchestra's string section. Later that year he took the orchestra on its first provincial tour and, as every musician knows, extended journeys are where friendships are made. Reed remembered Elgar arriving at Paddington Station to take the train for the start of the tour. A porter warned Elgar to stay away from a part of the train where:

> ... 'there was some sort of bloomin' band....'
> 'That's all right,' said Elgar. 'I'm one of them.'

In mid-1905 Elgar visited the USA for the first time. In all he made four visits, with his customary courtesy towards orchestral players travelling with him. The New World did Elgar a double service by welcoming him as both composer and conductor. A guest in America, he didn't have to do anything except be himself and America loved him for it.

The following year, while composing *The Kingdom,* Elgar wrote to Adolf Borsdorf, principal horn of the LSO, for advice on a horn passage. German-born Borsdorf (1854–1923) was a founder-member of the LSO and London's most influential horn player. He replied that the passage for four horns was 'not at all too difficult' and hoped to be in the orchestra when the work was performed. Significantly he added in his letter that he felt 'proud' and 'honoured' to have been asked for advice from Sir Edward.

Of all Elgar's relationships with orchestral players the one with Reed was the most significant. Initially, it was an easy association stretching over a decade, until it suddenly deepened into a close, lifelong friendship. Reed's story of how in early 1910 he met Elgar in Regent Street has become folklore. Casually Elgar asked if Reed had any spare time and if so would he come and see him in his New Cavendish Street flat. The composer was sketching out something for the 'fiddle' and wanted to discuss 'some questions of bowing', and 'certain intricacies in the passage work'.

Reed was flattered. He soon attended Elgar's flat and after only a morning's work learned much about the composer's highly individual methods of working. It was 'an education' to see how Elgar was putting together sketches for what was to become one of his most important works: the Violin Concerto. More visits to the flat were followed by Elgar and Reed working together on the concerto and at the country home of Frank Schuster, The Hut, in Bray near Maidenhead.

Jointly they continued working on the concerto. There was no problem about what to do for relaxation between sessions: they were both from the West of England and music-making was punctuated by long country walks. Reed increasingly found himself being taken into Elgar's confidence. A special relationship developed and Reed – by now 'Billy' – became one of the composer's most intimate companions. It was the best of friendships. They made music together both publicly and privately – Elgar's dedication of his *Sospiri* Op.70 to Reed reminds us directly of how close they were.

Much research goes into determining how composers want their music performed, but given Elgar's long conducting career both on the concert platform and in the recording studio, it was passed on through the players. That said, conductors like Sir John Barbirolli and Sir Adrian Boult were also in touch with the composer; but players experienced him over several decades, sometime on a daily basis. Elgar requires subtle tempi and flexible interpretation. Some conductors struggle to achieve this, but Britain is fortunate to have Elgar's style handed down through its orchestras.

Paul Beard, whom I encountered at the beginning of my career, belonged to the final generation of players who knew Elgar as a conductor. For the last quarter-century of his career, Beard led the BBC Symphony Orchestra. By this time he was close to being a national figure. He was the player you looked for when tuning in to early televised broadcasts of the BBC Proms. In post-BBC retirement he was a professor at the Guildhall School of Music where I was a student. On Wednesday afternoons he led the orchestra.

Imposing and authoritative, he seldom pulled rank, for example by telling you he had played for Arturo Toscanini – but this afternoon was different. The school was preparing a performance of *The Dream of Gerontius* with the Guildhall School's principal, Gordon Thorne, as conductor. But at this particular rehearsal Thorne didn't appear; instead, Beard mounted the podium and announced that he had persuaded the principal to let him take the rehearsal as, having played the work under Sir Edward's direction, he wanted to impart some of the composer's 'special points' in the orchestration.

In fact there was quite a catalogue of Sir Edward's 'special points'. My main regret now is that I didn't write them down at the time, but one item was unforgettable. Near the end of the afternoon, Beard arrived at rehearsal number 120, where the Soul comes before God; for many of us – performers and audiences alike – it is the most dramatic moment in any choral work. 'Sir Edward', said Beard, impressed the orchestra by instructing that the first beat of the bar with a dynamic of *fffzp*, must be as though someone had punched you in the stomach and winded you.

As remembered now, Beard's desire to pass on the composer's interpretation of his own work was more than a professional commitment. His career was long and the question of when he played for Elgar didn't much matter. He led several orchestras before joining the BBC. Yet the point was that after a lifetime of distilling the wishes of many legendary conductors, his early recollections of Elgar were still strongly felt. He had the luck to discover Elgar the man and Elgar the artist in a single encounter.

Some would argue that the player's job is not to become emotionally involved with the music. Others would argue that with Elgar this is not possible. The American conductor and composer Bernard Herrmann was an Elgarian of renown. In *Edward Elgar Centenary Sketches*, he noted that 'one of the most splendid things about this music is the pleasure and joy that sweeps over the faces of the players as one of the great climaxes of his music is reached'.[1]

A few weeks before Elgar died, his old friends the London Symphony Orchestra assembled in HMV's Abbey Road Studios to record the 'Triumphal March' and 'Woodland Interlude' from *Caractacus*. They were conducted by Lawrance Collingwood; Elgar lay in his sick bed at home in Marl Bank, Worcester, connected to the studio by a telephone line relay. He was thus able to direct the rehearsal on some points of interpretation. His close acquaintance – Reed – led the orchestra. Even at a distance of nearly 150

1 H.A. Chambers (Ed.), *Edward Elgar Centenary Sketches* (London: Novello & Co., 1957), 20.

miles, Elgar's voice alone was enough to invoke the old magic. He asked who was present and Reed replied that 'all his best bandsmen were there' adding that they sent their love. It was a bittersweet moment. Even if they hadn't been told, the players must have guessed this was the end. It was an afternoon's work lasting a few hours, but it brought all concerned great satisfaction.

Elgar was the first British composer of substance to appear for nearly 200 years. That is one piece of his importance. The jigsaw fills out with his cultivation of the orchestra. An expert on the orchestral world from which he himself had emerged, Elgar understood its need for professionalism. He gave players a new pride in their work and they were grateful. Yet Elgar's importance is not found in any one thing. It breaks down into many parts. Beyond those favoured hundreds of orchestral players who knew him in person are the millions who rejoice in his music today. He can be spiritual and he can be comical. He enthrals us and entertains us. The conductor Constant Lambert, who was also a perceptive commentator on music, wrote simply, yet brilliantly, that 'Elgar was the last serious composer to be in touch with the great public.'[2]

2 Constant Lambert, *Music Ho!* (London: Faber and Faber, 1937), 273.

~ Andrew Litton

My conducting career began in January 1982, when I won the BBC Rupert Foundation Conducting competition. A 22-year-old New Yorker, I am embarrassed to admit that my Elgarian knowledge was pretty much limited to *Enigma Variations* and the piece played at every American graduation, *Pomp & Circumstance* No. 1. Suddenly, my career began and in England of all places! My new agent handed me a recording of *In the South* with Silvestri and the Bournemouth Symphony, and I fell in love! It was more than a little ironic that my relationship with the Bournemouth Symphony began four short years later (Principal Guest and then Principal Conductor). My London conducting debut, with the Royal Philharmonic, was set for January 1983, and *In the South* was on the programme. How amazing to experience that exhilarating music with such a great orchestra! I was truly in heaven!

At that point, I was Rostropovich's assistant conductor at the National Symphony in Washington DC, and the phone rang in November 1984 from the RPO enquiring if I could fly over immediately and replace an indisposed *Maestro* (I wish I could remember who) in a concert with *Enigma Variations* at the Royal Festival Hall. Even though I had never conducted it before, the brashness and fearlessness of youth compelled me to say yes, and next morning I was rehearsing the Royal Phil yet again. I remember feeling really shy at suggesting corrections to an orchestra for which this music was in its DNA, but I kept noticing details that were being overlooked – a short note, a tenuto, a dynamic – so I summoned up my courage and carried on. Of huge support was their leader Barry Griffiths, who quickly took me under his wing and said: 'Don't take so much time at the end of the phrase! Other conductors do and it is so unnecessary!' In the end it seemed like a really convincing performance and fortunately the critics agreed. My love for Elgar was cemented.

I went on to perform *Enigma* with the RPO on three more occasions in the next two years and then on 22 December 1987 we convened at Abbey Road Studios to record an Elgar album for Virgin Classics. The producer on that occasion was Andrew Keener. We had already collaborated on a handful of discs at that point, but he took it upon himself to start indoctrinating me on the Elgar Symphonies, *Falstaff* and *Introduction and Allegro.* He didn't have to work too hard. I was smitten. My initial Elgar First was in 1991 and I've conducted it 26 times since with orchestras as far afield as the Philadelphia, Melbourne Symphony, Vancouver Symphony and the Swedish Radio. My most-treasured performance was with the BBC Symphony at the Barbican in January of 2013. We had a great time rehearsing, and everything aligned for the performance. Performances of this standard are what one tries for every week, but one is lucky if they happen once a year.

Elgar 2 quickly became my favourite and it was the work I chose for my farewell to the Bournemouth Symphony at the Royal Albert Hall Proms in July of 1994, after six great years as Principal Conductor. Is there a greater valedictory farewell work? In September 2007, I conducted it with the London Philharmonic at the Royal Festival Hall, after which I received the Elgar Society medal – a great honour of which I am very proud!

Another great Elgar experience was performing *Introduction and Allegro* with the Dallas Symphony at Carnegie Hall and the Proms. I believe it was Andrew Keener again who inspired me to programme it! I hope someday to have an orchestra and a label interested in recording the two symphonies – it would be a dream come true.

Anyway, just to throw some additional fun stats at you, the Elgar works I have conducted the most are: *Enigma Variations* 38 times with 12 different orchestras and recorded it for both BIS and Virgin Classics. I've conducted the Cello Concerto 30 times with 11 different soloists. Elgar First Symphony, 26 times with ten different orchestras. Elgar Second, sixteen times with five different orchestras. *In the South,* 21 times with ten different orchestras, and the Violin Concerto seventeen times with six different soloists, including a recording for Avie Records. Finally, *Cockaigne* 31 times with ten different orchestras.

Elgar's music remains a vast treasure-trove of intensely satisfying music to perform. I look forward to increasing my numbers, but also hopefully adding some new experiences someday, like my first *Gerontius.*

~ Neil Mantle

I write the following shortly after being accorded the great honour of being awarded the Elgar Society's Medal in recognition of the efforts I have made in promoting his music in Scotland. I have interpreted the title, *The Importance of Elgar*, as an opportunity for personal reflection on what Elgar's music has meant to me over sixty years.

Coincidentally, the Elgar Society and I came to fruition in the same year, 1951. I confess that my knowledge of his music was sketchy to say the least for the first ten years of my life but all that changed dramatically on the evening of Sunday, 11 November 1962. Somehow, with school looming the next day, I persuaded my parents to allow me to stay up to watch a film about Elgar in the BBC's *Monitor* series. The director was the young Ken Russell, still, at that early stage in his career, relatively disciplined and accurate in his approach to subject matter. How keenly I felt Elgar's early setbacks and rejections, and the sadness of his final years when he felt his music was out of tune with the changing times. I could not have felt all this more personally! As the programme ended, sixty minutes later, there was no doubt: I was an ELGARIAN body and soul and so it has been ever since.

A few months later, walking home on a Thursday evening after choir practice, something caught my eye lying beside a dustbin, illuminated by a streetlight. It was a set of 78 rpm records – the gold titling on the front had helpfully caught the light. I read:

ELGAR, Symphony No. 2 in Eb, op.63
The London Symphony Orchestra
Conductor, Edward Elgar

Of course, fate had determined that these precious discs in their brown leather cloth album were destined for me and were duly liberated. I can still recall examining each disc nervously: were all the six records there and were they scratched or worse still broken? Happily, my luck was in and I silently blessed the kind people who had placed the album beside their bin and not inside it! I listened to those records over and over. I have them still and, yes, I can still play them! Serious decisions had to be made each birthday and Christmas as to which Elgar LPs might be purchased. They were still expensive items in the early 1960s with very few Elgar items on cheaper-priced reissues.

I had, a year or so later, discovered the excellent local music library and, by purloining my parents' tickets, I was able to borrow for study no less than a dozen miniature scores each week. The *Radio Times* was carefully scanned for interesting items – Elgar naturally eagerly sought – and off I would trot on Saturday morning in search of the scores. Amongst the items the library possessed were those of Elgar's two delightful miniatures *Chanson de Nuit* and *Chanson de Matin*. Their scoring for a small orchestra gave me an idea: rather than merely listening to these pieces, why not conduct them?

My kind grandfather organised the printed leaflets announcing the formation of a new orchestra, together with my contact details; in those far off days a simple telephone number. I posted the leaflets in the music library and a music shop, sat back and waited for dozens of eager musicians to apply. Twenty or so brave souls unwittingly took the plunge, not the hundred or so I had confidently predicted but it was a start. Quite what they made of this cocky fifteen-year-old schoolboy 'maestro' I now hesitate to think. I recall one of the violinists asking me if a school friend of his who played the double bass could join us. As we had no basses at all, I was delighted. Upon enquiring how long said friend had been learning, the reply of 'six weeks' was forthcoming. 'He's in!' I exclaimed, nothing daunted! That young player went on to become the longstanding principal double bass player of the Royal Scottish National Orchestra.

I had absolutely no idea from where I could obtain the necessary orchestral parts so, at a time when I should have been initiating myself into the mysteries of maths, physics and chemistry, I spent long hours copying out the parts by hand, including, of course, the aforementioned *Chansons*. With their restrained scoring they suited my little group well and much pleasure was experienced in working on them. As our numbers swelled to a more useful forty or so players we were able to proceed to the *Three Bavarian Dances*. The reason for this choice were simply that, having discovered the St Andrews Orchestra music library, this was their sole set of Elgar parts!

By 1970 many of the young players had departed for pastures new and a rethink was necessary. I was then studying horn at The Royal Academy of Music in London and found that the first orchestra was due to play Elgar's Second Symphony at a repertoire rehearsal. I had only graduated to the humble second orchestra but was so desperate to take part that I bribed a friend with the princely sum of £1 (this was over half a century ago!) to call in sick and allow me to take his place. Later, being frustrated at Elgar being most remiss at composing no pieces for horn, I 'deranged' his beautiful *Chanson de Nuit* for horn and piano and have since performed it several times.

I wanted to be able to explore the larger-scale Elgar works, requiring many more players than I had previously. Accordingly, I started recruiting for a brand new orchestra, the grandly named *Scottish Sinfonia*. The first few years were difficult as many of the local players were committed to other orchestras but, by 1974, we had sufficient numbers to tackle Elgar's Second Symphony during the Edinburgh Festival Fringe of that year, with the First Symphony and Cello Concerto the following summer. Although we lost money more often than we broke even, it was all tremendously exciting.

In 1993 I assumed conductorship of choral societies in Edinburgh and Dundee, which enlarged our repertoire considerably. We performed the majority of Elgar's choral works, often more than once, and I especially remember with delight numerous members of both orchestra and chorus expressing their excitement at discovering this wonderful music, together with bewilderment that it was not better known. The strangest experience around this time was conducting *The Music Makers* in the magnificent Orléans Cathedral when that city generously invited my Dundee Choral Union to visit and perform. I never did discover if the look of permanent bewilderment on the part of the members of the French orchestra was caused by the unfamiliar idiom of the music or my mangling of their language during rehearsal. This changed to outright astonishment as they encountered Elgar's witty musical reference to their *Marseillaise*!! Over the fifty-three years since I founded the Scottish Sinfonia we have given over sixty performances of Elgar's works. If this sounds less than impressive, it is worth bearing in mind that on average we only give four performances per season and also that the overall repertoire has to be a balanced one.

My wife and I have been frequent visitors to 'Elgar Country' imbibing that very special atmosphere, including of course, his beloved Malvern Hills. An occasion that we both treasure is that of sitting in our car, on a hot summer's afternoon, listening to the opening of part two of *The Dream of Gerontius* in a performance we had recently given in Dundee with their splendid Choral Union. We were parked directly outside the location of its composition, Birchwood Lodge.

The Importance of Elgar? I know not if listening to his music cures backache or mitigates the effects of influenza. What I do know is I cannot imagine my life without his music. It has been my inspiration and delight in good times and a solace when things were not going so well over the sixty years since that cold, dark November evening.

~ Antonio Pappano

The first language I spoke at home was English but there was also an incredible patois in use by my family, a Southern Italian dialect. When I say patois, it was more like an invented language because certain words were always in English. This caused me trouble later because I never officially studied Italian. As with most dialects, the meaning of some words tends to be changed or the endings of words are cut off. This one, akin to Neapolitan, was actually from the Benevento, which is inland from Naples in Campania, and has its own twang. Of course, being around and hearing two languages at the very beginning of life is very stimulating and, although I did not know it at the time, very helpful for a prospective musician: the colours, sounds and structure of language are hugely important, certainly for a future opera conductor!

I moved to the USA when I was thirteen, a formative age from an educational point of view as I went straight into the American education system; into first year High School. Of course it was something of a culture shock watching American TV as I grew up hearing different sounds for my language. You know it is English, but it is spoken in a completely different way and so your ear must adjust. My younger brother lost his accent in what seemed like a couple of days; I never really lost my English accent. Of course, in England people think I sound American with an accent that is difficult to pin down, but when I go to America they think I sound British!

This appreciation of the sounds of language both verbally and musically was a useful background when I worked with an Italian orchestra, the Santa Cecilia, in the music of Elgar. The players were not familiar with the music, with Barbirolli's performance of the First Symphony in Rome more than 60 years before but a memory for the archive. It had not been performed there again until I conducted it in the early 2000s. This amazing music that is so expressive, so melodic, it seems extraordinary that it was not in the repertoire of an orchestra such as the Santa Cecilia.

Teaching the players the music was quite an adventure, and I went about this by selling the music in an almost messianic way – selling the message as a kind of disciple. Elgar writes diatonically and of course chromatically, his harmonies not unlike Puccini's, each one however uses very personal handling of chord inversions that go a long way in creating their respective sound worlds. The harmonisation of even simple tunes can reveal so much. Of course, the melodic aspect of Elgar's music immediately appeals to Italians. When you hear them play the slow movement of the Symphony, you can hear something Mediterranean in the way melody is treated. That comes very naturally to the players, but I also included the audience, telling them about the piece and its history and how long this work had been missing from their concert halls. I am no longer music director of the Santa Cecilia Orchestra and if I have one regret it is that I did not perform *The Dream of Gerontius* there.

I conducted the Symphony, first in London with the London Symphony Orchestra (LSO) and then took it to the Romans with my accrued wisdom. The *cantabile* in Elgar's music is clear in pieces like *In the South* which is of course Italianate, reflecting the landscape of Liguria, which is an incredible mix of water, rock, sunshine, and history. The Straussian, virtuosic treatment of the music was 'up the street' of my orchestra. Their type of fiddle playing is very much about beauty of sound and lightning velocity.

Elgar's 'sound' is based on what he learned from the Germans: Schumann of course in particular, and Brahms, and then Wagner and Strauss. The Italians are not used to sustaining the sound and I had to work very hard with them to try to get all the facets of making a proper Elgarian aural environment. Sustaining a melody is one thing because it's protagonistic. On the other hand, sustaining harmony means groups of people playing together with no individual being more important than another, and that was not in the natural DNA of the Italian players. But we got there! I was so proud to have somehow converted them to this music I love so deeply.

Many years ago I conducted the *Enigma Variations* for the first time – I think it was with the orchestra in Cologne – and of course I have done both Symphonies and the two concertos, the Violin Concerto being a most important piece for me. I have conducted *In the South* and the *Introduction and Allegro for Strings* and I have played in the Piano Quintet. Naturally, I am looking forward to conducting *The Dream of Gerontius* which is 'on the books'. I have a long history of being close to Elgar's music for I was Daniel Barenboim's assistant in Bayreuth and elsewhere. He has always been a champion of Elgar's music since early on, so I think I got the infection from him, probably when I was forced to come to grips with the Symphonies. I realised there is such a depth of feeling there and, for me, what makes Elgar's music personal is the attachment he has to relationships. For example, the Violin Concerto is obviously a love song: an extended expression of incredible sensual passion and basic human care and kindness. To the degree that this happens in Elgar's music is, I think, special. As we know he had a few entanglements, and I think they inspired him, but he had these incredible friendships too and you know there are these little love letters to each one of them in the *Variations*. When you know about who these people are, the human component becomes so important in understanding the music. It blows the dust off all those musty English clichés. That is so very important. Of course, Elgar was born at a certain time, and he dressed in a certain way, cultivating his signature moustache. However, I think psychologically he was a very complicated, complex, human being. I suspect under the surface he suffered a lot and that suffering is most definitely funnelled through his music, some of which is heartbreakingly poignant, such as the last two pages of the Second Symphony. There is a *fortepiano* accent that just shoots you through the heart. I certainly become very emotionally involved in this music.

The Violin Concerto was the one piece I have always coveted, but I never got a chance to conduct it until very recently, and luckily with Vilde Frang. Her recent recording is an absolutely wonderful performance. The sheer length of the piece, the demands it places on the soloist and the accompanying players, is considerable. I had to bring out all my armoury – all my knowledge of conducting singers to create a warm and appropriately alert environment for the violin. Of course the orchestra has a prominent role to play in the piece too. It took me a long time to learn the concerto because of its unusual harmonic sequences. Even though it is in a romantic musical language that we all know and love, I find the music unpredictable. And that's why I find it interesting, but also very challenging. I fell in love with the concerto from hearing the famous recording with Menuhin and the LSO, which, of course, was Elgar's orchestra. That is a tradition preserved by the orchestra and of which one is immediately aware when they play two notes of this music. The players just know how it should sound and how it should go. That is why I am looking forward to doing the *Enigma Variations* with the orchestra because the musicians know the piece ten times better than I do. Perhaps…

When a piece is so well known, that is when you must take nothing for granted. Recently I recorded the Cello Concerto which is, I suppose, with the *Variations* Elgar's calling card around the world. Cellists have the Dvořák, Schumann, Haydn and the Shostakovich concertos but with the Elgar it is very hard to say the words 'Elgar Cello Concerto' without bringing up the name of Jacqueline du Pré and the poignancy of what happened to her. She had a unique way with the concerto, but if you try to imitate this it sounds ridiculous. With her, it seemed as if the music could only be played her way.

Now there is no greater compliment to Elgar than soloists from all over the world playing his music. I turn back to Daniel Barenboim again who recorded both symphonies with his Staatskapelle Orchestra in Berlin and the Cello Concerto with Alisa Weilerstein. He also recorded *Falstaff* with the same orchestra. The story goes that he got the orchestra to really admire and come to love Elgar's music.

I heard Mark Elder conduct *The Kingdom* with the LSO about ten years ago. It was a wonderful performance, but I have to conduct *The Dream of Gerontius* first before considering pieces such as *The Apostles* and *The Kingdom*. All the same, with my work with the LSO I am putting a strong and obvious accent on British music. Elgar's symphonies are going to be very important, and we want to travel with this music, taking our heritage abroad as ambassadors for our heritage. On one of my last tours through Europe with the LSO one of the pieces we played was the Fifth Symphony of Vaughan Williams. I was worried how this was going to be received because the music was virtually unknown to our audiences. Happily, it was very warmly received: that feeling of benediction in the piece with its natural spirituality really got to the audiences. We went on tour to America in the spring of 2025 and took the *Enigma Variations* and Walton's First Symphony with us. Certainly, in the future, Elgar's music will feature prominently in my programming.

~ Adrian Partington

There are several ways in which this title could be interpreted. I am not an academic, but after over fifty years of performing Elgar's music, and for almost as many years reading about the man and his music, I can offer a few thoughts. (These may of course be disputed by people better qualified than I.)

Elgar was a famous national figure in the first few decades of the twentieth century: he received every honour which the nation was able to bestow on him; his music was played everywhere from the Royal Albert Hall to the humblest dwelling where there was a piano; the 'man in the street' knew Elgar's name and could whistle one or two of his tunes. He was also a part of that subjectively entitled phenomenon known as the 'English Musical Renaissance', which was much discussed in the twentieth century, when musical historians believed that nothing had happened in British musical life since the seventeenth century. This interpretation is now viewed as too glib; there were many developments in the eighteenth and nineteenth centuries: Parry and Stanford, for example, were significant national composers well before Elgar's name was known.

Apart from Elgar's public achievements in the years before the First World War, and apart from the large body of music that he left, much of which is still enjoyed today, Elgar was not a figure of great *historical* importance. He did not start a musical movement, nor did he develop one. His brief but spectacular career was brought to a sudden halt by the Great War. Public taste moved away from Elgar and other 'late Romantic' composers as a result of this conflict, and its many social and economic consequences. (Elgar's music was perceived after 1918 as being part of the 'old order', which had caused so much suffering; people wanted something new, e.g. jazz.) Elgar was arguably the best of a group of British composers of the late nineteenth and early twentieth centuries whose art owed much to German 'Romantic' music; in Elgar's case, his debt was to Wagner, Brahms and Schumann. The music of his contemporaries, for example Parry and Stanford (the latter Irish by birth, but British by education and career), has fared less well than Elgar's because their musical personalities were not as strong.

Thus, Elgar's music is a final flowering of a nineteenth-century aesthetic; he had no significant musical successors; and, unlike Stanford and Parry, Elgar did not teach composition, or even involve himself in the world of musical education to any great extent, apart from an unsuccessful period as nominal Professor of Music at Birmingham University. It is thus arguable that *historically speaking,* Elgar is less important than both Stanford and Parry, whose pupils and 'grand-pupils' dominated British musical life for the rest of the twentieth century: Vaughan Williams, Holst and their many pupils.

Elgar was a wonderfully gifted composer whose music has brought pleasure to thousands of people over the past hundred years or more; but he finished an epoch and did not contribute to the flow of musical history. I contend therefore that Elgar is not a figure of historical importance compared to his younger contemporary Vaughan Williams or his near contemporaries in Europe, Debussy or Bartók, for example. The question is, does Elgar's music continue to give pleasure now?

There is no doubt that the UK has radically changed in the past decade or so, demographically, geopolitically and culturally. Classical music has not fared well through these changes: national and private funding for most musical institutions has plummeted, audiences continue to decline in size, choirs are smaller, fewer children are learning to play musical instruments and so on. The decline in interest in 'Classical' music of course began in the 1960s with changes in education policy, which meant that fewer and fewer children were taught anything at all about such music. The prioritising of 'core' subjects and a change in emphasis towards popular music in the music curriculum have together accelerated to the point where there is now a national ignorance about Classical music which did not exist fifty years ago. Moreover, Classical music, because it is now appreciated by so few people has gained a reputation for being 'elitist', and it has become politically unimportant, so few people in authority are interested in speaking up for it. (I should add that private schools have continued to invest in Classical music, which has meant that although there are still plenty of young musicians seeking to enter the profession, they come from a smaller and smaller section of society. This has added to the atmosphere of 'elitism' which is one of Classical music's most obvious problems; and is ironic considering Elgar's own humble beginnings.)

As a result of the new ignorance, interest in Elgar has declined nationally to the point where he is not perceived as an important national figure; in fact, where people have actually heard of him, they may see him in the same way as, for example, Winston Churchill, i.e. a representative of an old white, Anglo-Saxon, male, imperialist culture. It is hard to deny that

Elgar was such a representative, with his social climbing, his collecting of national honours and his reactionary political views and snobbery. It is hard to defend Elgar in our current cultural climate on these grounds, a climate which has caused Elgar's most famous tune, the Trio of the first *Pomp and Circumstance* March, to be seen as a symbol of everything which the UK should not now be. (Possibly the tune in its choral version will be banned from the Last Night of the BBC Proms.)

I would thus argue that Elgar is no longer a person of any importance in the UK. Sadly, he has never been an important musical figure elsewhere. However, his music is still loved by many of that small proportion of our population who still have an interest in Classical music. It is up to us to continue to defend and promote the work of Elgar, otherwise in the future it may be forgotten.

I cannot see an end to the decline in the public funding of Classical music; the Arts Council of England has other priorities now. Similarly, I cannot see an end to falling attendances at concerts; and I cannot see a change in attitude of those who decide the nation's education policy. I cannot see a recovery in the fortunes of the traditional churches, the Anglican church in particular. (This matter may seem tangential to an essay about Elgar, but I believe that the disappearance of church choirs and congregations has impacted greatly on British life: fewer and fewer people are involved in public music-making, that is to say hymn singing, now. And for many people in former times, singing in a church choir as a child was their introduction to becoming practical musicians, and their initiation into Classical music.)

I cannot see an end to the view among the general public that Classical music is not for them (that is, if they even give the subject any thought). Appreciating Classical music requires a certain level of patience and knowledge. In recent years, the proliferation of electronic devices has provided too many easy alternatives to listening to any music which lasts longer than a few minutes; and to be blunt, most people's ability to concentrate has been seriously impaired. Thinking these depressing thoughts made me consider why I became interested in Elgar as a child, and why he has been a central figure in my life for over fifty years. I have come to the inescapable conclusion that it was because I had a privileged upbringing, not financially speaking, but culturally. My parents cared about the arts and considered them as important. Neither of them went to private schools and both were brought up in council houses. But Classical music was definitely part of their upbringing in the 1930s because of the prevailing cultural climate, not because their parents were musical.

It was thus my privilege to be born into an Elgar-loving household: my parents had met and courted in Malvern so, as young professional musicians, they could not escape the influence of Elgar who had died only a few years before their arrival. My father was a pianist and organist, and my mother was a violinist; as a duo, much of their repertoire was by Elgar. By the time I was born, they had settled in Nottingham, and my first clear musical memory was of being taken to hear the *Enigma Variations* in the Nottingham Albert Hall, played by, I think, the CBSO. I would have been five or six at the time (*c.*1964). I remember being overawed by the experience. My parents subsequently sent me to be a Chorister at Worcester Cathedral, partly because they were extremely impressed by the wonderful musicianship of the Cathedral's then Director of Music, Christopher Robinson, and partly because they were in love with 'Elgar Country', having enjoyed the best times of their lives there. As a Chorister, I had a full diet of Elgar experiences, from singing *The Spirit of the Lord* on a televised 'Songs of Praise' broadcast in 1968 to singing on an LP recording of Elgar's Church Music in 1969, which may have been the first of its kind, and is certainly still available, fifty years later. I heard my first *Gerontius* at the 1969 Three Choirs Festival, which fascinated me, partly because the solo tenor lost his voice about halfway through the performance.

With a solid Elgarian background from early childhood, my understanding of, and love for, Elgar's music has developed and intensified over the succeeding decades to a point where I feel very comfortable performing any of his music. Since returning to the world of the Three Choirs Festival as Director of Music at Gloucester Cathedral in 2008, I have enjoyed the enormous privilege of directing most of Elgar's large-scale works with world-class orchestras: the concertos, the overtures, and of course the oratorios: I conducted my third *Apostles* in 2023 and my fourth *Kingdom* on the last night of the 2024 Three Choirs Festival at Worcester. I have ten performances of *The Dream of Gerontius* under my belt now, too. Elgar's music is important to me because, as I have demonstrated, I grew up with it; it is like a member of my family, and I love it as such. The most pervading characteristic in his music is its nostalgia. I think he *knew* he was at the end of a musical era and regretted the fact, hence the deliberate nostalgia in the music.

It is more difficult to define precisely what I enjoy about Elgar's music, aside from its overwhelming sense of nostalgia. The only way I can briefly explain my love for the music is that there are aspects of Elgar's personality in it: his world view, his self-doubt, his humour, his generosity, his anxiety, his narcissism, and his *Sehnsucht* (yearning), all of which I feel accord strongly with my own personality. (I think all musicians are narcissistic to a greater or lesser extent!) In addition, I have become increasingly aware of the sheer professionalism of the music, the skill in its compilation; the consistent idiomatic writing for all instruments; the wonderful and inventive harmonic sense; and the most wonderful tunes, tunes which would 'knock 'em flat' to quote his promise about the tune of the Trio of *Pomp and Circumstance* March No.1.

Elgar was a thoroughly practical musician and composer; a man of the people despite his pretensions; and an obviously flawed human being struggling to make sense of the world. These are the reasons which make his music important to me.

~ Donald Runnicles

Like many of my contemporaries, my first encounter with Elgar was as a player in youth orchestras, then soon afterwards as a very impressionable sixteen-year-old conductor of the Caritas Ensemble in Edinburgh, soon to become the Caritas Orchestra. I remember we performed the *Serenade for Strings* and one of the *Pomp and Circumstance* marches. I founded Caritas with a couple of school friends back in 1970 when I was a pupil at George Watson's College under the benevolent eye of the inspirational music teacher there, Richard Telfer, who suggested we play a charity concert. Then, throughout my student days, there were the Friday night concerts at the Usher Hall, often with Alexander Gibson conducting the Scottish National Orchestra in the *Enigma Variations* with a deep understanding of the style. When I went to St John's Cambridge as a post-graduate student, I played third horn in the Cambridge University Music Society Orchestra. We played *In the South* there along with the Violin Concerto with Menuhin, conducted by Philip Ledger – both the work and the performance a spiritual journey for me. Learning from *inside* the orchestra teaches a young conductor what an orchestra needs from him or her, as well as offering insight into the hierarchy of orchestral life (and the hierarchy of intonation!). Those Elgar horn parts! People often cite the influence of Richard Strauss on Elgar. Well, perhaps, but the style of Elgar's horn parts is entirely his own. In the First Symphony, for instance, the writing is not only very virtuosic, but a great deal more chromatic than Wagner or even Richard Strauss. The flamboyance, the whooping gestures of Elgar's horn writing in the outer movements are not mistakable for anyone else – they are absolutely *Elgarian* – and quite unlike anything before him.

His approach to writing for strings is also very much his own, so often awarding equally important material to the second violins as to the firsts, which is why I try to persuade orchestras to seat the seconds on the right, opposite the firsts, rather than behind them on the left (not that every orchestra is comfortable with this!). I love what Elgar is supposed to have once said to the seconds: 'Enjoy this tune, gentlemen, I wrote it especially for you.' Then there is the delicacy and transparency of a kind not to be found in the tone poems of Strauss, a vulnerability of spirit, a feeling of existential *angst*, of 'what is my place in this world?' that was not part of that master's personality. Perhaps, in such a rapidly changing world as ours, Elgar's is a unique voice which more than ever we can recognise in ourselves.

I have to keep reminding myself, on looking at the subtlety and originality of his scoring, that Elgar was self-taught. A musically literate friend of mine whose score reading isn't at all bad once remarked to me that if he randomly opens a densely orchestrated page of a score that he knows well by, say, Mahler or Strauss, he can pretty quickly identify the principal melody. That is not, he says, always so at first glance with Elgar. The melodic line isn't always instantly apparent. I think this makes sense. It could well have something to do with the fact that Elgar had a working knowledge of a wide variety of instruments including the viola and so the layout of his scores reflects this 'middle-voice' mindset. He was not a pianist in the mould of Mahler and Strauss. They may not always have composed at the piano – Strauss certainly did not, especially later in life – but somehow as a result of the layout of Elgar's scores, the voicing, what is doubled, etc., the melody doesn't leap out at you visually. He was a supremely contrapuntal composer as well, but looking *into* the score to get an aural, inner-ear clarity requires a different kind of approach. Above all, perhaps, is his mastery of symphonic form and his handling of thematic metamorphoses (the transfiguration of the First Symphony's *Scherzo* theme into that of the slow movement standing as a particularly glorious example). It is as assured and subtle a process as anything by his illustrious Austro-German counterparts.

His music is, of course, in the blood of British orchestras, and there are still differences between the way British players and those outside the UK approach it, which in turn merits a different approach from the conductor. My first performance of Elgar's First Symphony was not with a British orchestra; rather, it was back in the late 1990s with the Atlanta Symphony.[1] It was during my time as Music Director of San Francisco Opera, and I wasn't doing very much guest conducting then. The Atlanta players had very little experience of this music, and there were many of the same challenges as when I conducted the work with the Berlin Philharmonic more recently. With that great orchestra, faced with its glorious, supreme sound, I found myself needing to concentrate often on the transparency of so many of the textures I mentioned earlier. The challenge with both orchestras was to bring it in two or three days to a point where the players were enjoying the performance as opposed to hanging on by the seat of their pants! But that's the privilege of bringing these great masterpieces which we know and love to players who perhaps do not perform this music

[1] Sir Donald was Principal Guest Conductor for over twenty years, until 2023. Eds.

that often. Having conducted, for instance, the *Enigma Variations* with great American orchestras such as the Philadelphia, I have found that there is something specific in this music which speaks on a subliminal level to American musicians. America is a country of immigrants after all, and very many people hear in Elgar a nostalgia, a need for *belonging*. In these times, this music is more 'exportable' than ever.

Leonard Slatkin

Why did English Music Disappear in America?

When I was a young boy in Los Angeles, I loved to listen to the radio broadcasts that emanated from the New York Philharmonic. The specific year is not defined in my memory, but my gut reaction to hearing the Fourth Symphony by Vaughan Williams has never gone away.

Sir John Barbirolli was a frequent guest conductor with the Los Angeles Philharmonic, and from the time he presented Elgar's *Falstaff*, I was hooked. These pieces by Vaughan Williams and Elgar, as well as myriad other works from across the pond, not only made a huge impression on me but were also part of the canon of regularly programmed works. Of course, Elgar's *Enigma Variations*, Cello Concerto, and ubiquitous *First Pomp and Circumstance* March were all ensconced in our collective consciousness.

These days, almost the only pieces of British music we experience often are *The Planets* and *The Young Person's Guide to the Orchestra*. Even *The Lark Ascending* seems to be off the radar. Gone are the days when Tippett and other English composers were eagerly anticipated by American concertgoers.

In 1974, I made my London debut, with the Royal Philharmonic in an all-English programme that included Walton's *Portsmouth Point* Overture, Delius's Violin Concerto, and Vaughan Williams's Symphony No. 6. That last piece would become one of my most often performed works. Along with André Previn, I championed and recorded much of the British repertoire and played these pieces often, even outside of their homeland.

I did not do very many contemporary works, only venturing into the worlds of Turnage and Birtwistle a few times. Since the earlier generations were underrepresented, I felt audiences really needed to hear the two Elgar symphonies, along with assorted Vaughan Williams, Walton, Finzi, and the lesser-known Holst pieces.

Recently, at Bard College in upstate New York, the intrepid Leon Botstein presented a festival featuring the music of Vaughan Williams and a few of his contemporaries. This was much needed, but in my view, had one flaw. To absorb and comprehend lesser-performed music, one needs to understand it in the context of the masterpieces. Hearing Vaughan Williams's *Job* or Concerto for Two Pianos and Orchestra only makes sense if one is aware of the works of greater stature, as was the case with previous generations.

What happened? Why is so much great music being neglected today?

My best theory is that the younger generation of conductors either does not know the repertoire or does not believe it will further their careers – quite the opposite of how I came to a modest degree of prominence in the field. This lack of intellectual curiosity is disturbing. Of course, we all want to be taken seriously within the standard repertoire, but do we really need yet another Brahms, Bruckner, or Sibelius symphony cycle on disc or other media outlet?

The situation is similar with the repertoire of my own country. Gone are the symphonists such as Schuman, Piston, Harris, Sessions, and so many others. It is as if the history of our musical pathway suddenly evaporated. The new podium minders are always on the hunt to find the next compositional voice, and in doing so, neglect the world that came before.

If I were starting my career today, I would focus on repertoire that is not presented very often on the concert platform. This is not limited to American and English music. What about all the wonderful French composers who were writing at the same time as Debussy and Ravel? When was the last time you heard Spanish masters Albéniz or Falla in the concert hall? I won't even get into the almost-forgotten Russian contemporaries of Prokofiev and Shostakovich.

As I approach my 80th birthday, I have narrowed the repertoire I will lead going forward. My list comprises about fifteen second-half pieces representing familiar masterpieces as well as works played less frequently. Among them are the two Elgar symphonies, Walton's Symphony No. 1, and Vaughan Williams's Symphony No. 5 and Symphony No. 6. These pieces helped define my career.

However, it will be up to the new kids on the block to discover and preserve the compositional traditions of earlier generations. I sincerely hope that curiosity will prevail and that we will once again see and hear these magnificent sonic edifices on a regular basis.

Which reminds me of something curious: Why didn't I ever perform *Falstaff*?

~ David Temple

The music in my house, as I grew up, was an odd mix of Methodist hymns, pop music and football chants. My parents owned a handful of classical LPs to throw into the mix alongside The Rolling Stones, The Beatles and The Kinks. It was during this time that I first heard Elgar's *Enigma Variations*, and in particular 'Nimrod'. My father would borrow a knitting needle and conduct it with great passion. Moving forward ten years, I came to London and was spotted by a singer in the church I was attending, who informed me a) that I was a tenor and b) that tenors are an endangered species. Even though I couldn't read music, she encouraged me to audition for the London Philharmonic Choir and to my surprise, the chorus director John Alldis miraculously allowed me in. This changed my life for ever.

Seven months after I joined (by this time I was nineteen) I was starting to understand the basics of musical notation but was truly flummoxed when I looked for the first time at the vocal score of Elgar's *The Apostles*, which we were to record with Sir Adrian Boult towards the end of 1973. I managed to navigate 'The Spirit of the Lord' but when we got to 'Let us fill ourselves with costly wine', which was in 9/8, I was totally lost and had to listen to those around me to mimic the rhythms. Despite all of this, I immediately fell in love with the work and the composer. Those around me were saying, 'Wait until you sing *The Dream of Gerontius*!' with the implication that *The Apostles* was somewhat inferior, and at this time, I hadn't even heard of *The Kingdom*. Incidentally, though I have a great affection for *Gerontius*, it is definitely No. 3 in my list, behind the two named above.

One of my tenor colleagues in the London Philharmonic Choir was the Elgar expert, the late Geoffrey Hodgkins, who – now that I had grasped the concept of 9/8 and had started conducting – suggested in 1979 that I form a choir from fellow LPC singers and record some Elgar Part Songs for Meridian Records. The album, named *Evening Scene*, is still available, and it was a great thrill at the age of 26 to have some songs compared in *Gramophone* to those conducted by Sir Adrian Boult.

Geoffrey always believed that my conducting of Elgar was too brisk for his liking and in 1990, when I conducted a performance of *The Apostles* and shaved almost 20 minutes off a recording around at the time, he shook his head. In truth though, I was going with my instincts and one thing in my favour was that the audience seemed to remain engaged by it.

It is not that I think I am right and everyone else is wrong, but I now have the self-belief to follow my instincts. In addition, I have listened to many recordings by Elgar himself and in these recordings, I noticed many surprises and revelations. First of all, if he recorded a work more than once such as chunks of *Gerontius* from concerts, the tempi and the interpretation were different each time, which leads me to believe that if you listen to a piece recorded only once by Elgar that this is not necessarily the definitive Elgar version, as he may well have conducted the same work completely differently a year later. Secondly, the rubato which is actually marked in the score is miniscule compared with the rubato shown by his conducting.

In preparation, to conduct the new *The Kingdom* recording, I was fascinated to hear Elgar's own recording of the Prelude, which I hoped would provide me with guidance as to how this and the rest of the work (which he didn't record) can be interpreted. His conducting of the Prelude is extraordinary in that, instead of the stereotypical view of the portly staid Englishman, it is far more like the film music which followed years later by such as Erich Korngold and Max Steiner. The word which sprang to my mind was 'swashbuckling'. Whilst recording *The Kingdom*, I wanted this feeling to seep into the more dramatic sections, e.g. the coming of the Holy Spirit and the 'speaking with other tongues' passage. Based on Elgar's recording of the Prelude, and also knowing his recorded passages from *Gerontius*, I wanted to imagine how his performance of *The Kingdom* would sound.

Another aspect I work on when conducting Elgar, is how I interpret the instructions *colla parte* or *Recit.* Very often, this is assumed to be *slower* than the tempo it is in the middle of BUT this is not always the case. I am a great believer in delivering recitatives at a speed as if they were spoken rather than sung. This helps the listener to engage and understand. It also helps with the flow of the narrative which is so important in Elgar's music. When there is a *rubato* marking (e.g. *accelerando, ritardando, piu mosso, allargando*) I often slightly anticipate it so that the process seems natural and not forced. In recording terms, it would be equivalent to a 'crossfade' rather than an abrupt edit.

Elgar confided to those closest to him (usually Alice Elgar or August Jaeger) if there were sections, within a piece, he wasn't sure the audience would understand and therefore their attention might drift. A very obvious passage is the start of Part 2 in *Gerontius* which begins very quietly and dreamily, developing to a recitative duet between the Soul of Gerontius and the Angel, ending with a lyrical duet before they encounter the Demons. This 10–15 minute passage can have the audience reaching down to read the soloists' biographies in the programme. With careful thought and imaginative preparation, such passages can be both intimate and magical. The difference between tedious and hypnotic is at the mercy of the performance.

Of the three major choral works composed in the 1900s, I believe that *The Apostles* contains Elgar's best music but there are also some sections which can be a little laboured. If I ever record this work, these are the passages which will take up most of my attention and preparation. *The Dream of Gerontius* is Elgar's most famous choral composition, but all in all, I feel that *The Kingdom* is the best of the lot. To convert many more is a lifetime ambition of mine.

4. In 1898 Rosa Burley, the Headmistress of The Mount School in Malvern, 'snapped' this image of Elgar in the porch of the school where he taught violin and piano for thirteen years.

3

Performing Elgar's Music

~ David Briggs

For as long as I can remember, Elgar has been a constant presence. Growing up in Birmingham in the 1960s and 70s, my parents often took me to the CBSO concerts at the Town Hall where the young, bushy-haired and extremely brilliant Simon Rattle was taking the orchestra by storm. I was aware, even in my early teens, that Elgar had a close relationship with the Town Hall, with many appearances as both composer and conductor. On Saturdays we used to frequently go on family trips to the Malvern Hills, usually taking a picnic but sometimes adding on a delicious cream tea at 'The Kettle Sings'. Even as a young teenager, I was aware of the symbiotic relationship between Elgar's music and this quintessentially British landscape. We visited Elgar's birthplace and I lightly carved my initials in a gatepost about half a mile down the road, which is still there – all to do with identity and perhaps a deep recognition of place.

I proceeded to Solihull School, on a Music Scholarship. One of our A level set works was the *Enigma Variations*, so I got to know these pretty much by heart. I loved the turbulent, rapidly changing emotional volatility of this music, and learnt all about what makes Elgar sound like Elgar, and nobody else. I often wondered why this music sounded so 'British'. If Elgar had lived in Paris, or Madrid, or Berlin, would it have sounded different? I suppose the truth is that Elgar's music, like that of so many great composers, was born out of a huge melting pot and he was influenced by so many composers whose music he would have perused, and no doubt completely internalized, in his father's music shop in Worcester. But the stamp of genius so often comes into play, so that it's much more than a mere conflagration of other composers' techniques.

As a Viola Player in both the Midland Youth Orchestra and the National Youth Orchestra of Great Britain, I had the privilege of getting to know numerous pieces from the inside out, as it were: relatively lesser-known pieces (*The Banner of St George*, *Spirit of England*, etc.) as well as *Enigma*, the Cello Concerto, *Froissart*, etc.

My first professional appointment was at Hereford Cathedral where, on 1 January 1985, I became Assistant Organist. I remember my first rehearsal as *repetiteur* for the Three Choirs Festival, which was for *The Dream of Gerontius*. It transpired that there were no fewer than six members of the chorus who had actually sung this piece under Elgar, as teenagers in the early 1930s. After the famous 'Demons Chorus,' a little old lady at the back of the second altos, wearing a tiny hat (pronounced 'het') and pink mittens, came up to me and said she thought I'd played it very well – and, referring to the famous 'Ha-Has,' that 'Sir Edward used to like it this way' and made this extraordinary snarling sound. The problem was, I suspect, that *everything* she sang sounded rather like that… but I soon became very aware of being part of a living tradition. Naturally I learned the wonderful G major Organ Sonata, which suited the Hereford Father Willis like the proverbial glove, rather appropriate as the 1892 specification was drawn up by George Robertson Sinclair (GRS, of *Enigma*), who was a close friend of Elgar.

In 1989 I went to Truro, where GRS was the first Organist, as Cathedral Organist and introduced many Elgar pieces into the repertoire of the Cathedral Choir (*Great is the Lord, Give unto the Lord, Light out of darkness, The Spirit of the Lord*, etc.). I recorded the Organ Sonata for BBC Radio Three – it sounded even more stupendous on the Truro Father Willis, which is more of a fearsome Maserati than the plush, rather oldy-worldly Bentley at Hereford.

From 1994 to 2002 I had the great privilege of being Director of Music at Gloucester Cathedral, which Elgar apparently described as 'the finest concert hall in Europe.' I remember conducting *The Kingdom* using Herbert Sumsion's score, which was full of markings which were (allegedly) instigated by Elgar. Memorising and conducting this complete masterpiece is something which I will never forget, especially that wondrous Prelude and 'The sun goeth down.' This music seems to take on a completely new life in an acoustical and architectural ambience like Gloucester. In 2000, I had the lovely experience of conducting *Gerontius*, for the Millennium Concert of the Gloucester Choral Society, with top-notch soloists. Michael Kennedy, the renowned Elgar biographer, wrote to me afterwards and said he thought I really understood the essence of Elgar. This affirmation, coming from a musician of the quality of Michael, meant a colossal amount at the time, and still does. At the Gloucester Three Choirs, I became good friends with Elgar's godson Wulstan Atkins and his wife and children. We visited their home in Surrey once, lovingly-adorned with much Elgar memorabilia. I remember he always described him as 'El-guh.'

In 2009–2011 I undertook two massive transcription projects, both commissioned by the Worcester Three Choirs Festival: Symphony No. 1 in

Ab and Symphony No.2 in Eb. These transcriptions were both premiered at Worcester TCFs on the new Tickell organ at Worcester, and subsequently recorded for the Acclaim Productions label. It was a moving experience, performing this wondrous music in Elgar's 'own' cathedral – it sometimes felt as if he was actually looking over my shoulder. The goal was, as always, to make each bar sound authentic in its new guise, which often meant making many changes. Perhaps the hardest aspect was playing the *Scherzos* of both symphonies up to EE's metronome mark. It took several months to make each transcription, cross-checking from the piano arrangements and the full orchestral scores. Holding the original manuscript of the First Symphony in my hand in the British Library was a curiously moving experience. I noticed that each note slanted slightly to the right, like little tadpoles, almost as if his hand could only just keep up with the sheer vivacity of his aural imagination.

As we now head further into the twenty-first century, it is wonderful to see Elgar's music being so fully represented. Having said that, I find it rather perplexing that much of it is so little known here in the USA. Perhaps it will become more so in the future, rather in the manner that Mahler has almost supersaturated the market in recent years. For certain, Elgar's music touches the heart in a unique way, and that is surely what makes music stand the test of time.

~ Neville Creed

I have been lucky enough to have encountered Elgar's music frequently throughout my life. One of the first recordings I owned was Adrian Boult's recording of the First Symphony which was played until the needle gouged the vinyl. It was the school choral society's rousing performance of *The Dream of Gerontius* which convinced me that music would be the path to follow. Little did I know that Elgar's choral works would feature so prominently in my working life. When conducting chamber choirs I have often programmed the exquisite part-songs, which choirs relish. In these miniatures Elgar displayed the same great virtuosity that was a hallmark of his orchestral writing. His attention to detail when writing for the choir is legendary. His use of texture and articulation bring out the details of text in a revelatory manner. The delicate simplicity of *My love dwelt in a northern land* becomes almost instrumental at the words 'And oft that month we watched the moon' – sustained lines are contrasted with linked staccato vocal accompaniment. In the intense setting of *Go, song of mine*, Elgar explores an extensive variety of markings in the vocal parts, particularly at the words 'To seek its maker at the heavenly shrine'.

However, my main encounters with Elgar's work has involved the great oratorios. In the 1990s, as Director of the Bournemouth Symphony Chorus, I prepared the *Dream*, *Apostles* and *Kingdom* for Richard Hickox's performances at the Barbican. More recently, as Director of the London Philharmonic Choir, I have prepared these works for a variety of performances – perhaps most notably for Sir Mark Elder in Manchester and London. It is always a demanding and special project when these three magnificent works are programmed in tandem.

The Apostles and *The Kingdom* form the first two parts of his incomplete trilogy – what a pity it is that he didn't continue with *The Last Judgement* and complete the cycle.

The Apostles, although not the best known, is possibly the most rewarding and inspiring for the choir. The opening 'Spirit of the Lord' establishes the intense level of expression, with an intimate yet powerful setting. The closing episode, 'In heaven', combines the on-stage choir, off-stage choir and soloists in what is surely one of the greatest moments in the choral repertoire. *The Apostles* is immensely challenging to prepare as the choir takes on so many roles – providing commentary on the scenes as well as reacting to the tumultuous events. Elgar achieves dramatic momentum with a plethora of short choral interjections which can be unsettling to sing unless they are virtually committed to memory. The longer choral sections provide an opportunity for the choir to give full reign to their voices and they always relish these moments.

The Kingdom is perhaps the least well known of the 'big three' but it stands worthily beside its illustrious neighbours. There is plenty for the choir to get to grips with: a huge variety of textures (at one point dividing into three choral groups), intimate choral interjections in the crowd scenes such as 'In Solomon's Porch' and splendid choral outbursts such as at the words 'so may thy church be gathered together'.

The Dream of Gerontius is clearly the most well-known and frequently performed of the three and offers tremendous opportunities for the choir: singers seem to relish the visceral power of the 'Demons' Chorus' and the ethereal beauty of the Angelicals. Elgar conjures a wonderful palette of choral colours and the demands on the choir are considerable.

Earlier in this article I mentioned Elgar's attention to detail in his choral writing. There is often much debate about what he meant with his variety of staccato, linked staccato, marcato and different accents. It seems to me that all these markings are offered in service to the text. By using staccato marks Elgar is offering an idea of how to deliver a particular word rather than just suggesting it should be short. I think he found the standard methods of articulation rather limiting and it is up to choral directors and conductors to interpret these markings in order to enhance the delivery of text. When preparing choral works, I start and finish with the text. Initially the choir needs to become intimate with the text, thoroughly understanding the messages within, and then finally deliver it with the utmost clarity and commitment. Elgar's music is a dream to prepare as he allows this process to happen with the most subtle and well-judged indications on his scores.

Elgar's music is a mainstay of the choral repertoire and barely a season passes without performances of his wonderful music. I consider myself to be privileged to have conducted so much of his work as well as preparing his music as a choral director for so many inspiring conductors.

~ Scott Dickinson

'Let's start with the Elgar, please', and with a particularly youthful flourish of E flat major, off we all head into the tumultuously sun-soaked pleasure that is the *In the South* Overture. The venue is the sports hall of Strathallan School, Perthshire, the conductor Martyn Brabbins and the date 8 July 2023; the much anticipated first day of the National Youth Orchestra of Scotland's summer course.

I am lucky enough to witness this encounter, this challenging yet joyous rite of passage, up close. As Elgar's love of the Mediterranean spread its infectious smile over the assembled company, we tutors caught each other's eyes with irrepressible grins of pleasure: what greater privilege could there be than to be present at the very moment when the next generation experiences the wonder of being right in the living, beating heart of this expression? So refreshingly far away from any complicating connection with imperialism or grandeur this is, quite simply, music of the most potent ardour, the most explosive description imaginable of living life to the full, the vivacity of Italy as seen through the eyes of an Edwardian English tourist – with nostalgia, poignancy, expectation and fulfilment coupled with that masterful paradox where simplicity and complexity collide: perhaps only a composer as self-taught as Elgar could muster this so tellingly.

Looking around the room, it is so obvious that these lucky young people are finding deep channels of connection with each other, with the past, with the inspiring presence of Martyn Brabbins, with the notion of travel, and certainly with their own futures, through the heart, mind and formidable technical challenges of Sir Edward Elgar. It isn't long before the cries of incredulity – cellists reaching for top E flats, 'let's try figure 26 slowly and calmly' – are replaced by an understanding and idealism that these demands are driven by a bigger picture: the huge sweep of passion that propels the overture's narrative. Almost all is forgiven when the flow is this strong, the journey this vibrant.

It is ever thus, playing Elgar: crazily demanding yet immensely fulfilling. Besides the regular joy we at the BBCSSO have of performing and recording Elgar under the consummate understanding of Martyn Brabbins, I was lucky enough to be part of several extremely meaningful (not that Elgar 2 ever couldn't be!) encounters with the Second Symphony last Spring from two other enormously passionate Elgarians: Ryan Wigglesworth and the BBCSSO in the claustrophobic intensity of City Halls Glasgow, the majestic Music Hall Aberdeen and on BBC Radio 3 and John Wilson and his Sinfonia of London in Snape Maltings (could there be a more perfect acoustic for this piece?) and on Marquee TV. The overridingly generous spirit of the first movement, the heart-breaking pathos with which the second unfolds, the way the wild energy of the *scherzo* transitions (figure 118) to a melody of questioning beauty which then turns on itself so terrifyingly (figure 120), and the resolution and final calm of the *Finale* add up, of course, to one of the greatest and most complete journeys of the orchestral canon. In this age of instant gratification, what could be more important than one hour's travel through hopes and fears, with every emotion from paranoia to heart stopping beauty: the very essence of what it is to be human, surely?

Later in July 2023, Martyn's instinctive, thoughtful and hugely emotional sweep couples with the passion of youth to make Elgar's masterpiece the centrepiece and highlight of the NYOS concerts: an orchestra member reports afterwards that they are now listening to *In the South* regularly 'to restore happiness'. What better rallying cry could there be for every one of us to do everything we possibly can to ensure that no generation misses out on the sense of communal wonder that this importance of Elgar can bring?

❧ Thomas Eisner

Growing up in the Peak District, the music of Edward Elgar was very much part of my musical life. By the time I left home I had already played the *Serenade for Strings, Introduction and Allegro* and his *Wand of Youth* and, of course, The *Enigma Variations* with my Cheshire Youth Orchestra. Years later I was to visit Elgar's birthplace in that tiny house surrounded by fields and, to a certain extent I found I could identify with how he must have felt, coming from provincial England with the wrong religion. He was born in 1857 close to Malvern Spa, I came into the world in 1957 in another Spa town – Buxton.

I have always been fascinated where Elgar's 'sound' comes from. In January 2024, as part of the London Philharmonic Orchestra (LPO), we played Schumann's Symphony No. 2. I was reminded at the start of the slow movement how much Elgar had been inspired by this work – what we think of today as the quintessential Englishness of his slow movements is strongly influenced by Schumann.

Two summers ago, whilst playing Wagner's opera *Siegfried* in Bayreuth, I suddenly heard a theme which sounds just like the last movement of Elgar's first symphony. Down in the pit I wondered if Elgar had discovered the opera from reading the score, or if he actually attended a live performance. Elgar of course knew his Wagner and was devoted to this music. However, it is not certain if he ever attended a performance of *Siegfried*.[1] It is clear to me that Elgar was an exceptional autodidact - he would have had to be, notwithstanding a thriving amateur scene. There was not much going on in Worcester and Malvern and, presumably, that made him all the more determined.

As an orchestral player I experience many different emotions when I play Elgar's music. I love the upward thrill of the opening of *In the South* and the ending of the First Symphony feels like we have put the world back together. The viola solo in *Introduction and Allegro* still makes me cry. To me, variation 13 of *Enigma* is all about loss – where is Helen Weaver now....?

In 2006 I gave a recital at Elgar's Birthplace Museum. Elgar, in the form of his great niece Margaret, was in the audience. Talking to me after the concert, she remembered fondly, as if it was just yesterday, walking around a lake with 'Uncle Edward'. I think he is still with us.

[1] In August 1893 Elgar heard *Siegfried* in Munich. Eds.

~ Kate Kennedy

The Nightingale Concerto

In the archives of the Museum of Music History there is a large cardboard box. It is one of many hundreds containing photographs, newspaper cuttings, and letters. Inside this box is a smaller, wooden one; plain but well made, varnished, and with neatly joined corners. Lifting the lid, there is a faded golden velvet drawstring bag. As I open it, a little book emerges, bound by the most ornately carved covers of silvery steel. It is unlike anything I've ever seen before. Turning it over in my hands, creaking open the tiny pages – not far, just enough to see a bar of neatly written music inked onto each miniature piece of vellum – I turn back to the arrestingly beautiful cover; the roughness of the uncut ruby that adorns its decorated metal clasp, the milky depth of the moonstones set into each corner, the filigree of silver and gold, intricately shaped. At the centre of the cover, carved into the metal, are the shape of a cello, a little bird in full song, and the letters B and V.

My eyes turn to the spine, to the oddness of the binding, which looks at first glance to have been done inside out – until I realise that the book is in fact laced together by a cello's A string. I can see the silver winding at the top of the gut. Strings do not last for ever and would be regularly replaced on a cello. This string has been repurposed and therefore saved from ephemerality – here it speaks of something new and enduring. It is in fact the A string on which the cellist Beatrice Harrison made the first recording of Elgar's cello concerto.

This little book represents a moment in which multiple factors came together to make history, with Elgar's music at its heart. It tells the story of two highly influential friendships, between Beatrice Harrison and Princess Victoria (sister of George V), and between Beatrice and Edward Elgar. The book contains, with a bar on each tiny page, the slow movement of Elgar's cello concerto. And on the last page is his signature. If we learn to read its symbolism, it can tell us how these relationships shaped the story of radio broadcasting, and established Elgar's cello concerto as one of the most loved pieces ever written for the instrument.

The book was a love gift, made with Elgar's assistance, and given by Beatrice to Princess Victoria. Just like the book, their relationship centred around Elgar's cello concerto. Beatrice had commissioned the book from the 'arts and crafts' miniaturist, metal worker, and enameller Hal Broun Morison. It was a gift that summarised everything that was most dear to her, and every detail of it was carefully crafted to represent the relationship that was the most important of her life. Princess Victoria owned a copy of the piano reduction of the cello concerto, given to her by Beatrice almost as soon as Beatrice herself had got to know the work. Beatrice and Victoria would regularly play through it, and enjoyed playing the slow movement so much they took over HMV studios to make a private recording of their duo. Beatrice referred to Victoria as 'her life, her music'. And the feeling was mutual. Princess Victoria's love of the concerto and her financial support of its performances and recordings, played a quiet but significant role in Beatrice's championing of the work. The central part the concerto plays in their book is Beatrice's grateful acknowledgement of this. The Elgar cello concerto was not only at the centre of their relationship, but it became established at the heart of the twentieth-century cellist's repertoire, at least in part due to Beatrice's life-long promotion of it, supported by Victoria. But as we shall see, in their hands, their rather eccentric early public exposure of the concerto's slow movement on BBC radio was to ensure the concerto would become as laden with symbolism as the little book in which they had so carefully transcribed it.

The book tells us about the centrality of the concerto to the two women's relationship, but it also holds a story that allows us to think about the quality of Elgar's much fabled and ineffable 'Englishness' from a slightly different angle. The singing bird, etched above the image of the cello on the front of the book, represents a nightingale. In May 1924, Beatrice, with the encouragement of Victoria, undertook the BBC's first major outside broadcast, bringing their microphones out of the studio to record her duetting with nightingales in her garden. The experiment was the most high-profile in radio's early years. It changed broadcasting history and opened up a world of possibilities for the new genre of radio. Beatrice played the concerto's slow movement, introducing it to one million listeners. The subsequent annual nightingale broadcasts and 1928 HMV recordings would bring the concerto to a vast public, but in a very particular light. By performing it to so many in such particular circumstances, Beatrice would harness the concerto to associations with the Arcadian, poetical, feminine, and pastoral. The link between the concerto and the nocturnal song of the nightingale so soon after the end of the war was read as mystical, with the suggestion of voices from beyond, alongside a popular nostalgia for a rural idyll that even then was under threat. This heady mix was augmented by the sense of excitement about the new technological innovation that made these broadcasts possible. Championed so publicly by Beatrice and her nightingales, it is perhaps no wonder that the concerto has never fully recovered from its early cultural associations with a lost era, and with a peculiarly English form of bucolic melancholy.

* * *

The cello concerto, finished in 1919, was premiered by Felix Salmond before Beatrice knew of the work. However, the premiere was famously considered a disaster, as Salmond and the London Symphony Orchestra were not given enough rehearsal time. Elgar was bitterly disappointed. There was no second London performance for over a year, and in consequence, eighteen months after it was written it was being referred to as 'strangely neglected since its original production last year'. Even by January 1921 it was still Elgar's 'little known' cello concerto. Had Beatrice not become so publicly associated with the work soon after this setback, its reception history could have been very different. It is no exaggeration to claim that Beatrice's championing of the work, supported by Princess Victoria and their mutual love of the piece were responsible for its speedy transformation from 'strangely neglected' to core repertoire.

The recording company HMV asked Elgar to record his concerto, with Beatrice as soloist (Salmond might have been a more obvious choice, as he had premiered the work, but Beatrice was one of HMV's recording artists). Alice Elgar recorded the progress of events in her diary that winter: '11 December 1919,... Nice to hear the Cello Concerto – Miss Harrison came to play through Cello Concerto with E. for Gramophone... 19 December, Beatrice Harrison (& her family) to play through Concerto... 22 December, E. left before 9 for Hayes, [...]. Conducted Cello Concerto into gramophone – Beatrice Harrison cellist'. Beatrice's mother had accompanied her on some of these excursions to the Elgar's home in Hampstead. Although Alice's diary entries are rather matter of fact, and do not gush with effusiveness for Beatrice's playing, Beatrice later wrote that she remembered Alice saying to her mother: 'I think your child will make people love this work when she has had an opportunity of playing it in public'.

There was a problem with the recording quality of the third movement, and after a return to the studio, the recording (albeit abridged) was completed in November 1920, almost a year after it was begun, and only released in 1921. From then on, Elgar always chose Beatrice to be his soloist for the concerto. Salmond had moved to America, and the concerto now belonged firmly to Beatrice. In fact, the 1920s were defined for Beatrice by her growing friendship and professional association with Elgar. They worked as a pair, with Elgar conducting her at several performances in London, including at the Queen's Hall and for the Philharmonic Society, as well as at the Three Choirs Festival in 1924, which that year took place in Hereford Cathedral. It was a memorable occasion, as, in her words, she was 'the first woman instrumentalist to play there, and I believe that Sir Edward had some difficulty in persuading some of the dignitaries that all would be well, as some of them seemed uncertain.' In the wings at one performance in Manchester, he urged her on: 'Give it 'em, Beatrice, give it 'em. Don't mind about the notes or anything. Give 'em the spirit.' It is interesting to consider, what, in Beatrice's hands, that spirit was, and whether her sense of it indelibly shaped the way the concerto was heard throughout the twentieth century. Championed by a woman, reviewers were universally approving, but some could not get past her gender, and the concerto inadvertently became a 'feminine' work by association.

For instance, in 1927 the *Tägliche Rundschau* reviewed Werner Wolff's performance of the concerto with Beatrice and the Berlin Philharmonic Orchestra. It was the first time the orchestra had played the work:

> It is a concerto specially suitable for lady players, soft with a melancholy rhythm, delicate in expression, a refined piece, even though a little colourless, but adapted to the nature of the instrument. Playful grace, a little pathos produce variety, lady cellists ought to take it up if they want to entertain their audience in a dainty and pleasant way. Beatrice Harrison by her interpretation gained for it a considerable success.[1]

Whilst Beatrice's playing was commended for its beautiful tone and great power, the fact of her sex has determined, for this reviewer at least, that the concerto becomes a work for a woman. However, coupled with the fame of the nightingale broadcasts, often written about in the most feminine terms, (we frequently find mention of the feminine delicacy of the birdsong, and even little wild animals clustering around the cellist's flowing skirts), does Beatrice's interpretation stamp a gender on the work that was never Elgar's intention?

To begin with, Beatrice and Elgar's relationship was rather formal on Elgar's part. Letters in the Museum's archive show Elgar writing in most respectful terms: 'My dear Beatrice: Thank you for your letter. I am very proud that the Concerto delights you and I am very happy when I conduct it for you.'[2] But as Elgar's familiarity with Beatrice increased, they began

1 25 February 1927.

2 Museum of Music History, 15 September 1923.

to bond not only over the concerto, but, perhaps somewhat unexpectedly, over dogs. Beatrice's obsession with everything on two claws or four paws was a passion that she shared with Elgar. She was at one point the owner of at least thirty highland terriers, among a whole host of other animals (at various points her Surrey home included a room full of birds, two alligators she had acquired on a tour of America, and a monkey). Elgar became the happy recipient of a number of these dogs, donated from the Harrison household's menagerie.

Elgar's own dog Juno had been a much adored feature of his sister Pollie Grafton's household for a decade, during which time, Elgar explains to Beatrice, 'she helped me with all my compositions for the last nine or ten years' (which included the cello concerto), and when Juno died in October 1923 Elgar turned to Beatrice for a replacement, to reside with his sister at her home at Stoke Prior near Bromsgrove. Juno mark II was introduced to the Grafton family, and Elgar was breathless with delight at

> 'the little goddess': She is a darling, very lively and happy and extremely vigorous and well in herself and a delightful bundle of mischief and the greatest joy to us all. She objects to the scratching sound of my pen on paper but does not mind music in the least;- she listens to a violin, viola, cello and piano with a sedate, critical air but thinks it all a sad waste of time and that digging for moles is much better worthwhile.

Other placements were less successful – Brenda, an Aberdeen terrier with which Beatrice supplied Elgar insisted on growling and barking at him and the gardener, and with much embarrassment on Elgar's part, had to be returned to the Harrisons in disgrace.[3]

When Elgar famously discovered the joys of cycling, and embarked on long road trips on his trusty bicycle 'Mr Phoebus' with his friend Rosa Burley, he was engaging with the sounds and details of nature as much as enjoying the exercise; Rosa remembered how he had particularly loved the birdsong. Beatrice and Elgar's love of birds and animals found its zenith in the nightingale broadcasts, which took place at the centre of the decade in which the concerto was rarely off Beatrice's music stand. This is perhaps the moment to look at this seminal moment of broadcasting history in a little more detail.

The BBC had been convinced by Beatrice (and, behind closed doors, by the royal family) to take its microphones out of the studio for the first time on 19 May 1924, and broadcast live from Beatrice's garden, as she duetted with a nightingale. The event was an instant popular success and

3 Elgar's love of dogs was not shared by Alice Elgar and it was only after her death in 1920 that he reverted to owning several during the remaining years of his life.

was repeated for years afterwards. She played the slow movement of the concerto, as well as Rimsky Korsakov's *Chant Hindou* and the Irish folksong *Londonderry Air*. Not only did her choice of repertoire guarantee that millions heard this hauntingly beautiful excerpt from the concerto, guaranteeing that it could never again be deemed 'little known', but she situated it in the most bucolic, gently melancholy framework one could imagine.

The idea had struck her and Princess Victoria the year before. In 1923 Beatrice had discovered that when she played her cello in the woods of her Surrey garden amidst the bluebells (seeds given as a royal gift from Sandringham when Beatrice had moved in), a nightingale would be attracted by the sound of her cello, and join her in a duet. In fact, by the winter of that year, the nightingale and the slow movement of Elgar's cello concerto were to become so important to the princess and to Beatrice that both were the defining features of the little silver engraved book that was made in 1923, months even before the first nightingale BBC broadcast.

With the encouragement (and perhaps some high-level string pulling) of Victoria, Beatrice suggested to John Reith, the Director General of the newly formed BBC, that he might send his sound engineers to broadcast the duet between her and the bird. Although the BBC had in fact already been interested in trying to broadcast birdsong, so the request was well timed, it was nevertheless an immensely risky and expensive decision. In 1924 there was no possibility of recording, so the cello and nightingale would have to go out live, which of course required the nightingale to perform on cue. It was also barely within the engineers' capacity to record out of a studio, and it had only been attempted once, with a short and muffled speech from the King, Victoria's brother, being broadcast from the British Empire Exhibition in Wembley Park a few weeks before. The whole expensive venture could not have taken place without the financial backing of the royal family. In fact, Victoria and her mother Queen Alexandra became so personally invested in the project that when HMV proposed making a recording in 1927, they put up the funds for a specially designed recording van kitted out with the most cutting-edge technology available and personally inspected it on its completion.

What transpired was to become the biggest event in broadcast history but not without its challenges. There were problems to negotiate such as insects in the microphones, and an escaped donkey. However, the technical challenges and unforeseen disturbances turned out to be the least of the BBC engineers' problems – Beatrice played, and the microphones recorded, but the bird refused to sing. Beatrice sat in her garden, playing Elgar, Rimsky Korsakov and folksongs for nearly two hours, with engineers at Broadcasting House poised to switch from the Savoy Orchestra who were filling the time, to go live to Beatrice's garden. Finally, almost at the point when they were about to give up on the venture altogether, the nightingale began. The relief amongst the engineers crouching in the bushes and those listening in London can only be imagined. The general public from Canada to Australia had been listening, waiting for the moment when they would hear the first birdsong broadcast on the radio. People had clustered around their radios for a nail-bitingly long time, waiting for the sound of the bird. Others had held telephones up to their radios, so family and friends without a device of their own could hear.

When the bird finally sang, listeners were transfixed by the ethereal duet. For many, living in cities, or living abroad, a nightingale was something they'd never heard, or had not heard for many years. Many of the BBC engineers and indeed John Reith himself were battle-scarred ex-servicemen, and listening in the dark was something they had done in the trenches, in the anticipation of enemy activity, rather than a shower of birdsong. For a nation still in deep mourning, to hear something so pure emerge from the dark, coupled with the plaintive tones of the cello, was transformational. The nightingale broadcasts were the antithesis of mechanised destruction and demonstrated that new technologies could be used for peaceful purposes, bringing natural beauty and hope to listeners.

The following morning Beatrice was swamped by tourists, fan mail, and emotional accounts of what the broadcast had meant to the general public. The broadcasts were repeated annually for twelve years, and HMV made several 10 inch disc recordings of the duet. They brought pleasure to many for a generation, and came to define Beatrice, who quickly became the 'nightingale lady', an eccentric identity that she actively encouraged, but came to overshadow her reputation as a serious interpreter of contemporary music, and a soloist with a formidable technique.

Beatrice always associated her nightingales with the Elgar concerto in particular. She wrote that they 'respond most readily to plaintive airs, and the piece with which I have had the most success is Elgar's cello concerto'. It was no coincidence that the music she chose to play in her garden was folksong, and Elgar (with a hint of the nocturnal and exotic provided by the Rimsky Korsakov). The Elgar concerto was absolutely embedded in the vision of Arcadia she went to some lengths to maintain in interviews and in her written accounts of the event. What better than the concerto, written in his cottage 'Brinkwells' in the Sussex woods, to complement Beatrice's carefully constructed rural fairy tale? Indeed, journalists eagerly took Beatrice's statements about the nightingale's love of Elgar to heart: the *Evening News* of 1927 reported that nightingales respond particularly to scraps of the Elgar Cello Concerto. The correspondent adds: 'I have often heard Miss Harrison lure the nightingale into song by playing scraps of this concerto.'

With the endorsement of the royal family, and in particular Princess Victoria, the BBC was able to bring both Beatrice and the Elgar to an audience across the Commonwealth annually over the next few years, establishing the concerto as a modern classic in the minds of countless listeners. However, the concerto that so many got to know intimately through Beatrice's nocturnal renditions was hardly the same work that audiences would hear in a concert hall. The fully orchestrated version is in itself pared back and intimate, with the orchestra supporting the cello in muted tones, and the slowly unfolding melody is folksong-esque in its touching simplicity. Played without accompaniment these qualities were enhanced. Set alongside the meandering unaccompanied Rimsky Korsakov and other folksongs (and bearing in mind that most listeners would never have heard the concerto with orchestra, only with nightingale) Beatrice was setting a generation's expectations of the work. Subsequently it became something of a modern-day folk song, a melody of nature; spun from the trees and night sky of her garden. Supported not by muted strings but by the noises of an evening woodland, it becomes something elemental. Beatrice had done Elgar an enormous service in making the concerto's slow movement such a prominent part of these extremely high-profile broadcasts, but she had presented it to the world on her very specific terms. But perhaps these terms were not so very far from Elgar's own sense of the work.

Near the end of his life, Elgar had fancifully warned one friend that if he were to hear the concerto's spectral melodies on the breeze whilst walking in the Malvern hills, he must not be scared – it would be him, from beyond the grave. Many newspapers likened the broadcasts to a seance; the hidden voice from the sky breaking through the dark in response to the cello calling it out of the silence. In fact, taking the voice from heaven motif to its extreme, Beatrice would have us believe that there was a 'divine' affinity between her, Elgar himself, and his concerto. In the Museum of Music History's archive is a draft sketch, in Beatrice's handwriting. She writes of a voice that apparently came to her in her sleep, six years after Elgar had died. '"You must not worry – you will play the Concerto, & Sir Edward will conduct it for you as he does for the Angels in Heaven". Said to me in a dream.'[4] Playing the Elgar was her divine calling (as well as essential for her career, particularly in its later years). She retained a letter written to her a year after this dream episode, in 1944, remarking that 'After all these years you

[4] MOMH Harrison Archive, 1943 (Box 32).

were able still to play that concerto as if it was a great and divine message'.[5] Whether it was divine intervention, or the result of a carefully cultivated relationship with the BBC and the influence of Princess Victoria, Beatrice's annual broadcasts gave her enough leverage with Lord Reith to ensure that full broadcasts of the cello concerto with orchestra regularly took place between 1928 and 1944. Nightingale or no nightingale, the concerto's place in the repertoire was firmly established.

In the decades after Beatrice's death her playing has been all but forgotten, although the nightingale broadcasts have entered cultural history as the moment that established radio as a serious cultural and artistic medium. These first 'outside' broadcasts opened the door to the possibilities of broadcasting nature and soundscapes external to the studio and brought a global audience together over the combined sounds of the cello and bird.

The little silver book created by Elgar and Beatrice for Princess Victoria holds within its heavily coded and symbolic pages the ghost of the relationship between these two women. It is a relationship wrought around the nightingale, cello, and Elgar's achingly intimate slow movement; a relationship so private that it is barely recorded in history, but with such a monumental outcome both for the history of broadcasting in the UK, and for the reputation of Elgar's cello concerto. Beatrice's (and Victoria's) broadcast cemented the concerto's associations with a romanticised English pastoralism and with a quietly patriotic Englishness: wistful, feminine and understated. Beatrice and her nightingales have largely been forgotten now. But the cultural phenomenon they represented in the inter-war years, establishing Elgar's concerto as one of the greatest in the repertoire, will always be present in our collective cultural memory, subtly shaping our understanding of the work.

5 MOMH archive from Frank Rushforth (Box 33).

~ Tasmin Little

Music of all varieties was always on in the household as I was growing up and by the time I had picked up a violin, aged 6, I already knew that there were certain composers whose works I was compelled to play. Elgar was at the top of the tree, alongside Delius and Walton. As soon as I was capable of getting my fingers around *Salut d'Amour*, around age 9, the piece became part of my very early repertoire. As I progressed into my teenage years at the Yehudi Menuhin School, I was playing other short bonbon pieces and the *Études Caractéristiques*, alongside the Piano Quintet and the Violin Sonata. The latter was a particular favourite of Yehudi Menuhin, who frequently performed it with the student pianists at his school, and many violin students learned this great work whilst they were there and benefitted from his wisdom. Yehudi's style greatly influenced me in my early performances of Elgar; the violin writing lends itself perfectly to the portamenti and nuance of expression that were Yehudi's distinctive and trademark style, and it is well documented that Elgar himself felt the young Yehudi innately understood his music.

In addition to the sweeping gestures, strength of harmony and grand scale frequently inherent in Elgar's music, there is an enduring elegance and charm to much of his violin writing and, at times, a real sense of vulnerability. This is especially the case with the Violin Sonata and the Piano Quintet, both composed in 1918. I believe it is this juxtaposition of intimacy and bold and sweeping gestures that make Elgar's music so powerful. It is also something that I believe makes his music very appealing, even outside the British Isles. There are certain British composers whose work doesn't 'travel' well. I have performed Elgar's music all over the world and he is by no means in this category. Even in works such as the Violin Sonata, which I performed globally over 60 times and where the proportion of pensive music greatly outweighs the more overtly dramatic moments, there is enough passion in the melodic and harmonic lines to sustain excitement and interest.

Elgar's ability to paint pictures of people and use skilful orchestration to imply characters is unsurpassed. His gift for melodic invention and the ability to write intensely memorable tunes is underpinned by generous harmonies which are well balanced between the expected and unexpected. Take, for instance, the famous transition between Variation VIII 'W.N.' and Variation IX 'Nimrod' in his *Enigma Variations*. Anyone who is familiar with this piece will anticipate the magic of what is about to come – but, for the first-time listener, this 'tingle factor' unexpected key change is truly momentous.

During the 1980s, his monumental Violin Concerto, by far the longest in the violin canon, was not often programmed in concert. At the time, it was not considered 'essential standard repertoire' for the self-respecting violinist, in the way that Beethoven, Bruch, Brahms and Tchaikovsky have been regarded for many decades. It was not until the late 1980s that I had the opportunity of hearing the work live in concert, in London's Royal Festival Hall. The soloist was Igor Oistrakh and, although there were some aspects of his playing that were not to my taste, his passion for the music shone through and I fell so in love with the piece that I was determined to learn it immediately. To my delight, the Royal Philharmonic Orchestra was keen to invite me to perform the work, and I gave my first performance with it in 1988 under the baton of Yan Pascal Tortelier.

Over the course of my career, I gave 73 performances of the work, in the UK, Europe, Australia, New Zealand, North and South America and Asia. The list of my conductors is lengthy and contains some of the great Elgarian interpreters: Richard Hickox and Vernon Handley (both of whom conducted me playing it at the Three Choirs Festival) and Sir Charles Groves, with whom I played it four times only a couple of months before he passed away. Other notable conductors include Leonard Slatkin (who knew the piece off by heart and barely needed the score!), David Atherton, Daniel Harding, Martyn Brabbins, Robin Ticciati, Jac Van Steen, John Storgårds, Jerzy Maksymiuk and Gerard Schwarz, among many others. Each conductor brought his individual approach and added something to my growing interpretation – a nuance here, an unexpected harmony there, a detail in the woodwind, a rapid *accelerando* – it all gave me an ever deeper understanding of the intricacies of this giant of a violin concerto.

During the early 1990s, as I was beginning to make a name for myself performing the concerto, which was still fairly under-represented in the recording catalogue. I was approached by several major record labels, each inviting me to put my rendition on disc. Many high-profile conductors and orchestras were suggested to me and, yet, I instinctively knew that I needed to wait a long time before committing to disc an interpretation that would truly reflect everything that I wanted to express. As the 2010 centenary of the premiere of the Elgar concerto drew closer, I finally knew the right time had come to record this work that I had carried within me and performed around the globe for some 22 years. I approached Chandos Records, as I had made some early recordings with them; they have always had a great reputation for British repertoire and they had on their roster the wonderful Sir Andrew Davis. I had collaborated many times in concert with Andrew both in the UK and abroad and I felt he would be a perfect partner for me. The highly positive answer came back within the hour – even better, Andrew Davis already had recording sessions scheduled with the Royal Scottish National Orchestra and the repertoire was to be some Elgar orchestral works. Andrew was very excited to record the violin concerto with me and happy to change the repertoire to make the concerto the main focus of the CD.

The sessions themselves could not have gone better. For a piece of this duration and difficulty, I fully expected that we would have to work non-stop and use every second of valuable session time. As it happened, the reverse was the case – it was almost as if the piece was 'playing itself' and these sessions are some of the most enjoyable and rewarding that I ever experienced. Andrew and I both knew the concerto intimately but, as we both commented on at the time, it was a surprising fact that we had never actually collaborated on it. I think it was this that contributed to the overall success of our combined interpretation – we had both performed the work with many different musicians over many years but had the excitement of finding out what we each felt about the structure, emotion and detail. In addition, the Royal Scottish National Orchestra rarely performed the piece and was full of enthusiasm, so the whole team felt very 'fresh' and the resulting animation of the performance is tangible. The recording, released in time for the 100th anniversary of the premiere, went on to garner hugely favourable reviews and won the Critics' Choice in the 2011 Classic BRIT Awards. Of the 45 recordings that I have made over the decades of my career, this recording is one of my favourites.

Bringing Elgar's works to life and experiencing the commitment of my fellow musicians on stage, alongside the appreciation and excitement of the many audiences around the globe, has left me with memories that I will cherish for the rest of my life. The concerto has finally found its rightful place in the repertoire, performed worldwide, appreciated by audiences and, just as importantly, given the admiration and respect by today's violin soloists that it truly deserves.

~ Julian Lloyd-Webber

'Music In the Air'

I was a teenager when my godfather, the composer Herbert Howells, presented me with a score of Elgar's Cello Concerto, which he inscribed: 'To Julian, from H.H. to whom E.E. once said of this work, "It's just an old man's darling"'. A few weeks later my interest in Elgar was further kindled by a performance of his First Symphony at the Royal Festival Hall during which the inspirational maestro, John Barbirolli, not only managed to drop his baton enough times to derail an entire Olympic relay race but also fashioned a performance of such emotional intensity as to be utterly irresistible.

Two such seismic events so close together marked the beginning of my absorption in both Elgar's music and the character of the man himself. I began 'borrowing' my father's luridly orange 850cc Mini to head west out of London towards Elgar Country. Along the way to Worcestershire, the contours of the land, the distinctive towns and villages, the lure of the valleys and the hills, and whatever else might lie beyond – all these things made a huge impression on an adolescent boy who had previously known very little beyond the confines of London.

Often, I only made it as far as the north Cotswolds, but whenever I could I would venture further towards the Malvern Hills along the glorious road from Stow-on-the-Wold to Tewkesbury that winds its way across hillsides which remain as cold and windswept today as when Elgar wrote those rustling semiquavers in the *Scherzo* of his First Symphony.

I sometimes wonder which of Elgar's works were most dear to his heart; the ones he would most want audiences to be hearing today? Or, to pose the question another way, which works are the essence of Elgar? Was the real Elgar the bombastic, tub-thumping composer of five *Pomp and Circumstance* marches, *The Banner of St George*, the *Imperial March* and much else besides? Or was the real Elgar the lover of the countryside who liked nothing more than to walk the hills – with or without his dog or dogs – and who liked to dream his dreams while fishing on the banks of the River Wye with his close friend the violinist W.H. 'Billy' Reed.

Reed was the leader of the London Symphony Orchestra, and he became a hugely important figure in Elgar's life almost as soon as they first met, when Elgar guest-conducted the orchestra. Reed was also my mother's violin teacher at the Royal College of Music and she recalled him as 'a lovely man with twinkly eyes who was always happy to talk about Elgar'. She also claimed it was Reed who began the tradition of audiences applauding the arrival of the orchestra's leader simply because 'they were so pleased to see him!'

From Reed we know that Elgar hated discussing the 'meaning' of his music:

> Elgar was always very reticent and unwilling to discuss the inner meaning of anything he had composed. There was nothing he disliked more. He would change the subject abruptly or retire into his inner self with some such observation as 'Oh, I don't know anything about music. Let us go out and see the river, or go up to the common, and do something sensible for once'. Occasionally, though, he let things slip out. I remember once when we were rehearsing the First Symphony, and ... a passage was being played in too matter-of-fact a manner to please him, he stopped and said, 'Don't play it like that: play it like' – then he hesitated, and added under his breath, before he could stop himself – 'like something we hear down by the river'. I never can play or hear that phrase but I am with him 'down by the river' again as I have been so many times.[1]

Much as Elgar disliked revealing anything about the source of his inspiration it is interesting that, whenever he did, he so often mentions nature: 'My idea is that there is music in the air, music all around us, the world is full of it and you simply take as much as you require'.[2] And writing to his friend and publisher AJ Jaeger: 'The trees are singing my music — or have I sung theirs? I suppose I have'.[3] Then there is Elgar's famous 'deathbed' comment to his friend, the theatre producer Barry Jackson, when Elgar 'rather feebly' tried to whistle the opening theme from his Cello Concerto. 'Barry', he said with tears in his eyes, 'If ever you're out walking on the Malvern Hills and hear that, don't be frightened, it's only me'.[4]

I believe it is no accident that Elgar's most internationally performed major work is his Cello Concerto – almost entirely misunderstood at its premiere yet, today, globally recognised as a masterpiece. It has no

1 William H. Reed, *Elgar as I Knew Him* (London: Victor Gollancz, 1936), 140.

2 Robert J. Buckley, *Sir Edward Elgar* (London: John Lane, 1905), 32.

3 Jerrold Northrop Moore, *Elgar and his Publishers: Letters Vol. 1, 1885–1903* (Oxford: The Clarendon Press, 1987), 212. Letter to August Jaeger, 11 July 1900.

4 Michael Kennedy, *Portrait of Elgar* (London: Oxford University Press, 1982), 334.

tub-thumping, no sense of triumphalism – it is the music of one human being expertly conveying his deepest emotions to his fellow human beings through the medium of music.

It is also nature music, something that seems increasingly remote in today's urban-centric world. As Gainsborough and Constable painted the British countryside, Elgar also had an extraordinary ability to portray nature through music in the same way that he allowed us to visualise his 'friends pictured within' in the *Enigma Variations*. Thus, his importance as a chronicler of the British countryside becomes ever more significant as the landscape, and the wildlife within it, that Elgar knew and loved so well continues to disappear at alarming speed. Present day farming practices lethal to wildlife (73 million birds lost in the last 50 years) and the habitats needed to sustain it have resulted in an increasingly barren land and the sights and sounds of the countryside Elgar recorded so often in his music are fast vanishing.

When we were rehearsing for our recording of Elgar's Cello Concerto the conductor, who had known Elgar so well, offered me just one piece of interpretive advice. As I started the lilting 9/8 first movement theme rather too loudly, Yehudi Menuhin interrupted me: 'Please play this as if it's coming from far away over the hills.'

I played this extraordinary piece of music many, many times and I can write, without hesitation, that it has been a constant, significant presence in my life. The slow movement in particular carries a spiritual depth 'beyond tears', resigned to its fate, and it is no surprise that Elgar chose to share his obvious affection for it with my godfather. In his Cello Concerto Elgar gives us his essence and, whenever he does that, his music will continue to reach minds and touch hearts forever.

↝ Rupert Marshall-Luck

'Especially Sacred': A Perspective on Elgar's Violin Writing

Few would argue that Edward Elgar was one of the most influential of all British composers. The emotional power of his music was profound in its time and continues to resonate today; and, although he founded no school and taught at no conservatoire, his influence upon the following generation of composers was evident and important. However, as a concert-giving violinist who has also had the privilege of editing a number of Elgar's violin works, what I have found increasingly interesting and remarkable is the potency of Elgar's notation in his music for violin, and what it can tell us not just about the music's intended execution but also about how Elgar himself viewed the instrument, as well as what might be termed the 'violinistic environment' in which he was working.

The care that Elgar devoted to the notation of his works is well known: anyone who leafs through an Elgar score, even casually, is immediately struck by the detailed markings, from the particularly placed tempo markings, through the carefully layered dynamics, to the precision of the articulations. This notational care extended throughout a work's genesis, often right up to the point of its publication: during the preparation of my edition of the Sonata for Violin and Piano for G. Henle Verlag, and as the sources relating to the first edition of 1919 were being examined, my colleague, Dr Norbert Müllemann, commented that he had never before seen evidence of a composer changing so minutely the position of pedal markings so late in the publication process. Elgar's precision in such matters was, naturally, driven always by a strongly held view of how he wanted his music to sound; and this view is especially evident in his string-instrument music. Just one example may be seen in the correspondence relating to the Piano Quintet, where, in a letter to Harold Brooke of Novello, dated 21 June 1919, Elgar proposed notating the following gesture

thus:

in order to convey precisely the length of the *f*.[1]

Elgar was himself a violinist of considerable ability; and the combination of the understanding of a high-level executant with an immensely fastidious attention to notational detail is, possibly, unique in the genre of string-instrument music. Elgar's music for this genre offers, therefore, an especially revealing insight into the mind of the composer. The published scores – especially the earlier works – contain a wealth of technical instruction, as well as other compositional and notational features, that reveal a great deal about Elgar's view of stringed instruments, as well as about the physical – and, therefore, sonic – characteristics of the violin at the time of the works' composition. This means that the very specific notation of the music can carry information about the mode of performance as intended by the composer. In examining these issues, this essay will begin with a discussion of Elgar's own credentials as a violinist and an overview of his contribution to the genre, before examining some particular examples of Elgar's notation and what these can tell us about the performance of the work in question.

Credentials

Elgar appears to have been largely self-taught as a violinist, although during 1877 he did receive some lessons from Adolphe Pollitzer, a musician of considerable repute who, after being awarded First Prize at the Vienna Conservatorium in 1846 at the age of fourteen, undertook further studies in Paris before emigrating to Britain in 1851, where he became concertmaster of the new Philharmonic Orchestra as well as holding a Professorship at the London Academy of Music.[2] This instruction, however, was not extensive, comprising as it did a 'course' of five lessons – although Pollitzer evidently had a high regard for Elgar's talent, encouraging him to return for further continuous study, Elgar gave up the lessons a little while later.[3] It seems likely that Elgar's experience of and exposure to violin writing gained as a result of his involvement with Worcestershire's amateur orchestras was at

1 Jerrold Northrop Moore, *Elgar and His Publishers: Letters of a Creative Life* (Oxford: Clarendon Press, 1987), 804.

2 Obituary of Adolphe Pollitzer, *The Era*, 17 November 1900.

3 Michael Kennedy, *Portrait of Elgar*, 3rd edn, (Oxford: Oxford University Press, 1987), 24–5.

least equally important as his formal lessons in informing him about the instrument's capabilities, thereby guiding him towards a mode of composition for the violin that is wholly idiomatic. He clearly possessed a high level of understanding as far as the violin's potential for technical dazzle is concerned:

Études caractéristiques, op. 24; D: bb. 1–2 and bb. 25–6.

The visual appearance of these two examples, from the fourth of Elgar's *Études caractéristiques*, op. 24, make their formidable technical challenges highly evident; yet the writing is admirably well-suited to the violin: the double-stopping allows for resonant tone-production as well as for clear delineation of the two melodic layers; and the arpeggios in the second part of the example make use of finger-patterns that lie easily under the hand. Such writing is possible only for a composer with intimate and detailed knowledge of the violin and the extent of its capabilities as well as an appreciation of the type of figuration that assists effective performance.

Further evidence of Elgar's detailed technical knowledge with respect to violin-playing may be seen in his *Study for Strengthening the Third Finger*. This, as a footnote to the manuscript score describes, was written in 1877 for his own use and it is possible, therefore, that it was created as a response to his lessons with Pollitzer; but what it shows most markedly is a more far-sighted approach to technical development on the part of Elgar than might have been expected from an amateur string-player of the time. While the fourth finger is, muscularly, the weakest of the fingers – and it is important to develop its strength as early as possible – third-finger independence is also necessary to achieve for the development of more advanced violin technique. The exercise also works to develop ease of expansion between the third and fourth fingers: essential for the spacing needed for fingered octaves and tenths. In this study, then, we can see Elgar's technical imagination vaulting into the future: envisaging a requirement that would enable him to excel in a particular musical field.

Study for Strengthening the Third Finger; opening.

The chords are not to be played:
the 1st, 2nd and 4th fingers remain
fixed in the positions indicated.

How Should It Sound?

Elgar's understanding of the violin, then, was considerable and detailed. That this understanding informed his composition for the instrument has been shown by the preceding examples, but it is also manifested in the performance instructions he gives in his works for violin. Many of these instructions concern instrumental colour: for instance, in his *Allegretto on GEDGE,* he uses *pizzicato* and harmonics to create a multidimensional range of instrumental colour:

Allegretto on GEDGE; bb. 72–5.

His ear for colour also led him to invent new techniques, most notably the *pizzicato tremolando*, which he used to telling effect in the accompanied cadenza of the Violin Concerto (Elgar's footnote in the Novello score explains: 'The pizz. tremolando should be "thrummed" with the soft part of three or four fingers across the strings'). The *tutti* string writing of the cadenza is also notable for its use of bowed *tremolando* and *sul ponticello* (where the string is bowed very close to or even right on the bridge, giving a thin, ghostly sound quite different to the violin's usual tone); and Elgar also layers sounds by doubling notes but with each instance having a different type of execution:

Violin Concerto, op. 61, 3rd movement; from rehearsal figure 101 (*tutti* strings).

But, for me, even more fascinating than Elgar's use of instrumental colour are his performance directions that imply a tonal effect based on an implicit acknowledgement of the violin's technical basis. This, in turn, gives performers valuable clues regarding the practical realisation of the music. In his early works for violin, Elgar was profuse in marking technical instructions, and *Salut d'Amour*, op. 12, has an especially revealing set of fingerings. The violin's very first bar contains a puzzle:

Salut d'Amour, op. 12; b. 3.

Having indicated a 4th finger on the first g-sharp^2 of the bar, why does Elgar repeat the fingering for the second? The fingering indication is redundant if the violinist plays the entire bar in one position (that is, without moving the hand along the strings), as, in that case, the second g-sharp^2 would 'automatically' be played with the 4th finger, and redundant fingerings are usually frowned upon in marking violin music unless a special reinforcement of a desired fingering is judged to be necessary. (In fact, editors are usually guilty of omitting *necessary* fingerings, rather than of supplying them when they are not!) I believe that Elgar intended the b-natural^1 to be played with the 1st finger and, as this necessitates a change of position between the g-sharp^2 and the following b-natural^1, the indication '4' on the second g-sharp^2 implies another change of position between the b-natural^1 and the following g-sharp^2 – in other words, Elgar intended this melodic figure to be played on one string (the A string), the omission of the indication '1' on the b-natural^1 being simply an oversight. If this is correct, it also implies that Elgar intended a unified tone-colour for this bar (and, indeed, for the rest of the phrase, as his fingerings in the following bars make it clear that they should, also, be played on the A string).

Another example of the potency of Elgar's markings with respect to technical realisation occurs in the third movement of the Sonata for Violin and Piano, op. 82. Bars 126 and 127 of the violin part consist of rhythmically parallel figures which carry, apparently, inconsistent articulation markings: the second of the paired semiquavers in the first half of each bar (the g-natural^1–d-natural^2 and the e-natural^1–b-natural^1) have no *staccato* dot, whereas the analogous notes in the second half of each bar (f-sharp^1–c-natural^2; a-natural^1–d-sharp^2) do:

Sonata for Violin and Piano, op. 82, 3rd movement; bb. 126–7.

It might be tempting to attribute the missing *staccatos* to a mistake, but I feel that would be to dismiss their omission too lightly. A *staccato* dot means that the note on which it is given should be separated from that which follows, and, assuming the first note of bar 126 is played on a down-bow (which is, violinistically, the only sensible option), this separation would need to be effected in the upper half of the bow by means of a *martélé* ('hammered') stroke – by no means impossible, but requiring considerable muscular effort and control. On the other hand, to follow literally Elgar's given articulation, with a smooth join between semiquaver and following quaver, is entirely idiomatic when played in the upper half of the bow. A separation between notes *is*, however, relatively easy to achieve in the lower half of the bow, where it is entirely natural to lift the bow slightly from the strings to give the required articulation; and beginning the second half of each bar on an up-bow allows just such a stroke to occur. Elgar's given articulations, then, imply a bowing – and the bowing itself makes achieving the articulation as physically easy as possible: an important consideration, given the passage's placement at the end of a long and strenuous Sonata!

Sonata for Violin and Piano, op. 82, 3rd movement; bb. 126–7, showing bowing indications implied by the given articulation.

How Did It Sound?

Elgar's technical instructions sometimes also reflect the 'violinistic environment' within which he was working; and, where they occur, these, too, can impart valuable information about a work's intended manner of performance. There are instances where they reveal something of contemporary performance practice: for example, the notable direction *vibrato* in the second movement of the Violin Concerto, which implies that the application of an almost-continuous *vibrato* was, in England in 1910, still far from being a violinistic norm:

Violin Concerto, op. 61, 2nd movement; from 5 bars before rehearsal figure 54.

(Ironically, the Concerto is dedicated to Fritz Kreisler, who was famous for playing with a continuous *vibrato*!)

More frequently, Elgar's directions are informed by contemporary characteristics of the violin, and an effective realisation of such directions must take into account the characteristics of the instrument on which the performance is made alongside an awareness of the implications of Elgar's instructions. Turning again to *Salut d'Amour*, there are two points where the specified choice of strings looks odd to a modern violinist: bar 28, where Elgar indicates the e-natural[2] to be played using the open E-string; and bars 35 and 36, where the harmonics are, likewise, given to be played on the E-string:

Salut d'Amour, op. 12; b. 28 and bb. 35–6.

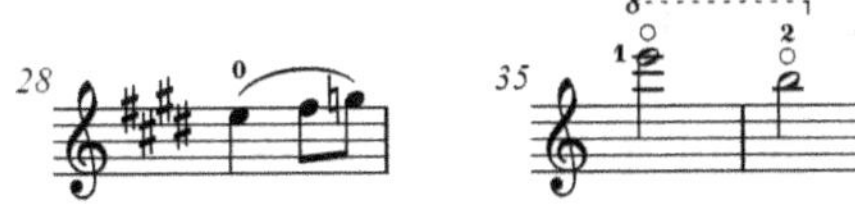

However, at the time of the composition of *Salut d'Amour* (1888), gut strings were almost invariably used – indeed, Carl Flesch, in *The Art of Violin Playing* of 1924, states that the use of 'wire' (that is, metal or metal-wound) strings became widespread only during the First World War, and recommends their use both from the technical side and from the standpoint of public performance in terms that suggest that advocacy on the subject was still required:

> Nowadays an artist, whose instrument is provided with a steel E, an aluminium-covered steel A and an aluminium-covered gut D may step onto the concert platform with the comfortable feeling, not to be at the mercy of the too capricious gut strings, whereas in former days a violin recital looked sometimes very much like a circus show, the performance being suspended a few times, the artist rushing from the platform to the green room and the artistic impression of the public being irremediably destroyed.[4]

Metal strings, though, have a more strident tone-colour than gut strings, particularly so in the case of the open E-string, which loses a rounded softness of sound for a more penetrating, 'cutting-edge' quality. This can be advantageous in some contexts; but to follow Elgar's specifications in this respect in a performance using modern strings of an intimately tender work such as *Salut d'Amour* is a mistake. Rather, we should make a choice of strings that better imitates the more pliable E-string tone-quality that Elgar would have known and probably had in mind when he made his technical specifications. In this solution, the e-natural² of bar 28 is played as a stopped note on the A string, lending it a mellower character; whilst the harmonics of bars 35 and 36 are played as artificial harmonics, also on the A string:

Salut d'Amour, op. 12; b. 28 and bb. 35–6, with altered fingerings and string selection.

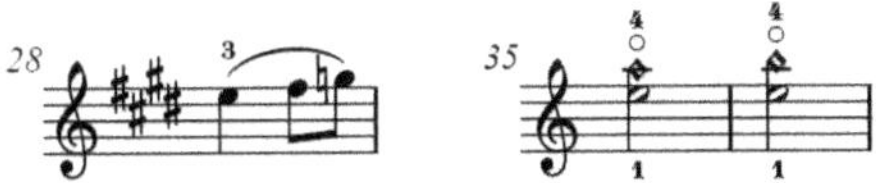

4 Carl Flesch, *The Art of Violin Playing*, trans. Eric Rosenblith (New York: Carl Fischer, 1939), 11.

'Especially Sacred'

Elgar's music for violin has a special place of importance in the genre. May Davidson, the daughter of Marie Joshua, the intended dedicatee of the Violin Sonata, wrote to Elgar after her mother's death: 'She had a feeling that anything you wrote for the Violin was especially sacred to you.'[5] The finely detailed nuances of Elgar's notation in the violin works corroborate that view; and, although it might be said that Elgar lavished a similar level of diligence on all his works, I feel that, in this context, his care carries a particular significance. His first-hand knowledge of the instrument – born partly of traditional instruction and experience but also of a deeply thoughtful and considered approach – means that his technical instructions carry many layers of meaning which violinists can feel entirely justified in honouring when shaping their own interpretations. This characteristic – possibly unique – is, for me, a major consideration when assessing The Importance of Elgar.

5 Jerrold Northrop Moore, *Edward Elgar: Letters of a Lifetime* (Oxford: Oxford University Press, 1991), 317.

~ Stewart Mcilwham

Printed above the opening bars of the score of Elgar's Concert Overture *Froissart*, Op. 19 (his first large scale orchestral work) is the Keats quotation, 'When Chivalry Lifted up her Lance on High'. Having previously only had a vague notion of the definition of 'Chivalry' I consulted the *Oxford English Dictionary* to find the precise meaning. What stood out were the words *honour* along with *unselfish and kind behaviour.* This suggests that the 'Knightly' subject and 'moral code' were of great interest to Elgar at this early stage in his career.

Nearly 45 years after playing in my first performance of the *Enigma Variations,* in a 1980 concert with the National Youth Orchestra of Scotland in Lerwick on the Shetland Isles, my lasting impression of Elgar's music is of its spirit of honesty, positivity and sincerity. What follows has nothing to do with musical scholarship but a purely practical and emotional response as an instrumentalist to performing his music here and abroad for more than four decades. I have been extremely fortunate to view all of this from the front row of the woodwind section of many orchestras, but particularly two with a long history of playing and recording Elgar's music; the Royal Philharmonic (RPO) and, for the last 30 years, the London Philharmonic (LPO). I am also fortunate that from this vantage point I sit virtually in the middle of the action with an excellent view of the conductor, often with many bars rest in which to listen and observe.

So, in reconsidering my experiences for this essay, one of the main things that strikes me most is how enduring and truly internationally recognised Elgar's music continues to be since it was written. So many of his fellow British composers (with the obvious exceptions of Vaughan Williams and Britten) have failed to establish a foothold beyond these shores let alone retain a presence on the concert platform here. There is also an impressively diverse roster of conductors and instrumentalists that have embraced and championed his music, taking many of his works into their repertoire.

The first piece of Elgar I played was the Concert Overture *In the South* for a Sunday evening play-through with the sadly long-gone Glasgow Unitarian Orchestra. From the opening flourish I was swept along on what at the time felt like the most exhilarating orchestral rollercoaster ride. I was totally captivated with what was going on around me and the unexpected wealth of technicolour orchestral detail. It revolutionized my perception of this composer which up until this point had only been based on hearing 'Nimrod' and 'Land of Hope and Glory'. This launched what has turned out for me to be a lifelong love of Elgar's music and an extremely fruitful and privileged journey performing the majority of his orchestral and choral compositions.

From the perspective of a young flute and piccolo player Elgar was not really one of the main composers I was heading nervously to study in the orchestral excerpt books. That's not to say his music does not have its technical challenges and there are certainly many moments of great virtuosity for a wind player such as in 'The Little Bells' from his Second *Wand of Youth Suite*. Often, while performing his music I get the feeling of being no more than a cog in a much bigger machine: there is not so much individual exposure but more of being a part of a bigger ensemble. I love the way Elgar uses his forces and blends different groups of instruments across strings, wind and brass into various combinations and textures, a true mixed palette of orchestral colour such as the beautiful autumnal sound world he creates at the opening of the First Symphony with low flutes, clarinets, bassoons and violas in octaves.

As a schoolboy my early curiosity was greatly aided by the acquisition of many recordings on LP and cassette. In particular I enjoyed the advocacy of Vernon (Tod) Handley and his 'Classics for Pleasure' cycle. Most of these set me back no more than a pound each at the time and I collected them all as they were released during the late 1970s and early 1980s. While taking further study in London I played in my first performances of the First Symphony, *Falstaff*, the Violin Concerto and *The Dream of Gerontius* with the Young Musicians Symphony Orchestra under a much-underrated Elgarian conductor James Blair. Sir Edward ('Ted') Downes and the BBC Philharmonic in Manchester were my next champions on my Elgar journey. Under his baton I played in my maiden Second Symphony and in many subsequent performances. During that time Ted made a much underrated studio recording of the *Enigma Variations* and *In the South*. It is still worth seeking it out on a now deleted CD on the Conifer label. In Manchester, I also took the opportunity to hear the Hallé Orchestra perform Elgar's music and was, of course, reminded of their special Elgarian connections through Richter and Barbirolli.

Joining the RPO in 1990, the presence of Yehudi Menuhin as the orchestra's President and Principal Guest Conductor, added another unique link. There was something about knowing he was almost certainly the last living person to have had an important musical relationship with the great man that transcended any technical limitations he may have had to conduct the complex scores in front of him. It was extraordinary how this willowy 80-year-old man could generate so much energy and conviction in his performances. I recently re-listened to his recording of the Second Symphony (Virgin Classics) made in Abbey Road studio No. 1 in 1990 (the same location where he recorded the Violin Concerto under the composer in 1932) and was amazed at how spontaneous and vital it sounds; the mercurial *scherzo* is miraculous.

Without doubt the Cello Concerto, the *Enigma Variations* and *The Dream of Gerontius* have and continue to be the works that are way ahead in terms of popularity and number of performances. What is most encouraging though is how often performances of the two symphonies still appear in concert and the recording studio. If I had to limit myself to just one part of Elgar's music these two symphonies, for me, contain his greatest music: the height of his compositional creativity and mastery of orchestral forces.

The great Austro-Hungarian conductor Hans Richter standing in front of the London Symphony Orchestra before the London premiere of the First Symphony in 1908 (the world premiere had been given four days earlier in Manchester under his baton with the Hallé) famously said 'Gentlemen, let us now rehearse the greatest symphony of modern times written by the greatest modern composer - and not only in this country'. It is not unreasonable to say, as far as this country is concerned, that this statement about the First Symphony is still true over a hundred years later. However, there is one possible exception: the Second Symphony!

On joining the LPO I have had the benefit of sitting in the orchestra that has perhaps performed and recorded Elgar's music more than any other. My shelves are weighed down with recordings of the orchestra playing virtually every major work of his under a truly international line up of artists including Van Beinum, Boult, Barenboim, Haitink, Handley, Solti, Mackerras, Slatkin and now Edward Gardner, the orchestra's current Principal Conductor and latest champion of his music.

As I write this at the beginning of 2025 there is a continued list of forthcoming concerts and recordings. In January we undertook a New Year tour of China where we played the *Enigma Variations* to a standing ovation in Beijing under the baton of Paavo Järvi who lavished real care and fresh insight through his interpretation of this much played work. Looking further ahead there are a reassuring number of more LPO performances including a new recording of the Violin Concerto and a German tour with my first love, *In the South*. There are also performances of both Symphonies on consecutive evenings in another German festival later that season.

Elgar's music has had a long and cherished place in my heart. I even named one of our dogs after him: Elgar, the black labrador! I am also still hoping that I will get further opportunities to play some of his less performed repertoire, particularly *Falstaff*. This 'Symphonic Study' for me runs the Symphonies close in terms of greatness. My last outing with it was an LPO performance conducted by Vladimir Jurowski in the Royal Festival Hall in 2019. Jurowski gave an outstanding interpretation really getting to the heart of this underrated and under-performed work. I still hope this performance may appear on disc at some point in the future and that one day Jurowski will conduct more Elgar, a composer he has largely resisted performing until now.

Other lesser performed works on my wish list are another *Kingdom* and maybe something from comparative rarities like *Caractacus* or the *Starlight Express*. In the meantime, recordings continue to suffice in the absence of live performances. More importantly there seems to be no waning of the Elgar flame and I think we can be safe in the knowledge that here and abroad artists, orchestras and conductors who will continue to 'Hold up on high' Elgar's 'Lance' for many future generations to come.

~ Alice Neary

An edited transcript of a conversation between cellist, Alice Neary, and the singer and researcher, Richard Strivens. Their discussion of Elgar's relationship to the cello starts with the second movement of the Piano Quintet, Op. 84. [The Figure numbers below refer to the musical scores, which are available on IMSLP].

Alice
I think there are particular voices that Elgar chooses to use to express certain emotions or to communicate certain things. The viola is possibly the other of the string instruments that he felt the most attuned to, for example, there's a wonderful solo viola moment in *In the South.*

Richard
How does that compare with his use of the cello?

Alice
There's a certain kind of heroism that Elgar brings out when he writes for the cello. In very broad terms, there's a vulnerability that he chooses for the viola. The slow movement of the Piano Quintet begins with the most wonderful pure viola melody, which could easily have been a violin, but he chooses the viola. The timbre in that particular register of the viola makes it incredibly personal, or perhaps vulnerable. The cello also has a huge role in the slow movement; there's a lot more freedom of expression given to the cellist. There's the contrast: the intimacy of the viola, and the cello being allowed more expressivity. As soon as the violin has the melody, it has a warmth and openness rather than that intimacy.

Richard
You mentioned freedom given to the cello.

Alice
It is more cadenza, or fantasia, like; for example, after Fig. 31, when the cello is on its own. Then, just before Fig. 32, the dominant voice is the cello even though it's doubled, no, tripled. Elgar's using the cello in the higher register and that dominates the overall sound. The cello is separated out,

rhythmically as well and in its expression markings. There's also a great counter-subject for the cello, around Fig. 37, that seems very Elgar.

Richard
At Fig. 38 you have the viola taking the melody ...

Alice
... it's the one time the viola has that figure. Otherwise, it's always the cello. This refers back to what you asked at the beginning. As a player, you get what you're given, obviously. Then you read into what you're given: try to work out composer's intentions. If the cello's role is to have more freedom, that's the cellist's gift: you take that and play with it. It is also part of preparation and performance to think, why did Elgar choose the cello here, and the viola there?

Richard
It's a complicated idea 'the composer's intentions', but that's a shorthand, isn't it?

Alice
A very limited shorthand, there's a limit, practically, to the number of instructions on the page. Elgar, actually, is one of the most busy: there's a lot that he's asking for. It's all very neat, ordered. I think that is intentional and so it is very important to respond specifically to each instruction.

Richard
May I ask you more about the unison melodies across multiple instruments in the Piano Quintet?

Alice
Like the beginning of the last movement, [Fig. 44] after the introduction? It's almost 'Pomp and Circumstance'-like. It feels very British, somehow, don't you think?

Richard
Yes, although there's a sense of French chamber music and Brahms too. I wonder why we feel it to be British. Is this something that we have overlaid on the music?

Alice
It's hard to put your finger on it. It says *con dignità*; there's a dignified swing to it. One always wants to play it faster than the relatively slow tempo marking [*Allegro*, ♪ = 126]. There's a restraint to it.

Richard
And something about the circles of fifths?

Alice
Yes, it's very structured; and the eight-bar phrases, a sense of safety.

Richard
Could we move on to talk about the *Enigma Variations*, notably Variation XII. B.G.N.? You have used the word 'heroic' as an adjective to describe Elgar's writing for the cello. Can you take that further?

Alice
There's certainly also a tenderness, although he rarely uses the cello as a tentative character. The solo cello at the beginning of Variation XII is bold, it's the big intervals, Elgar is using the cello as an advocate, a real voice. With the big intervals come the big distances you physically travel.

Richard
Can you broaden that out to the way Elgar writes for the cello?

Alice
When Elgar's using the cello more as the advocate I mentioned earlier, he's likely to use bigger intervals.

Richard
Any intervals in particular?

Alice
A lot of sevenths, I would say. Although, in the *Enigma Variations*, it's upward sixths and downward sevenths.

Richard
Elgar seems very willing to take the cello up above a G [on the A string] ...

Alice
... in fourth position? Yes ...

Richard
... where it's not only exuberant or extrovert, there can be a sudden tenderness; he takes (inserts) you up there and then suspends you there.

Alice
I think that's true. The clever thing, balance-wise, is that that range on the cello is much more easily heard because it rings very well. If you're at the bottom of the D string, you really have to work to make the sound, to make

it project. Whereas up there, there's the possibility of finding that tender, *dolce* quality, without worrying about not being heard.

There's another interesting aspect to Elgar's cello writing. He uses solo cello at the beginning and end of this Variation, then the *cello section* for the majority of the movement. He clearly loved the sound of the cello section.

That reminds me of the slow movement of the First Symphony which is unusual with its two-cello solo. Again, he achieves a very beautiful quality: it's the particular quality of two players, two instruments sounding together. Yes, it's less individual, less spotlit somehow; you need be able to blend evenly, there's a more collaborative feeling. Tchaikovsky does the same in the Piano Concerto, but most people don't perform it that way, it's usually done as a solo.

In the Cello Concerto, he uses the cello section *with* the solo cello. In the first movement, the theme at Fig. 6 starts with solo cello and moves into unison with the cello section. And then there's a big moment in the last movement [at Fig. 59] when you almost allow yourself to be swallowed up into the section.

Richard
And what does that moment feel like? I know that you've played it relatively recently at the Wiltshire Music Centre with the West of England Youth Orchestra conducted by Tim Redmond.

Alice
In that instance, I found myself just encouraging them to enjoy joining in the character of the solo instrument and that we would all go for it in the same way.

Richard
With a professional orchestra, I presume it's different?

Alice
I've done it both ways: as principal cello, you go with what the soloist wants, because sometimes they might want to dominate more, wanting to keep their sound above the orchestra, or sometimes they're happy to be submerged within it.

Richard
I guess that's a conversation between principal and the soloist, or even, is it a silent conversation?

Alice
It can, or cannot, be silent!

As the soloist, I've never felt overpowered by the cello section. I'd rather at that moment feel we are all playing together: you try to match bowings and which string we're on, because it will sound better if we're all doing the same. There's a *nobilmente* marking, and up to *fortissimo* when the basses join [at Fig. 60]. Elgar is definitely wanting the power of the whole section.

Richard
Elgar uses the cello in so many different ways, and yet it's always within a certain late romantic manner of composition.

Alice
Yes, I think it's relevant that the Cello Concerto was one of the last pieces he wrote; autumnal, a retrospective feel. Even though there is a heroism to the character who is the soloist in the concerto, I think there's a wistful longing for the past, especially at the beginning and end of the Concerto.

Richard
Previously, we've talked, briefly, about the Concerto being a 'journey'. You start somewhere and that's where you return to?

Alice
You return to the same place. I mean, a very similar place. The Concerto's opening statement comes back at the end of the 4th movement [at Fig. 72] which is so powerful, but it's changed by the journey you've been on. As a player, you really feel it. Here's an example of Elgar's subtlety: in the opening statement there is no *rit.*, when it returns at Fig. 72 there is. The other main difference is the accompaniment. At the opening, it's accompanied very tentatively. At Fig. 72, it's much more powerful and there's a sureness, a result of the journey that the piece has taken you on.

Richard
I'm not going to ask you to describe your journey with the piece, I think that's far too personal, but are there things you want to say about moments on that journey?

Alice
After the very bold opening statement, you're left ... there's a real reaction to that bold statement ... emotionally slightly drained, and then very naturally, it takes you via the *ad lib.* scale into the main subject of the movement [Fig. 1]. The emotional effect is very clear, as is what it demands of the player.

Richard
As opposed to the big scale up just before Fig. 5. That one must be exhilarating.

Alice
Oh yes, absolutely exhilarating. But this first one, where you're just left, alone – such tentative music.

Richard
What about feelings of performance nerves?

Alice
The emotion of the big scale up is so written into the music, it's not a place I feel nervous, no, because it's a natural place that you're reaching for. It's very well-written on the instrument; of course, you need to have practised your scales ...

It's the quiet moments where there's a tentative nature to the music, a hesitancy, a wondering, a finding-your-way that I find the most demanding. Because you have to be vulnerable at those moments. You have to allow a vulnerability into the sound. So, for example, the first time you play the main theme [Fig. 2], that is very hard to play well. When you get to the the *fortissimo* version at Fig. 4, that's so satisfying to play. It's beautifully orchestrated with horns and low winds. Overall, the Concerto is orchestrated brilliantly, there are generally no big balance problems.

Richard
When you play the Concerto, are you able to separate out you, the performer, and you as the central character of the music?

Alice
There's such a strong emotional attachment to the piece for me. I'm sure it's inherent in the music. The journey you go on, I really do *feel* it as I play it. You do have to be careful as a performer that you're not *only* feeling the emotion that you're communicating. These amazingly beautiful and proud moments – or sad, or longing – the piece can truly conjure up these feelings and that's good *up to a point.* I definitely have had to learn to focus on the music needing to speak to someone else. It is not just what I hear in my head.

Richard
Take us to another point where there's clearly some change of direction in the journey.

Alice
The main theme of the first movement is repeated six times. Each repetition has a context, and each context changes the journey. In some instances, say, following a very loud moment, there might be some left-over energy. But when it comes at the end of the movement, [Fig. 17], it needs to be

incredibly vulnerable. That makes the first movement quite a searching journey.

Things really change when you get to the transition to the second movement [from Fig. 18], which is ingenious: the way he combines themes, bringing things back. It's pretty obvious in some ways: for example, the second movement begins with the same chords as the opening of the whole piece, but its context is very different, being pizzicato and with a huge dynamic range. It's trying to find a new way through, almost like solving a problem. The first movement didn't solve anything. And you're left: 'what are we going to do now?' Start again and see what happens.

This is another place where Elgar's specificity is so evident. When I'm teaching this section, but also when I'm practising, these little snippets of scherzo material [from the *Allegro molto* after Fig. 18 to Fig. 19] are all marked differently. He is giving lots of indications as to how he wants the journey to continue.

Richard
That gives, strangely, a sense of freedom?

Alice
That's how I read it. It's limited what '*pianissimo crescendo* to *forte*' tells you [two bars before Fig. 20], but it's a big gesture and different from the first time you played that snippet. The chords in between each of these scherzo snippets are ingenious, like little comments. What they say affects what happens next. I'm only saying out loud what Elgar writes. It is very satisfying as a performer to have this much detail, because what we're always doing is trying to 'speak' the composer's voice, in this case, Elgar's.

Richard
This takes us into the scherzo [Second movement, Fig. 20].

Alice
First, let's sum up where we have got to: the first movement has this incredibly longing. Yearning is the overall mood. It's nostalgic, weighted down by the past. Suddenly, through the transition you get into the very light-hearted music of the scherzo. The playful character feels to me like we're looking at a life – looking back on a childhood. There's an easiness, a lack of that weighty worry. Yet there are occasionally memories: the outbursts at Fig. 22 when the cello is suddenly back to being that melodic instrument. Most of the time it's virtuosic in this movement.

Richard
What does being 'melodic' indicate to you?

Alice
It's proud music, it has more grandeur to it. These are fleeting moments, though. Actually, like the whole scherzo: fleeting, incredibly short.

Richard
Is there some link between these melodic moments and the dignity of the unison tune in the Piano Quintet [3rd movement] that we pointed out earlier?

Alice
Yes, but I don't think it's as reserved. Because most of second movement of the Concerto is effective when it's very quiet, dynamically these break out from that and again there are bigger intervals.

Richard
You use the word proud.

Alice
He doesn't write *nobilmente* there, he's after something a bit wilder. Overall, a much more youthful spirit than the first movement and then at the end it flits off, really, with such fun and lack of worries.

Richard
Do you find a response in the second movement, given you say the first movement didn't solve anything?

Alice
You have found *some* response. It doesn't feel totally satisfied. The piece works well pretty much without breaks between the movements because one thing responds so much to what's just happened.
The third movement is *so* incredibly beautiful. It has less of the yearning, longing and looking back of the first movement, there's more hope. There are rising phrases, rising intervals, the music calls for an opening up of possibility rather than the closing sense of the descending phrases in the first movement.

It's got a fairly fast metronome marking. When you try it at ♪ = 50, it actually feels really fast. It's in 3/8 not 3/4, there's more of a feeling of it being in one-in-a-bar, a very slow one, never being too heavily beat-y. When I played it with Tod Hanley conducting, he was *insistent* – I was quite young – that I should play it faster. I found it hard, but I think he was absolutely right.

I think Elgar was looking for something quite spoken in the opening of the third movement. The way that it begins, these short phrases, in a faster tempo, allows for separations within phrases to be felt more. If it's slower, then you're waiting for everything. But with a flowing tempo, a phrase might stop more abruptly and that's more effective.

The movement is mainly about hope, but it is not without angst. There are certainly more painful moments, like Fig. 36 with more falling intervals. This is in contrast to the rest of the movement with its big intervals, rising sevenths. They're seeking ... yes, optimistic. The other character that comes into this movement, not present in the rest of the piece, is an anger in the middle of the movement at Fig. 38: there's a real sense of fighting against something. The first movement, despite its sadness and yearning, doesn't have that much fight in it.

Richard
Turning to the end of the movement, if the opening had a faltering, spoken quality ...

Alice
... the end gives us more fluent sentences. Here those short phrases, from the start of the movement, are joined together, with the rests removed in the solo line. Elgar has beautiful and subtle ways of repeating the same music *nearly.* I think he's a genius at that. Although this is a satisfying conclusion, the third movement ends on the dominant which propels you straight into the last movement.

Richard
I'm struck by the fact that the last movement starts with an orchestral introduction. The cello has led before.

Alice
But it's more a transition into the cello starting the movement proper at Fig. 44! This 'transition' is *allegro* but when the cello plays that material at Fig. 44, it sets up the tempo for the rest of the movement which is *allegro, ma non troppo,* slightly slower. I find that Elgar's markings only reaffirm what you're thinking, encouraging you down your path further. I do really believe him!

It's ingenious the way the fourth movement works in that he uses this declamatory material in the introduction, referring to the beginning of the Concerto. It's more heroic here and has less regret. This theme then becomes the folk dance at Fig. 44. Structurally it is very clever. Literally using the same material, that little *ad lib.* section just before Fig. 1, becomes the outward-looking cadenza at Fig. 43. It's a clever way to bind the piece together, even for someone hearing it for the first time. As a performer, it's really valuable to notice these things. The vulnerability in the first movement and then the searching, clearly becomes in the fourth movement a great declamation, but interestingly it keeps losing confidence.

Richard
Tell me about the folk dance.

Alice
There's something very rustic about it. It might feel a bit Edwardian if he hadn't written all the off-beats and quirkiness. What this more simple, rustic music does is set up the end of the piece and that is what really stands out in this movement: the end and how Elgar journeys from this joyous playful music to something so intensely moving.

Although there are some tricky aspects to navigate too: to be together with the flute, some of the passage-work is the most difficult section of the whole piece, even though the cello is in the background at, say, Fig. 50, I find that music quite tough. Mostly, the Concerto is beautifully written for the cello, but this is slightly more awkward. You have melodies which mustn't dominate, the little things going on in the strings are all quite playful.

Then it's the big build to that moment that we spoke about before, the solo cello with the cello section all marked *nobilmente*. Different from the *nobilmente* at the opening of the Concerto ...

Richard
... so even the expression markings have taken a journey!

Alice
This is the folk dance, but now it's got stature, not much harmony ... a unison version ...

Richard
... again, like in the Piano Quintet ...

Alice
... going into unison, yes, it really punctuates the movement.

We have to talk about the end. Fig. 64 is the start of a natural wind-down, Elgar lightens the texture, puts the theme very high in the wind and everyone's pizzicato. It's starting to break down from that obvious rustic, simple character; it's losing its identity as he changes the rhythm. The simple personality of that folk dance is disappearing and it's becoming something more melodic. Although Fig. 66 is the beginning of the end, Elgar's metronome marking is fast. He's asking for a very gradual process. It's very tempting in performance to let it immediately be very slow, but he's so clear it's *poco più lento*. It doesn't say *adagio*, it's winding down until we hear the *lento* of the slow movement again.

And this coda isn't all quiet and slow. It has the biggest of all climaxes with this rising seventh at Fig. 69. One of the defining moments of the piece. At that moment, you feel very alone, you *are* the voice. You're set up by a big orchestral tutti.

Richard
You're saying there's a sense of loneliness on stage, or aloneness?

Alice
Aloneness, yes. Not lonely, that's right. It's more you are the lone survivor, the lone voice. The responsibility of that moment. You're suddenly thrust forward to say something. It's a most exhilarating feeling. To reach that point of the piece, this journey we've been talking about. The build is so … it's absolutely the moment to spill, to open your soul. Everything has led to that moment.

Richard
It feels as if you've been led to a place where you feel like you and the character – Elgar's character – are one.

Alice
Yes, that's what Elgar writes into the music, but it's so much the job of the performer to lead the audience to this place, to allow things not to finish before, not to say everything too soon. You're suggesting things and you're finding your way through. But this is the moment …

… but it's not even the end. That's where – because we've had this huge outcry – the intimacy can return. You can have 'intensely intimate' *because* you've had 'intensely extrovert' …

It's incredible, how close he can then put so many themes, he puts the slow movement immediately into the opening of the whole piece, and then it's immediately back to the last movement. It's like a Fabergé egg!

There's something still perhaps pent up about the character, something that's left over, even, from the first movement. There's something – a certain restraint – that is finally allowed out at the very end of the piece.

Richard
A final question: how long has it taken to get to a point where you feel like you've developed *your* way of telling this 'story', playing this Concerto?

Alice
It's probably the first piece that I felt most sure about. Every time I come back to it, the preparation is finding your way into the story *now*. Actually, it's more about emotional reactions; an emotional journey, rather than a told story. You're communicating music: it has to be reactive to the moment.

With a different orchestra or conductor, they'll present something slightly different. You have to be adaptable to be able to take that on board.

Richard
You can't have your core swayed too much, though. You have to have strength to be able to take whatever emotional impulse you receive.

Alice
But you also don't want to be a cold, unaffected presence as a soloist; you need to be part of the whole.

Richard
So, if your core is slim and weak, they don't have anything to respond to.

Alice
Absolutely. And obviously, as you're one and they're eighty, you've got to be strong. Yes, because otherwise the character won't 'speak'. It's too small a voice. You have to have strength.

Here's an example from the first movement, the violas have the theme first; how they play it determines how I then play. If it's quite assured, you might want to give a less sure response. And vice versa, if it's very tentative, you can develop it further.

Yes, experience gives you a freedom, because you've tried these things. You've thought about the ways thing could go, it isn't just totally spontaneous. It's spontaneous in that there are lots of options and almost subconsciously you find your way through. If I bring out *that* C sharp, because the violas played a C natural just before, I believe the audience will feel it somehow, because of the intention behind my decision.

~ David Owen Norris

In his book, *Elgar as I knew him*[1], the violinist W.H. Reed describes visiting Elgar to play over the sketches for the Violin Concerto: 'I found E. striding about with a lot of loose sheets of music paper, arranging them in different parts of the room. Some were already pinned on the backs of chairs, or stuck up on the mantelpiece ready for me to play. ...what we played was a sketchy version of the Violin Concerto. He had got the main ideas written out, and, as he put it, "japed them up" to make a coherent piece. ...this morning's work was a unique experience to me: it gave me a very intimate view of Elgar as a composer, revealing the singularity of his mental processes, the originality of his methods, and the surprising speed at which he worked.'

Reed describes another play-through: 'I found the studio in the state I had become accustomed to at the London flat: music paper all over the room, scraps at any vantage point, many different versions of the same thing with the different bowings to be tried for each. At once we plunged into it. Passages were tried in different ways: the notes were regrouped, or the phrasing altered. The Cadenza was in pieces; but soon the parts took shape and were knit together to become an integral part of the concerto.'

In *Edward Elgar A Creative life*,[2] Jerrold Northrop Moore surmises that 'the idea was clearly to get a view of the whole pattern in the sequence of sheets placed round the room – with the chance to change, add to, or take away from it.' The most interesting aspect of this procedure is the possibility of changing the sequence of the sheets, perhaps at first by simply walking to a different sheet, and only later confirming the change by pinning it to the back of a different chair. Reed does not specifically mention such re-ordering. (The phrase 'the notes were regrouped' does not mean 'the sheets were re-grouped': the meaning becomes clear in a separate article on the Concerto, in which Reed writes of 'these arabesques, and deciding whether they should be demisemiquavers or whether the groups should be written as broken triplets.') But the idea of 'knitting together the pieces' of

1 William H. Reed, *Elgar as I knew him* (London: Victor Gollancz, 1978).

2 Jerrold Northrop Moore, *Edward Elgar: A Creative Life* (Oxford: Oxford University Press, 1984).

the *Cadenza* certainly doesn't rule out arranging the sheets in a different order, and Moore's tripartite interpretation of 'change, add or take away' is generally accepted. It fits in with the comment of Rosa Burley, at whose school Elgar taught the violin, that he 'did not write the work in the order in which it would be played.'

Some readers may recall the advent of Cut & Paste as vividly as I do. I found it enabled me to improve the presentation of a logical argument. It's perhaps unfortunate that Cut & Paste tempts us to begin writing before we've worked out the final shape of our argument, but even this can be seen as an extension of the generally benign power of notation. An analogy from poetry is useful, I find, in reminding us of what notation makes possible. Improvise a poem beginning 'There was a young person from Bewdley.' Easy! But if I were to ask you to write a sonnet beginning 'My favourite composer, Edward E,' or even 'It is a beauteous evening, calm and free,' you would probably require pencil and paper. Notation, whether of words or music, makes it possible to put more thinking-time into something than the something takes to perform. Cut & Paste is an extension of that. Elgar's separate sheets pinned up around the room harness the same power.

If we were to regard brainstorming – the jotting down of ideas, whether musical or verbal – as a two-dimensional method of mining the unconscious mind, then Elgar's procedure, like Cut & Paste, adds a further dimension to it, a sideways look at those ideas. There's a three-dimensional analogy ready to hand. If you've read *The Art of Memory* by Frances A. Yates[3] (or Cicero's *De Oratore*, for that matter), you'll know all about the notion of imagining your facts as being placed in various locations in a building that you know well, and then constructing your arguments by mentally walking round that building in a certain way. The technique degenerated into a mere Kim's Game[4], but at its mediaeval height it was much more subtle, becoming an Art of Composition. A passage about this sort of 'composing' from the scholar Mary Carruthers resonates uncannily: 'It is possible for one with a well-trained memory to compose clearly in an organized fashion on several different subjects. Once one has the all-important starting-place of the ordering scheme and the contents firmly in their places within it, it is quite possible to move back and forth from one distinct composition to another without losing one's place or becoming confused.' The 'memory' aspect of this is replaced by notation, of course – those pinned-up sheets

3 Frances A. Yates, *The Art of Memory* (London: Routledge and Kegan Paul, 1966).

4 A game or exercise, in which a selection of objects must be memorised. The game develops a person's capacity to observe and remember details. The name is derived from Rudyard Kipling's 1901 novel *Kim*, in which the protagonist plays the game during his training as a spy. Eds.

of manuscript paper – and Carruthers is not speaking of musical composition; but there's no doubt that Elgar's possibly unwitting adaptation of this ancient art of walking from one idea to the next, enabled him, too, 'to compose clearly in an organised fashion'.

Although Moore quotes most of the extracts from Reed given at the beginning of this essay, he does not quote the passage I find most interesting: 'revealing the singularity of his mental processes, the originality of his methods, and the surprising speed at which he worked'. To begin with those 'mental processes', Elgar's well-known dictum – 'My idea is that there is music in the air, music all around us, the world is full of it and you simply take as much as you require' – would mean, if taken literally, that his mind, conscious or unconscious, had nothing to do with his music. Elgar, of course, was perfectly aware of his mind's role. In 1922, he recalled how the 'strong, characteristic stuff' (in *King Olaf*) had 'been conceived and written (by a poor wretch teaching all day) with a splitting headache after dinner'.

The inspirations of *In the South* make it clear that the music 'all around us' was in fact implicit in his inner self. One passage was inspired by the Roman bridge near Alassio. As Elgar wrote: 'the massive bridge and road still useful, and to <u>a reflective mind</u> awe-inspiring'. (He himself underlined the words 'reflective mind'.) Dan the bulldog, famous for falling into the River Wye in the *Enigma Variations*, was pressed into service here, too, but *In the South* is no more about a dog-fight than the Prayer motive in *The Apostles* is about Dan snuffling in his sleep. Elgar knew that his susceptibility to the natural world was merely a stimulus to his 'reflective mind', as his beautiful description of the germination of *In the South* makes clear: 'The exhilarating *out of doors* feeling arising from the gloriously beautiful surroundings – streams, flowers, hills: the distant snow mountains in one direction and the blue Mediterranean in the other. The idea came in a flash. In that time I had composed the overture – the rest was merely writing it down'.

'The <u>idea</u> came in a flash'. And 'that there is music in the air, music all around us' he also characterised as an 'idea'. Where did the ideas come from? It seems to me that Elgar's unconscious mind, though undeniably deep, was also unusually close to the surface – barely submerged, and most 'singular' indeed. Reed's key words 'mental processes', 'methods' and 'work' (note the thoughtful order) put the slightly comical story of walking round the room playing the fiddle into a more serious light. Elgar has discovered how to do musical brainstorming in three dimensions.

I never did learn the surname of the charming man who used to live in the house where Elgar improvised his Enigma, but thank you, John, for showing me Elgar's study. Obviously originally a small bedroom, with what would have been a cosy little fireplace. How do we know it was the study? Well, the light hanging from the ceiling is not in the middle of the room, but in the corner by the fireplace. If you had a desk in that corner, that's where you might instruct your electrician to put the light when electricity was first installed in the house. More significant were the drawing-pins. Stripping off the old wallpaper in preparation for re-decorating the room, John discovered a constellation of tiny holes in the plaster, apparently the imprint of drawing-pins. They ebbed and flowed across the walls, confirming that Elgar's desk was indeed in that cosy corner, and showing how he would pin things up as far as he could reach without getting up, and then rise to pin up still more in more distant parts of the room. What were those drawing-pins pinning up?

The answer's pretty clear. Elgar developed his Cut & Paste technique a decade before Reed experienced it. Could it be significant that he developed it in the very house where he made his Enigma breakthrough? Can it have contributed to his journey from being a good composer to becoming a great one? It would certainly have helped him follow his own advice about the importance of deciding where to place the climax – he could just pin it elsewhere until he found the perfect spot. Those drawing-pin holes remind us that convincing musical forms require strategy. Tick-tacks rather than tactics, as it were.

I am indebted to Richard Westwood-Brooks for bringing this information to my attention.

~ Christian Tetzlaff

It was on a sunny day in Cheltenham in July 1985 that I first made the acquaintance of Sir Edward Elgar's violin concerto. A lovely lady gave me the violin part, inscribed with nice words about my performance, and an invitation to look at the piece; she thought it might suit me! Unfortunately, I wasn't yet ready for it. (The same would have applied had I met my present wife at that time – somehow the two seem to me to be connected...)

Raised in Germanic musical culture in the 70s certainly meant, concerning the twentieth century, a focus on Alban Berg, Béla Bartók and Arnold Schoenberg – as opposed to Jean Sibelius, Edward Elgar and Dmitri Shostakovich. Things have changed – in that culture – and, even more so, in me. (That day in Cheltenham was also my first scone with clotted cream...)

Moving forward to the year 2012, I was now a resident of Putney, in South-West London, living with my new wife (who adores everything British), enjoying British cultural life, playing regularly at the Proms – arguably the most wonderful concert series possible – and getting involved also with British Pop culture of the 70s and beyond. So, I was now ready for the big piece: and these days it has become, together with the Brahms, my favourite concerto.

One attraction is the beautiful, amazing violin writing – difficult but rewarding, composed with a total understanding of the nature of the instrument. But there are more important aspects than that, of course: the projection of a deep sense of longing, of wild inner turmoil in the first movement; followed by a song of peaceful acceptance and love that can turn the violinist into a medium that talks to the audience of everything that is (or could/should be) the most important in our lives; and finally the last movement, which recaptures the nervous energy of the first but is full of fresh miracles, especially the astonishing *cadenza*. That it finds its way to a triumphant ending is almost surprising – but very satisfying for both performers and listeners.

I do have a sense of mission with this concerto, for the above reasons – but also for another. Coming to it without any performing tradition, I fully trust Elgar's score: for instance, the mesmerizing second theme in the first movement is marked *pianissimo* throughout – it's not supposed to be a show of violinistic power. Then the tempi: as indicated by Elgar (far more flowing than those usually taken) the atmosphere seems to be less 'Empire' than 'Jugendstil' – these tempi bring out, for all the strong, at times violent emotions, a beautiful elegance and flexibility. As a result, I discovered – to my surprise – that my performances take about 45 minutes (which feels quite indulgent for a violin concerto!), as opposed to the 50-55 minutes duration which I encounter in most other performances.

Above all, I see the concerto as a major composition by a major composer. I like the words of a reviewer, who wrote that Elgar 'came late to the party' (the party being one of romantic, tonal and very personal statements) 'but had very important things to say'.

Even though I will not be able to have had as many years with it as I have had with Brahms and others, I hope to enjoy living with this concerto for a while yet – at least until the 100th anniversary! This year (2025) I will be playing it in Chicago, New Zealand and (after the joy of playing it at the Proms last year) back in Britain with the BBC Philharmonic in Manchester, where a few years ago I played it for the first time. And finally: this performance will be tied to a CD production – my wish for so long.

~ William Vann

Some Thoughts on Elgar

Whilst I remember being well aware of the work of many composers as a child, Elgar was not one of them: as a chorister, English church music of his era was all about Parry and Stanford, save, perhaps, the occasional dubious renditions of *Land of Hope and Glory*. I first came to his music as a young adult whilst attempting to sight-read my way (badly) through the bass part of *The Dream of Gerontius*, later performing it (with a little more success) as part of a chorus of massed Cambridge college choirs in Ely Cathedral under the baton of Christopher Robinson. Subsequently I sang in a memorable performance of *The Apostles* as a choral society bumper in Canterbury Cathedral, but in terms of studying his music in depth, a breakthrough moment was when I accompanied performances of his songs as a pianist at the Royal Academy of Music. The harmonic language, textures and audacious compositional techniques deployed in the writing of *Sea Pictures* (and in this instance I refer to the version for voice and piano) are not only striking, but they become even more astonishing the more they are experienced. That piqued my interest, and I went back to listen to *The Dream of Gerontius* and much more, performing other works in the meanwhile such as the Violin Sonata, many more songs and a fair few of the choral works.

Compositional techniques aside though, what I adore about Elgar's music is an unashamed Romanticism and emotional honesty, coupled with the compositional brilliance to transmit consistently those profound feelings with integrity, and a structure that allows (but, crucially, doesn't force) the listener to be transported. In that sense, at his best he is like Bach or Brahms. He didn't always achieve that, but then nor does Brahms: perhaps, if he had been trying too hard to achieve greatness all the time, his music might have rather less meaning.

It has been a delight to get to know his choral music in much more depth over the last few years as Director of Music of the Royal Hospital Chelsea, where I am lucky to oversee one of the best professional church choirs in the UK. My predecessor, Ian Curror, recorded a disc of Elgar's

5. A studio photograph by J. Russell & Sons of London and Windsor. The German critic Otto Lessmann published an enthusiastic review of *The Dream of Gerontius* in the *Allgemeine Musik-Zeitung* following its premiere in Birmingham in October 1900, after which he applied to Elgar for a photo to illustrate a general piece on the composer's works. Elgar sent him this image from the Russell Windsor studio.

choral music in 2004 called 'Perfect Love': that recording was, unlikely as it sounds, presented by Manfred Mann, and included a fascinating selection of lesser-known works. Collaborating with SOMM Recordings under the guidance of Siva Oke and with enormous help from Andrew Neill, we conceived a programme ('The Reeds by Severn Side') that explored the scope of Elgar's choral music, from early – and humble – beginnings to his final choral work, the memorial ode to Queen Alexandra: *So many true princesses who have gone.* Humble seems such an appropriate word to use about Elgar, because he never seems to have blown his own trumpet, nor was he a child prodigy, nor even recognised as a young adult – he found his voice gradually, through respecting the work of others, and this is exactly why his music is so attractively honest.

We chose to record 'The Reeds by Severn Side' in the church of Holy Trinity, Sloane Street, just half a mile down the road from the Royal Hospital Chelsea: it has a superb Harrison & Harrison organ that can cope with the demands of music such as *Give unto the Lord,* a sumptuous acoustic and enough distance from the Heathrow flight path. The opening two pieces we chose to record are notable as the musical material was in fact written by two Classical composers: a *Gloria* based on a Mozart Violin Sonata, and a *Credo* on themes of Beethoven. To hear a composer getting under the skin of two great masters in this way is instructive, enlightening and, perhaps surprisingly, musically rewarding too, with countless delicate touches revealing Elgar to be already some way towards mastering his art. There are works on the disc that most audiences will have heard, of course, and they are superb: *Give unto the Lord* is a masterpiece and one of the finest of all English church anthems; *They are at rest* is one of the most touchingly reflective *a cappella* works; and *There is Sweet Music* is a stunningly innovative part-song; but what really took me aback was the lesser-known repertoire. *I Sing the Birth* is a beautifully crafted and touching modal carol that deserves to be part of the regular Christmas choral repertory; his *Angelus,* setting Elgar's own translation of a Tuscan text, is another clever concept, brilliantly executed, with a bell-like figure in the internal parts gloriously wrapped in another quasi-modal tune in the soprano and bass, binding Elgar's intensely Catholic faith with the soundscape of a secular part song. Even in the relatively simple world of an Anglican psalm chant (*Psalm 68,* in this instance), he displays touches of harmony and melodic lyricism that are recognisably his.

Since then, I have enjoyed hugely delving deeper into Elgar's music; take his songs, for example, which I used to find a little saccharine, but now often appreciate for that very reason. *Speak, music* is a good example: when performed without guile or showiness it can be the most wonderfully touching of songs (as it was when I was lucky enough to perform it in an Elgar-only recital with the mezzo-soprano Kathryn Rudge in 2022). Making assumptions about composers from a small part of their *oeuvre* is always dangerous, but with Elgar it seems to be particularly so, as every new discovery forces you to re-evaluate the man and his music: and what a delicious feast of music it is.

6. Numerous cartoonists delighted in drawing Elgar as exemplified by this 1914 sketch of the composer conducting in Queen's Hall. The artist was Edmond Kapp. Although Kapp said this was the finest of the many drawings he did of Elgar, it was never exhibited because the pen went wrong leaving small deposits on the paper, later successfully removed. Though not exhibited, the drawing appeared as Number 10 in *Personalities* published by Martin Secker in 1919 and was reproduced in the 11 November 1932 issue of *The Listener*.

4

The Dream of Gerontius and Other Religious Music

～ Janet Baker

The Role of the Angel in *The Dream of Gerontius*

(*This essay was first published in 2007 in Elgar* An Anniversary Portrait *by Continuum Books With an introduction by Sir Nicholas Kenyon. We are grateful to both Dame Janet, Sir Nicholas and Bloomsbury Books, the successors to Continuum, for their permission to reproduce this essay.*)

Some years ago, HRH the Princess Margaret came to see me during the interval, just before I went out to sing the role of The Angel in Westminster Abbey. We chatted for a while and then as she left the Green Room, she turned at the door and said with a twinkle in her eye, 'Good luck, Janet, be an angel.'

Be an Angel, yes indeed, any role we play we have to 'be'; it has become such a part of us that, for a time, we really feel we are that person. The Angel is special, and I was lucky to have the chance to play her and explore her character very deeply, through Elgar's marvellous score and the ideas expressed in Newman's wonderful poem.

It tells of Gerontius on his death bed in agony of mind, surrounded by his friends who pray for him. As his soul departs, the priest joins with them in speeding Gerontius on his way out of this world.

Part Two, where we meet the Angel for the first time, paints a completely different scene. Here, the atmosphere is peace, light; a timeless quality emerges through the music and Gerontius wakes from a sleep sensing the changes which now surround him, and gradually realizes that he is held in the arms of a mighty being, borne along at tremendous speed and listening to a wondrous sound of singing.

The voice he hears is that of his Guardian Angel who has been guiding him, watching over him all his life, and who now is carrying him towards the seat of Judgement, where he will be subjected to the unbearable glance of God; finally he will be taken by the Angel to be healed and to sleep in the waters of oblivion until she comes again to waken him.

This conversation between Gerontius and the Angel is nothing short of sublime and raises some interesting questions. Elgar, great composer that he is, has thought of everything: the performer has only to obey the markings and directions he has written on the score – these are many and one ignores them at one's peril.

Gerontius is different from the Angel: he is a human soul, newly dead; she is a being of eternity. The two singers have to make this clear. It is done for us in the music, each character having a personal tempo, and the conversation works as long as Elgar's instructions are scrupulously observed. It quite often happens that Gerontius invades the timespace of the Angel and vice versa, in which case the exchange between them loses some of its magic and shape.

Gerontius feels himself 'changed': he is refreshed, free, more himself than he has ever been. The Angel is unchanging. The important difference for her is that at last she can communicate with Gerontius directly in a way which has not been possible during his earthly life, and he is able to answer the questions he wishes to ask her. She has a stillness about her and radiates joy because she knows the truth of her very first words, 'My work is done, my task is o'er', and she is taking him home. She says he is both her child and her brother; perhaps in some far-off past she has herself been human and has now attained the exalted purpose of being responsible for the welfare of another soul.

There is something very beautiful in Newman's teaching that we all have a guardian angel who is within us or beside us every step of the way. The bond between the Angel and Gerontius is significant and the thought of some force in our lives which can make us feel valued and loved is a tremendously comforting one.

Gerontius is asking many questions. 'I fain would know a maze of things', he says, 'were it but meet to ask'. She replies on the most simple, transparently written phrase, 'You cannot now cherish a wish which ought not to be wished'. Something about the triplets Elgar has written always made this phrase full of meaning for me. The whole piece has moments which I found so affecting, they are almost impossible to sing. Two pages later there is another, this time on the words, 'It is because then thou didst fear, that NOW, thou dost not fear'. The music rises to a top F sharp and is physically exhilarating to sing.

Another example of these special moments and one which never failed to move me is the moment when Gerontius asks, 'Shall I see my dearest Master, when I reach His throne?' Elgar writes a phrase which hangs in the air, as if the phrase is too important to answer without a pause. The Angel pauses with it, and after what seems like an eternity replies 'Yes'. The one word, 'yes', has so many levels of meaning for me; the Angel knows what the sight can do to the unprepared human soul, and tells him that although he will see his Lord, he will be both gladdened and yet pierced unbearably.

All through the work it is as though the composer and poet are unified so closely that the world they inhabit becomes just that bit clearer and one is spellbound. At certain points this collaboration is lifted from an already wonderful level to an even more inspiring one. Each time one performs the piece, it is possible to find more and more of such moments because life changes us and we discover ever deeper meaning in the familiar, well-loved works we sing. It is like a journey and one of the greatest privileges the musician has.

Actors recognize this process – each time we play, special nuances, different vocal colours make for a unique, creative experience for the re-creative artist.

When one remembers how much European music has used Christian thought and liturgy, it might be difficult to understand how performers who are neither Catholic nor believers in the Christian faith can bring truth to this work.

Just as painters see the world more vividly, more significantly in terms of light than the rest of us, so musicians are affected by sound, so the starting point must always be the notes on the page of a score. If singers also develop a sensitivity for words, then these two forms of 'truth' enable them to enter the world of composer and poet to a sufficient degree that they have authenticity. Unlike any other musicians, vocalists have this singular benefit of a two-pronged basis which the music and words give them.

Newman's poem has different levels. The outer and most immediately accessible is the story which is based on Catholic doctrine; but the story can be seen in a wider sense, in that the journey of Gerontius is one we all undergo. The trials, the agony, his death-bed distress of conscience are all trials we understand and share in some measure. The idea of a companion who loves us unconditionally, who will be there to guide us both in this life and, hopefully, in the next, strikes a chord in the heart of many people.

The performer needs to play many parts in the course of a career and try to enter into them all. There can be no more inspiring and compassionate role than that of the Angel; it is difficult to judge in this work, which is the most important influence – the music or the ideas which are expressed through it.

The greatest challenge awaiting any singer is the resolution of the constant battle between words and music which rages within every work we approach. If the composer is of the first rank the decision is, to a great extent, made for us, but every so often we are given a certain leeway where the boundaries of the musical phrase give way and present us with a kind of freedom. This is where the performer shows his stature, choosing for himself which precise word is to be stressed and the depth of meaning it will be given – all will depend on the individual's personal understanding and intelligence.

Years ago, the fully trained singer in 'bel canto' was weighed by the audience in such moments and judged accordingly. To articulate words clearly without disturbing a beautiful sound and to invest supreme meaning to them equally is the highest art to which any singer can aspire.

There are all sorts of tricks to be learned using the organs of articulation in the face, a skill undervalued today when even ordinary speech of every day is slovenly, lazy and difficult to understand. But for the few students who are willing to do the colossal and never-ending work involved, there are great secrets to uncover and the powers of interpretation can rise to immeasurable heights.

I can't begin to count the number of times a stranger has stopped me in the street to say how much this work has meant to them or a member of their family in times of trouble.

There is deep power of comfort and hope in *The Dream*, which reaches out beyond the outward expression of Newman's poem and Elgar's music and satisfies a need in the human heart. We all, performers and audience alike, touch the fringes of something indescribable and inexplicable, and find ourselves able, for a little while at least, to face the world.

For a moment the power of music allied to the power of words is placed in the hands of the singer as the medium between composer, poet and audience, bringing with it the most awesome responsibility and the most sublime joy.

~ David Cairns

An Introduction to *The Dream of Gerontius*

(*Reprinted from a 1983 programme note.*)

In the blazing summer of 1900 Elgar completed *The Dream of Gerontius* and walked in the cool of the Malvern Woods. 'The trees are singing my music' – he wrote exultantly to his friend Jaeger – 'or have I sung theirs?'

Though the words refer ostensibly to the 'Woodland Interlude' in *Caractacus* they bring irresistibly to mind the wonderful passage in Part 2 of *Gerontius*, where, with a sound like the voice of primeval forests, the great Chorus of Angels 'Praise to the Holiest', gathers towards its first mighty C major utterance; but they could stand for the whole work. As Elgar himself sensed, a special presence breathes through it. He acknowledged it by the quotation (from Ruskin) that he wrote on the manuscript score, after the final bar: 'This is the best of me; for the rest, I ate and drank, and slept, loved and hated. Like another; my life was as the vapour, and is not; but *this* I saw and knew ...'

No other work of his carries so strong a feeling of having been *given*. With all its sophistication of technique and rich complexity of texture and motivic relationships, with all its elaborately contrived harmonic language (far more chromatic than in anything he had yet written and fruit of his immersion in Wagner's music), it has an inspired naturalness and an inevitability as though it could not have been other than what it is, almost as though it did not have to be composed but was always there, 'before the hills were born'. The masterly word-setting, combining natural speech-rhythm and lyrical song into a single perfectly flexible style of 'heart subduing melody', argues long and careful study, as does the skilful use of earlier styles of church music. Yet the work seems to have come of its own accord from deep and ancient wells of human experience.

There was no precedent in English choral music for the work's grandeur, beauty and imaginative scope; there was no precedent either in Elgar's own music, except that the year before *Gerontius* he had suddenly 'found himself', in the *Enigma Variations*. At the age of 42 he had produced his first work of fully mature and awakened genius. The 'friends pictured within' who form the matter of the *Variations*, are, however, a rather less awesome and audacious subject than that of *Gerontius,* which deals with the last earthly moments of Everyman and his 'progress from death to the threshold of eternity' (to borrow Michael Kennedy's description). Yet Elgar evokes this unknown world, brings it to vivid life, with the inspired conviction of a visionary and the assurance of an artist in complete command of his inspiration.

Gerontius, we can at least say, came at precisely the right time in his development. Its subject conspired with the particular moment – the final emergence of his genius in the *Variations* and the fame they brought the middle-aged provincial composer almost overnight – to release hidden springs of power in him. He was ready for what he called 'my chief work'. The Birmingham Festival had commissioned a major choral piece from him for the autumn of 1900. He chose Newman's poem 'The Dream of Gerontius' which the priest at St. George's, Worcester, where Elgar had played the organ, had given him as a wedding present ten years before. It had been, as he said, 'soaking in his mind' since then. 'All that time I have been gradually assimilating the thoughts of the author into my own musical promptings'.

This is just how the work sounds. Elgar has lived the poem and made it his own, until he is completely at home in it, both in the fevered, intensely dramatic emotions of Part 1, where Gerontius dreams his death, and in the calmer, more measured sublimities of Part 2, where his soul meets its maker. The very opening of the work – the mysterious, pervasive Judgement motif, scored for unison clarinets, bassoons and muted violas – plunges us into a new and strange yet recognisable world. In the fifth bar Elgar adds a cor anglais, the instrument whose rich, plangent sound colours the score at some of its most expressive moments. Throughout, the orchestration has a splendour and a subtlety which never lose their fascination and become more apt with each fresh hearing. Again and again, Elgar's 'musical promptings' create complete sound-images which take possession of the words, and once heard, seem the only possible response to them.

One thinks of the hushed premonitory death-rattle of tremolo violas and drum roll (played with wooden sticks) at Gerontius's first whispered cry, 'Jesu, Maria, I am near to death'; the exquisite translucent stillness of the string writing at the beginning of Part 2, as in his dream he awakes in the 'undiscovered country' beyond death; the inspired doubling by the cellos of his 'To the God of earth and heaven' (one of many superb opportunities that the part offers a heroic tenor); the thrilling trumpet crescendo which joins the sopranos' sustained high A in the first great outburst for full chorus in 'Praise to the Holiest in the height'; the brief but equally memorable effect of the sudden sharp accent on divided violins and violas (above the solemn sound of the Judgement theme on clarinets and bassoons) which suggests 'the moment when the struggling soul quits its mortal case'; the radiant sound of three solo cellos which accompanies the Angel's warning that 'the sight of the Most Fair will gladden thee but it will pierce thee too'; the sweep and tumultuous power of the full orchestra's 'grand mysterious harmony ... like the deep and solemn sound of many waters' as the soul and its guardian approach the threshold of eternity.

Such examples could be multiplied many times. But the handling of the vocal forces is no less masterly. Elgar writes for soloists and chorus with the same imaginative flair and technical assurance as for orchestra. The range and variety of choral sound is extraordinary – from the disembodied effect of the semi-chorus stealing in with their healing 'Kyries' to the nightmarish roar of the Demons and the immense, full-throated shout of the Angelic Host. The passages for double chorus or sub-divided voices in Part 2 create a sense of the infinite space of the spirit world, through which the listener seems to move in a series of vast ascending planes. By contrast, the sonority of the four-part choruses is glowingly solid and compact. As for the writing for the soloists, Elgar's ear for speech-rhythms, his sense of word-setting and his harmonic mastery combine to create a style of wonderful flexibility, responsive to every changing thought or mood in the text.

As with the orchestral writing, the effect is to bring each moment of the drama intensely before us and burn it 'on our consciousness.' Even for the most staunchly Protestant listener, the Catholic trappings of Newman's text – the thrones and dominations, the Holy Marys, the *Subvenites* – fade, transcended in a vision that is timeless and that touches us all, believer and agnostic alike.

~ Neal Davies

The Bass Roles in *The Dream of Gerontius*

I first became acquainted with the music of *Gerontius* in my first year at university, listening to the Barbirolli recording with Richard Lewis, Janet Baker and Kim Borg. I was sitting in the basement library at King's College London with an LP and headphones, and I have never been more moved by a first hearing of a great work. I was overwhelmed and thrilled with equal measure and even at that stage, when I still had few thoughts of being a professional singer, I knew this was a piece for life; and so it has proved. My singing teacher, Kenneth Bowen, was a distinguished interpreter of *Gerontius*, and I suppose that at that time and stage in my life, I simply trusted that one day I would sing it. I did in fact sing it five years later at the age of 23, in the company of giants; Robert Tear and Alfreda Hodgson.

I sang the Priest's 'Proficiscere, anima Christiana' at my final singing lesson with Ken at the RAM and spoke the words 'Go forth upon they journey Christian soul' at his funeral many years later at St. David's Cathedral. It has guided me, consoled me and uplifted me throughout my life and career.

Whatever one feels about Cardinal Newman's words (and there are many for whom they prove an impenetrable barrier to the work as a whole), there can be little doubt that Elgar created a supreme masterpiece in *Gerontius*. For musicians and singers in particular, it is there for us at times in our lives when we are faced with the immense questions of life, death and eternity. As a performer we have the privilege of observing audience reactions, from individuals for whom the work stirs up powerful, latent memories, to the cumulative effect that 'Praise to the Holiest' or 'Softly and gently' can have on a mass of listeners, captured in that very moment of a visceral, live experience in a concert hall or cathedral. We as performers are not left unmoved by this; a performance of *Gerontius* is often a profoundly draining, but ultimately uplifting, experience which will stay for us for many days and weeks.

The bass soloist is required to sing two different characters, one earthly, although by virtue of being a priest, nonetheless spiritual in nature, and an angel who most definitely inhabits an unearthly plain: the Angel of the Agony. It is sometimes argued that these two characters call for two different singers and different voice types. A baritone for the Priest in Part One and a bass for the Angel of the Agony in Part Two. A largely unaffordable luxury and, I would argue, an unnecessary one. Both parts call for a well-focussed, rich bass-baritone with a free easy top, but also one capable of tenderness and real sensitivity to the words. It is notable just how many *piano* and *pianissimo* markings there are in both parts. As with all of Elgar's scoring for voices and orchestra, if his dynamics are observed to the letter then the singer will be heard.

Elgar keeps the bass waiting; nearly 30 minutes in total. Thirty minutes of being swept along by the drama of the tenor, the chorus and orchestra and Newman's text, but eventually the great brass chords sound and it is our turn. This moment represents the precise transition between the earthly and spiritual sphere; Gerontius himself yields up his spirit 'into thy hands O Lord, Lord, into thy hands' and he dies. In Part Two, we encounter his soul moving towards the presence of God and judgement.

Solenne et con elevazione (solemn and elevated) is Elgar's marking and interestingly the first line sung is marked merely *forte*. The temptation to go at it, all guns blazing, must be resisted. 'Full, not loud' is a marking I still have in my score from that very first performance. And a very useful one it is. The music calls for great reserves of power. The vocal lines are long and lie rather high. Start pushing at the beginning and you will soon be in trouble. Like a jet on take-off, we reach our cruising altitude when the voice re-enters with the chorus at the words 'Go forth upon thy journey'. The chorus sings of patriarchs, prophets, holy monks and hermits, but the soloist keeps it direct and simple, God the Father, Son and Holy Spirit.

As the Angel explains to the Soul in Part Two, 'it is the voice of friends around thy bed, who sing the Subvenite with the priest'. It is this simplicity amongst the incense-rich density of Newman's text which enables Elgar's music to overwhelm us, to envelop us and ultimately, whatever our beliefs, to give us hope and to give us comfort when we most need it in life. After the initial proclamation of 'Go forth upon they journey, Christian soul', the music settles into a regular, 4/4 heartbeat as the Soul is launched into the world to come; exultant on 'Go in the name of Jesus Christ', then hushed on 'Son of the living God who bled for thee', receding further still on the 'Holy Spirit', the orchestral accompaniment a barely whispered *ppp*. This spirit eventually pours forth as a tidal wave of sound and ecstatic emotion into the choral entry 'Go in the name of angels and archangels' and from that moment on all doubt is cast aside and the soul of Gerontius is borne upwards. There can be few more exhilarating moments for a performer to stand on a stage surrounded by hundreds of voices and players, particularly when the chorus divides into eight parts, seemingly floating above the cushion of the orchestral sound, once again moving with that steady 4/4 heartbeat. It is music of utterly transcendent beauty which hangs in the silence at the end of Part One.

The second section for the bass emerges out of the great chorus 'Praise to the holiest in the height' as the Soul moves close to judgement and into 'the veiled presence of our God'. It is here that both the bass roles are brought into contact with each other as the Soul hears the echo of the voices of his friends on earth together with the priest. Standing before the throne of God is the Angel of the Agony who strengthened Christ in his own passion in Gethsemane and who will now plead for the soul of Gerontius.

He does so with vivid, richly Catholic imagery, re-telling the night in Gethsemane with all the doubts and 'shudd'ring dread' suffered by Jesus in his last hours. This is a very human picture of Christ, of a man quite literally beaten down and wounded, assailed by doubts, worn down by our sins, but nonetheless 'girdled' with innocence, strengthened by the 'sanctity which reigned' in him. Anyone who has watched and waited at the bedside of a dying loved-one cannot fail to be moved by the plea to 'hasten Lord their hour, and bid them come to thee ... to that glorious home'. It can be almost unbearably moving to sing. The responsibility to express the inexpressible.

Again, as in Part One there are many phrases marked *piano 'teneramente'* (tenderly), *molto espressivo* (very expressively), *dolce* (softly). I always find the *poco affrettando* (a little hurrying) particularly moving at 'Jesu by that pang of heart which thrilled in thee' as it melts into 'that mount of sins which crippled thee'. There is a bleakness in the orchestration at the 'sense of guilt which stifled thee' also marked with a *teneramente*. Perfect attention to detail by Elgar ensures that nothing becomes generic or commonplace; everything is meaningful, both musically and poetically. Immediately the music becomes intensely personal and private as the soul sings 'I go before my Judge'.

And with that, the bass part finishes, and we are left to contemplate the final sections of the work: 'Take me away', requiring almost superhuman endurance from the tenor; and 'Softly and gently' for the mezzo soprano, surely one of the most beautiful and moving endings to any great choral piece. The perfect mirroring of the end of part one, a great mass of voices singing very quietly together. Perfection.

~ Bernard Longley

'The Best of Me'

Sir Edward Elgar and the Roman Catholic Archdiocese of Birmingham

Shortly after my appointment as Archbishop of Birmingham I was invited to be Michael Berkeley's guest on his BBC Radio 3 programme *Private Passions*. It was broadcast on Easter Day 2010, a few months before Pope Benedict XVI came to Birmingham to beatify Cardinal John Henry Newman and, with this very much in mind, I chose my final piece of music from Elgar's Oratorio *The Dream of Gerontius*. Greatly to its credit, on the night before the beatification ceremony in Cofton Park, Birmingham City Council sponsored a performance of *The Dream of Gerontius* in the Town Hall (where it had first been performed – though poorly received – on 3 October 1900).

From the outset I was conscious of the many links binding the Roman Catholic Archdiocese of Birmingham with the person and music of Sir Edward Elgar. Among these are his upbringing as a Roman Catholic in Worcester and the lifelong challenges that this brought, the inspiration he drew from the Malvern Hills, close to his birthplace and his home of many years, and his final resting place beside Lady Elgar in the churchyard of St Wulstan's Church in Little Malvern. (Worcestershire is one of the five counties within the Archdiocese of Birmingham.)

When we are drawn to a composer and the themes that have motivated his life's work it is natural for musicians and music-lovers alike to want to discover and understand as much as possible about the artist's life and the significant influences upon it. There is no doubt that for Edward Elgar the teachings and practise of the Catholic Church and the liturgical life of St George's Catholic Parish in Worcester, where he and his family worshipped, were among the important elements that influenced the way that his life unfolded and that had a lasting impact on his music, adding to its beauty and its depth.

Elgar was at home in the neo-classical church in Worcester served by the Jesuit Fathers. During some of his most formative years he was familiar with the life of the little Catholic community worshipping in St George's. Before he succeeded his father as organist in 1872, for a number of years he shared with his father the duties of supporting the liturgical worship at St George's. In such a setting the musical, if not the spiritual, bond between father and son must have grown stronger.

Those who would wish to understand the deepest influences on a composer's life, whether they are the things of God or the earthly realities that He has created, must first of all attune themselves and listen intently to the music itself, which is also a fruit of God's creation. No one who listens to *The Dream of Gerontius*, I believe, could doubt the impact of Elgar's personal faith in Christ and his confidence in the merciful judgement and forgiveness of God. The original manuscript score of the oratorio, one of the treasures of the Birmingham Oratory, offers Elgar's own assessment of his work on *Gerontius* as 'the best of me'.

Elgar was not obliged to choose a poem of Saint John Henry Newman to find suitable material to match his own genius, but he was drawn to the sublime beauty of Cardinal Newman's vision of God's abiding goodness and His tender outreach to the erring soul. It is notable that he received a copy of Cardinal Newman's poem from the Parish Priest of St George's as a present on the occasion of his marriage to Alice Roberts in 1889. In his oratorio Elgar's music is fused with Saint John Henry's spiritual insights and becomes itself a prayer which we can make our own.

When I was ordained bishop by Cardinal Cormac Murphy O'Connor at Westminster Cathedral in 2003 I asked the Cathedral choir to sing an anthem by Elgar from another of his Oratorios, *The Apostles*. Elgar set this text from the prophet Isaiah: 'the spirit of the Lord is upon me' – a text of scripture which Our Lord Himself used in reference to His own mission and ministry. Whenever I hear that setting I sense Elgar's awareness of the Holy Spirit at work in his own life and enabling his creativity to flourish.

In 2011 a permanent memorial was blessed and dedicated to Elgar's association with St George's Church and the mission of its Catholic community within the city of Worcester and the surrounding countryside – albeit 150 years after Elgar's time of service as organist of St George's. On many subsequent visits to St George's I have celebrated Pontifical Mass when the entrance procession has invariably been prompted on its way by Elgar's setting of the antiphon *Ecce sacerdos magnus*.

A few years later, in 2017, St George's hosted a concert of Elgar's liturgical and devotional choral music, largely written for use at St George's. It was the late Dr Donald Hunt, whose collection of Elgar's Music for the Church had just been published by Cramer Music, who originally conceived the idea of celebrating that music in a unique concert and festive gathering.

Elgar's music for the Church has enhanced both Anglican and Roman Catholic worship. In a development which surely would have pleased him, the last sixty years of ecumenical engagement has witnessed an increasing exchange of music across our two traditions. Aside from his great oratorios, whenever we hear Elgar's music for the Catholic Church it was clearly composed for either liturgical or devotional use, depending on the texts that he was commissioned to set. A brief survey of some of this music demonstrates Elgar's dedication to the relatively modest office he held at St George's – compared, for example, with the much grander choral tradition of nearby Worcester Cathedral.

The first choral piece by Elgar that I recall hearing in the liturgy was *Ecce sacerdos magnus – Behold the great priest.* It is an antiphon and responsory from the Divine Office commemorating saints who were bishops, but it is frequently used at the ceremonial entrance of a bishop into a church. It was written for a visit of one of my predecessors, Bishop Edward Ilsey, newly appointed successor to the ailing Bishop William Bernard Ullathorne, when he came to St George's in 1888 – his first year in office.

It dates from Elgar's early years of composing as the organist of St George's – the same period of his life which resulted in a wide range of devotional pieces. They betoken a fruitful time of collaboration between the organist and his Jesuit Parish Priest, Fr Thomas Knight SJ, who had been appointed to St George's in 1886, the year of Elgar's own appointment as organist in succession to his father.

The choral pieces he wrote include three *Ave* motets. *Ave verum corpus* reflects Catholic belief in the Real Presence of Christ in the Eucharist and was sung during Exposition and Benediction or in processions of the Blessed Sacrament. The other two motets are in veneration of the Blessed Virgin Mary. *Ave Maria* is the popular devotional prayer *Hail Mary, full of grace,* setting the words of the Archangel Gabriel in St Luke's Gospel, spoken to Mary and announcing the forthcoming birth of Jesus. *Ave maris stella,* or *Hail star of the sea,* is a Vespers hymn from the Office of Our Lady dating to the 8th century.

Much of the liturgical action during Elgar's time as organist required the accompaniment of choral or organ music, including the Vespers Voluntaries for use during evening services at St George's. Another piece for organ with strong Worcester associations is Elgar's *Cantique,* a transcription of a piece originally written for wind quintet and dedicated to Hugh Blair, a former organist of Worcester Cathedral.

Elgar's Latin hymn, *O salutaris hostia – Oh saving victim* – is sung in adoration of the Blessed Sacrament, and was also probably written for use at St George's during Elgar's tenure of office as organist there. Elgar's music reflects the serenity of Catholic faith in the presence of Christ in the Eucharist, seeing this sacrament as the gateway to everlasting salvation and eternal life. It is most frequently sung during Benediction of the Blessed Sacrament, then a popular devotion in Catholic parishes on Sunday afternoons.

It is often argued that Elgar's Catholicism, as well as his modest social origins, caused him to feel something of an outsider, despite his nationally recognised stature as a composer and the knighthood he received in 1904 from King Edward VII. Despite this he continued to receive commissions from the established Church, such as *Give unto the Lord*, a choral setting of Psalm 29. This was written in 1914, on the cusp of the First World War, for the Festival of the Sons of the Clergy at St Paul's Cathedral in London.

By this stage Elgar had long been accustomed to seeking inspiration not only from the words of the liturgy but from the Scriptures themselves. This is very evident in his use of both the Old and the New Testament Scriptures in his great oratorios *The Apostles* and *The Kingdom*. He was not only following in the footsteps of Handel and Mendelssohn – he was clearly responsive to Protestant sensitivities requiring all prayer and devotion to proceed *sola scriptura*.

Elgar's religious music was not confined to church or concert hall but also found its way into the drawing-room. In 1928 he set Ben Jonson's carol *I sing the birth*. In his article 'Sir Edward Elgar's Church Music' written for the May 2017 edition of *Laudate*, the magazine of the Guild of Church Musicians, Donald Hunt offers us an illuminating insight:

> Elgar looks back to earlier times. The carol is particularly interesting in that it adopts a modal language which was always claimed to be anathema to the composer. There is almost a suspicion of attempting to join the new group of composers such as Holst and Vaughan Williams, who were deeply involved in the folk-song and Gregorian chant revival.

In a similar vein, the English part-song *Good morrow* is one of Elgar's final pieces of Church music dating from 1929. Again, according to Donald Hunt, it is what Elgar 'described as a "Partsong carol sort of thing" … written for "the King's happy recovery from serious illness"'. We are reminded of the composer's obligations as Master of the King's Music. But the part-song also transports us right back to the beginning of his professional life, where it draws on a hymn tune written during Elgar's time at St George's.

In art there can be few stronger affirmations of Catholic faith in eternal life than the sublime setting of *The Dream of Gerontius,* accompanying the soul of the dying man on its journey as a pilgrim of hope through Judgment and into Purgatory. In the Archdiocese of Birmingham, we cherish those roots of Catholic faith that were influential in the life of Sir Edward Elgar and we offer praise to the Holiest for enabling us to hear and appreciate the particular gift of music which first flourished in the city of Worcester through the genius of Edward Elgar.

~ John Quinn

Some Personal Observations on Recordings of *The Dream of Gerontius*, Op. 38

(This essay is an abridged and updated version of a survey first published by MusicWeb International where the full version, in which I explain my judgements in greater detail, can be found.)

The Dream of Gerontius is, deservedly, a staple of the choral repertoire; since I began singing in choirs some thirty-eight years ago, I have taken part in 15 performances, including one in Germany. When I first started collecting recordings, more than fifty years ago, I believe there were only two versions of *Gerontius* in the catalogue: the 1964 Barbirolli reading and the 1954 account conducted by Sargent. How things have changed! What follows is a necessarily brief survey of complete recordings, all of which I believe are currently obtainable. So far as I know, I have heard all the recordings which have been issued commercially on CD.

Three conductors are particularly associated with *Gerontius* on disc: Sir John Barbirolli, Sir Adrian Boult and Sir Malcolm Sargent. In 1945, Sargent made the first complete recording of the oratorio in Huddersfield Town Hall. The town's celebrated Choral Society and the Liverpool Philharmonic Orchestra served him very well. There's a good solo team, chief among whom is the peerless Heddle Nash. Incidentally, this is the only recording which uses different singers for the two bass roles. In 1954 Sargent, now knighted, returned to Huddersfield to make his second recording. This time Richard Lewis took the title role. Sonically, this is an advance on the 1945 version, of course, but I think that the earlier recording is interpretatively stronger. In 2018 Pristine Audio released a BBC broadcast of a 1961 Sargent performance, again from Huddersfield and with the same soloists as in 1954. The sound has come up well and there's more urgency in the performance, though I find Lewis's cavalier attitude to note values is an irritant.

Lewis was the soloist for the famous 1964 Barbirolli recording. To be honest, he's not my favourite interpreter of the role but he does well here, even though he was suffering from a cold. I'll draw a veil over Kim Borg's singing. The undoubted glory of the performance is the young Janet Baker as the Angel. I suspect I'm not alone in being unable to dispel the memory of her distinctive timbre and interpretative insights from many phrases. Barbirolli conducted with warmth and, at times, fire, obtaining a fine response from choir and orchestra. Sir John can also be heard in two live recordings: a 1957 performance in which he conducted the forces of RAI, the Italian state broadcaster, the chief interest being in Jon Vickers as Gerontius. The Angel is Constance Shacklock and it's good that this fine singer's excellent performance of the role has been preserved; she never made a commercial recording of it. Apparently, Sir William Walton, listening to the live broadcast at his home in Capri, was enthusiastic about the Italian choir; I'm afraid I can't share his view. There's also a 1959 Barbirolli performance in which he conducts the New York Philharmonic; this is better on all counts than the Italian reading. Lewis is again his Gerontius and the fine Canadian singer, Maureen Forrester impresses as the Angel, a role she never recorded commercially. The Canadian bass soloist is emphatically not to my taste. The latest incarnation of this recording on SOMM shows this valuable performance to best advantage.

When Sir Adrian Boult recorded the work – at last – in 1975 there was controversy over EMI's choice of Nicolai Gedda for the title role for there are several tenors on record who are better suited. Helen Watts offers a warm, 'central' reading of the Angel's part and Robert Lloyd is arguably the best bass on disc. Boult's interpretation bespeaks wisdom and understanding; I'd describe it as 'dedicated' but I feel the drama is somewhat underplayed. In some ways, Boult is better served by a 1968 BBC filmed performance which was issued on DVD in 2017. The male soloists are Peter Pears – the performance pre-dates his Decca recording with Britten – and John Shirley-Quirk. The latter is excellent. Much of what Pears does is good, especially in Part II, but I don't care for his distracting theatrical gestures. The standout feature of this recording, though, is the contribution of Janet Baker. I can only repeat what I said when I first reviewed the performance for MusicWeb: 'I have heard her audio recordings many times but I was completely unprepared for the extent to which I would be moved by not just hearing her but also by once again *seeing* her sing the role. She was 34 when she gave this performance and so we get the full flower of her understanding of the role allied with freshness of voice. She stands almost completely still and sings gloriously and with great intensity. She identifies completely with the words and with the music. I have been fortunate enough to hear a number of very fine mezzos in this role over the years but this performance reminds me why Dame Janet was – and is – an incomparable Angel'. For this reason, all lovers of *Gerontius* should seek out this performance, though be warned; the sound quality is not great.

By my count, there have been recordings by a further 17 conductors, including a 1960 performance conducted by Hans Swarowsky, which The Elgar Society issued in 2008. The chief interest lies in the fact that the work is sung, uniquely on disc, using the German translation by Julius Buths. Many will be intrigued by the fact that Julius Patzak sings the title role. Sadly, he's something of a disappointment. His commitment to the music is not in doubt and he sings with feeling. However, he was 62 at the time of making this recording and I'm afraid it shows. On the plus side, Ira Malaniuk is very convincing as the Angel. Her tone is rich and full and she sings the part with fine expression and understanding. Ludwig Welter does the bass solos well. Swarowsky conducts well and gets a good response from the orchestra but, sadly, the choir isn't much to write home about.

Space only permits me to discuss a few other recordings, which I will consider mostly in alphabetical order of the conductors. Daniel Barenboim's 2016 Decca recording was made live at two performances in the Philharmonie in Berlin, the first of which I attended. Prior to the concert, several soloists were obliged to withdraw. The originally advertised Gerontius was Jonas Kaufmann but, in the end, Andrew Staples stepped in at very short notice, to good effect. His tone is clear and very focussed. His may not be the most opulent of voices, at least as here recorded, but it's well-suited to this role. Catherine Wyn-Rogers, another replacement soloist, was the Angel. She gives a performance that is full of maturity and sensitivity. I am disappointed by Thomas Hampson. Barenboim's choir comprises professional singers; they are excellent. The playing of the Staatskapelle Berlin is simply magnificent. Barenboim's conducting is very individual and some of his tempo selections will be controversial. However, it seems to me that everything he does is in response to the spirit of the music; he has clearly thought deeply about it and has reached his own, very musical, conclusions.

Benjamin Britten's recording has a special place in my affections because it was the first recording of the work that I bought for myself on LP (I'd grown up with my father's LPs of the Barbirolli recording). Britten's recording was made in The Maltings, Snape, in 1971, after an Aldeburgh Festival performance. One of Britten's many insights was to use the Choir of King's College, Cambridge for his semi-chorus. The different timbre of this choir set against the London Symphony Chorus is telling – in a wholly positive way. On no other recording, until Sir Mark Elder's 2008 version, was the vital semi-chorus contribution so individually defined. The use of the King's choir in this way suggests to me that Britten had thought about *Gerontius* very deeply. His conducting is very fine. Peter Pears's assumption of the title role won't be to all tastes. He was 61 when this recording was made and, arguably, the recording came a few years too late in his career. That said, I like a lot of what he does in Part II, where the more intimate music suits him. Yvonne Minton is an underrated Angel. She may not tug at the heart strings in the way that Janet Baker does, but she's at all times tasteful and sensitive. John Shirley-Quirk is in sovereign voice as the Priest. The Angel of the Agony is not entirely within his best compass but he sings the part well.

Sir Andrew Davis recorded *Gerontius* in 2014. Stuart Skelton sang Gerontius. His reading of the role has been widely praised elsewhere and I also found much to admire. That said, I remain unsure that in Part I he conveys the sense of Gerontius as a man *in extremis* as convincingly as some other tenors on disc. However, much of what he does is very good indeed and he convinces in Part II. Dame Sarah Connolly is a first-class Angel, bringing very expressive and expertly controlled singing to the role. Her admirers may have regretted that it took so long for her to make a studio recording but it was worth the wait. The BBC Symphony Chorus offers one of the best choral contributions on disc, though there's a minor disappointment in that the semi chorus isn't as distanced as I'd have liked. In all other respects, though, the Chandos engineering is superb. The contribution of the BBC Symphony Orchestra is consistently excellent. Sir Andrew Davis has the complete measure of the score and his grasp of Elgarian style seems as instinctive as it is complete.

There are two recordings by Sir Colin Davis. His 2005 LSO Live reading (now licenced to Alto) need not detain us long. The LSO and London Symphony Chorus both perform superbly and, one or two points excepted, I find Sir Colin's interpretation convincing. The soloists, David Rendall, Anne Sofie von Otter and Alistair Miles are unsatisfactory, however. Happily, a much better representation of Sir Colin in *Gerontius* is available on the Profil label. This also derives from a live performance, given in Dresden on Palm Sunday, 2010. The soloists are excellent. John Relyea does both of the bass solos very well indeed. Paul Groves sings Gerontius and I think that here he achieves greater spontaneity than was in case in the Mark Elder studio recording of 2008. The Angel is Sarah Connolly who sings marvellously, bringing out many expressive nuances in the score. The Staatskapelle Dresden, an orchestra with which Davis had enjoyed a long association, plays superbly. The Staatsopernchor Dresden makes a notable contribution too. Sir Colin conducts with great understanding and also with a fine dramatic sense. Some of his tempi are a little more urgent than we hear from many conductors but I am completely convinced by his way with the music throughout

Sir Mark Elder's recording dates from 2008. As Gerontius he has Paul Groves, who had sung for Elder in a rather special 2005 Proms performance. He's impressive, too, in this recording, though perhaps he was just a little more spontaneous in the Prom performance. On the other hand, studio conditions and, no doubt, further experience in the role, enabled him to be more nuanced in 2008. He's equally successful in both Parts I and II Alice Coote is a distinguished Angel. She sings with feeling and commitment as well as musicality. Bryn Terfel is magisterial as the Priest and predictably imposing as the Angel of the Agony. The Hallé Choir and the Hallé Youth Choir (as the semi chorus) sing splendidly while the orchestral contribution from the Hallé is terrific. Elder's conducting is masterly. His command of detail is extraordinary, as you can tell if you follow with a score, but equally memorable is his command of the big picture. He is arguably the leading Elgar conductor of our day and this *Gerontius* is one of the very best things he's done on disc.

Moving back in time, Vernon Handley's version appeared in 1993. In a neat reversal of the Sargent recordings, the Huddersfield Choral Society travelled to Liverpool to link up in Philharmonic Hall with the RLPO and its chorus. Anthony Rolfe-Johnson offers an excellent portrayal of Gerontius, albeit one that emphasises the lyrical aspects of the role but without short changing the dramatic moments. Catherine Wyn-Rogers is, perhaps, a little understated as the Angel and certainly doesn't "do" as much with the words as do some of her rivals – or, indeed, Rolfe-Johnson. However, her portrayal is unaffected and sincere. Her subsequent appearance in Daniel Barenboim's recording does her greater justice. Handley draws marvellous playing from the RLPO and he's very well served by the combined choirs. The performance benefits hugely from Handley's attention to detail and his profound understanding of the work. I bought this recording when it first came out and I have always felt that it's been underrated.

For his 1998 recording, Richard Hickox has the benefit of the LSO on top form, and the London Symphony Chorus offers some of the best and most thrilling choral singing of this work on disc. The trademark Chandos sound is also a big plus for this set. Arthur Davies sings Gerontius. I don't feel he evidences sufficient identification with the character he is portraying in Part I. There's much to admire about his contribution in Part II. In the last analysis, however, I don't think that his Gerontius, for all its merits, quite matches the leading exponents of the role, especially in terms of characterisation and feeling for the text. Felicity Palmer's singing is impressive and expressive, not least her very good account of the Farewell. However, at certain key points I don't feel she brings the same level of intensity to the music as, say, Sarah Connolly or Janet Baker. Her portrayal of the Angel impressed me but didn't move me. Hickox's conducting is admirable and shows empathy with and understanding of the score. I have to admit, though, that I was disconcerted by his spacious treatment of several episodes. The performance has much to commend it but I don't believe that it disturbs the leading recommendations.

Sir Simon Rattle recorded *Gerontius* in 1986 in Birmingham; I have often wondered what he'd make of it nowadays. John Mitchinson, a former pupil of Heddle Nash, sang the title role. Around this time, he was Rattle's tenor of choice for such works as *Das Lied von der Erde* and *Gurrelieder.* He was thus ideally equipped to be among the most manly exponents of Gerontius on disc and he fulfils amply that expectation. However, he was also a noted singer of art songs, with a particular expertise in the field of English song so, unsurprisingly, he was equally alive to the many sensitive nuances of the role, especially in Part II. Janet Baker had, by this time, over 20 years further experience as the Angel since recording the role with Barbirolli; this shows in a reading of great maturity. That said, there are trade-offs with the Barbirolli set. To my ears her voice had darkened over the intervening years and I also find a greater degree of freshness in her earlier traversal of the role. Nonetheless, her portrayal of the Angel is deeply satisfying. Arguably, her earlier rendition for Barbirolli remains preferable but I still wouldn't wish to be without this marvellous example of her singing this role in the full maturity of her career. John Shirley-Quirk sings the bass roles with the eloquence and dignity that one came to expect from this distinguished singer. Rattle's famed attention to detail is consistently in evidence and, in fact, in terms of sheer beauty and refinement of orchestral sound this is one of the finest recordings the work has received. The CBSO is on top form throughout, as is the CBSO Chorus, and in consequence all the big moments make their full impact. Rattle is equally successful in realising the more intimate sections of the score, such as a gossamer-light account of the Part Two Prelude.

There have been two very recent recordings. The first of these (2023) is conducted by Paul McCreesh. This is notable on several counts. The excellent chorus, 150-strong, was mainly comprised of young singers from the Gabrieli Roar project and the Polish National Youth Choir; they acquit themselves admirably. The freshness of the choir's sound is striking and there's no lack of body when it comes to the big chorus moments, though ideally there should be more snarl in the Demons' Chorus. The orchestra is the Gabrieli Players, who use instruments of Elgar's time – including the composer's own trombone. This is the first time a recording of *Gerontius* has used period instruments and the result is a complete success. There's absolutely no suggestion of thin tone; the climaxes have power and presence, while the many passages of quiet, refined music are imbued with delicacy, subtlety and transparency. The bass-baritone, Andrew Foster-Williams is satisfactory but doesn't challenge the best of his predecessors. Anna Stéphany may not quite match the eloquence of Dame Sarah Connolly or leave an indelible mark on phrase after phrase in the way that Dame Janet Baker did, but hers is nonetheless a fine and convincing portrayal of the Angel. Nicky Spence is outstanding, giving one of the finest, most nuanced performances of Gerontius on disc. I think he is successful in all aspects of the role. Paul McCreesh conducts the work very well indeed. For the most part his tempo selections are appropriate, and I was consistently convinced that his conducting conveyed the *spirit* of the music. This recording of *Gerontius* is a considerable achievement.

In 2025 the Ondine label, issued a recording in which a combined Anglo-Finnish chorus and the Finnish Radio Symphony Orchestra were conducted by Nicholas Collon. This is a live performance given in April 2024 and recorded in excellent sound. The orchestral playing is of a very high order indeed and the chorus work is consistently excellent, though as is so often the case, I'd like to hear a bit more venom in the Demons' Chorus. Roderick Williams is the baritone soloist. He sings well, as one would expect, though I don't think he has quite enough vocal heft for the Angel of the Agony. Christine Rice is a good Angel. She sings with poise and sincerity and her diction is excellent. There's much to admire in her performance, even if she doesn't challenge the primacy on disc of Janet Baker and Sarah Connolly. John Findon sings the title role; I understand he was a late replacement for an indisposed colleague. He has a strong, clear voice and excellent diction. If I'd attended the concert, I think I'd have gone home satisfied but for repeated listening on a recording I fear his performance is too generalized; there's insufficient nuance and attention to detail. Nicholas Collon conducts well. His pacing of the score is, for the most part, judicious and idiomatic. His conducting displays welcome attention to detail and much empathy with Elgar's music. He conveys the drama very successfully and he's also good in the more intimate passages. In the last analysis, though, despite many merits, this recording does not challenge the best.

Everyone will have their own favourite recordings of *The Dream of Gerontius*. A version that is ideal in all respects is inevitably out of reach and, of course, the work's discography continues to expand. Among the recordings I have discussed, I believe a few stand out from the rest.

The inclusion of a recording involving Dame Janet Baker is surely mandatory. Her performance on the Boult DVD is special but there are drawbacks, not least the sound quality. The fine Rattle performance offers better sound and greater role maturity than the famed Barbirolli set. Yet, despite the drawback that Kim Borg is a grievous disappointment, for vision and inspirational conducting I keep coming back to 'Glorious John'. Richard Lewis is a very considerable Gerontius, even when slightly indisposed, and in the young Janet Baker Barbirolli had an incomparable Angel. Barbirolli's choir and orchestra perform as if their very lives depended on it. It is this version that has always moved me the most and, surely, emotion as well as objective assessment is a major part of the evaluation of any musical performance. I'd also want Heddle Nash in the 1945 Sargent account. No Elgar enthusiast's collection should be without this performance: Nash is simply *hors concours*.

Several other versions have much to commend them; those by Britten, Boult (1975 EMI), Handley, Rattle and Sir Colin Davis (Dresden 2010). However, I think that the best all-round modern versions are those conducted by Sir Andrew Davis (Chandos), Sir Mark Elder and Paul McCreesh. Davis has superb recorded sound and an exceptional Angel in Sarah Connolly. All aspects of the Elder performance are very fine, though as time passes, I have become a little less convinced by Bryn Terfel as The Priest; he is an imposing Angel of the Agony, though. Elder's conducting of the score is deeply satisfying. I continue to find his Gerontius, Paul Groves, very impressive but Nicky Spence, who sings for McCreesh, is exceptional; he offers one of the finest, most nuanced interpretations of the title role that I have ever heard. The McCreesh performance, presented in excellent sound, is a great achievement. A choice between these three distinguished performances of *The Dream of Gerontius* is well-nigh impossible to make, but by the finest of margins I choose Sir Mark Elder's recording with the Barbirolli, now over 60 years old, as an 'historic' choice. These two recordings, both featuring the Hallé Orchestra and Choir, belong in any serious Elgar collection.

(The time between submitting the material for this book and its publication means that the Collon recording covered above was the last one to be issued and considered by John Quinn. We are aware that further recordings such as those by Martyn Brabbins, Edward Gardner and Sir Antonio Pappano will have been issued in the meantime. Eds.)

~ Andrew Staples

My journey into the world of Elgar's music began deep in the crypt of St Paul's Cathedral, where, as a young chorister in the late eighties, I first encountered his choral music. I had (and still have) a slight obsession with the physical copies of music that I use, and I remember the colours of the protective binding in which our copies were enclosed by the Cathedral Librarian. 'Dyson in D' was in deep red, 'Dyson in F' was blue/green, Elgar's *Give unto the Lord* was a leathery beige... but within the outer cover I remember being struck by the two-tone burgundy etching of Elgar's face. His splendid moustache and slightly furrowed gaze peering out at us from a copy so dog-eared and well-thumbed that it seemed as if it had been printed long before it was written. Perhaps this is why I always had a feeling of a timelessness, of 'always having existed-ness' whenever we sang his music.

I can still remember the chills as the immense St Paul's organ leant slowly into the opening chords of 'The Spirit of the Lord' – harmonies of an epic cinematic scene that rose like musical incense above us. I loved the feeling of singing those languid, arching melodies in the second section and the simple unison phrases which refused to be governed by tempo or harmonic structure. I didn't realise at the time that Elgar was teaching me about *leitmotif, rubato* and about modes of vocal expression that brought the performer into the role of advocate and evangelist for the spirit and message of the music, rather than merely its salesman. This was a musical language that was immediately more multi-dimensional and dramatic than much of the other music that we sang. Here were visceral feelings of tension and release, of escape and cadence, all underpinned by an emotional depth and scope that was available to Elgar – and now also belonged to us as performers. The extra time and the harmonic intricacy that he was able to pack into a phrase offered an expanded world of intriguing possibility. It showed us that there was more to be found within the perceived limits of harmony and structure. It taught us that you didn't need to break the rules, you merely needed to understand them so well that you could bend them to your will. Perhaps not a good thing for choristers to realise. We strode gladly into Elgar's ancient and modern world, and as we did so, we hoped that his burgundy moustachioed visage would crack just a hint of an approving smile as we endeavoured to conjure his vivid sweeping landscapes.

Another work that left an indelible mark on me was not one of his larger choral pieces, but rather the regal strains of the *Pomp and Circumstance* Marches. Performed during the Queen Mother's 90th birthday celebrations at Horse Guards Parade, at which St Paul's was invited to contribute, this music, with its majestic grandeur, seemed to encapsulate the essence of Britishness. It was a regal and imperious sound that evoked the glory of empire, the very fabric of a nostalgic, idealised and timeless Britain – one steeped in optimism, generosity and splendour. This initial impression would later evolve as I grew to know Elgar's more complex and subtle compositions, but the memory of that music piping out over a sun-drenched St James's Park from grey bullhorn speakers, rendering in the open air the textures and fragrances of an ineffable Englishness, evoked as Wordsworth puts it,

> ... a sense sublime
> Of something far more deeply interfused,
> Whose dwelling is the light of setting suns,
> And the round ocean and the living air,
> And the blue sky, and in the mind of man;
> A motion and a spirit, that impels
> All thinking things, all objects of all thought,
> And rolls through all things.

A performance that gave Elgar increased hero status – at least in my mind – was again given in St Paul's, in 1997. The BBC broadcast a performance of *The Dream of Gerontius* with Philip Langridge, Sir Andrew Davis and the BBC Symphony live from the cathedral. It was inspiring to me in a number of ways – not only in Langridge's intensely human and subtle performance (as was his trademark) but also in the way that the performance was captured for television. Even at the time it seemed a treat that a concert such as this was broadcast live at primetime, 7.30pm on BBC2 and simultaneously on Radio 3. It took me nearly twenty years until I was lucky enough or able enough to sing Gerontius and a few more until I was allowed to record or broadcast it.

Simply put, it's a tough sing. It's not a piece that rewards the attempts of a young singer. Not only because of the vocal stamina required, but more that the piece demands such a degree of risk and vulnerability from the singer. You need to be vocally assured to 'go' where Elgar wants to take you, to take that leap. Listening back to the 1997 Langridge performance, it's his unique qualities of risk and vocal vulnerability that I think offer the best explanation of what it is to sing this piece. On the one hand it's about range; literal range in terms of the notes Elgar chooses. It's a stretch for any tenor – anyone who tells you otherwise is fibbing. It's also a stretch in terms of volume. You have to make an enormous noise at times to soar over the lush strings and reinforced winds and percussion. But more than simply providing enough volume and high notes, you need to find the excitement without letting that define the quality of the sound. This is a constant struggle with singers and to an extent for orchestras. The problem is that as you approach the limits of volume, the sound quality tips towards an angry, red 'loud'. What Elgar requires of the singer and the players is to live at these extremes of expression and to have access to a radiant spectrum of colour, with which he paints the otherworldly scenes of celestial blinding light. For Elgar, loud and exciting doesn't always mean aggressive. 'Never louder than lovely' as the adage goes. Of course, when he's depicting demons baying for blood, he knows exactly how to enact aggression. But on the whole, within the terror and blaze of his heightened moments you still need to maintain something of the enchanted beauty and honesty of expression that exist so easily in the quieter, more reflective passages – such as the opening of the second part.

On the other hand, another consideration in the vocal production is that of challenging the assumed notion that everything you sing needs to be 'beautiful'. Sometimes it's more important to be honest, and sometimes honesty isn't beautiful. It can be painful, or angst-ridden, or determined and repentant. Here I think Langridge's example is peerless. The beauty is found in the honesty and the unvarnished struggle at the core of the piece. As an audience, we need to feel the struggle and trial of the music and feel not simply moved by it but moved along by it, as if we're party to it. I think for example of the viola da gamba obligato in 'Komm süßes Kreuz', from the *St Matthew Passion*, where Bach is depicting Simon of Cyrene labouring under the weight of the cross. The music he writes is so unplayably hard that surely Bach is attempting to enact that struggle at the same time as commenting on it in a poetic manner. Thus, for a performer to make it sound too easy or smooth or beautiful would be to miss Bach's point. Elgar was, of course, a disciple of Bach, even going so far as to 'write' his name (B, A, C, H(Bb)) in the bass line as Gerontius faces his ultimate judgement at 'Take me away…'. Is Elgar here admitting that Bach is his ultimate judge and that when his music comes face to face with Bach it will be tried in his fires?

The final stretch required to perform Gerontius is one of faith. If you're going to mean everything you sing, you need to be able to see through the lens of Elgar's music, which magnifies and reveals the meaning of Newman's text. This is key to all the potential technical problems mentioned above. If you mean the words entirely, all the musical difficulties melt away.

You don't need to believe it yourself, but you need to know that Elgar damn well did and if you want that burgundy moustache to twitch even a little bit, you had better not shortchange him when it comes to meaning what you sing. His belief affects every phrase and note of this piece. Once you tap into that power, the emotional carrier-wave that Elgar provides in the orchestra suddenly supports you through the piece instead of overwhelming you. You can't fight it anyway.

As my journey through Elgar's music has continued, so has my appreciation for his work and my understanding of its place within the broader tapestry of European classical music. A pivotal moment in this journey occurred when I had the dubious honour of stepping in for an indisposed star-tenor at very short notice in Berlin. The task was to perform in *Gerontius* alongside Daniel Barenboim for a concert and live recording for Decca, for an audience which was there to see Jonas Kaufmann. You've never seen a more disappointed bunch of Germans when I walked on – but by the end I think they forgave me. On the day, there was only enough time for a twenty minute 'seating' rehearsal before the Philharmonie's doors were flung open. Barenboim (whom I hadn't met previously) calmly shook my hand as we walked on stage to meet the Staatskapelle for the first time. 'Have you sung this before?' he asked. Attempting to reassure him, I replied 'many times...' to which he said, 'Oh no! So you've got many bad habits!'

Further confidence was instilled when a well-meaning producer quietly said to me that I shouldn't be offended if they didn't end up releasing the recording – 'after all you've not had any rehearsals...' I'm glad to say that my many bad habits and lack of rehearsal notwithstanding, they did in fact issue the disc.

This experience, among subsequently some other less stressful ones across Europe, underscored for me how Elgar's music, which I initially perceived as quintessentially English, resonates with a much wider audience. Performing *The Dream* in cities such as Leipzig, Paris, Budapest and Stockholm with great European orchestras, I've been struck by the universal admiration that the piece receives. Elgar's music comfortably bridges the worlds of Mendelssohn, Mahler, Strauss and Wagner, and is celebrated and embraced as if it were their own. Each performance, whether it feels like revisiting an old friend or introducing a premiere, never fails to connect deeply with players and audiences, affirming Elgar's place in the pantheon of great European classical music – and as one of our once proud nation's most valuable exports.

~ Roderick Williams

The following thoughts are an instinctive reaction to this subject heading and are not supported by academic research or musicological evidence. They are the musings of a practitioner.

Not long ago I was invited to sing the solo baritone part in a performance of the *Five Mystical Songs* by Ralph Vaughan Williams at the Concertgebouw in Amsterdam. To my knowledge, this could easily have been the first performance of this work in that famous hall. Certainly no one from the chorus or orchestra could remember a previous performance there (or indeed in the Netherlands – but I defer to anyone who actually knows the facts).

As I stood on that impressive, renowned stage during the rehearsal, my gaze fell upon the names of composers written on plaques high up on the walls, surrounding the inside of the Grote Saal. The Greats are there, from Lassus through to Stravinsky, the names of genius composers of Western Art Music throughout the ages. High up behind the choir, for example, next to the organ and thus visible to most of the audience if not to the performers, you can find the name Bach. He hardly has the most honoured position in the room but he is at least counted amongst this elite band of creatives. Several Dutch composers are honoured in this way; names with which I am not familiar but may be better known to the native audience.

As we began work on RVW's beautiful music, it occurred to me that there wasn't a single British composer's name to be seen. Not Byrd, Purcell, Elgar, Vaughan Williams or Britten. It gave me cause to consider how British composers are regarded within this temple to Western Art Music. Was this testament to an early twentieth-century German critic's description of Britain as 'a land without music'?

A major piece of British music that I have sung outside the United Kingdom is Elgar's *Dream of Gerontius*. Richard Hickox conducted us in it in Bamberg, Bavaria with the city's chorus and orchestra, and on another occasion in Toulouse, when the BBC National Chorus of Wales travelled out to join the city's symphony orchestra. I remember thinking then that these were terrific opportunities to showcase something of the very best of

English grand choral music. We performed with a sense of pride and our audiences listened and were, I think, impressed.

More recently than that, in the summer of 2015, Simon Rattle was invited to conduct the Vienna Philharmonic at the penultimate night of the BBC Proms. He was delighted to further his relationship with this mighty orchestra, given that he was then the principal conductor of the Berlin Philharmonic, so a guest appearance like this gave him a chance to programme something special. He asked the members of the Vienna Phil what they would like to bring to the Proms; the answer came back that they would like to play *The Dream of Gerontius.* They had played it (once?) before and were eager to do so again, especially at the Royal Albert Hall in London. If there is an Austrian equivalent of bringing coals to Newcastle (*schnitzel to Vienna?)* then this was it.

I'm sure Simon enjoyed the experience of conducting that wondrous orchestra in that particular piece. I certainly made a conscious note, as I sat within the well of the upper strings during Part One, to remember the sheer quality of the sound in this piece I knew well. The Vienna Phil played the music with respect, with warmth and generosity. Those aspects of the writing that were more obviously Germanic in influence (the opening of the prelude, for example, reminiscent of Wagner's *Parsifal*) sounded especially *echt* in their hands. Having said that, the essential British characteristics of the piece were not lost; this was not *Gerontius* with an Austrian accent.

The compliment the orchestra paid us by choosing and playing this piece was really appreciated by the Proms audience, I'm confident of that. The care and attention they lavished on this music suggested an acknowledgement that this piece could stand its ground alongside any of the Austro-German classics. And this is at the heart of my thoughts about Elgar's *Dream of Gerontius* and where it stands in comparison to other giants of the choral repertoire, not just within the United Kingdom but more specifically on an international stage. I have performed plenty of British music that stirs me, most probably because I am English, but which I presume will have less or no appeal to an international audience. I imagine I might almost find myself apologising for such music outside these shores. Emphatically not so with the *Dream of Gerontius.*

Each time I experience a *Gerontius* performance and the rehearsals leading up to it, I find myself marvelling at how it is that Elgar came to write a piece of such depth, breadth, profundity and vision. I can scarcely believe how modern the piece is even today, and imagine how extraordinary it must have appeared to the Birmingham audience in 1900 (despite the limitations of that premiere) and the extent to which it pushed the boundaries of composition in its day. I have fairly rudimentary experience of British music of this period and of what came before – the music of Parry, Stanford and Sullivan for example – but I can't think of other music that has the ambition of *Gerontius*, that makes such intense demands on all of its performers.

Let me begin by focusing on the title role. I'm not sure that tenor soloists had been required to sing such a demanding, quasi-operatic solo role in a British oratorio before this. The polite, modest scale in which previous solo repertoire (that I know of) is written gives me the impression that a late nineteenth-century British lay clerk, trained in one of the UK's cathedral choirs, could have an honest stab at most oratorio solos up to this point. Gerontius, however, is in a different league. The stamina and *bel canto* technique required for the *Sanctus fortis* aria separates the Italian opera-school singer from the gentleman amateur.

To sing the role of Gerontius, however, requires more than just vocal heft; there are other moments that benefit from an ability to sustain an even tone in *pianissimo*, and some of these passages come close on the heels of more declamatory sections. The end of the *Sanctus fortis* aria, for example, suggests pale tone colours to match both the anxieties within the text and the delicate orchestral textures that accompany. A tenor who has managed to battle his way through the earlier orchestral *tuttis* can find himself awkwardly exposed towards the end of this aria.

The quality of the tenor writing impresses me as being something out of the ordinary, on a grander scale than much else I know in British music of the era. While I can guess that it did not appear out of a vacuum and that a musicologist could chart the development of Elgar's solo voice writing, it always strikes me as an unusual and courageous bit of writing.

Meanwhile, I was paying particular attention recently to the orchestration of *Gerontius* when we were preparing the oratorio for a live recording in Helsinki, under the baton of Nichols Collon. My specific interest this time was to learn as a composer and orchestrator myself; I had been working on a commission for the Bach Choir for a companion piece to *Gerontius* and so was even more receptive than usual to the orchestral textures Elgar explored. I often find it especially invigorating to be seated on stage close to the players during rehearsals and performance so that I can understand at close quarters what challenges they face. (Because the Priest and the Angel of the Agony are relative cameo appearances when compared to the role of Gerontius or the Angel, this gives me time to appreciate what else is going on!)

Many players within British orchestras have the benefit of experience with this score so it was interesting to watch the members of the Finnish Radio Symphony Orchestra come to terms with it for the first time. I noticed how involving and intricate the string parts are, not just for the first violins but throughout the whole string section, including many moments of thoroughly independent *divisi* writing (particularly in the violas and cellos), much rapid passage-work throughout each instrument's register, even when acting as less essential accompanying texture to something more soloistic in the winds. I enjoyed moments of solo string writing, not just for the section principals but sometimes for several members of the front desks, resulting in multiple solo sonorities. Elgar's attention to the smallest detail of articulation and orchestration I find fascinating and leaves me with the impression of a composer who had a highly developed sense of orchestral colour and the possibilities offered by a full symphony orchestra.

I especially enjoyed Elgar's writing for percussion, in particular moments such as the glockenspiel 'icing on the cake' during the demons' chorus or the long-held solo bass drum roll that links the huge choral climax 'Praise to the Holiest' with the introduction of the Angel of the Agony. And elsewhere, Elgar's spotlight on instruments such as the bass clarinet and the contra-bassoon gave me inspiration; both of those instruments were to feature at prime moments in the orchestration of my own piece.

This wide range of orchestral texture and Elgar's remarkable willingness to experiment with unusual instrumental colours, all in support of his depiction of Cardinal Newman's text, still leave me awestruck. From the first unison note of the prelude to the final rolling out of the last D major chord, there is a real sense that this piece is majestic, epic, profound, that it is music of value, of worth. I propose that *Gerontius*, of all British music, stands tall in refuting the claim that Britain is a 'land without music'. Even granted that it would not have existed in this form without musical influences from the Continent, it still manages to exemplify for me aspects that feel quintessentially English or British.

I choose to focus on *The Dream of Gerontius* because of the large scale of the work, its nature as an extended meditation on a point of Roman Catholic theology, its reputation amongst performers both in this country and especially abroad, and for its extraordinary level of musical craft and inspiration. I have discussed aspects of the work with various orchestral players on my trips abroad and also some members of the audience who often tell me they have only encountered Elgar through his first *Pomp and Circumstance* March. They were all stunned with admiration when they became acquainted with this masterpiece.

And so I return to the stage of the Concertgebouw and the composer plaques decorating the walls. Which of our composers deserve to join these worthy names and what pieces might we present as evidence to support our claims? I have already listed some other British composers who I think are deserving but, especially in this most famous of concert halls with its world-renowned symphony orchestra, my money would be on Elgar as our ambassador. And if I had to choose one piece as my Exhibit A, it would be his *Dream of Gerontius*.

~ Catherine Wyn-Rogers

I was lucky enough to have teachers and conductors who were devoted to Elgar's music. Even at school, where I was in the choir, we sang *My Love Dwelt in a Northern Land,* and then when I was a member of the Derbyshire Singers, we sang *The Snow,* songs from the *Scenes from the Bavarian Highlands* and more. The conductor of that choir, Joseph Clark, had been a member of the Hallé choir when Sir John Barbirolli was at the helm and who, of course, was such a wonderful interpreter of Elgar. When I was a student at the Royal College of Music, my singing teacher recalled begging leave to go to the Royal Albert Hall to watch Elgar rehearse *The Dream of Gerontius* and my director at the College was Sir David Willcocks who had been conducted by the great man when he was a choirboy at Westminster Abbey.[1] Later I watched Sir David conduct that magnificent work at Worcester's Three Choirs Festival. I felt that I had so much experience surrounding me when it came to approaching Elgar's extensive repertoire for the mezzo-soprano voice, which helped me to really get inside these works.

My first two performances of *The Dream of Gerontius* took place during one weekend in the early 1980s, the first at Tonbridge School and the second at the Mayfield Festival, with my beloved Bach Choir and Sir David conducting. Kenneth Bowen sang the role of Gerontius. He was extremely nice to me, telling me where to stand and sit. What a treat it was to hear him, such an expert in the role and with the perfect voice for it too. Since then, I have been privileged to perform the Angel many times, along with the other Elgar oratorios and of course *Sea Pictures,* all of which have their various joys and challenges. I write, having only just taken part in a concert of both *Sea Pictures* (numbers 1, 4 and 3) as well as *The Music Makers.* Elgar has provided me with much employment!

However, far more important, I feel, is the spiritual and musical fulfilment offered by being able to sing Elgar's music. There have been memorable occasions of course – singing each of the trio of Elgar's oratorios, *The Dream of Gerontius, The Apostles* and *The Kingdom,* at Three Choirs

1 Sir David sang under Elgar's direction as a choir boy in June 1932 for the premiere of the composer's *So many true princesses who have gone* (Queen Alexandra Memorial Ode). Eds.

Festivals and at the Proms. Collaborating with Sir Andrew Davis, Richard Hickox, Sir Mark Elder and others on these works were always highlights for me. I have also been lucky enough to perform *The Dream of Gerontius* with Zubin Mehta in Munich at the Staatsoper, where Sir Peter Jonas was the intendant and whose devotion to the work began when he heard it at the age of seven, and then with Daniel Barenboim and the Berlin Staatskapelle orchestra, the latter also being recorded live – these were really wonderful experiences.

Vocally, I feel there is a particularly British sound which lends itself to Elgar's music. I know he wrote for voices he had heard in Bayreuth and elsewhere on the continent, yet it is hard to get away from the native sound which is hugely affected by language. Just as Italian singers have an Italian brightness in their voices because of the Italian vowels (which we emulate as singers), British singers have something which inevitably owes so much to the English language. I recently heard the opinion that music itself is influenced by the language of a country and I really do agree. However, that in no way precludes British singers singing other languages and other nationalities' music (and vice versa of course). We just have to be aware of the differences, many of which are simply the sounds of different languages. There is also a very British passion, which is not histrionic but is nonetheless very deeply felt. Maybe it comes from the inherent humour of the British, or the compassion and yet restraint, or even from the landscape itself, which I feel infuses so much of Elgar's work, along with the intensity of his faith which underpins *The Dream of Gerontius* in particular, and which demands a similar intensity from his singers.

My favourite remark, which I have never forgotten and heard after a *Dream of Gerontius* performance, was when a lady came up to me and said 'my husband died three weeks ago – I hope he had an angel like you'. I was so touched by this and have always thought that the role of the Angel and Elgar's *Gerontius* has a special function, no matter one's beliefs: it is a comforting and heartfelt work.

5

Writing About Elgar

7. A *Daily Mail* press photographer took this photograph on 29 October 1919 of Elgar pouring tea for Edward German in the Adams Rooms of the Piccadilly Hotel. Standing behind them are HMV staff members George Colledge, William Manson and three unidentified employees. The occasion was the launch of the first Heifetz records to be released in Britain, one of which included the first recording of *La Capricieuse*.

~ John Bridcut

Elgar the Modernist

The mutual admiration of Edward Elgar and Richard Strauss is well-documented. It was after the second German performance of *The Dream of Gerontius* in 1902 that Strauss publicly toasted 'Meister Edward Elgar, the first English progressivist', while Elgar some years later called Strauss 'the greatest genius of our age'. When Strauss's music moved into ambiguous and then confused tonality later that decade, Elgar did not defect. He was in New York in 1907 to conduct *The Apostles* and *The Kingdom*, when a deputation asked him to lead a prayer meeting, to pray for the failure of Strauss's *Salome* at the Metropolitan Opera. Even 26 years later, he described this as 'so staggering and screamingly absurd that I don't think I have recovered from the shock even now'.

I don't know whether Elgar ever saw *Salome*. But in 1910, a year after visiting Strauss at his home in Bavaria, he did go to Covent Garden to see the even more harmonically and tonally adventurous *Elektra* – the first Strauss opera to be given in Britain. Elgar's wife said that he had been 'much impressed' by it, but had kept on saying 'the pity of it!' – presumably a reference to the plot rather than the score!

I wonder to what extent *Elektra* emboldened Elgar in his mid-50s to embrace modernism in his 'symphonic study', *Falstaff*. The audiences at its first outings in 1913 were bewildered by the evanescent tonality, the dissonant irruptions, the strange orchestral colourings and the lack of sustained Elgarian melody. Applause was faint and seats empty. The critic Ernest Newman spotted 'quite a new Elgar and one that the public used to the older Elgar will not assimilate very easily'. Robin Legge in *The Daily Telegraph* said 'I do not think that even Elgar has ever written more complicated music ... here again Elgar has given us a masterpiece of music, prodigiously stamped with his own remarkable personality'. I like his choice of the word 'even': he recognised that Elgar's music was by then far from straightforward.

To a public that had grown to love the heart-warming but comfortable diatonicism of the *Serenade for Strings*, the *Enigma Variations*, or the main theme of the First Symphony, the rollicking, sometimes barbarous chromaticism of *Falstaff* was a shock. But Elgar himself said that writing *Falstaff* had given him more enjoyment than any of his other music. He was depressed that it didn't catch on, and at the peak of his career was reduced to appealing to Thomas Beecham, who had premiered *Elektra* in Britain, to take up the piece. Beecham never replied.

Although performances today are still infrequent, *Falstaff*'s reputation is much more secure. It ensconces Elgar firmly in the twentieth century, looking forward rather than back, and happy with that. But his questing modernism was interrupted by the Great War, and the consequent appetite for music that fed patriotic sentiment. Thereafter came the Cello Concerto, novel in form but nostalgic in language. Perhaps only the Piano Quintet, with its proto-Shostakovich opening, kept the modernist flame alight until he started work on the Third Symphony.

There had been many signs of Elgar's adventurousness before *Falstaff*. His Second Symphony two years earlier, with its eerie, throbbing passage of what Elgar called 'a malign influence wandering thro' the summer night in the garden', and violent interruptions from brass and percussion, went over some heads in the audience. Elgar was dismayed by their reaction: 'they sit there like a lot of stuffed pigs'. Further back too – the very concept of the *'Enigma' Variations*; the use of the Jewish shofar in *The Apostles* (in which he briefly covered the trial of Jesus, offstage with stage directions and an almost cinematic flair, and focused instead on the ordinary folk, the apostles – appropriate in what was to become the people's century); the thrumming strings in the cadenza of the Violin Concerto; the nihilistic part-song *Owls*, which effectively has no ending; the key of the First Symphony – who else of note had (or has) written a symphony in A flat major? – and then subverting it with the second theme in the most unrelated key, D minor. All these point to Elgar's playfulness and departures from convention.

Contrary to the colonialist image that he sometimes cultivated, he was moving away from the Victorian certainties of Parry and Stanford, magnificent though they can be, to the musical and psychological ambiguities that were an intrinsic part of the twentieth-century zeitgeist. If he had had a conventional music education, and had studied composition at one of the academies, would he have charted his own path in this way? As it was, he never had a composition lesson in his life. Instead, his music comes from personal experience – whether helping tune pianos or sell music in his father's shop in Worcester, or learning the fiddle, organ and bassoon, running a wind band at Powick asylum, or playing first violin professionally in new music by Dvořák at the Three Choirs Festival under the composer's baton. He also travelled widely to hear concerts and opera whenever he could. This accumulation of experience took an alarming while to bear fruit – his first big success (*Enigma*) had to wait until he'd just turned 42 – but it was a wise investment. His own orchestration was a marvel of imagination, ingenuity and practicality, and his musical ideas had matured 'deep in his soul'.

On top of that came his own personal hang-ups. Socially awkward, alternately charming and boorish, sometimes ecstatic, sometimes suicidal – we would say today that he was 'on the spectrum'. His complicated but passionate personal relationships, his tank of self-confidence sometimes overflowing, sometimes empty… he worked out these tussles in his music. As a result, it is open to fresh interpretation and assessment in every generation, and way beyond English shores. As Daniel Barenboim once said, when conducting Elgar in Germany: 'I get mad at people who say we will be playing music by "the British composer Edward Elgar". Does anyone ever say we will play music by "the German composer Johannes Brahms?"'

Sometimes the ambiguities are *en clair*. With his love of riddles, Elgar set hares running with the supposedly hidden 'enigma' theme in the *Variations*, or the triple asterisk with which he concealed the subject of Variation XIII: was there a clue about a female traveller (as Elgar himself once hinted) in the quotation from Mendelssohn's overture *Calm Sea and Prosperous Voyage* coupled with the sound of a ship's engines which Elgar arranged by asking for a timpani roll 'with side-drum sticks' – or was it just superstition about the number thirteen? But then that number was no accident: Elgar had moved it there from its original position at number six. It's hard not to suspect Elgar of mischief. Later on, an 'immortal beloved' was perhaps suggested by the unnamed soul he said was enshrined in the Violin Concerto. But Elgar wrote this in Spanish, presumably to enhance the mystery.

There are obscurer ambiguities too: what does he signify in the Second Symphony when the percussion's violent hammering tries to destroy the music for a while? (This was five years earlier than Carl Nielsen's destruction by timpani in his Fourth Symphony.) When he says he has 'shewn himself' in this symphony, as well as the Violin Concerto and the choral ode *The Music Makers*, what does he mean, and how much does this relate to the peak of his affair (whether platonic or not) with Alice Stuart-Wortley, his 'windflower', which was only revealed when Michael Kennedy burrowed deep in the correspondence at the Elgar birthplace many years later?

In many ways, Elgar was the English Mahler – not because their often nervously intense music sounded alike, but because both composers, consciously or not, relish musical ambiguity to house both irony and melancholy. But there is one piece of Elgar which does sound like Mahler, and is unambiguous. *Sospiri*, the short, anguished work for strings, harp and harmonium, escaped beneath the jingoistic radar of 1914. It was written before war broke out, but inappropriately first performed ten days after, sitting oddly beside a tub-thumping rendering of 'Land of Hope and Glory'. It has a kinship with the *Adagietto* in Mahler's Fifth Symphony, first performed in London by Henry Wood in 1909. *Sospiri*'s unrelieved intensity, with the continual disjunction between the violin line and the accompaniment, speaks of a deep, unresolved longing, even despair – certainly something much stronger than the 'sighs' of the title. It had nothing to do with the war, but was probably the most nakedly personal statement Elgar ever made. In later years, he seems to have been embarrassed by the nakedness, as he effectively disowned the piece. But even here there is a riddle: why had he given it to the German publishers, Breitkopf & Härtel, with whom he hadn't worked for almost twenty years? Perhaps he was thinking of the German origins of his dear friend, the music patron Alfred Rodewald, whose shockingly premature death ten years before had caused Elgar some sort of breakdown.

Elgar's method of composing often involved pegging sketches randomly to a washing line, and then harnessing his self-taught musical intelligence with his often-complex motivations to rearrange those sketches into a coherent, if sometimes ambiguous, whole. That seems to me to be part of a modern mindset. But he was also a modernist in curating his work. He knew how to use photography to promote himself, and he was fascinated by new technology. While some musicians chafed at the implications of audio recording, Elgar embraced it. Once it became possible to record an orchestra, Elgar was on the case. From 1914 on, he was often in the recording studio, even though it meant scaling down his orchestra's original size, and adjusting his scores. Full-size orchestras could be captured after 1925 thanks to electrical recording, which Elgar hailed as 'the greatest discovery in the history of the gramophone'. He became the first composer ever to commit almost all of his orchestral works to disc (some of them more than once), doubtless seizing the financial moment, but also bequeathing the sound, not just the pages, of his scores to posterity. But then the man who had himself photographed on his deathbed, 'pretending' in David Owen Norris's words, 'to be dead already', had a keen sense of legacy. He recorded *Falstaff* with the LSO in November 1931, in the brand-new EMI Abbey Road studios, and the result is staggering. It positively fizzes with nervous energy and fierce rhythms, even though Elgar was then 74, and the performance is faster than any of the modern recordings, perhaps because of the five-minute limit for each side of a 12-inch 78rpm disc. One of the HMV engineers described how Elgar 'lost himself in the music' in these sessions. This recording shows that, almost 20 years on, there was no mellowing in his *Falstaff*, and he was right proud of it.

~ Hugh Cobbe

In July 1937 Benjamin Britten met William Walton for lunch and recorded in his diary that he found him charming but 'I feel always the school relationship with him – he is so obviously the head-prefect of English music, whereas I'm the promising young new boy. Soon of course he'll leave & return as a member of the staff – [Vaughan] Williams being of course the Headmaster. Elgar was never that – but a member of the Governing board'.[1] Here we find a young man, destined to become a great British composer of the twentieth century, setting up a hierarchy of three of his predecessors. Walton was an older contemporary, Vaughan Williams very much belonged to the previous generation while Elgar, of the generation before that, was thus at highest level in his hierarchy.

Britten was not at ease with the works of these predecessors of his – after Britten's death Walton told Michael Kennedy that whatever some people might say 'we were always on good terms and I much admired many of his works, even if he detested most (not all) of mine'. His discomfort with the music of Vaughan Williams is well known, and in May 1931 he wrote in his diary that he was absolutely incapable of enjoying Elgar for more than two minutes! Walton, for his part, was much interested in the works of both Vaughan Williams and Britten (though he did refer to Vaughan Williams in 1942 as 'a really big pussy with very sharp claws'),[2] while in a newspaper interview he said: 'I have an unbounded admiration for Elgar. I like even *Salut d'Amour*. There's no other English composer to touch him. He's bigger than Delius, bigger than Vaughan Williams. He's becoming bigger all the time'.[3]

Vaughan Williams of course represented a different, and new, strand in English music in contrast to those such as Parry, Stanford and especially Elgar who followed the Germanic tradition (this strand initially also included Vaughan Williams's early music before he eventually found his own voice with the help of his work on *The English Hymnal* and by collecting

1 As quoted in Humphrey Carpenter, *Benjamin Britten: A Biography* (London: Faber & Faber, 1992), 110.

2 See VWL1641, at https://vaughanwilliamsfoundation.org/discover/letters/.

3 Interview in *The Yorkshire Observer*, 21 December 1942.

English folksong). The new strand was often dismissed as 'pastoral' by some contemporaries. Nonetheless Vaughan Williams regarded Elgar as a sort of founding father of English music, alongside his own teachers Hubert Parry and Charles Stanford. Elgar and Vaughan Williams were not close friends. Vaughan Williams had approached Elgar in the early 1900s asking for lessons in orchestration but was turned away by Alice Elgar on the grounds that Elgar didn't take pupils; she suggested he went to Granville Bantock. Writing about this Vaughan Williams observed: 'Though Elgar would not teach me personally he could not help teaching me through his music. I spent several hours at the British Museum studying the full score of the *Variations* and *Gerontius*. The results are obvious in the opening pages of the finale of my *Sea Symphony*'.[4]

Elgar's overall importance was perhaps made most clear by Vaughan Williams in a passage in his 1934 lecture 'The Evolution of the Folk-Song: the Folk-Song and the Composer' where he is discussing how composers had or had not used folksong: 'A stronger case perhaps is our own English composer Edward Elgar. I have some hesitation in discussing in public or venturing to appraise the music of one whom we, in England, all revere as our leader, but the case of Elgar is always quoted by those who oppose the theory of what is known as the 'folk-song school of composers'.[5] Here we have a firm acknowledgement of Elgar's position as the figurehead of English music at the time of his death. To pursue Britten's simile, he was not just a member of the governing board but its chairman.

4 Reprinted in Ralph Vaughan Williams, *National Music and Other Essays*, 2nd edition (Oxford: Oxford University Press, 1987), 188.

5 Ibid., 41.

~ Jeremy Dibble

Elgar and the *Topos* of the March

Perhaps one of the most pervasive aspects of the seventeenth, eighteenth and nineteenth centuries in musical composition was the influence of dance characteristics, essentially established through the court of Louis XIV. In so much of the baroque and classical eras we witness not only the presence of dances in their unadulterated forms, such as for example in dance suites, the concluding movements of overtures, serenades, *divertimenti* and the third movement of symphonies and string quartets, but also of their overwhelming influence in other idioms such as cantata, oratorio and opera, where arias and choruses abundantly adhere to the rhythmic and metrical features of dance style-forms. In the nineteenth century this 'dance' mindset continued – the *Saltarello* finale of Mendelssohn's 'Italian' Symphony is one such potent example – but it was also augmented by other style-forms, perhaps the most prominent of which were the waltz and the march (though other style-forms such as the barcarolle and nocturne also became popular). Throughout the nineteenth century, the march became an increasingly conspicuous genre. Schubert's *Marche militaire*, Mendelssohn's 'Wedding March' (from *A Midsummer Night's Dream*) and 'War March of the Priests' (from *Athalie*), Berlioz's 'Rakoczi March' (from *The Damnation of Faust*) and Wagner's 'Kaisermarsch' and 'Wedding March' (from *Lohengrin*) being some of the most enduring, and the subgenre of the 'funeral march' would for ever be epitomised by Handel's 'Dead March' from *Saul*, the second movement of Beethoven's 'Eroica' Symphony, Chopin's 'Marche funèbre' (from his Second Piano Sonata) and Wagner's 'Siegfried's Funeral March' in *Götterdämmerung*, one of the most arresting examples of the genre as a dramatic vehicle.

In the late nineteenth century, the march robustly retained its links with the military and with national ceremony, but its character, connotations, meanings and symbols also began to proliferate with a wider sense of artistic purpose. In British music of this period this is particularly evident in the music of Sullivan, Stanford and Parry who used the march in a variety of contexts in opera, oratorio, symphony and incidental music. Parry's well-known 'Bridal March' from his incidental music to *The Birds*, the ceremonial gravity of Part II Scene 3 of *Judith* ('The Exploits of Judith'), the ritornello-like opening (and closing) idea of *Job* (which Elgar greatly admired) and the slow march in his late symphonic poem *From Death to Life* are four such examples; and Stanford's particular affinity, typically infused with his penchant for the dramatic, for the funeral march in his opera *Savonarola*, his incidental music to Tennyson's *Becket*, the slow movement of his Second Organ Sonata, and his masterly symphonic adaptation in the 'Agnus Dei' in his *Requiem* (to name but a handful of instances) reveal a fertile versatility for this sub-category. Yet, without doubt, the most fecund exponent of the march in late Victorian, Edwardian and Georgian Britain was Elgar.

One can of course identify him almost synonymously with the genre through the considerable popularity of his *Imperial March*, written for the Diamond Jubilee of Queen Victoria in 1897 which, along with the *Festival March* of a year later (now lost or destroyed), were almost certainly key precedents for the four *Pomp and Circumstance* marches of 1901-7, notably the first which occupies such an iconic position in the 'Last Night of the Proms', and the paradigm of the march's ternary form allowed Elgar to exploit his flair for virtuoso orchestral colour in the outer symphonic sections while accommodating his other undisputed aptitude for rousing (and fundamentally diatonic, vocally-orientated) melody in the central 'trio'. It is also perhaps worth pointing out that the extensive reprise of the 'trio' material in the tonic key in the final sections of Elgar's large-scale concert marches more closely resembles sonata practice; indeed, the symphonic framework of Elgar's marches as orchestral works also accentuates their essential conception as *concert*-pieces, a property which is further emphasised by the substantial, muscular proportions of the *Coronation March* of 1911, the less well-known *Empire March* of 1924 and the late *Pomp and Circumstance March* No. 5 of 1930, arguably his finest essay in the genre.

These marches are the most visible corroboration of Elgar's abundant incorporation of the genre within his larger output, but it is evident from the earliest phases of his maturity in the 1890s that the march as an element of stylistic focus was already important to his creative imagination. The opening of the chivalric *Froissart* (1890) is a march theme as are parts of the transitional material to the second subject, and this same sentiment is echoed in Scene II of *The Black Knight* ('To the barrier of the fight') of 1889–93, essentially Elgar's 'First Symphony', the ternary microcosm of the opening to Scene IV ('To the sumptuous banquet') and much of the music which forms the finale. In the two large-scale choral works of 1896, we observe Elgar embryonically assimilating the march into a more intrinsic feature of his developing Wagnerian canvases where the orchestra (key to the process of symphonic propulsion) and the dramatic vehicle of integrated leitmotif is so inherent to his dramatic thinking. This is more effectively deployed in the more fluent pages of *Scenes from the Saga of King Olaf* where the changing phases of the narrative form an important part of both solo and choral delivery. Here, the march, besides its familiar association with marshal illustration (as, for example in the 'Death of Olaf'), provides an important symbol of procession and spiritual fervour, especially in scenes such as 'The Conversion' (notably Olaf's impassioned adherence to Christianity) as well as in the depiction of ceremony and invocation (such as in 'Sigrid'). In *The Light of Life*, which is broadly reflective, it is significant that Elgar harnesses the march, not as a military projection, but as an expression of resolution ('Light out of darkness') and defiance ('The wisdom of their wise men shall perish'). This proliferation of the march *topos* as a dramatic and syntactical agency in Elgar's music has major implications for how we understand the aesthetic of the composer's musical language, for not only does it indicate how fundamental were the incorporation of genres within his style, but how quintessential was the march as a malleable means of both emotional and structural enunciation within the fabric of his semiological armoury.

For the framing material of the *Te Deum* (1897), Elgar used a march-like theme to articulate an appropriate sense of eulogy, but for his two more overtly nationalist vocal works of 1897 and 1898, *The Banner of St George* and *Caractacus*, the march plays a seminal structural role as the finale. In the former, very much in the style of a narrative ballad (so vigorously established by Stanford's *The Revenge* of 1886), Elgar marks his last choral section 'Epilogue (March)' which, as the title suggests, functions as a non-diegetic commentary after the action of the cantata has concluded. For the more highly developed *Caractacus* (1898), however, Elgar predicated the entire first part of his finale (whose powerful focus is Caractacus's monologue in Rome) on a march ('the 'Triumphal March' of the Roman soldiers as they process with their enslaved British prisoners into Rome) in the form of a choral overture, in which the customary ternary form took on more ambitious attire. Indeed, both the more extended march and 'trio' paragraphs, with their copious amounts of thematic material, anticipate the manner in which Elgar's structural practices, particularly those of a sonata type, would evolve.

After the precedent of *Caractacus*, with its greater structural and thematic involution, the *topos* of the march in Elgar's music became increasingly diverse in its manifestations and contexts. Particularly illuminating in this regard are the years 1899 to 1901 in which the composer unequivocally confirmed his reputation as a master of the orchestra. In the *Enigma Variations*, there are strong suggestions of the march ethos in 'Troyte', but as with *The Banner of St George* and *Caractacus*, the ebullience of the march is reserved for the 'autobiographical' finale. Here Elgar's structure is a fascinating extension of ternary structure – again the familiar juxtaposition of rhythmic dynamism and the 'big tune' of the 'trio' in the subdominant together with the presentation of the 'Enigma' theme. A recapitulation of the march idea then yields to a cyclic 'memory' of the first variation (topically depicting Elgar's wife) before the march structure is resumed with restatements in the tonic of the 'trio' tune and, as a peroration to the movement and the entire work, a reprise of the 'Enigma' theme. In 'Sabbath Morning at Sea' of the *Sea Pictures*, a march idea (marked 'molto maestoso') plays a more rhetorical role as a projection of the final line of the second verse ('Of holding the day glory!') and its cadence in C major. Even more powerfully, later in the song, Elgar deftly incorporates it into the recapitulation of C major ('He shall assist me to look higher') as a melodic expansion of the secondary idea (from verse three) and as part of a developmental process of thematic reprise (including the opening melody of the first song). Perhaps, most decisively this march idea is used for the resolute coda, a transformation of which is then expressed in the final song (again autobiographical in sentiment) as the main thematic material.

In *The Dream of Gerontius* the Wagnerian techniques of earlier choral works had become more finely tuned and erudite in terms of their contrapuntal and structural functions, and concomitant with this refinement, the *topos* of the march also became a much more sophisticated component of Elgar's leitmotivic and thematic menagerie. One need only scrutinise the opening 'Judgement' theme in Part I to see how this, by degrees, metamorphoses into the foreboding, march-like progress towards Gerontius's glimpse of the deity in Part II. His treatment of the chorus, moreover, had also become more elaborate as a dramatic agency in its range of roles across the spectrum from the reflective commentary to the vivid *turba*, and in this context the march infuses several choral utterances including the two slow processionals, 'Go forth in the name', 'Be merciful, be gracious', and the vibrant, more animated choral reprise ('In the name of angels and archangels') of the Priest's acclamation 'Proficiscere, anima Christiana'. As mentioned above, in October 1901, the first two *Pomp and Circumstance Marches* were premiered in Liverpool under A.E. Rodewald, and, in the same month, the more neglected but exceptionally fine funeral march for W.B. Yeats's and George Moore's *Grania and Diarmid* was performed in Dublin's Gaiety Theatre. But before these marches saw the light of day, Elgar's preoccupation with the rhetorical potential of the march was enshrined in his overture (or short symphonic poem) *Cockaigne*. Characteristically rich in thematic material, the exposition of Elgar's sonata structure is dominated by a march theme,[1] and the second thematic phase of the tonic is a typical type of spacious 'trio' melody. But perhaps the most significant corroboration of the role of the march in *Cockaigne* (and its intrinsic part of the sounds of 'In London Town') is the central march of the 'brass band' which appears first as a new thematic departure of the protracted development and later as part of the recapitulation juxtaposed with the majestic reprise of the 'nobilmente' 'trio' melody replete with a striking late modulation away from the tonic (C major) to E flat major, underpinned by the entry of the organ.

Cockaigne and the first two *Pomp and Circumstance* Marches undoubtedly had the effect of consolidating Elgar's bond both with march form *and* its rhetorical gestures, and the appearance in 1902 of the *Coronation Ode*, which not only incorporated the 'trio' of *Pomp and Circumstance* No. 1 but also projected the march ethos in its outer movements, served to universalise the composer's confident integration of the style-form. (It is also tantalising to imagine whether a second *Cockaigne* overture, contemplated during 1903,[2] might have continued the exploration of the march *topos*.) Moreover, these works were a significant prelude to a substantial series of march-inspired music which permeated his mature works, especially those of his most fertile before the First World War. In his two later oratorios (essentially *operas-manquées*) for Birmingham, in which the intensification of Wagnerian leitmotivic methods reached a new height of syntactical intricacy, Elgar used the march in a number of original contexts. In *The Apostles*, for example, the genre is used to colour the vividness of the 'Dawn' scene, replete with shofar. There are also other ideas which seem to invoke the march's character – the motive associated with teaching the gospel, the selection of the apostles ('The Lord hath chosen them'), the hymn-like section based on 'Turn ye to the stronghold, ye prisoners' (which could easily be a 'trio' theme), the more animated parts of 'The Betrayal', Judas's tragic realisation of his part in Jesus's arrest in 'The Temple' which takes the form of a solemn funeral march ('O Lord to whom vengeance belongeth'), and this same solemnity recurs with the huge quasi-operatic choral and orchestral architecture of the finale ('All the ends of the world shall remember and turn unto the Lord'), arguably the most grandiose statement in all of Elgar's music. Similarly, *The Kingdom* is heavily pervaded by march themes. A number of these, of course, were already inaugurated in *The Apostles*,

1 See Dibble, J., 'Narrative and Formal Plasticity in the British Symphonic Poem, 1850–1950' in Allis, M. & Watt, P. (eds), *The Symphonic Poem in Britain 1850–1950* (Woodbridge: The Boydell Press, 2020), 23–4.

2 See Kennedy, M., *Portrait of Elgar*, 2nd Edn. (London: Oxford University Press, 1982), 358.

but in addition Elgar skilfully and strategically augments his thematic reservoir with new march ideas such as the 'arrest' material and the thrilling 'Pentecost' chorus 'He that walketh upon wings of the wind'. Perhaps the most significant idea, however, is the 'New Faith' in D flat major, a deeply moving 'slow processional' and theme which lies at the very epicentre of the composer's individual interpretation of the Acts of the Apostles. It also plays a central role in the opening prelude.

In Elgar's later orchestral works the march was no less important. The 'grandiose' section of *In the South,* somewhat less cohesive in structure than *Cockaigne,* is strongly suggestive of a 'slow march' (depicting the belligerence of the Romans) and this particular sub-genre also proved to be quintessential to the cyclic design of the First Symphony whose opening march forms the apotheosis of the last movement. Furthermore, one should also not ignore the spirit of the 'quick march' in the *Scherzo,* especially the secondary idea in C sharp minor marked *marcato.* The Second Symphony is also heavily imbued with contrasting march material in its outer movements, but it is the elegiac slow movement, styled as a funeral march, which stands out. One should also not overlook what is arguably Elgar's orchestral masterpiece, *Falstaff,* whose pages are full of march themes used in this context of a 'symphonic study' as an illustrative means of the character depicted in Shakespeare's *Henry IV.* In addition, Elgar's series of deft march transformations are supported by an orchestral palette of true mastery and a tonal scheme which surpasses those of his symphonies and earlier overtures.

In Elgar's later music, the march continued to be an influential style-form though it would be beyond the scope of this essay to identify all the instances of its application and function. Nevertheless, to stress how critical the march remained in Elgar's creative psyche, the citation of a few select examples is indicative of the composer's continued inventive dexterity. Among his assemblages of shorter pieces, his music for the masque, *The Crown of India* (1912), included a fine example, and the somewhat neglected incidental music for *Arthur* (1925) contains several march-infused ideas. *For the Fallen* (1916), the third part of *The Spirit of England,* is a moving choral embodiment of a funeral procession, a work comparable with Stanford's later neglected ternary commemoration in march form of the 'Unknown Warrior' in *At the Abbey Gate* of 1921. The last movement of the Cello Concerto (1919) is a unique example of a vigorous march used as the pivotal first theme in a highly modified sonata structure (pungently laced with cyclic references) which, as the most substantial essay of Elgar's four movements (indeed the first three movements, in their comparative brevity, have the effect of being a 'suite' of pieces), provides the end-weight to a highly unconventional concerto scheme. Another intriguing experiment can be witnessed in 'The wagon passes' of the *Nursery Suite* (1931), a march uniquely based on a short ostinato figure.

As if to adumbrate the significance of the march *topos* in his music, Elgar returned to the paradigm of *Pomp and Circumstance* in 1930 and it is perhaps no coincidence that one of his last tasks in 1933 was to undertake an orchestration of Chopin's 'Funeral March' which Adrian Boult recorded at the EMI studios at Abbey Road on 30 May 1933 and which had its first performance at Queen's Hall on 25 February 1934 as part of a Philharmonic Society memorial concert, two days after the composer's death.

~ Ronald Grames

Elgar has been long acknowledged as the first British composer after Purcell to have a major international reputation. He was praised and befriended in his time by Richard Strauss, fulsomely complimented by Hans Richter, who declared him 'the greatest modern composer', and Arthur Nikisch, who considered his First Symphony 'a masterpiece of the first order', admired by Nicolai Rimsky-Korsakov, who declared his *Enigma Variations* 'the greatest since Beethoven', and eulogized by composers as disparate as Jean Sibelius and Igor Stravinsky. Though he was most influenced by the European continental music that dominated British musical culture in his time – by Wagner, Liszt, Berlioz, and to a lesser degree Brahms – he developed a musical language of such quintessential Englishness that in retrospect it seems to have served as a musical backdrop to the Edwardian British empire and its pomp and celebration.

I could, I suppose, disclose that Elgar was one of the composers who first introduced me to classical music, but I suspect that another's experiences would make far better reading. Vaughan Williams began his career when Elgar was at the height of his acclaim in Great Britain. He famously sought lessons from Elgar in the early 1900s as he strove to find his compositional voice in a world where Elgar's music largely defined British national music. This was before English folk songs, Tudor hymnody, and studies with Ravel took him on a different path. When he was informed by Lady Elgar that her husband's schedule would not allow it, Vaughan Williams turned to study of Elgar's scores, the *Enigma Variations* and *The Dream of Gerontius* in particular.

It was some time before the two met beyond chance encounters at festivals. The turning point may well have come only after C.V. Stanford died in 1924. The involved story concerns a spiralling sense of betrayal between Stanford and Elgar which spilled over onto those, like Vaughan Williams, that Elgar saw as being in Stanford's circle. An early conversation did find Elgar rather sarcastic over criticism from a musicologist friend of Vaughan Williams, but when he attended a performance of the oratorio *Sancta Civitas* some years later, the conversation was much more congenial. Elgar was 'generous' in his praise. In fact, he said that he had considered setting the text himself but 'shall never do that now, and I am glad I didn't because you have done it for me.' Vaughan Williams told him that 'this made me sorry that I had ever attempted to make a setting myself.' That is a remarkable statement, even allowing for polite deference and the younger composer's tendency to self-deprecation. It was, after all, a work which Vaughan Williams declared to be his favourite among his own choral works. Between these are increasing hints of additional conversations, at least one informally set in a pub, and one must assume the two occasionally discussed music over those beers and not just the Reformation and clergy celibacy (a Vaughan Williams joke). We know of an exchange between them regarding a work by Hubert Parry while attending its rehearsal, and Elgar's influence clearly extends to Vaughan Williams's 1935 *Five Tudor Portraits*, which largely owes its existence to Elgar's suggestion that RVW should make an oratorio of John Skelton's ribald poem *The Tunning of Elynour Rummyng.*

Despite the warmer relationship of later years, there are only three letters known to have been sent by Vaughan Williams to Elgar, all dating from the last years of the latter's life. One from June 1933 congratulates Elgar on his Royal Victorian Order honours. Two are of greater substance to this discussion. An earlier one, from 1931, has several signatories, and light-heartedly but pointedly encourages Elgar to return to composing and complete his third symphony and write the third of the sacred oratorios. The last letter was sent by Vaughan Williams on 23 February 1934. It informed the terminally ill Elgar that he had been preparing *The Dream of Gerontius* for performance at the upcoming Leith Hill Festival, something Vaughan Williams 'had been longing to do ... for years.' He poignantly asked for Elgar's blessing. The performance was broadcast, but sadly Elgar, who died three days after he received the letter, did not live to hear it.

Vaughan Williams wrote, by way of a tribute, an article for *Music and Letters* titled 'What Have We Learnt from Elgar?' In it he describes Elgar's brilliance at choral and orchestral writing and finally acknowledges its influence on his own works with a candour and generosity – not to mention wry humor – that is less common than perhaps it should be. The article, published in *National Music and Other Essays,*[1] is go-to reading for anyone who wants the question of Elgar's importance answered with authority. Of course, other English musical luminaries including Arnold Bax, Yehudi Menuhin, Malcolm Sargent, Hamilton Harty, Walford Davies, Constant Lambert, and Henry Wood, offered tributes as well, and like Vaughan Williams affirmed Elgar's greatness and his significance to his country's music

1 Ralph Vaughan Williams, *National Music and Other Essays*, 2nd edition (Oxford: Oxford University Press, 1987), 188.

and people. Benjamin Britten is, perhaps, the exception to this acclaim that proves the rule, as his disparaging remarks regarding Elgar's music, made early in his career, are well known. 'I am absolutely incapable of enjoying Elgar for more than two minutes,' he said in 1931 as a cheeky teenager. This acerbic dismissal puts Elgar in good company, for four years later he stated: 'Certainly the best way to make me like Elgar is to listen to him after Vaughan Williams.' In the 1930s, Elgar, and for that matter Vaughan Williams, cast a long shadow over the efforts of this ambitious newcomer with his equal measures of vanity and insecurity. Time and experience seem to have mellowed Britten towards Elgar though, for decades later, in 1968, he recorded a gripping and insightful account of the *Introduction and Allegro* and three years after that led a searingly powerful recording of *The Dream of Gerontius* that suggests that his attitude had changed.

There does not seem to be any school of composition today that draws directly from the works of Elgar, though some romantic nationalists, American and Russian as well as British, carved out parallel paths in the stylistic turmoil of the twentieth century. But what of the importance of Elgar now, to a world immersed in popular culture? As Vaughan Williams pointed out in his 1935 tribute, Elgar had been able to speak not only to the musicians of his time, but to the British people, as well. Certainly, such a connection would now seem more tenuous, outside of The Last Night of the Proms, when general music education and artistic awareness are at a lamentable nadir and the ephemeral is the product of the day. Still, where there is popular interest in serious music, Elgar's importance is still evident. Classic FM's Hall of Fame, though often disparaged by cognoscenti, serves as a barometer of popular sentiment. In the 2023 listener poll, two Elgar works are among the top 20 – the *Enigma Variations* and the Cello Concerto – and eight are included in the full list of 300. I suspect there may be similar polls run by some of the ever-smaller number of classical music broadcasters in the US, but just about every American will be familiar with one work by Elgar: the trio of *Pomp and Circumstance March No. 1*. Absent A.C. Benson's words, it has been played at almost every high school and college graduation ceremony for many decades. Few but the musicians who perform it – often over and over – know who wrote it, but the memory is nearly universal and the tune instantly recognized.

There is another institution of American life that owes a debt of gratitude to Elgar, and that is Hollywood. His influence might be less than that of the fascists who drove so many fine Jewish composers out of Europe and into the waiting arms of the American film industry, but it is collaterally more benign. One has but to look at one of the most celebrated of film composers, John Williams, to be aware of the importance of Elgar's nobly expressive, lushly orchestrated, often uplifting music. Could one, for instance, imagine the music of the throne room scene of *Star Wars: A New Hope* without Elgar? Or the tour of Cloud City in *The Empire Strikes Back*? True, Williams has many British influences: William Walton is certainly one, and Gustav Holst's *Planets* is an obvious inspiration as well. Even Vaughan Williams seems to hover over a scene or two. But the influence is no less real for being second-generation or for being unrecognized by most moviegoers.

Beyond the music itself, Elgar's life story appeals greatly to egalitarian instincts and makes Elgar important as a model of 'success-through-perseverance' and 'humility-with-fame'. Many of those I've named who, at his passing, extolled Elgar's musical brilliance also noted this quality of character. Admirers of Vaughan Williams will point with justifiable pride to the many instances of modesty, charity, and liberality in a life that, because of its rather privileged beginnings and subsequent successes and recognition, could have produced a different – dare I say more familiar? – personality. Elgar, the fourth of seven children of a small-town music-store owner and organist, had fewer privileges at the start. The son of a tradesman of limited means, he gained none of the advantages of prestigious schools and music academy training, and that, and his Roman Catholic upbringing, made him an outsider in Protestant British society. He did not, of course, climb to the highest echelons of British music and society unaided. Besides his musical family and some important friends, a fortunate marriage to a devoted wife with social connections and an unshakeable belief in his abilities was enormously helpful. Yet, his hardscrabble achievement of recognition was essentially built on supreme merit and relentless effort. There was occasional moodiness and an inclination to initial aloofness, conceivably for self-protection, but the autodidact Elgar showed little tendency to faults that have been known to afflict some self-made persons, notably excessive self-regard or a predisposition to bitterness over past prejudice and opposition. (Elgar's and Stanford's mutual enmity is one significant exception to the latter.) Rather, his hard work, good humour, kindliness, and loyalty were all noted by those who knew him well.

Perhaps I should give the last word on Elgar's importance to such a person: contemporary Sir Richard Terry, famed Catholic musicologist, choral director, and organist. 'So passes England's greatest composer, a noble life nobly lived; a peaceful rest well and truly earned. To the young musician Elgar leaves an example of high endeavour and fine achievement. To those privileged to enjoy his friendship he leaves memories of a sweet and pleasant savour'.

~ Andrew Green

An early morning in the winter of 1966/67. On waking, I reach for the family transistor radio, which my bedroom has on virtually permanent loan. A sudden passion for classical music has invaded the brain of this previously sport-obsessed fifteen-year-old, and days now start with the BBC's Third Programme (shortly to be re-named Radio 3).

The sounds heard as I switched on were new to me, yet somehow familiar. Was this – Elgar? It was indeed, revealed as the *Introduction and Allegro* for strings. I was as pleased as if some complex riddle had been solved. Clearly, the devouring of such Elgar standards as the Cello Concerto, *Sea Pictures, Enigma Variations* and *The Dream of Gerontius* had somehow absorbed and distilled the musical language enough to inform my guesswork.

By this time, plenty of 'core' classical repertoire by all the obvious legendary 'foreigners' had been assimilated, but it was also pleasing to note that my own country wasn't without its composers of a certain standing. For me there was a particular identification with Britten and Vaughan Williams. The former, because he was writing magical music in my very own time and Vaughan Williams, because many of his later works seemed 'modern' – the fourth and sixth symphonies, for example – and thus, again, felt 'present'. There was much to love in the music of Elgar and Delius, but it wasn't (or so I naively felt) 'relatable' in quite the same fashion, being from an earlier chapter in British musical history.

Early on, though, I somehow picked up the idea, from the musical ether around me, that I should think of our native composers as something of a niche interest. A few years on, as a Cambridge undergraduate, my enthusiasm for Vaughan Williams was regarded as mildly eccentric. Much later, during my years presenting for Radio 3, one senior producer greeted even modest expressions of enthusiasm for British music with rolled eyes – perhaps it was all lumped together under the damning 'English Pastoral' nomenclature. Argue your case quietly with such individuals and you felt you would be ignored. Raising my voice even a little and ears would be covered as if I had hollered.

Thankfully, that wasn't the whole story and British composers (not least of the present day) have been well represented on both Radio 3 and Classic

FM, down to the present. *BBC Music* magazine has British music of all periods firmly in the mix. And we can hardly complain that British musicians have sold us short in terms of concerts and recordings of this repertoire.

However, what of the view of this music exhibited abroad? It remains hard to detect signs of widespread serious interest in properly exploring the *breadth* of music by British composers – beyond, that is, the advocacy of British performers on their travels, who have done what they can. We might note that while British musicologists/music writers have made many a distinguished contribution to research on the 'great' composers, precious few of their literary counterparts overseas have taken up the cause of British composers, Elgar included. Of course there have been exceptions – in the USA, for example. How fortunate that Elgar enthusiasts have been to be able to turn to the exhaustive work of New Jersey-born (and recently deceased) Jerrold Northrop Moore, who went so far as to settle in Elgar's own county of Worcestershire.

Over the years, high-ranking conductors from outside the UK have embraced amounts of Elgar's music while holding positions with British orchestras. As far as first-hand experiences go, I recall (for example) a finely measured Festival Hall performance of the Symphony No. 1 with Bernard Haitink conducting the London Philharmonic. As big an Elgarian thrill as I have ever had came on entering the same hall while Sir Georg Solti was in the middle of rehearsing the self-same LPO in a work I then barely knew, the concert overture *In The South (Alassio)*. I arrived to be knocked backward at that point where Elgar imagines the ancient Romans as (in his words) 'the relentless and domineering onward force of the ancient day'. What a passage that is! In recent times, we have (for example) the enthusiastic embracing of Elgar's music by Vasily Petrenko during his tenure as principal conductor of the Royal Liverpool Philharmonic Orchestra. But how far have such conductors championed – or been *able* to champion – a meaningful *range* of major Elgar works away from the UK in concerts with non-British orchestras? Vladimir Ashkenazy's library of Elgar recordings with the Sydney Symphony Orchestra is a rarity.

That teenage perception of mine that British music, not least by Elgar, was a 'niche interest', not to be trumpeted too loudly, persisted for all too many years. From my spell as an artist manager in the late 1970s/early 1980s, I remember a dinner table conversation with the 'cellist of an Austrian-based string quartet of some note, during which I raised the subject of the Elgar Cello Concerto. Very good, yes, he agreed – but it was the only Elgar he knew. I remember the shyness with which I then suggested to this flag-bearer for Austria's distinguished place in musical history that there might be other Elgar repertoire he could sample … you know, if he had a spare moment now and again. Occasionally, as a journalist, I've had cause to raise the subject of British music in conversations with contacts on the Continent. One concert promoter in Germany shrugged her shoulders at the inability of audiences there to stand for anything more in Elgarian terms than, maybe, the *Enigma Variations* if you were lucky. Elgar's fundamentally 'Germanic' musical language counted for nothing. I just nodded feebly in a 'Well, what can you do?' kind of way.

Well, I'm more impatient these days. In my advancing years I'm less and less inclined to nod feebly, to settle for such equivocation. For one thing, I'm increasingly irritated by the very notion of attaching national labels to music. For heaven's sake, when it comes down to it, there are only individual composers, each with a greater or lesser ability to touch the hearts and minds of individual listeners. Person to person.

On the day I write this, I happen to have been discussing the subject of promoting the music of Vaughan Williams outside the UK with conductor Andrew Manze. He told me that he has abandoned describing RVW to orchestras as 'the British composer, Vaughan Williams', in favour of simply 'the composer, Vaughan Williams'. I would venture to suggest that if this should be the approach with Vaughan Williams (and Manze reckons his bold stance helps the cause) then it should all the more be the case with Elgar – to my mind, beyond any other of his British actual and near contemporaries. A lifetime of savouring Elgar's music leaves me placing him ever higher among the composers of his day, of any nationality. In his own right, he gives the lie to those endlessly quoted, odiously shallow words penned by German critic Oscar Schmitz in 1904, describing Britain as 'Das Land ohne Musik': 'The land without music', for goodness' sake.

It's not that I would choose to describe Elgar as a 'great' composer. If such adjectives are not to become devalued, the appendage should surely only be attached to the very few who either substantially/dramatically changed the trajectory of musical expression or whose work is possessed of a certain monumentality of achievement. But to pick up the brief for this essay – for this volume – Elgar can emphatically be described as 'important', as long as that word can be applied across all national boundaries and not refer just to his standing in his native country.

How then to define 'importance'? Oh, I could do my best to break down in detail the constituent elements of Elgar's craft, from his ability to shape meaningful melodic lines and his ear for sound to his complex explorations of human emotion and his undoubted mastery of the technical nuts and bolts of composition. But the more you try to tie down compositional talent in such a fashion the more it slips through your fingers. To put it simply: whatever his means, Elgar was possessed of all it took to fashion richly satisfying music of profundity and humanity which can speak to anyone, anywhere, not ignoring his ability to spin lighter music of charm and elegance. And unlike my teenage self I certainly no longer compartmentalise Elgar in the confines of a previous musical era. He speaks to my emotions in the present. We connect.

To sum up. Elgar's 'importance' is such that no explorer of the music composed during his lifetime, no student of that period, can possibly consider themselves fully informed if they have not delved deep into the proper breadth of his music. The massive expansion of the scope of the recording industry's output has gratifyingly brought to our attention a host of composers active in Elgar's lifetime who have languished in the shadows as far as an international audience is concerned, whether it's the likes of the Swede, Kurt Atterberg, Russia's Alexander Glazunov or Johan Wagenaar in the Netherlands. But how many among them approach the stature of Edward Elgar as a craftsman and a distiller of human emotion? So what if he didn't write as many symphonies as Sibelius, or any operas or copious amounts of chamber music and song? He gave the world a sizeable enough body of work of sufficiently high quality across a range of genres to be taken seriously as 'the composer Elgar' – without the prefix of 'British'.

If we're not careful, being shy about Elgar's true 'importance' can prevent us from appreciating *just how* remarkable, by any standards, are familiar Elgar works. We can easily take them for granted. *What* an astoundingly imaginative work is the Cello Concerto! How truly breathtaking to inhabit the unique world of *Gerontius* for an evening. What searching substance there is in the two symphonies. On a lesser scale, the intense introspection of the Piano Quintet, the dazzling brilliance of the concert overtures *Cockaigne* and *In the South*, the fabulous anthem *Great is the Lord* ... and so on and so on.

It doesn't have to be the big Elgarian musical statements that display his extraordinary skills: his 'importance'. Which brings us full circle, to the *Introduction and Allegro*. A work displaying all the technical skill Elgar had at his disposal, from the immaculately conceived structure and his contrapuntal mastery to that acute ear for string sonority and the breadth of feeling. But don't take my word for all that. In one of very many Elgar-related discussions I savoured with the afore-mentioned Jerrold Northrop Moore, I happened to make the most passing of references to the *Introduction and Allegro*. Before I could begin my next sentence, Jerry interjected just three words: 'A perfect work'. And so it is.

~ Daniel Grimley

Elgar's Instrumental Alchemy: Colour, Value, Timbre in his Orchestral Music

Richard Strauss's cordial toast, following a performance of *The Dream of Gerontius* at the Lower Rhenish Musical Festival in Düsseldorf on 20 May 1902, to 'the health and success of the first English progressivist, Meister Edward Elgar', has often been cited as one of the breakthrough moments in Elgar's international reputation.[1] Yet the basis for Strauss's rare encomium – the question of what had drawn him so powerfully to his English colleague's work – is unclear. Contemporary German critics commented widely on the intensely mystical 'post-Parsifalian' atmosphere of Elgar's oratorio, and on the solemnity of Elgar's musical treatment of Newman's text. Strauss may further have been struck by the innovative, *sui generis* formal structure of the work, its deft handling of a sophisticated *Leitmotivic* texture, and its through-composed narrative arc, tracing the dying soul's journey toward purgatory. But it is difficult to believe that, for a committed Nietzschean and the composer of *Salome*, it was the devotional aspects of Elgar's work which appealed primarily to Strauss's imagination. What surely caught his ear instead was the sheer sonic impact of Elgar's music, especially his treatment of the orchestra. It was in this respect, above all, that Elgar could justifiably claim to be at the front rank of modern European composition. And it was his orchestration, not only in *The Dream of Gerontius* but throughout his work from *Froissart* onwards, that announced him as such a fresh and distinctive presence in English music. As one of his closest musical friends and collaborators, the violinist Billy Reed, recalled, on hearing Elgar's work for the first time: 'I was so thrilled by the music, and by what was to my ear the newness of the orchestral sound'[2]

1 Jerrold Northrop Moore, *Edward Elgar: A Creative Life* (Oxford: Oxford University Press, 1999 [1984]), 368–9. Strauss's toast was widely reported in the British press, for instance in *The Times* on Friday 23 May 1902 (p. 10), and in the same day's *Manchester Courier* (p. 4).

2 W.H. Reed, *Elgar as I Knew Him* (Oxford: Oxford University Press, 1989 [1936]), 21.

It is curious, then, that the orchestral timbre of Elgar's music has not received more systematic investigation. Extensive attention has focused on biography and critical reception, aspects of Elgar's distinctive harmonic syntax, and his approach to large-scale musical form. And, at the time of writing, a digital humanities project is seeking to stimulate renewed interest in the concept of the 'Elgarian theme'. But beyond passing references (often of a highly insightful kind) in the wider literature to specific instances of textural realisation or orchestral layout, there has been no dedicated study of Elgar's instrumentation that has sought to explore how timbre plays a formative role in his work. Such a study is beyond the limitations of the current essay, but it is hoped that thinking more intensively about the use of timbre in Elgar's orchestral scores might support greater understanding of other parameters of his work and its place within early twentieth-century European composition.

One reason for the absence of more sustained discussion of Elgar's orchestration is that there is no widely accepted theoretical framework for the analysis of musical timbre comparable with the well-established and familiar methodologies for harmony or motivic development. Alexander Rehding and Emily Dolan remark that timbre has traditionally been regarded as little more than 'an afterthought';[3] it remains an elusive concept. One of the earliest attempts to formulate a definition, by Jean-Jacques Rousseau in his entry for Denis Diderot and Jean le Rond d'Alembert's 1765 *Encyclopédie*, as David Blake notes, recognised that 'differences between sounds are produced from sonic qualities distinct from pitch, rhythm, and dynamics', yet was unable to move beyond basic descriptive ways of referring to particular timbres and their practical use.[4] Growing insistence in the nineteenth century on sound's fundamentally non-representational character promoted the idea of music's essentially 'neutral' quality; orchestration was hence a colour or tincture to be applied once the purer, more intellectually elevated work of composition was done. Yet developing interest in programme music challenged such platonic notions of musical meaning, and for late nineteenth-century composers, pre-eminently Richard Wagner, orchestral timbre assumed an altogether more essential role, one that lay at the core of music's value and significance.

3 Alexander Rehding and Emily I. Dolan, 'Timbre: Alternative Histories and Possible Futures for the Study of Music', in Rehding and Dolan (eds), *The Oxford Handbook of Timbre* (Oxford and New York: Oxford University Press, 2018), 2–20, at 2.

4 David Blake, 'Timbre', in Alexander Rehding and Steven Rings (eds), *The Oxford Handbook of Critical Concepts in Music Theory* (Oxford and New York: Oxford University Press, 2018), 136–59, at 139.

It is precisely its ability to move listeners in powerful and immediate ways that lies at the root of timbre's complexity. As Blake suggests, 'timbre is not simply acoustical but *psychoacoustical*';[5] it is an emergent category, determined both by the physical properties of the sound-object and also by the acoustic response of the listening subject (which is in turn shaped by the conditions of their auditory environment). This ambiguity is captured by the linguistic associations of the relevant terms in French and German. The French *sonore/sonorité*, for example, refers simultaneously to the sound itself and to the act of (re)sounding, as well as to a sound's qualities or characteristics, combining noun, verb, and adjective. The German *Klang* works similarly, with the added complication that the term was also used in music theory to refer to chord formations, principally the triad, which formed the basis for elaborate theories of harmonic function and musical relation (from Hugo Riemann to Heinrich Schenker). Twentieth-century composers became increasingly preoccupied with the metaphysical associations of this idea of *Klang* or *sonore* as a resonant, vibrating acoustical phenomenon, one that could assume a quasi-mystical significance beyond the boundaries of linguistic representation.[6] This was the context in which Strauss understood timbre's role, and in which his younger contemporary, Arnold Schoenberg, coined the phrase *Klangfarbe* (usually translated as 'tone-colour') in his 1911 treatise *Harmonielehre*. 'Farben', the third of Schoenberg's *Five Orchestral Pieces*, op. 16, composed in 1909 and first performed in London in 1912, applied the principle of *Klangfarben* creatively by exploring the shifting colours and affective associations of a single (non-diatonic) chord through a series of gradually changing instrumental combinations.

Elgar was highly attuned to the affective properties of musical timbre. In an undated manuscript account of childhood memories in Worcester, visiting a family in the cathedral precinct, for instance, he recalled:

> The drawing room was lined with books, books, all leather-bound & faded: the curtains also & the silk bands which held them, all were faded to a soft golden brown, as was the piano. When Broadwood sent it by long & weary road fifty years before, its mahogany had surely

5 Ibid., 141.

6 See, for example, Christopher Hailey, *Franz Schreker: A Cultural Biography* (Cambridge: Cambridge University Press, 1993); James Hepokoski, *Sibelius: Symphony no. 5* (Cambridge: Cambridge University Press, 1993); Karen Painter, 'The Sensuality of Timbre: responses to Mahler and Modernity at the Fin de Siècle', *Nineteenth-Century Music*, 18/3 (1995), 236–56; John J. Sheinbaum, 'Adorno's Mahler and the Timbral Outsider', *Journal of the Royal Musical Association*, 131/1 (2006), 38–82.

> been a rich red: but time had shaded all the tints to one mellow tone – & I played in a golden-brown room.[7]

Elgar's reminiscence is striking not simply for the Proustian precision of its description, but the way that colour, sound, time and place become merged into a single shade or mood, gathered up in the instrument's tone: it is a process of timbral intensification.[8] This pattern of strong association was characteristic of much of Elgar's thinking about the relationship between music, sound and his creative environment. His oft-quoted letter to Sidney Colvin of 13 December 1921, for example, in which he confided 'I am still at heart the dreamy child who used to be found in the reeds by Severn side with a sheet of paper trying to fix the sounds & longing for something very great – source, texture & all else unknown', is as much about the significance of timbre (the evocative sound of the reeds on the river bank) as a wistful reflection on the mythic origins of musical creativity.[9]

At the same time, Elgar's interest in timbre was also sharply practical. He learned the essential principles of orchestration from the standard texts of the time (both translated from French), Anton Reicha's *Orchestral Primer* and Hector Berlioz's *Treatise on instrumentation and Orchestration* (which Strauss updated and revised in 1904), as well as from practical experience: Elgar's friends and contemporaries attest to his fine ear for instrumental layout and scoring in multiple empirical contexts. Wulstan Atkins, for instance, recorded his admiration for Handel's orchestration in *Messiah*, in particular the use of the second violins to double an alto line, 'bringing that part into prominence by throwing it into the upper octave', and praising 'the wonderfully resonant effect Handel obtained by the spacing of his chords in a chorus like "Their sound is gone out"'.[10] Elgar similarly wrote glowingly to his Yorkshire friend Dr Buck about Dvořák's music, describing it as 'simply ravishing, so tuneful & clever & the orchestration is wonderful; no matter how few instruments he uses it never sounds thin'.[11] Elgar had been deeply moved by a performance of Dvořák's *Stabat Mater* at the 1884 Three Choirs Festival in Worcester, and the opening pages of

7 Moore, *Edward Elgar*, 24.

8 On Elgar and Proust, see Byron Adams, 'A Far Country: Elgar, Proust and Modernity at the Fin de Siècle', lecture read at Gresham College, 14 December 2007, available online at https://www.gresham.ac.uk/watch-now/elgar-musical-modernism-fin-de-siecle [accessed 14 January 2025].

9 Matthew Riley, *Edward Elgar and the Nostalgic Imagination* (Cambridge: Cambridge University Press, 2007), 85–6.

10 Moore, op. cit., 57.

11 Letter dated 28 September 1884, quoted in Jerrold Northrop Moore (ed.), *Edward Elgar: Letters of a Lifetime* (Rickmansworth: Elgar Works, 2012), 15.

the Czech composer's score offer a particularly striking example of timbral design: the work begins with a single pitch (F sharp), *pianissimo*, scored for horns, violas and cellos, which is then registerally and texturally amplified by the gradual addition of oboes, clarinets, violins, flutes and bassoons. These timbral shifts create a slow process of colour modulation which is only later revealed as a giant dominant preparation for the work's actual tonic (B minor).

Further evidence of Elgar's approach to instrumental timbre is evidenced in his correspondence with Herbert Brewer concerning the orchestration of Brewer's oratorio *Emmaus* with which Elgar generously assisted. Elgar's letters record how he '*fattened* out the p.f. arrgt' at the climax of the orchestral introduction, and queried the effect required at a later passage: 'I gave this wholly (except final chords) for strings – I don't think it wants *colour* but you may have meant it for *wind* – but I give the soft wind a chance (contrasting) at letter R'. His correspondence also addresses matters of doubling and balance between instruments and singers: '2 bars before S. I struck c in first Vio: to avoid clashing with vocal part – also in the *rall* What is notable here are Elgar's references to weight or body of sound ('fatness'), colour, and texture ('soft' winds), alongside other matters of practical realisation, such as his comments that 'the harp is effective but *ad lib*, and 'thinking you will use the organ in other more likely places I've not put it in except a ped: or two in introduction':[12] Elgar's sparing use of the organ to underpin pivotal moments of timbral arrival in his own works, not merely the oratorios but also (poignantly) the finale of his Second Symphony, was in this sense the refined application of an already familiar procedure.

Elgar was notoriously reluctant to speak publicly about his working methods, but he did offer a rare insight as part of the lectures he gave during his tenure as Peyton Professor of Music at the University of Birmingham. In his talk on Brahms's Third Symphony, given on 8 November 1905, for example, he described the work's orchestration as 'noble and restrained', but commented more negatively on the 'curiously "casual" passages – ending *pp* fiendishly difficult to get "level" – doubling the third', noting that 'where special effects are intended – such as "solo" passages for any instruments – we must not cavil but accept what is given us, but where we see a Tutti – full force and the effect is thin we may enquire where the disappointment lies'. Turning his attention to the final chords of the first movement in particular, he noted that 'the third appears nine times', resulting in a 'dull, heavy effect',

[12] Letter dated 30 June 1901, quoted in ibid., 114–15.

and parsing the specific instrumental layout of Brahms's score to conclude: 'Trumpet parts – cruel.'[13]

Elgar's criticisms of Brahms's orchestration underline the difficulty of blending different instrumental timbres and of obtaining intonational consistency (more difficult for the third of a triad than the tonic or fifth because of the fundamental frequencies of the harmonic spectrum), as well as different instruments' ability to speak effectively at particular dynamic levels (softer, sustained sounds are easier for the strings and woodwind than for the trumpets, where maintaining constant lip pressure at that dynamic in such a low register is challenging). His remarks stand in sharp contrast to a passage from his final lecture of the first term, 'In Retrospect', given on 13 December, where he quoted at length from Tchaikovsky's correspondence. Writing of his Fourth Symphony, Tchaikovsky claimed: 'I never compose in the *abstract*, that is to say, the musical thought never appears otherwise than in a suitable external form. In this way I invent the musical idea and the instrumentation simultaneously'[14] In this light, it is tempting to draw parallels, for example, between Tchaikovsky's delicately pointillistic scoring in the second movement of his *Manfred Symphony* with that of the scherzo in Elgar's own First, which he would complete just three years after his lecture.

It was only in his (foreshortened) second series of lectures, however, that Elgar turned to the question of timbre and instrumentation as a primary topic, explaining in his talk on orchestration, given on 1 November 1906, that 'orchestration in its highest sense, is the art of *composing* for an orchestra; Not the perfunctory matter of ARRANGING ideas for instruments.' For Elgar, orchestration was properly 'a real, living branch of creative art, not (as the erroneous definition would *lead an enquirer to think*), a mere labour: a transference of ideas from one medium to another, – or painting, as *it were*, a picture in colour from a mezzotint.'[15] He then pointedly echoed the passage he had quoted from Tchaikovsky's letters the previous year by suggesting that 'I find it impossible to imagine a composer creating a musical idea *without defining inwardly, and simultaneously*, the exact means of its presentation.' For Elgar, the overriding concern was a question of harmony, understood here not in its conventional sense but specifically *as* timbre: the

13 Percy M. Young (ed.), *Edward Elgar: 'A Future for English Music' and Other Lectures* (London: Dobson, 1968), 103.

14 Ibid., 221. The quotation is not identified in Elgar's text (nor in Young's volume), but is taken from a letter to Nadezhda von Meck, 5/17 March 1878, quoted in Modeste Tchaikovsky, *The Life and Letters of Peter Illich Tchaikovsky*, ed. with an introduction by Rosa Newmarch (London: John Lane, The Bodley Head, 1906), 281.

15 Young (ed.), op. cit., 235.

overall impression made by the sounding-together of different instruments. On this basis, he juxtaposed piano music with the richer palette of an orchestral score, arguing: 'It is too easily assumed that the piano is capable of reproducing not only the orchestral EFFECTS but orchestral harmony also *and pianists expect* an orchestra piece to sound well on their favourite instrument.' Thinking perhaps about his own limitations as a performer, Elgar explained that 'the rigid piano is capable of only two *qualities of tone simultaneously in the hands of a moderate player*', whereas 'the modern orchestra is capable of an unending variety of *shades of tone*, not only in succession, but in combination.' Anticipating Schoenberg's emphasis on *Klangfarbe*, Elgar then suggested that 'a whole world of new *harmonies is at* the disposal of a composer for orchestra: harmonies which may sound execrable and impossible on the piano but which may give the greatest pleasure when scored for instruments.' Unlike Brahms, he described how 'the dissonant notes *of a chord* may be merely suggested by the soft-toned instruments, or they may be thundered *out by the heavy-toned ones, while the principal notes* of the chord – the backbone – is *merely suggested*.'[16] In the final section of his lecture, he commented on the orchestra's development, referring to it as a 'complex machine'[17] that evolved through the addition of new instruments, alluding to his own desire at one stage to include four saxophones in the orchestra for *Caractacus*. Elgar swiftly abandoned the idea for reasons of availability and expense, but the saxophone would soon find a prominent place in later orchestral scores, from Ravel's *Bolero* to Vaughan Williams's Sixth Symphony.

Attempting to account fully for the distinctive sound of Elgar's orchestration would require a far more in-depth study than is possible here and inevitably pose wider questions of historical performance practice and realisation. The remainder of this essay instead reviews a few selected instances of Elgar's approach, drawing attention to three broad timbral principles which underpin his orchestral practice: first, colour or special effect (the use of solo or unusual instruments); second, blend or registration (the mixing of different instrumental configurations to obtain a specific sound); and third, stratification, depth or volume (namely, the arrangement of instrumental layers so as to increase or decrease the impression of size or scale). At one end of that spectrum, Elgar's use of solo instruments within an ensemble context frequently followed established nineteenth-century practice, where a particular instrument is briefly 'spotlighted' to create a heightened feeling of emotional intensity. A normative example is the

16 Ibid., 237–9.
17 Ibid., 239.

passage for solo violin at b. 70 in the first movement of the *Serenade for Strings*, op. 20. Marked *espress.*, the soloist states a variation of the movement's lyrical second subject in dialogue with the rest of the first violins in the middle section of the movement, leading to the reprise of the opening subject at b. 92. The fleeting sense of introspection, however, is later enhanced by Elgar's nostalgic recollection of the same solo, now restfully in the tonic major, on the closing page of the finale (b. 52): a characteristic gesture of thematic recall he would develop in many of his later works (notably the Cello Concerto).[18]

Greater emotional impact is achieved by the clarinet solo in Variation XIII, '***', of the *Variations for Orchestra ('Enigma')*, op. 36, which quotes a three-note figure from Mendelssohn's Overture *Calm Sea and Prosperous Voyage*. Elgar himself is supposed to have alluded to the emotional connotations of this passage and its association with one of his Worcestershire friends and patrons, Lady Mary Lygon. Yet the clarinet figure's effect relies on its unusual musical context, heard against a gently rocking 16-bar viola ostinato, solo cello pedal, and timpani roll played with hard sticks. The passage's intensity is further amplified when it is taken up by the trombones, *pianississimo*, with the viola ostinato and cello pedal (now in *tremolo*) spread across the full string section, accompanied by the (unpitched) bass drum: an eerie effect which, according to Ernest Newman, Elgar compared to the 'throbbing engines' of an ocean liner, 'dwelling in imagination on somebody or something the parting from whom and which had at some time or other torn the very heart out of him.'[19] Whether or not it refers to Lady Lygon, it is one of several passages in Elgar's work that suggest the noise of some enormous but hidden machine moving inexorably unseen.

Other instances of solo instrumental writing in Elgar's orchestral music are no less emotionally marked. The clarinet solo at the end of *Falstaff*, for example, has a similarly poignant quality to that of Variation XIII in op. 36: a sense of reluctant departure or regretful reminiscence, in this case implied by the pain of Falstaff's banishment and the fond memory of his former relationship with the young Prince Hal. Earlier in the same work (at Fig. 76), an extended 'Dream Interlude' for solo violin serves as a plaintive portrait of the work's protagonist himself as a young man, 'Jack Falstaff, now Sir John, a boy and page to Thomas Mowbray, Duke of Norfolk.' For this episode, which Elgar originally sketched as a piano miniature, he pares back the accompaniment to a walking bass in the lower strings, delicately

18 Riley, op. cit., 32ff.

19 Julian Rushton, *Elgar: 'Enigma' Variations, op. 36* (Cambridge: Cambridge University Press, 1999), 53 and 76.

punctuated by harp and horn, omitting the heavy brass and percussion which dominate the more belligerently modern sounding passages associated with the new King that frame the work's conclusion. The association between the solo violin and childhood is a timbral theme that Elgar adopts elsewhere, for instance in the final movement, 'Dreaming – Envoy', of the Nursery Suite, which might cautiously be identified with the autobiographical figure of Elgar himself. A different effect again is achieved by the entry of the solo viola with the first statement of the so-called 'Welsh theme' in the *Introduction and Allegro*, op. 47. Here, the theme's emergence is made more telling by the way the solo viola appears unexpectedly out of the ensemble: an 'inner voice' seemingly summoned from within the concertante group that suggests a sudden connectedness with a deeper emotional layer after the stern neo-Baroque gestures of the opening page and the fleeting evocation of the sounds of an aeolian harp that follow.

These passages differ again from the role of solo instruments in a larger, more ambitious work such as *The Apostles*, op. 49. The oratorio itself begins with a striking timbral image: after a swelling initiatory pedal tone on the organ, timpani and lower strings, a gently swaying curtain of sound quietly announces the opening motif, scored for woodwind choir (that is, the whole section including contrabassoon but minus piccolo, oboes and cor anglais), horns, harp and multiply divided strings. After the conclusion of the Prologue, a contrasting scena entitled 'In the Mountain – Night', borrows from earlier nineteenth-century evocations of wild alpine environments, pre-eminently the third movement ('Scène aux champs') of Berlioz's *Symphonie Fantastique*. Scored for an imitative group of oboes and solo cor anglais, played 'outside the orchestra' (i.e. offstage) and accompanied by a pedal in the cellos and double basses and hollow strokes on the timpani and bass drum, the passage creates a Mahlerian sense of wilderness and desolation. The solos return symmetrically at the end of the sequence but then give way to an even more striking effect: the entry of a solo trumpet evoking the sound of the shofar and summoning the first glimmers of dawn on the temple walls at Hebron. Elgar specified that a 'straight' (or 'herald') trumpet should be used to heighten the brilliance of the sound.[20] But the effectiveness of this transition relies equally on the abrupt timbral contrast between the trumpet's shining metallic timbre and the softer reeds, and by the way that the shofar's initial summons is echoed by the clarinet and horns and the re-entry of the chorus ('It shines!'), punctuated by the strings, upper woodwind, and percussion. As the dawn light grows, the resonant sound of

[20] See, for instance, Elgar's letter to Hans Richter, dated 28 August 1903, quoted in Moore (ed.), *Letters of a Lifetime*, op. cit., 154–5.

the shofar's call is amplified by the addition of the main trumpet group after Fig. 26, functioning in effect as a 'hyper-instrument', ushering the morning psalm. It is only as the sun itself rises, several pages later at Fig. 35, however, that Elgar finally releases the full orchestra, *fortississimo*, in a spectacular sequence marked *più lento, solenne*. Here, the trumpets are integrated as part of a multi-layered tutti, where the pulsating triplet writing for horns anticipates their role (along with the side drum) as this figure returns in the carefully terraced approach to the work's radiant final climax, at Figs. 232–3, celebrating Christ's ascension. Little wonder that Jaeger, Elgar's friend and confidant at Novello's, was moved to write: 'really, there is nothing in music like this', and described the temple sequence as 'colour most gorgeous & new, effects most astounding & bewildering, organ! &c&c'.[21]

Elgar's timbral innovations in *The Apostles* suggest the suffusion of light, but timbral saturation of a different kind is evident in pages of the Second Symphony. Though the scoring is dense throughout, a number of key passages particularly stand out. The first occurs in the central development section of the opening movement at Fig. 28: the strange *più lento* sequence, relatively slow moving but insistently propelled by the timpani, bass drum and double basses, over which spectral fragments of the symphony's opening theme and the 'Judgement' motif from *The Dream of Gerontius* drift past alongside rising chromatic figures in the flutes and violas. Elgar's employment of solo alongside tutti strings and the independent writing for two harps further complicates the stratification of the multiple timbral layers: an ingenious and seemingly irresistible mechanism which he once compared to 'a love scene in a garden at night when the ghost of some memories comes through it'.[22] If feelings of a supernatural presence are seemingly banished by the reprise of the opening subject and the movement's buoyant conclusion, they return with much greater violence in the central episode of the third movement, a rondo whose essentially playful ebb and flow is briefly seized by a much more ominous and belligerent feeling of forward momentum. Here, the ostinato figuration initiated by the wind and timpani at Fig. 119 is passed over to a 'rhythm battery' comprising two harps, bass drum, cymbals, side drum, tambourine and lower strings, with the trombones in counterpoint with fragments of the *scherzo*'s principal subject in the woodwind and upper strings at Fig. 120: a layering that ensures maximal potential for accumulating depth, weight and

21 Letter dated 8 July 1903, quoted in Jerrold Northrop Moore (ed.), *Elgar and his Publishers: Letters of a Creative Life, vol. 1, 1885–1903* (Oxford: Clarendon Press, 1987), 457.

22 Letter to Ernest Newman, 29 January 1911, quoted in Moore (ed.), *A Creative Life*, op. cit., 603.

volume. The sequence reaches timbral and dynamic overload at Fig. 121, as though the orchestra is momentarily captured by a completely ulterior agency (memorably evoked in Sir Charles Mackerras's 1994 recording with the Royal Philharmonic Orchestra).

After this terrifying encounter, what Elgar referred to as the 'smoothing out' offered by the finale is as much timbral as tonal/rhythmic: the restoration of a more regular hierarchic textural order, including Elgar's distinctive 'nobilmente' sul-G writing for the first violins.[23] But the movement's most touching gesture of timbral reconciliation is where the transfigured reappearance of the 'Spirit of Delight' motif from the opening movement (Fig. 168), luminously scored for winds, harps, and strings, and surely modelled on the final bars of Brahms's Third Symphony, gives way to a much sparer, more fragile texture for strings alone with two tiny harp interjections (Fig. 170^{+5}) as the finale's closing figure returns. It was perhaps this passage that Alice Elgar had in mind when she wrote in her diary of the 'wonderful music of the end of the 4th. movement', and of the symphony's concern with 'our human life, delight, regret, farewell, the saddest word & the strong man's triumph'.[24] But triumph is hardly the mood suggested by the timbral quality of these bars: they instead suggest a deeper feeling of openness and acceptance, an acknowledgement of their own contingency, which is ultimately more compelling.[25]

Thinking through timbre thus offers key insights into the colour and value of Elgar's orchestral music and its distinctive affects. The magically alchemical ability of Elgar's work to mix and combine very different emotional states and conditions is motivated by his foundational concern with the modern condition, and its complex contradictory streams, impulses and impressions. And it is through the sound of his orchestral scores, pre-eminently works such as the Second Symphony, that Elgar offered his most searching insights into that state of being. It was perhaps this quality that prompted Strauss's accolade at the Lower Rhenish Musical Festival, as he raised his glass to Elgar and the 'young progressivist school of English composers'.

[23] Elgar's expression occurs in a letter to Alfred Littleton at Novello dated 13 April 1911, quoted in ibid., 609.

[24] Diary entries dated 22 and 21 February 1911, quoted in ibid., p. 610.

[25] For a more sophisticated reading of this gesture, see J.P.E. Harper-Scott, 'Elgar's Deconstruction of the *belle époque*: interlace structures and the Second Symphony', in J.P.E. Harper-Scott and Julian Rushton (eds), *Elgar Studies* (Cambridge: Cambridge University Press, 2007), 172–219, at 219.

~ Stephen Hough

Marches abound in musical cultures all over the world and were usually written for ceremonial or military purposes, to regulate the step of soldiers' boots or arouse patriotism in the spectators – striding towards war and destruction or shoring up courage for defence. Then there are Wedding Marches celebrating with joyous exuberance a new life of two-made-one; and, at the other end of life, Funeral Marches which suggest the slow tread of a dead life's final journey, a coffin aloft before a descent into the grave.

I don't think it's an exaggeration to say that Elgar's *Pomp and Circumstance* March No. 1, from 1901, gave this old form a new purpose. Not only does its swagger lift the spirits with a patriotic surge as marches had done before, but it lends a special novel tug of emotion to the central section: the uniform's sleeve now wears a heart as well as epaulets. Elgar knew he'd written a winner: 'I've got a tune that will knock'em – knock'em flat', he said, and a year later words by A.C. Benson were added: 'Land of Hope and Glory'. It is now sung all over the world with gusto and affection.

The orchestral March itself began its life in Merseyside, in a performance conducted by the composer, dedicated to his friend Arthur Rodewald and his Liverpool Orchestral Society. Two days later, on 21 October 1901, it was played at the London Promenade Concerts. Sir Henry Wood recalled that the audience 'rose and yelled ... the one and only time in the history of the Promenade concerts that an orchestral item was accorded a double encore'.

Over a hundred years later they still rise and yell, and every year at the BBC Proms, its 'encore' unfailingly occurs as an unbreakable tradition, never ceasing to thrill and intoxicate. Why is that? The words have caused controversy over past decades with their late-Victorian imperialism, but any response to those sentiments by an audience is hugely overshadowed by the appeal of the music itself. The text would bite the dust of history with a different tune, but the tune would still enchant with other words – a tribute to Elgar's unique mix of rhythmic thrust, melodic genius, and harmonic alchemy. And structure. The central section would not work in the same way unless we'd arrived there after facing the javelins of the opening swashbuckling section, with the composer's characteristic major sevenths and heart-tugging suspensions.

A suspension, or an appoggiatura, is a built-in yearning present in Western classical music across the ages. A dissonant note is held and then released, and the brain responds to this exquisite 'torture' with pleasure. It's one of the main building blocks of all expressivity in music, and Elgar's use of it throughout his works is extra-strength, gold label, turbo-charged.

As we begin to hear the March, with its flare of unison E flat trumpets leading to the spiky darting violin figure, our hearts surge again, not with the violence of war, or the toxic exclusion of nationalism, but as citizens of a world of music which is universal. We await the central tune where, finally, we can sing together with open mouths and open hearts. 'Wider still, and wider'; every voice is welcome.

~ Andrew Keener

My parents' modest collection of classical LPs rested against the wall behind the radiogram in the front room of the house in South Wales where I grew up. The sleeve of Jascha Horenstein's *New World* rubbed shoulders with Cor de Groote's Rachmaninov, while a Sophia Loren lookalike inviting us to experience the delights of Rimsky-Korsakov's re-telling of *A Thousand and One Nights* sat uneasily beside Sir Malcolm Sargent's Tchaikovsky Fifth. I was disdainful, preferring my 45rpm single of B. Bumble and the Stingers' take on Tchaikovsky or the enticingly raunchy *House of the Rising Sun*, Eric Burdon's rude-boy vocals awakening something in my pubescent self which I was only beginning fully to recognise. But nestling behind that radiogram was also a 7" EP of the first two movements of the *Three Bavarian Dances* and Elgar's *Serenade for Strings* conducted by Lawrance Collingwood, HMV producer and conductor of those poignant sessions of excerpts from *Caractacus* which the dying composer supervised via a Post Office line from his death bed at Marl Bank. A seminal discovery, that small piece of vinyl.

To this day my mind's ear can never hear the end of the second Bavarian Dance without recalling the radiogram's auto-stop mechanism nudging the closing bars, causing them to repeat *ad infinitum*. Other Elgar recordings followed, quickly becoming embedded so deeply in my consciousness that I could mentally 'lip-synch' them. Prominent were Sir Adrian Boult's Lyrita accounts of the symphonies from the late 1960s, recordings which tend to be rather overlooked these days. Why? There's an energy and sweep in these performances beside which Boult's EMI remakes always strike me as if conducted in carpet slippers. It seems that Sir Adrian had a temper, so perhaps it was the insistence of Kenneth Wilkinson, doyen of Decca recording engineers on those Lyrita sessions, that Boult seat his second violins beside rather than opposite the firsts which provoked that venerable Elgarian to the incandescent result. Not that I can support such provocation. Elgar would say to the second violins, 'enjoy this melody, I wrote it especially for you', and there are surely few orchestral scores, from Haydn onwards, that fail to benefit from placing first and second violins antiphonally – '...two equal shoulders on either side of a head', as Toscanini described it.

And of course there was Jacqueline du Pré's 1965 EMI recording with Barbirolli of the Cello Concerto which, while my schoolboy contemporaries kicked a ball about in summer sunshine, I played in the privacy of my bedroom until the LP grooves were grey, comparing du Pré's generous *portamenti* with Pierre Fournier's patrician restraint, Pablo Casals's integrity and earthy sound, and Paul Tortelier's range of colour within a fast, focussed vibrato (wonderful partnership with Boult). For these I owe gratitude to the long-defunct Cardiff Record Library, and with score in hand as I listened, they and other Elgar recordings of the day offered irresistible ear-training for a future career as a recording producer. And what a superfine orchestral inner ear there is at work in these miraculous works by this self-taught genius. My schoolboy self marvelled at his subtle use of timpani at such moments as bar 8 in the slow movement of the Second Symphony – little *ppp* groups of three semiquavers, not audible as such, but adding, subliminally, the subtlest of meaning and extra sound to these bars, Elgar's sombre march of grief at the recent death of Edward VII. Another moment which opened my adolescent ears to Elgar's sound world came with the passage at the final climax of the opening movement of the First Symphony (from four bars before Fig. 47), where the *in extremis* character of the trumpets' and first violins' line is heightened by *tremolando* cellos, doubling the same line at the top of their register, defying standard treatises on orchestration. How much less climactic these bars would be without these added colours, tokens of the richest imagination, originality and sensitivity. A gradual awareness followed of Elgar's structural mastery, the thematic cross references, head indivisible from heart in their effect. Playing my grubby-sounding Pye LP of Barbirolli's Hallé Elgar's First Symphony, I marvelled, as all Elgarians do, at the metamorphosis of the scurrying semiquaver theme in the *scherzo* of the First Symphony to one of the most sublime slow movement themes in the repertoire.

Later, during my earliest days in London at the beginning of the 1980s, Sir Charles Groves, most self-effacing of distinguished Elgar conductors, told me that he could never decide at one bar before Fig. 30 in the first movement of the A flat Symphony whether or not to sub-divide his beat (not to do so might risk passing ensemble chaos, while the alternative might endanger the crucial sense of time suspended). With the score in front of me that evening, I turned to the final minute of the same movement and realized for the first time that here was the same theme, now consolatory in the home key. As with Brahms, such discoveries, more subtle yet than the above, are inexhaustible, lasting a lifetime. I'm still finding them. Such Damascene moments threatened to unhinge my younger self. Half a century later, they still do.

One hot day in 1970, that even younger self set out for Broadheath with his schoolfriend driving a battered Land Rover. The Second Symphony blared from a cassette recorder on the back seat. These were the days before the advent of the Visitor Centre at the Birthplace, and we straightaway entered the serenity of the cottage, the Dream Interlude from *Falstaff* a soft presence as we climbed the narrow stairs to the birth room. Insects buzzed in the hot tranquillity of the garden, evoking the second movement of the String Quartet. Never mind that the Land Rover broke down in the blistering heat on the way home, triggering a crippling headache. That pilgrimage to Broadheath was seared for ever.

For those to whom Elgar is part of one's musical DNA, does any composer more potently evoke past times in one's life? My susceptibility to his sound world, appreciation of the subtlety of this auto-didact's vision, has only increased with time. Producing recordings of his music over several decades has frequently resulted in an almost unbearable emotional response. One day, alone in a hotel room between producing sessions of music by another composer, I began editing a recording I had produced of the overture *In the South*, headphones clamped to my ears, contact with the music intimate and exclusive of all distracting surroundings. The transition which leads to the viola solo, *divisi* strings descending in misty pianissimo, suddenly brought tears at once healing and troubling, and I called the conductor of the recording, blusteringly wondering to him whether it was possible to go mad listening to music. 'Of course it is, my dear', he said. 'But you know I'm in Chicago at the moment, and it's 3am here'. I returned to the work, choosing – I hoped – the best take, objectivity restored.

~ Christopher Kent

Kenneth Howard Leech (1892–1995) ardent Elgarian

'Do you know Mr. Leech', asked the driver of the Calne branch line train in Chippenham station. 'No not yet', I replied. 'He invariably wears a trilby hat', continued the driver. A few weeks later again at Chippenham where, during my teens, I was aware that steam traction was in decline and the dark clouds of Beeching's economies were gathering, I spotted a slightly built man in a trilby hat and an old raincoat descending from the footplate of a locomotive. Little did I know that I had glimpsed a man who for the next 32 years was to be a fount of friendship, wisdom and understanding to me. He was truly a polymath: mechanical and design engineer, composer, author, mountaineer, photographer and a devoted Elgarian.

We first became acquainted through GWR steam locomotives, which following his retirement from Westinghouse in 1957 he drove unofficially, to which the authorities turned a blind eye as they deemed him 'a most responsible gentleman'. Kenneth arranged footplate rides for me: most memorably on an express from Chippenham to Bath. He drove and I fired, we roared out of Box tunnel at nearly 80 mph!

Shortly before this I had received an invitation to Kenneth's home, to meet Gladys, his wife, and sample her own brew of blended Lapsang Such-ong tea. It was not long before my attention was drawn to a miniature score of Tchaikovsky's Symphonic Fantasy *Francesca da Rimini* on the treble end of his pianola keyboard. Our minds met again but on another dimension, and on the regular Saturday morning visits that followed over the next four years Kenneth unassumingly introduced me to much of his collection of scores and recordings, the latter comprising discs and tapes recorded from broadcasts. His genius as a mechanical and electrical engineer had led him to record on discs of different materials such as Bakelite, coated steel or aluminium at 64 rather than 78 rpm. To reduce 'crackle' he would either fashion a needle from a garden thorn bush or treat some discs with lubricating oil. On his retirement as Chief Mechanical Engineer at Westinghouse, Kenneth was presented with a fine Ferrograph tape recorder. He bequeathed his scores and recordings to me, the latter I immediately placed into the care of the British Sound Archive.[1]

I owe Kenneth my early reverence for Romantic music. It was not always easy to find teachers and musicians to encourage this in the cynical *avant garde* world of the 1960s. Knowing me to have been deeply moved by my first hearing of the closing movement of Mahler's *Resurrection Symphony* Kenneth appreciated the strength of silence – he just shook me gently and warmly by the hand. That moment sealed our friendship. When I was fourteen he treated me as an adult, which was of great value and encouragement. His scores of works by Bax, Bruckner, Dvořák, Elgar, Franck, Mahler and Richard Strauss were lent to me according to their imminent performances on the newly inaugurated BBC Music Programme (Radio 3).

Although not a musicologist, as early as 1958 Kenneth anticipated the study of a composer's working methods when he visited the British Museum's Department of Manuscripts to note differences between the published score of Elgar's Violin Concerto and the holograph manuscript. He showed me his annotated score with these details, and it undoubtedly sowed the seed in my mind for future research into Elgar's compositional processes.

More was to follow, which was to influence me further in the direction of my future research. Whilst I was preparing an essay on Elgar to be submitted as part of my GCE 'O' level at Chippenham Secondary Modern School for Boys in 1964–5, Kenneth produced a fair copy manuscript in Elgar's hand given to him by Mrs Hill of Worcester. This was the cello part of a trio for violin, cello and piano of c.1889 which was subsequently revised and published as *Rosemary, that's for Remembrance* in 1915.

Following his service in the Railway Operating Division of the Royal Engineers during the Great War, Kenneth became a pupil for five years of Richard Walthew (1872–1951) of whom he wrote: '…he must have found me a trying handful, but his loveable character, his patience and skill, stripped me from the tangle of errors in which I had tried to write music, and eventually provided me with a new and thoroughly sound foundation of technique These qualities Walthew had previously assimilated from his own revered and generous teacher Hubert Parry.

Notwithstanding the economic depression and that he drove trains during the General Strike, Leech composed five string quartets, three violin sonatas, two piano quintets, two piano trios and aonatas for both viola and violoncello. Many received professional performances by such distinguished musicians as George Stratton and the Griller String Quartet. The largest genre comprises 164 songs composed between 1916 and 1989.

1 Now part of the British Library.

During the broadcasts of the BBC from Bristol in 1940 the bass-baritone Sinclair Logan performed two of Kenneth's settings of texts by the poet laureate, John Masefield, together with songs by George Butterworth, George Dyson and Ivor Gurney.

Eight of his ten scores for full orchestra are extant. They are fine examples of music calligraphy with the consistency and proportion becoming of a fine piece of engineering draughtsmanship. They include *To the Mountains* op. 29, dedicated to the two climbers who perished in the Mount Everest expedition of 1924. It was first performed at Morley College conducted by Michael Tippett. A decade later came his op. 32: *A Benediction in Farewell – To the memory of Sir Edward Elgar*. Kenneth conducted the premiere at the Kingsway Hall and, in 1938 following further public performances, it was broadcast by the BBC Symphony Orchestra conducted by Leslie Heward. The score is prefaced by these words from the magazine *Punch*: 'He passes from the shadowy daylight here, into the sublime dream.'

This work stems organically from phrases of sobriety but culminates in two climaxes before receding into the initial mood of tranquillity. In view of the acceptance of his recordings by the British Sound Archive it is regrettable that the same honour was not bestowed on his manuscripts by the British Library. It is fortunate that these have now been received into the collection of the Wiltshire and Swindon History Centre in Chippenham.

Kenneth's dedication and reverence for Elgar's music are nowhere more apparent than on the copiously annotated flyleaves of his copies of the miniature scores of the two symphonies as follows:

Appendix 1: Symphony No. 1

Chronicle of performances attended or recorded, 1923–92. Annotations transcribed from the flyleaves of his miniature score signed:
K H Leech, 1st August 1923.

Note. There were no London performances between Autumn 1919 and October 1923.

1. October 1923 Prom. Concert, Queen's Hall, Henry Wood.
2. December 1923 Queen's Hall, Aylmer Buesst.
3. December 4th 1924 Philharmonic, Queen's Hall, Bruno Walter. (Elgar present & called on 4 times).
4. February 20th 1926 Symphony Concert, Queen's Hall, Henry Wood.
5. April 26th 1926. LSO, Queen's Hall, Elgar.

6. September 8th 1927 Prom. Concert. Queen's Hall. Henry Wood.
7. September 4th 1928. Prom. Concert. Queen's Hall. Henry Wood.
8. August 15th 1929. Prom. Concert. Queen's Hall. Henry Wood.
9. October 24th 1929. Birmingham Symphony Concert from 5GB. Malcolm Sargent.
10. January 30th 1930. Philharmonic. Queen's Hall. Elgar.
11. September 11th 1930. Prom Concert. Queen's Hall. Henry Wood.
12. August 13th 1931. Prom Concert. Queen's Hall. Henry Wood.
13. December 7th 1931 LSO Prom Concert. Queen's Hall. Beecham (no coherence).
14. April 13th 1932. BBC Concert. Queen's Hall. Henry Wood.
15. November 30th 1932. BBC (Elgar Festival Concert). Landon Ronald (tempi?).
16. December 8th 1932. Birmingham Symphony Concert. Midland Region cond? (Very good)
17. December 4th 1933. LSO Queen's Hall. Hamilton Harty.
18. January 10th. 1934. BBC (Orchestra). Queen's Hall. Landon Ronald.
19. September 6th 1934. Prom Concert. Henry Wood.
20. September 5th 1935. Prom Concert. Queen's Hall. Henry Wood.
21. November 10th 1935. Broadcast. BBC Orchestra. Landon Ronald.
22. January 22nd 1936. Broadcast (Special Concert) BBC Orchestra. Boult (good).
23. August 18th 1936. Prom broadcast. Queen's Hall. Henry Wood.
24. December 7th 1938 Radio (house full) Queen's Hall. BBC Orchestra. Henry Wood (pulled about).
25. May 15th 1940. BBC Orchestra, Hamilton Harty (Radio from Bristol). Last movement poor others good.
26. April 22nd 1942. BBC Orchestra, Henry Wood (Radio). A race with Big Ben (dead heat!) 1st movement very fast.
27. November 11th 1942. BBC Orchestra, Boult (radio).
28. September 14th 1946. BBC Orchestra (radio) prom.
29. July 16th 1947. Raybould & Liverpool Philharmonic Orchestra (radio). Malvern Elgar Festival. Not much breadth.
30. August 7th 1947. Sargent & London Symphony Orchestra. (Prom). Very good, alive.
31. April 3rd 1948. Boult and BBC Orchestra (radio).
32. March 23rd 1949. Boult and BBC Orchestra. Scrappy, last movement bad.
33. August 16th 1949. Sargent and BBC Orchestra (prom).A magnificent performance, as near perfect as possible. Full of life yet with deepest feeling.

34. November 6th 1949. Boult and BBC Orchestra (radio).
35. November 29th 1950. Sargent and BBC Orchestra (radio). Not perfect. Tempi a little bit wrong.
36. November 30th 1950. Sargent and BBC Orchestra (radio). A little bit too slowly, but the slow movement was good.
37. August 16th 1951. John Hollingsworth and BBC Orchestra Prom (radio). Tempi and spirit excellent. A few details smudged.
38. May 28th 1952. Sargent and BBC Orchestra (radio). 1st very good, 2nd fast, 3rd slow, last scrappy.
39. December 3rd 1953. Sargent and BBC Orchestra (Radio). Exaggerated.
40. July 9th 1992. Andrew Litton and Bournemouth Orchestra (Radio?). Good.

Appendix 2: Symphony No. 2

Chronicle of performances attended or recorded, 1921–92. Annotations transcribed from the flyleaves of his miniature score were signed:
K H Leech, 1st August 1923.

1. Dec. 1921. People's Palace, Mile End. Saturday afternoon concert. Adrian Boult.
2. Nov. 1923. Queen's Hall. Saturday symphony concert. Henry Wood.
3. Dec. 8th 1923. Queen's Hall. Philharmonic. Landon Ronald. Specially fine performance.
4. March 7th 1924. Central Hall (BBC Concert). Landon Ronald.
5. Oct. 21st 1927. Queen's Hall (BBC Concert). Landon Ronald.
6. Dec. 12th 1927. Queen's Hall (LSO Concert). John Barbirolli.
7. Nov. 8th 1929. Queen's Hall (BBC Concert) Landon Ronald.
8. January 24th 1930. Queen's Hall (Halle Concert) Hamilton Harty. 1st movt. slow. 2nd movt. exceptionally good.
9. October 2nd. 1930 Queen's Hall. Edward Elgar (sat to conduct) BBC Prom. Concert. Finest possible performance. Elgar called on 5 times.
10. October 30th 1930 (via Radio Midland Region) Leslie Heward. Birmingham Symphony Concert.
11. February 18th 1931. Queen's Hall. Adrian Boult. BBC Symphony Concert.
12. October 1st. 1931. Queen's Hall. Sir Edward Elgar (stood to conduct: BBC Prom. Concert. Very good but not quite as good as 1930. Elgar called on 5 times.

13. December 7th 1932. Queen's Hall. Sir Edward Elgar (stood to conduct). Elgar Festival Concert (as good as, or better than 1930) Elgar called on 5 times.
14. August 17th 1933. Queen's Hall. Sir Edward Elgar (sat to conduct). (Elgar called on five times).
15. October 18th 1933. Queen's Hall. Adrian Boult. BBC Symphony Concert. Very good performance, especially Rondo.
16. March 1st 1934. Queen's Hall. Adrian Boult. Elgar Memorial Concert (Philharmonic) (A little disappointing).
17. October 22nd 1934. Queen's Hall. Hamilton Harty. LSO.
18. February 3rd 1935. Broadcast Concert. Landon Ronald. BBC Orchestra.
19. October 19th 1935. Broadcast Concert. John Barbirolli. Leeds Philharmonic.
20. November 8th 1935. Queen's Hall. Landon Ronald. LSO (Rather pulled about).
21. October 18th 1936. Broadcast Concert. Adrian Boult. BBC Orchestra.
22. February 4th 1937. Broadcast Concert. John Barbirolli, Halle Orchestra.
23. May 9th 1937. Broadcast Concert. Adrian Boult, BBC Orchestra.
24. February 2nd. 1938. Broadcast Concert. Adrian Boult, BBC Orchestra.
25. April 19th 1939. Broadcast Concert (Wolverhampton) Adrian Boult BBC Orch.
26. January 3rd. 1940 (Radio) Bristol Coop. Society Warehouse. Hamilton Harty BBC Orchestra.
27. October 2nd 1940 (Radio) Colston Hall, Bristol. Adrian Boult. BBC Orchestra.
28. October 7th 1942 (Radio) Bedford. Adrian Boult. BBC Orchestra. Reception bad as usual, switched off.
29. September 18th 1943 Broadcast (Sat. afternoon) Boult & BBC Orchestra. Very careful performance, but lacked the vital spark.
30. February 23rd 1944 Broadcast (Wednesday evening) Boult & BBC Orchestra lovely performance, every detail, but full of life.
31. May 14th 1945 (after VE day) Broadcast Boult & BBC Orchestra (Monday evening) Slightly dragged here and there & a domino in 1st. movement.
32. October 30th 1946. Broadcast, Goossens & BBC Orchestra. 1st. movement especially brilliant; rest rotten.
33. August 31st 1947. Broadcast, Edinburgh Festival. Barbirolli and Halle Orchestra. Rotten, Italian Opera.
34. November 16th 1947. Broadcast (Brighton). Boult & BBC Orchestra; mostly heavy and slow, without the vital spark, except at the close.
35. November 28th 1948. Broadcast. Boult and BBC Orchestra. Excellent except for slight drag in one or two places in 1st movement.

36. May 1st 1949. Broadcast. Boult and BBC Orchestra. Very good except for slight drag in a few places.
37. September 7th 1949. Broadcast. Boult and BBC Orchestra. (Bad reception) 1st movement rushed apparently the Mike for the strings had completely failed. general effect.
38. August 30th 1950. Broadcast. Sargent and BBC Orchestra (prom). Good general effect.
39. December 23rd 1950. Broadcast. Raybould and BBC Orchestra. 1st movement a little slow. 2nd a little fast. 3 & 4 lacked cohesion.
40. February 2nd 1952. Broadcast. Sargent and BBC Orchestra. 1st and 4th movements much too slow and dull.
41. February 23rd 1952. Broadcast. Sargent and B.B.C Orchestra. Slow movement and scherzo good.
42. April 30th 1952. Broadcast. Sargent and BBC Orchestra. 1st rather too slow. Slow movement and scherzo good.
43. May 13th 1953. Broadcast. Barbirolli and Halle Orchestra. Very good but not quite Elgar.
44. May 20th 1953. Bath Pavilion. Barbirolli and Hallé Orchestra. Dragged out, a wretched affair.
45. August 12th 1953. Broadcast. Sargent and BBC Orchestra (Prom.). 1st rather too slow, 2nd a little too fast. Good but not just there.
46. March 4th 1955. Broadcast. Sargent and BBC Orchestra (Symphony Concert.) Played very well, lacked spirit throughout.
47. January 1958. Broadcast. Sargent and BBC Orchestra. 1st movement too slow, others good but not 100%. Tape recorded and deleted.
48. November 14th 1958. Broadcast. Barbirolli and Halle. 1st and 3rd excellent, 2nd and 4th hurried.
49. December 2nd 1959. Broadcast. Sargent and BBC Orchestra. 1st too slow, 2nd rather fast, 3rd brilliant, 4th started too slow but finished 1st class.
50. March 1972 Broadcast. Barenboim and BBC Symphony Orchestra. 1st perfect, 2nd, 3rd and 4th very good. Altogether fine, one or two tempi blemishes.
51. 1974 Daniel Barenboim, really excellent.
52. 1990–91 Andrew Davis. Unbelievably BAD.
53. February 1st 1991. Edward Downes. Not as bad as Davis, but not good.
54. February 24th 1991. Good in parts.
55. June 26th 1991. Libor Pešek. Royal Liverpool Philharmonic Orchestra. Mostly glorious and thrilling.
56. December 25th 1992. Solti, London Philharmonic Orchestra (tape) not good at climaxes.

~ Robert Matthew-Walker

The Transcendental Elgar

Today – that is to say, in the third decade of the 21st century – there is universal acceptance that Elgar is a great composer, with his music performed regularly across the musical capitals of the world. As I write, a correspondent reports a fine performance in Paris of Elgar's Violin Concerto, by an international soloist, the Norwegian Vilde Frang, with l'Orchestre Philharmonique de Radio France conducted by the French-born Fabien Gabel.

It was not always so, for, as with the music of all great composers, the perception and final realisation of any work of art has, it seems, to go through a refining process, initially one of being buffeted by the slings and arrows of outrageous fashion until the inherent qualities of the music – those that seemingly possess immortality – finally resolve into that universal acceptance mentioned in our opening sentence.

It not yet one hundred years since Elgar died; as recently as 2022, the passing of Her Majesty Queen Elizabeth II removed the final living link to Elgar – the Queen had met Elgar, as a child, in 1932, when she attended with her parents the recording sessions for the composer's *Nursery Suite* – dedicated to her and her sister and mother.

Elgar was then Master of the King's Music, a position both popularly acknowledged and manifestly deserved as a consequence of his earlier orchestral celebrations of Britain's standing in the world in the dozen or so years of the late-Victoria and Edwardian eras – it was this popularity, which had made his music known from King to butcher's boy, that ensured his eminence during his lifetime.

For very many people, including professional musicians, that was the sum total of Elgar's achievements, reinforced by the global upheavals wrought in civic and personal life within a dozen years or so of the Abbey Road recordings.

The rise of Nazism, the consequential World War and the cost of post-war rebuilding betokened changes of the most profound proportions – it seemed to many artists that the social and aesthetic mores that had led to such catastrophic destruction were but symbols of what was previously wrong; they had to be either done away with or changed forever.

But the phrase 'many artists' does not constitute everyone. The post-war reactions – virtually across the globe – against the standards of earlier times was evident in new national and political formations, coincidental with the rise of new means of mass communication – television, especially, and the long-playing record, with the younger generations, as always, seeking to announce their post-war arrival by doing away with the standards of their predecessors.

In such circumstances, therefore, the music of Elgar, alongside that of most of his contemporaries, could not fail to be side-lined: for many, his music epitomised the standards that were, in post-war eyes, to be done away with: Empire, Pomp and Circumstance – these were relics of the past, not the golden, beckoning future.

Such profoundly superficial assessments of Elgar's music – not merely his music, but also that of his contemporaries, Richard Strauss especially – were often readily accepted by those to whom genuine musical thought is too challenging a process to go through, preferring to adopt a fashionable, more readily available, stance.

The centenary of Elgar's birth in 1957 provided a timely opportunity for reassessment, but it was surely the case that this did not happen – at least, not in the manner that we today might have wished. Elgar's cause was certainly helped by the remarkable series of gramophone recordings he made of his own music in the final decade of his life: these were, in one sense, living testaments to how his music should be performed, and a number of them were indeed reissued in the still relatively new long-playing format to mark his centenary.

1957 was not a quarter of a century following Elgar's passing, and as the 1950s came to an end, there were a fair number of musicians still alive who knew him – and younger generations, too, not just in Britain, whose aesthetic senses had been alerted to the qualities of his music, unconnected and unconcerned by superficial associations with the British Empire – after all, Elgar did not initially set the words 'Land of Hope and Glory': those were written later, to match his already-composed music.

There is the essential truth about Elgar: it was his music – his *music* – that fired people's imaginations, and if it could have fired Rachmaninoff in Moscow, or Mahler in New York – both of whom conducted the *Enigma* Variations in those cities – or the local butcher's boy in East London, or the King himself in Buckingham Palace – we are talking of purely *musical* qualities, inherent in a self-educated genius, not those of the contemporaneous nation in which the artist lived.

And as with the music of all great composers, it is the essential qualities that make their art individual and relevant to human experience across generations; we have seen Elgar's work accepted at the level which it demands. When Mahler, Rachmaninoff, Richard Strauss, Sir Georg Solti and Daniel Barenboim, Jascha Heifetz and Pablo Casals, Toscanini and Stokowski, amongst so many others, deem it necessary to perform Elgar's music, even the doubters should stop and ask themselves 'Why?' It has nothing to do with the one-time British Empire.

In some ways, of course – as I hope to have hinted at – it has more to do with fashion in music; essentially a temporary thing, but almost impossible to rile against when it is in full flow, and especially when one puts forward alternative composers and art-forms other than those considered at the forefront of contemporaneous musical excellence.

That it was always thus is demonstrated by the acceptance of the music of composers who were once dismissed or disregarded – usually, one has to say, on the grounds of ignorance. For in those first decades following Elgar's death, his was not the only music that was, at best, side-lined.

In the 1940s and 1950s, the symphonies of Mahler and Bruckner were unheard in this country. On a large scale, as were Elgar's, and calling for the fullest orchestras, redolent in language associated – wrongly, of course – with pre-war Imperialism, concomitant with the British and Austro-Hungarian Empires, it was all-too-easy and downright simple to dismiss their immortal masterpieces as the product of what today would doubtless be termed overbearing white supremacy.

What music-lover would willingly pay money to hear music that fashionable criticism would deem 'out-dated'? Even today, with composers (not all of them British) whose music goes unheard, but whose works were once hailed as being of the greatest interest and significance, we can see what happened to Elgar half a century and more ago being relived through the neglect of music by the more gifted of his successors.

We, today, can rest assured that Elgar's finest works are now part of the international concert repertoire in a way they were not always considered to be. What Elgar's music possesses, from the symphonies, the concertos, the oratorios and the late chamber music, are the qualities of immortality in art.

It may be easy to make that claim, but what do we mean by such a statement? The qualities of all great music are, no doubt, self-evident to the musician and the musical person: the non-musical individual we can safely ignore. In an attempt to answer that question, we must go back to basic principles.

Music is a living organism in time. It does not exist in space, although musicians need room in which to play their instruments or sing their parts. Music starts, continues and comes to an end. In that regard, it is virtually unique. One says 'virtually', as one can make a similar, if not identical, claim for a staged play.

Drama, especially theatrical drama, needs more than speech of course, whereas music needs performance – which should equally demand an attentive audience.

Art – painting or sculpture – exists only in space, not in time. A new painting in a gallery might well cause raised eyebrows at first: if one does not grasp it, the viewer can go away, think about it and come back for another look – *it is still there, unchangeable.* But with a new symphony or string quartet, one cannot go away and think over what one has been hearing and come back, expecting it still to be there, picking it up from where one left. The musicians will have likely packed up and gone home.

So music demands attention, and listening to music is, as always, an acquired taste. A symphony by Elgar lasts an hour, and an hour's attention is not to be given lightly: the demands of such music that are placed on the listener move this way and that in accordance with the fashion of the time. Elgar may have reflected at one level the significances of life in pre-World War I Britain and Europe – that part is demonstrably true, especially in such works as *The Crown of India* (a work whose *concept* was as unthinkable in post-1947 Britain as it is today) – but the language, the expressive force of the music itself was not akin to background film music: the *emotional* content of the work is, I submit, immortal – as was demonstrated to me during my time at RCA Records in London fifty years ago.

I had entered into a contract with the Scottish National Orchestra and Sir Alexander Gibson to make a series of recordings of Elgar's music. RCA of course, in those days, was an American company, and the international headquarters were in New York. The American global head of classical recordings was thrilled to learn of the new contract and told me, in no uncertain terms, that the one work of Elgar's the American market wanted was – *The Crown of India*. I was astonished. 'We need that work, Bob, more than the symphonies or concertos. The music is so fine and always makes a big impression when it is broadcast on WQXR.

So there you have it – music *cannot* express Imperialism, or white supremacy, or anything other than music – and the finest music always makes the deepest impression on listeners who are musical. But – as my American boss demonstrated – it has to be made available, either in public performance or through broadcast or recording media. The 'impression' Elgar's music makes, the demand for his music today is as strong as it ever was during his lifetime – I would suggest, even more so, in that the recent programming of the Violin Concerto in Paris, or Barenboim's performance of the Second Symphony several years ago in Berlin with that city's Staatskapelle which – to the astonishment of a friend, who was in the audience – earned a standing ovation, fully demonstrate.

Today, thankfully, Elgar is as accepted as Richard Strauss, Bruckner or Mahler. It may have been some time in coming, but the inherent nobility and humanity of his music, its character of being able to 'speak directly' to sympathetic listeners through committed interpretations by dedicated musicians, has never been in doubt. This very great British composer has, demonstrably, achieved the one goal all creative artists strive for, but so few achieve – transcendence, the transcendence of time and place, now and for all time.

~ Diana McVeagh

Suppose Edward Elgar had never lived? How would the history of music differ? And what would we as listeners miss? If there were no *Enigma*, would we hear Parry's *Symphonic Variations* of 1898 more often? Or Holst's *Planets* (1919)? If no Elgar Violin Concerto, what about Stanford's? No *Cockaigne*, more *London Symphony*; perhaps Ireland's *London Overture*?

If no *Gerontius*, maybe Delius's *Mass of Life* (1909)? Holst's *Hymn of Jesus* or Vaughan Williams's *Sancta Civitas* (which Elgar heard and admired)? Or would we have waited till 1961 for Britten's *War Requiem*? Would Vaughan Williams's *Tallis* be more accepted as European? Would symphonies by Bantock and Cowen be now in our repertory? Would *Peter Grimes* be the new *Enigma*, in terms of an international breakthrough? Would 'I vow to thee, my country' be sung at the Proms last night? What would be played at the Cenotaph? Would any composer, other than Elgar, have formed such a bond of unity with his countrymen, would enter so firmly our national consciousness?

Such speculation, though tantalising, is only a parlour game. More significantly, few composers have been as fully documented as Elgar. He left his own 'records', in sound and sight. There are copious photographs, and he was the first great composer to adopt the gramophone, memorials both finely assessed by Jerrold Northrop Moore. Though he moved house frequently, he kept full archives, even after his devoted wife's death: letters, diaries, programmes, press cuttings.

Jerry's magnificent five volumes of Elgar's letters (1987–90) are being supplemented by ongoing collections edited by Martin Bird and others, beginning in 2014 with the enchanting letters between Carice and her parents, and the publication of the Elgar family diaries. How one wishes Alice had been as perspicacious as she was diligent, with more pen-portraits of the notable people they knew, and less about the weather and Edward's bad colds!

Elgar's Birmingham lectures have been published (1968) and his manuscripts in the British Library have been scrutinised (1990). His letters too are now safely in the British Library. The handsome scholarly edition of his compositions is nearing completion. Also, thanks to John Norris, scores and books pour out from Elgar Works. Both Elgar's wife (1978) and his mother have books to themselves. Novels and plays have been written about him. Along with Holst and Britten, he has a museum devoted to his life.

So his life's artefacts are being well preserved. Such attention presupposes considerable importance. At some level, he knew his own worth.

Five books were written about Elgar during his lifetime, and several soon after his death by friends who had known him well. Those naturally concentrated on his most attractive qualities.

There are now something like fourteen shelf-feet of books *about* him, including symposiums and chapters in books. As he recedes into history, changes have taken place in his critical reception. David Cannadine and Michael de la Noy have shown how disagreeable Elgar the man could seem, if his musical achievement is ignored. He could be tiresome, rude, self-pitying. His complaints about his shortage of money have been looked at fairly in the context of contemporary writers and artists.

One of his most notorious remarks – 'I am still at heart the dreamy child ... as a child and as a young man no single person was ever kind to me' – has always shocked me. It is so untrue. He received great kindness all through his life. But he wrote it in 1921. His wife had died the year before. His daughter had just married and left home. He had sold the great house in London they'd bought when he was at the height of his fame. He had torn up papers, got rid of books and furniture: it must have seemed like destroying his past. He had just moved alone into a service flat in St James's. That was his state of mind when he wrote that bitter comment. It does not excuse it, but it may explain it.

I have a small personal irony. The reason I, a young unpublished woman, was commissioned to write about him was that no academic or well-known figure in the late 1940s regarded him as a worthwhile subject. He was too easily branded as an imperialist. Now it is the academics who write most about him. (The exception was Richard Taruskin, who never even mentioned him in his six-volume 2005 *Oxford History of Western Music.*) Young British academics can now apply rigorous analytical techniques to Elgar's music, as if he were Debussy or Schoenberg, unencumbered by the Malvern Hills, the British Empire, the identity of the five dots.

In my day Elgar was called a late-romantic. Now writers rate him a modernist. Does such classification matter? Obviously the music remains unchanged. So is it more than just semantics? Or should we be more aware of key structure, sonata deformation, hermeneutics, as James Hepokoski teaches us. Right from the start perceptive listeners heard Elgar's nerviness beneath the grandiloquence. Under that self-confidence lies loss and uncertainty. But the revisionists put even more stress on his inner turmoil.

But let not the life-affirming, positive, glowing, exuberant Elgar be under-estimated. The Spirit of Delight came rarely, but came it did, and we should share it. His achievement was so tremendous. The sheer quantity of first-class music he produced is amazing. He was such a late developer, had such a short composing life. His first big work, *Froissart,* came at the age of 33, by which time Britten had composed *Peter Grimes* and *The Rape of Lucretia.* His last major work, the Cello Concerto, came when he was 62, at which age Vaughan Williams was composing his Fourth Symphony.

And neither let us belittle Elgar, the man or the composer, by over-emphasizing his self-pity or his melancholia. It is the ambiguity of his style that is so original and so all-embracing; the tension between passion and inhibition, the emotional extremes, that make him so compelling. No one who engages fully with one of Elgar's symphonies is the same at the end as at the beginning. The fusion of celebration and elegy enlarges and refines our own sensibilities.

~ Christopher Morley

The ease of railway access between Birmingham and the various places where Elgar lived during his career (Worcester, London, Malvern, Hereford, London again) made the Second City a frequent magnet for his musical activities. Only Fittleworth in deepest Sussex, chosen by Alice Elgar for its remoteness as a retreat from the cacophony engendered by the Great War, had no direct transport connections, and after Elgar's bereaved return to the West Midlands the link to Birmingham seemed hardly to matter – apart from one auspicious occasion.

His first regular trips from Worcester Foregate Street to Birmingham Snow Hill began in 1879, when he joined the first violins in the orchestra William Stockley had formed in 1873, and which gave the first-ever regular series of concerts in Birmingham Town Hall. Elgar was still with the orchestra in 1889, when the programme on 7 February included Raff's Italian Suite, *In the South.*

Elgar's desk-partner was Frederick Ward, to whom he dedicated *La Capricieuse* Op. 17 for violin and piano (1891), and the two of them obviously grew very close, because after Ward's death his widow approached Elgar with a request for money – which he refused.

Stockley himself played a significant part in Elgar's development as a composer, conducting the first performance of his *Intermezzo Moresque* at Birmingham Town Hall in 1883 (though in his autobiography 'Fifty Years of Music in Birmingham' Stockley mistakes the date as 1880). Elgar also dedicated his *Sevillana (Scene Espagnole)* to Stockley; it was premiered in Worcester Public Hall by the Worcester Philharmonic Society on 1 May 1884, the Cathedral organist William Done conducting, and given in London eleven days later by the Crystal Palace Orchestra conducted by August Manns.

Subsequent relations with Stockley would not be so cordial, as a result of the debacle surrounding the premiere of *The Dream of Gerontius* at Birmingham Town Hall on 3 October 1900…

His fame increasing as a composer, with several works for choir and orchestra now under his belt, in 1898 Elgar was approached by the Birmingham Festival Committee to produce the major new work for the 1900 Triennial Festival. Though accepting the commission, Elgar had difficulties finding a subject, toying with the idea of the life of St Augustine (we had to wait for Tippett to climb that mountain), and after that subject was rejected by the Committee he turned to the possibility of an oratorio on the life of Jesus. He had problems finding a librettist, and, as the deadline approached, he at last settled on John Henry Newman's epic, incense-scented poem *The Dream of Gerontius*. He had been given a copy of the poem, complete with General Gordon's annotations, on his wedding day in 1889 by Father Knight, priest at the Worcester church in which Elgar was organist, and now he launched into discussions with priests at the Birmingham Oratory on the Hagley Road, founded by Cardinal Newman.

Dvořák had been offered the opportunity of setting this poem for an earlier Triennial Festival, but instead produced *The Spectre's Bride*. Any objections that Elgar's suggested text was aggressively Catholic were refuted by the fact that Stanford's *Requiem* had been commissioned for the 1897 Festival. There remained qualms, however, about the veneration of the Virgin Mary (and in fact when *Gerontius* was first performed at Worcester Cathedral all references to Her were bowdlerised), despite which the composition went ahead with white-hot speed. Novello, the publishers, responded with similar alacrity, printing the choral parts as they received them piecemeal and sending them up to the various choral groups who were to make up the Festival chorus.

Then disaster struck. Barely had rehearsals begun than Charles Swinnerton Heap, successor to Stockley, who had stepped down as director of the Birmingham Festival Choral Society in 1895 (possibly before he was pushed), and a brilliant musician and teacher, was taken ill and died suddenly on 11 June 1900. In a panic the Committee hauled Stockley out of retirement to take over the choral rehearsals.

A less suitable appointment could not have been imagined. The elderly Stockley was out of touch with the latest trends in music, not least the Wagnerian language of Elgar's score (*Parsifal* would have meant nothing to him), and he plodded through the choral rehearsals with little understanding, obviously more at home with the straightforward idioms of Handel's *Israel in Egypt*, selections of which were to make up the second half of the *Gerontius* morning concert, after a performance of Schubert's 'Unfinished' Symphony.

Elgar yelled at the chorus during a rehearsal very close to the performance date. Sometimes this resource works (I have used it myself), but not in this case. At the premiere the semi-chorus entered a semitone flat, and the die was cast for a performance which failed to take off.

The composer's bitterness was expressed in typically self-pitying terms in a letter to Jaeger at Novello & Co.: 'I have worked hard for forty years and, at the last, Providence denies me a decent hearing of my work; so I submit – I always said God was against art and I still believe it… I have allowed my heart to open once – it is now shut against every religious feeling and every soft, gentle impulse *for ever*'.

Except it wasn't. Elgar was by now the go-to composer, and, returning to his Jesus idea, but in a posthumous way, he composed *The Apostles* for the 1903 Birmingham Festival, and *The Kingdom* for that of 1906, both conducted by himself. The planned completion of the trilogy, *The Last Judgment*, never transpired, but he returned to the Festival in 1912 with his autobiographical *Music Makers*, the Festival's final major commission before the Great War brought an end to its existence almost forever (there was a half-hearted attempt at resuscitation in the 1970s).

In the midst of all the compositional activity for Birmingham, Elgar was involved in a far-reaching project involving the city which ensures his name will be remembered even beyond his artistic creations. Richard Peyton, the immensely wealthy head of a company of manufacturing chemists, was a major benefactor of the arts in the Midlands. At the age of 21 he had been present at the premiere of Mendelssohn's *Elijah* under the composer's baton in Birmingham Town Hall, and he had subsequently become a major and influential supporter of the Birmingham Triennial Festival. As his long life was nearing its end he formed the idea of establishing a Chair of Music at the recently founded University of Birmingham, and made it clear that he would only endow it if Elgar were to be appointed its first incumbent.

Despite deep initial misgivings, Elgar was persuaded by Peyton to take up the position for the sake of posterity. Elgar had had no formal musical education at all; his lecture-room had been the meadows at Claines, just outside Worcester, where he munched on bread and cheese whilst studying scores as a boy; his shoulders had chips on both sides as he simmered resentment at the academic status of Parry and Stanford, firmly ensconced in two great London music colleges, as well as Stanford's Professorship at Cambridge; he decided that accepting the Birmingham Professorship with its attendant obligation to deliver a series of lectures would give him the opportunity to swipe back at the musical establishment.

And so he did, his diatribes given in his robes as Doctor of Music of Cambridge, addressing packed audiences in the Birmingham and Midland Institute (just across the road from the Town Hall), for whose School of Music he was already a Visitor. The national press was present in abundance, reporting back on the outspoken nature of Elgar's lectures. Controversial they may have been, but his lecture notes reveal the depth into which he had researched his subject matter and the many august references he cited.

His inaugural lecture, 'A Future for English Music', was delivered on 16 March 1905, his final one (on orchestration and the Mozart G minor Symphony he had studied so assiduously in his youth) on 8 November 1906, by which time Elgar had had enough of the imposition and indeed politics of his professorial requirements. Having successfully established a Department of Music at the University of Birmingham and launched its library with the acquisition of the complete works of Purcell, he resigned, to be succeeded by Granville Bantock, already Principal of the Birmingham School of Music.

Soon after Elgar's resignation the main buildings of the University came into being, on the Bristol Road, where leafy Edgbaston merges into the seedier bustle of Selly Oak. His name lives on, with the Elgar Room in the old Arts Faculty building (how many times have I rehearsed and performed there), and now with the magnificent Elgar Concert Hall in the superb Bramall building giving a new, spacious home to the Department of Music.

Elgar's connections with Birmingham are also cemented in an organisation which has brought worldwide recognition to the city's musical life. We began with Stockley's orchestra, giving regular concerts in Birmingham Town Hall. Other enterprises were to follow, such as the orchestra founded and conducted by George Halford, but the feeling grew that there should be a municipal orchestra, following the example of places such as Bournemouth, and one founded by the City Council. And thus the City of Birmingham Orchestra was formed, with the worthy Appleby Matthews as its first conductor. Matthews had conducted the premiere of the long-awaited first movement of Elgar's *The Spirit of England*, 'The Fourth of August', on 4 October 1917. After a few preliminary concerts given in city theatres and cinemas, the CBO gave its inaugural symphony concert in Birmingham Town Hall. The date was Wednesday 10 November 1920, and the conductor was the country's most renowned musician, Sir Edward Elgar.

It was a long and demanding programme, beginning with *Falstaff*, the Cello Concerto with Felix Salmond the soloist and the Second Symphony. Reviews were ecstatic, and thus was born an orchestra, rechristened the 'City of Birmingham Symphony Orchestra' at George Weldon's insistence in 1948, which has become one of the greatest in the world.

The legacy Elgar left to Birmingham has been of crucial importance to me throughout my life. I cherish the Honours Degree I obtained after graduating from the Music Department he founded at the University of Birmingham. And for well over half a century I have reviewed performances from the orchestra he launched so generously, now well over a century ago, an orchestra which means so much to me and whose reputation I value so greatly.

~ Arthur Reynolds

The importance of Sir Edward Elgar's life and music to me has its origins in a far-off place and time. The place, a small-town suburb of Philadelphia; the time, my 1950s youth. On the summer nights of my boyhood, before the advent of television and air conditioning drove my neighbours indoors, a social life flourished on the salient porches that fronted the houses lining the street where I lived. Most of the menfolk reposing on those porches had seen their lives momentarily dramatized by wartime military service in Europe, so they had tales to tell. Many of their stories began in Britain, where they had been billeted in the months prior to D Day. Author Lynne Olson summed up their collective viewpoint in *Citizens of London*,[1] her account of life in the United Kingdom during the Second World War: 'To a number of Americans who spent time in wartime Britain, the country and its capital seemed to resemble Brigadoon – a magical place where courage, resolution, sacrifice, and a sense of unity and common purpose triumphed, if only for a few short years.'

What I absorbed from those porch encounters kindled a nascent Anglophilia that has never stopped expanding. By the time I was a teenager, my fascination with Britain had begun to find expression in my fascination with Elgar's music. My father had brought back from Britain an assemblage of 78 discs that included recordings of the Cello Concerto and the *Enigma Variations*. Sargent's *Gerontius* and Menuhin's Violin Concerto were to arrive by mail order not long afterwards.

At school, we recited passages from the plays of Shakespeare that reinforced my vision of Britain as a magical place. The sounds of Elgar's recorded music merged with my classroom recitations to leave me with a transcendental sense of connection between Shakespeare's diction and Elgar's scoring. Years later I would find support for that reflection in a line from Alice Stuart of Wortley's letter of condolence to Elgar's daughter Carice: 'He is our Shakespeare of music, born and died on the soil in the heart and soul of England…'

1 Lynne Olson, *Citizens of London: The Americans who Stood with Britain in its Darkest, Finest Hour* (New York: Random House, 2010).

Other neighbours included members of the Philadelphia Orchestra attracted to the town's easy commuting distance to the city. Music-making sounded from their porches; some of it from gramophones, some from live performance. The subjects of their stories were the soloists and conductors they esteemed. Chief among them was Eugene Ormandy, the Hungarian violinist then at the helm of the Philadelphia Orchestra. The first time my father took me into town to attend an Ormandy-led concert, the programme included my first hearing of a live performance of an Elgar work. A next-day reviewer had this to say: 'Eugene Ormandy, in his element, is an unbeatable conductor, and since his element includes Elgar's "Enigma" Variations, the Philadelphia Orchestra concert at Philharmonic Hall Tuesday night ended gloriously. Whether dealing with the grandeur of the "Nimrod" variation or the playfulness of the lighthearted ones, Mr. Ormandy was an imaginative and convincing interpreter...'

I wanted to know more and hear more, but what was available was meagre. Determined to gain a greater knowledge of Elgar's life and music, I had hoped to come out of a desert into an oasis when I took up a place as an undergraduate at Emmanuel College Cambridge in 1965. Alas I had arrived in England at a dark time in terms of indigenous interest in Elgar's music. To my knowledge, David Willcocks, who presided over music at King's College performed none of Elgar's compositions during my time at Cambridge. Travelling to London, however, I could hear Jacqueline du Pré's account of the Cello Concerto and what a glory that was. Regrettably I spent the summers of those years working in the USA, so I missed the chance to attend the Three Choirs Festival, where I would have heard memorable performances of Elgar's works.

In 1967, my last Cambridge year, I made a pilgrimage to Broadheath. What I found at the Elgar Birthplace Museum alarmed me: letters stuffed in shoeboxes; original-print photographs gathering light and dust on the Birthplace walls. Worse, I later learned that offerings of important artifacts were being turned away for lack of repository space. As I learned more about this lamentable state of affairs, the prospect of a journey opened up to me. During Elgar's lifetime – June 1857 to February 1934 – those who knew him saved everything that could be construed to be an item of Elgarian memorabilia. After his death, a small percentage of this material – what I call the 'trophy' items' – found its way to the Birthplace, the British Museum (later the British Library) and other public collections, or to the private holdings of wealthy collectors. Much of the rest belonged to Elgar's surviving contemporaries, many of whom, in the course of downsizing their dwellings, scattered their surplus possessions far and wide. In those days it was not unusual to find booksellers offering Elgar letters for as little as half a crown. If these orphaned artifacts could be acquired while their present or former possessors were still alive, information could be harvested that might produce penetrating insights into aspects of Elgar's life, particularly his creative process. Before me stretched the vista of a prospective adventure, comprising the excitement of treasure hunting, the gratification of building a collection, the fulfilment of scholarly ambition, together with the voyager's delight in embarking on paths previously untravelled.

A decade after leaving Cambridge, I returned to the UK to live in London during the years that saw the restoration of Elgar's rightful place as Britain's greatest composer since Purcell. During that time, and subsequently during the years that followed my eventual return to America, the results of my Elgarian odyssey, now spanning more than half a century, have proved fruitful beyond my loftiest expectations. I cite a few examples:

> A letter from the composer to the artist John Singer Sargent, tucked obscurely into the pages of a book I acquired by chance, provided the basis for an essay exploring the hitherto unknown relationship between the two artists. Who knew that JSS possessed the capacity of an outstanding musician?[2]
>
> A sheaf of discarded Novello meeting notes revealed the full story of the conflict between Eugène Ysaÿe and Novello over the performance of Elgar's Violin Concerto.[3] The discovery of correspondence between Elgar and August Manns produced new insights into the contribution of the Crystal Palace concerts to Elgar's self-teaching.[4]

Following trails of clues led to discoveries even Elgar sought but missed. He composed his *Civic Fanfare* for the 1927 Hereford Three Choirs Festival. Three years later came a request for a repeat performance; but Elgar could not remember what he had done with the manuscript. Fortunately, HMV had been on hand at the 1927 Festival to make a few experimental recordings, including of the *Civic Fanfare*. The recordings had not been published, but a single test copy had been sent to the composer. The extreme wear on the surface of that test pressing is evidence of Elgar having played the disc an uncountable number of times in order to reproduce the work. Over a period of years, I was able to discover where he had misplaced the original. There will be no further ambiguity because both the manuscript and the test copy of the recording now reside safely in my archive.

Offerings of Elgar material came thick and fast during the past decades. A descendant of HMV Photographer Fred Hempstead sold me

2 Elgar Society *Journal*, Vol. 14, No. 1, March 2005.

3 Elgar Society *Journal*, Vol. 23, No. 2, August 2022.

4 Elgar Society *Journal*, Vol. 24, No. 1, April 2024.

Hempstead's signed copies of his photos of Elgar bed-ridden in the South Bank Nursing Home. I acquired Alice Elgar's recipe book from the husband whose recently deceased wife passed on vivid memories of the tales of her grandmother's life as a member of the Craeg Lea kitchen staff.

One my most satisfying adventures arose from joining forces with Elgar biographer Dr Jerrold Northrop Moore to reproduce Percival Hedley's bronze bust, arguably the finest likeness of the composer and the representative example of his image chosen for display at the National Portrait Gallery. In 1904, Hedley sent the work to a foundry in Stroud for casting. Before producing the final copy, however, Hedley requested a test copy in wax. Duly satisfied, he gave the final order. The bronze bust was much admired; it won the Sculpture prize in the Royal Academy's 1905 Summer Exhibition. The wax version was broken into three sections for reuse. Unaccountably, they never reached the kiln. Instead, Dr Moore managed to acquire two of the three sections. He took them to the head modeller at Madame Tussauds who replaced the missing section using contemporary photographs. Carice Elgar Blake pronounced the result to be superior to the original owing to a slight change in the positioning of the head. Having acquired the wax copy, I went back to the Stroud foundry – still going strong – to see if a bronze version could be produced. This was achieved with complete success; now copies can be cast at will.

One day word reached me that a forthcoming Christie's Book Department sale was offering several items of correspondence from Elgar to the pianist Fanny Davis. I duly arrived at the Book Department and asked to see them. The clerk produced a small blue shopping bag with two letters and two postcards suggesting alterations to the score of Elgar's *Concert Allegro*, his largest composition for solo piano. When, as the successful bidder. I returned to collect my items, the clerk handed them over and said: 'By the way there's another, larger white bag that came with the little blue bag. We were going to throw it away, but you're welcome to it.' Inside the white bag I found a treasure trove in the form of crucial correspondence dating from Davis's time as a student in Germany. The letter presenting her eye-witness account of a concert at which Brahms gave the first performance of his Second Piano Concerto and his Third Symphony with Clara Schumann in the audience, following with the MS score, is a real show-stopper. The loss of this material, scheduled for the dustbin, is a prospect I dread to contemplate.

Over and above my manifold collecting adventures, Elgar's music has never ceased to enrich my life with solace and meaning. My friends ask, when will Arthur's Elgarian journey end? My answer: it will end with my end.

~ Wolfgang-Armin Rittmeier

Towards the end of his life, on 22 December 1933, Elgar dictated a letter to Ernest Newman, who had visited him two days before. Elgar refers to this visit, when they had – among other things – talked about the Third Symphony. After the visit Elgar put the opening and the final bars to paper and sent them to Newman, saying: 'With this I send the opening four bars (introductory) of the slow movement. I am fond enough to believe that the first two bars (with the F# in the bass) open some vast bronze doors into something strangely unfamiliar'.[1]

It is not clear, what Elgar meant exactly by the 'strangely unfamiliar something' into which these 'vast bronze doors' were opening. What kind of room or space did he have in mind? The fact that he uses this picture while he was facing death certainly suggests that the unfamiliar space he had in mind was death, and that the vast bronze doors – a good many west end portals of churches and cathedrals come to mind – sealed off this 'undiscovered country' and are opened only when you were to pass the threshold from life into eternity. Regardless of what Elgar might have meant or did not mean; by using the symbol of the door, he was dipping into human collective consciousness and chose to use a picture which is probably as old as humankind. Since the Egyptians, who painted false doors in their tombs about 4,000 years ago,[2] doors have been a powerful symbol in most cultures. Although the door is an everyday object, which we generally pass through unnoticed, its symbolic potential is always there[3], and thus it is much more than a 'movable barrier', which is simply used to open and shut a hole in the wall.

1 Jerrold Northrop Moore, *Edward Elgar: Letters of a Lifetime* (Rickmansworth: Elgar Works, 2012), 535.

2 See Doha Mohamed Sami Abdel Hamid, 'A Chronological Study of the False Door Concept' in *Journal of Association of Arab Universities for Tourism and Hospitality* 11(3) (December 2014): 110–17.

3 Nato Giorgadze, 'The Greater Reality behind Door. Study on perception of Doors' in *Ethnographica* 8 (2004): 19–28, at 24: 'People live in the world of Symbols and the world of symbols lives inside us'.

According to the German philosopher and sociologist Georg Simmel a human is the one being on the planet, who is – according to its nature – able to understand that all things in nature can be seen as either connected or separated from each other. The human species recognises this and understands that by 'selecting things from their natural situation in order to call them "separate", we have already related them to another in our consciousness, we already have contrasted those two against all that lies between them. This is true vice versa: things must first be separate in order to be put together. [...] We are at any moment – in the immediate or symbolic, in the physical or mental sense – beings who separate what is related and who relate what is separate'.[4]

The door is a symbol of this idea. Simmel continues, stating that the first hut which had a door, cut a part out of the whole and separated it from the whole. But it is important to understand that the door is not solid. It is not a piece of the wall. Thus, the room that it shuts is not *irrevocably* separated from the outside. In fact, the door 'cancels the separation of the inside and the outside because it constitutes a link between the space of the human and everything which is outside of it'.[5] As we choose to open the door, those things, from which we have been separate, merge into each other and the rooms which have been apart are made one room again, offering a permanent possibility of continuous alternation'[6] – as long as the door is kept open.

Now, it is important to appreciate that not all doors *look* like doors. In fact, they do not always have the 'physical characteristics of objective doors or gates'.[7] It is quite common that those people and what they stand for or what they do or have done fulfil this exact role. It is not by chance that in John 10:9 Christ describes himself thus: 'I am the door: by me if any man enters in, he shall be saved, and shall go in and out, and find pasture'.

In his book *The Hero with a Thousand Faces* Joseph Campbell[8] discusses his theory of the archetypal structure of the hero's journey found in mythical narratives all over the world, a journey which is also a symbolic representation of man's passage through life. One of the necessary events

4 Simmel's original essay 'Brücke und Tür' was published in *Der Tag: Moderne illustrierte Zeitung*, No. 683, 15 September 1909 (Berlin). The quotations used here were taken from Michael Kaern's essay 'Georg Simmel's "The Bridge and the Door"' in *Qualitative Sociology* 17(4) (1994): 397–413, at 407.

5 Kaern, op. cit., 409.

6 Kaern, op. cit., 410.

7 Giorgadze, op. cit., 25.

8 Joseph Campbell, *The Hero with a Thousand Faces* (New York: Pantheon Books, 1949).

to enable the hero to start the journey and cross the threshold into the 'undiscovered country' is the meeting with an aiding mentor. Without this aiding (often supernatural) acting as the doorway, neither the journey of the hero nor his return could take place.

In my view, Elgar and his music play this part in the musical relations between England and Germany. They are the door, the catalyst, the mentor. This is because, when Elgar was played in Germany for the first time, (and the situation has not changed) England had been thought of as 'Das Land ohne Musik' ('The Land without Music') in Germany. Although the musical scene in England has always been very lively, it had – in a way – been separated from the field of great musical history since the death of Handel who himself had also been a door through which continental music came to England. But the way from England (for English music) out into the world was more or less shut. Elgar and his music were the first powerful link between English music and music from the continent – mainly from what was then Germany. As Elgar was rooted in the Austro-German tradition of the Romantic Age, he brought this tradition to England and blended it with his very individual voice.

Consequently, both nations found his music attractive. While in England he was hailed as a most interesting Wagnerian at a time when Wagnerism was very *en vogue*, Germany greeted him as 'Meister Elgar', the first composer of progressive music, which – in addition and contrast to the music of his predecessors (e.g. Parry or Stanford) – had a very new and special ring to it. This was the somewhat strange individual colour, which is often called *English*, a colour which defies definition, although it seems to be very much there.

Elgar paved the way for those who came after him and who established an English tradition of composing in its own right, which has since then been recognised not only in the UK, but worldwide. If we look towards Albion today, we see 'The Land *with* Music'. Still, the process of paving is still necessary, and thus Elgar and his music continue to do so. Why is that so? Because there is a difference between being accepted and being performed. Sadly English music is underrepresented in German concert halls. While in the past few years some pieces by Ralph Vaughan Williams have turned up in concert programmes (*A Sea Symphony* seems to be a favourite) it is hard to find live performances of Stanford, Holst, Bantock, Delius, Bridge or Bliss – to only name a few. While it is probably *known* that since the late nineteenth century much music has been produced by renowned English composers, the greater part of this body of works remains *undiscovered*. But it seems that the image of 'The Land without Music' has – over the decades – been so internalised by many artists, planning directors and audiences that the idea that there might be interesting or even fascinating music lurking on the far shores of the Channel, simply does not come to mind.

There is one exception: the music of Edward Elgar. In the past ten to fifteen years, Elgar's music has become a regular visitor to German concert halls. The Cello Concerto has always been there, because cellists liked to play it. The *Serenade for Strings* has always been a favourite of school orchestras and *Pomp and Circumstance* No. 1 has been a highlight at German mock 'Last Nights' for decades, even if the Symphonies, the *Enigma Variations*, the Violin Concerto or *Falstaff* have not. But now they are gradually finding their way into the repertoire of German orchestras. An important part in the popularisation of Elgar's music in Germany has been played by the German choral scene – not only in 1901 and the following years. In the last decade I have accompanied many choirs on their journey through a work of Elgar's. Apart from *Caractacus* I have attended and supported wonderful and highly dedicated performances of all the great choral works from *The Black Knight* to *The Music Makers* throughout the country.

I have been fortunate to contact many conductors who have conducted one Elgar work after the other, just because they loved the music so much. I have also spoken to soloists and many members of many choirs. It was frequently the case that the work they were rehearsing was their first practical encounter with Elgar and generally they were fascinated by the music. Often, I hear statements along the lines of 'I had not imagined that Elgar composed such wonderful music. I always thought he was not much more than a Victorian jingo. But now I will start exploring'. Personally, it is *this* which constitutes the importance of Elgar from a German perspective. First of all, he opens the door to his works, his life and his times. But the experience of Elgar's work does more. For many people – either musicians or lovers of music - his work is the gateway to English music – and that is to English culture in general. The man and his music act – to quote Georg Simmel a last time – as a 'relating being'[9] as a communicator between great European musical traditions and countries.

Can there be a greater accomplishment?

9 Kaern, op. cit., 412.

~ Eleanor Roberts

The Hallé and Elgar

There are few composers as closely associated with the Hallé as Sir Edward Elgar. Not only was he President of the Hallé Concerts Society from 1930 until his death, he conducted the Orchestra a number of times, notably stepping into the breach for the Hallé's opening concert in 1914–15 season in the wake of Michael Balling's absence.[1] In the year of his 70th Birthday, Elgar chose to conduct the Hallé on 20th January 1927, in a concert of his own music: *In the South, Froissart, Sea Pictures, Enigma Variations* and the Violin Concerto, for which Adolph Brodsky came out of retirement as soloist. In the Manchester Guardian Samuel Langford wrote: 'Sir Edward Elgar himself seemed more inclined to indulge the orchestra than to rule it, as though he himself was savouring the delight of hearing the most lovely touches of the music given leisurely on beautiful instruments by first-rate players.'

The first work by Elgar to feature in Hallé concert programmes was *King Olaf*, on 1 December 1898.[2] (Not a work that the orchestra has performed since!) That concert was conducted by Sir Frederick Cowen, but it is with Dr Hans Richter that Elgar is most closely associated. Richter was an enthusiastic promoter of Elgar's works in all his concerts. The development of their resulting friendship is documented in a series of letters 1899–1913 that form part of the Richter-Loeb Archive.[3] They had come into contact initially through the Birmingham Triennial Music Festivals but it is unlikely they met until the London rehearsals of the *Enigma Variations* in June 1899.[4] Within his first season as Principal Conductor Richter brought

1 Michael Balling (1866–1925) was the Hallé's conductor from October 1912 until the outbreak of war in September 1914. A German by birth he was in Bavaria at the time but, because he was a British citizen, he was interned and stayed in Germany until his death, eventually resuming conducting there.

2 *Scenes from the Saga of King Olaf*, Op. 30 (1896).

3 Also part of the Richter-Loeb Archive are the scores that Elgar gave to Richter, all of which contain affectionate personal dedications and signatures.

4 Christopher Fifield, *True Artist and True Friend: A Biography of Hans Richter* (Oxford: Clarendon Press, 1993), 309.

two works to Hallé audiences for the first time: *Sea Pictures* (18 January 1900) and *Enigma Variations* (8 February 1900). *Sea Pictures* was part of a concert conducted by Charles Villiers Stanford, but it was Elgar who conducted his own work. I am confident that was the first time he conducted the orchestra; it certainly was the first time he did so in Manchester. Richter conducted the *Variations,* and it was his championship that Elgar credited with making that work a success. The correspondence provides some fascinating insights into Elgar's music, the following are a few examples. In the first letter, dated 5 October 1899, the composer refers to his revised ending for his *Variations*:

> I am so very delighted to see that you are playing my Variations again: thank you many times for taking an interest in my work. Since you introduced the work in the spring, following the advice of my friends, and I think your own view, I have added to the Finale making a more symphonic movement of it* in place of the original abrupt ending. This will not entail any long rehearsal as many of your orchestra played the new ending at the Worcester Festival so that the orchestral parts are quite correct. I hope you may approve of the additional music which I feel is an improvement in form.
>
> *It only adds between 2 & 3 minutes to the length – not more.

In April 1901 Elgar refers to a new overture:

> If you have not completed your programmes for next season would you keep a little 12 minutes for my overture: I have written it for the London Philharmonic[5] where it will be produced on June 20th – I shall conduct. The score is not yet ready or I wd [sic] send it to you, but I trust it not be long delayed. The work is not tragic at all – but extremely cheerful like a miserable unsuccessful man ought to write.

In a later letter he added to his description:

> here is nothing deep or melancholy – it is intended to be honest, healthy, humorous & strong but not vulgar: I hope I have not quite missed my aim & trust I may one day hear the overture under your conductorship – I need not tell you what a joy that would be.

The work was the *Cockaigne* Overture and Richter duly included it in his Manchester Concerts during the 1901–2 season, receiving its Manchester premiere on 24 October 1901. A letter dated from Liverpool on 25 October reveals that Elgar had his wish and had attended the concert in Manchester:

5 Royal Philharmonic Society. The London Philharmonic Orchestra was not formed until 1932, 74 years after the Hallé.

> The performances last night were truly magnificent – the Coriolan was sublime. My own overture was most exhilarating & I was glad indeed to hear it under your sympathetic & most masterly direction – but it has taught me that I am not satisfied with my music & must do or rather try to do something better and nobler. I hope the symphony I am trying to write will answer these higher ideals & if I find I am more satisfied with it than my present composition I shall hope to be allowed to dedicate it to my honoured friend Hans Richter: but I have much to do to it yet.

This is of course an early reference to the Symphony in A flat that was indeed dedicated to Richter 'True Artist and True Friend' and received its world premiere in Manchester on 3 December 1908 when Richter conducted the Hallé. In a letter dated 14 December 1908 Elgar thanked Richter for his 'splendid reading' before going on to say:

> I have been through the parts & have put the very few minor points right only one note have I altered & that is in the Timpani 5th bar after 136 – this bar should be a rest and so the note B is gone. Please insist that from four bars after 29 to 31 and from 53 to the end of the movement must be played in a veiled, mysterious way – a sort of echo: there is only one *f* (in the strings) for a moment throughout these two sections.

The early decision to dedicate the symphony to Richter – given that their friendship at this date was comparatively new – shows how sincere the regard on Elgar's side was. A letter dated 4 February 1902 addressed 'My dear Friend' begs Richter to dispense with formalities: 'One thing – please do not call me Dr Elgar – I would like you to call me Elgar, or even Edward:– the Dr is too formal… Please another time no prefixes.'

In March 1903 Richter was preparing for the first Hallé performance of *The Dream of Gerontius*, but the illness of soloist John Coates meant the performance was postponed for a week, until 13 March. Elgar was unable to be there, but sent a congratulatory note 'I hear the performance was the best.'

It feels significant that during Richter's time in Manchester, Elgar only conducted the Hallé on that one occasion in 1900, for it seems that, having heard Richter's performance of the *Variations*, he was happy to leave the interpretation of his own works in Richter's hands. The archive correspondence has other more light-hearted references to the first symphony in a letter dated 11 October 1903:

> My dear friend:
>
> You will be glad to hear that we are quite safe after our Motor journey.
>
> Will you please tell Mr Beale[6] that the bill for the following small things will be sent in to the committee.
>
> Six (6) babies, run over at one pound (£1) per baby.
>
> Two men knocked down; – I have guaranteed them wooden legs, to be provided by the Committee – Seven (7) dogs killed at two pounds (£2) per dog. You will see that infants are cheaper than dogs around here.
>
> There are several miles of fencing carried away & two lots of masonry knocked off the canal bridges – about 3 cwt: – an estimate for replacing this will be sent in.
>
> You will see we had a peaceful & happy journey & all the incidents are being worked into the symphony in E flat dedicated to Hans Richter
>
> By his friend

In late 1903 and early 1904 there are references to the fact that Elgar had not been able to complete the symphony and, instead, he provided *In the South* as his newest work. It was premiered by the Hallé at Covent Garden as part of the Festival of Elgar's works. Elgar conducted as the score and parts had not been produced in time for Richter to study them. On 26 February 1904 Elgar wrote: 'Would it be possible (perhaps next week) to devote 15 minutes with your orchestra to read through the new overture? I will get all parts as correct as possible but it's rather nervous work to leave late. I think the parts will be ready soon. I will bring them to you.'

When the Festival was over both the Elgars wrote to Richter:

> When I was listening to my husband's works last week, & hearing the wonderful way in which you penetrate the very inward meaning of his thoughts & give to the world such a revelation of what was in his heart in writing, I suddenly thought, now, what have I, good & precious enough, to send Dr Richter, as a remembrance of the beautiful moments I am living through? Then my mind turned to a portrait of my husband which I like so much – & then Mrs Richter assured me you would like a picture of him, so I have sent it to be packed & sent off to you, & trust you will like it. It is a very serious picture but looks as if he were seeing visions! If you do not like it as a picture of Edward you must please frankly say so, & send it back & I will get another one to replace it.

6 A member of the Three Choirs Festival Committee.

> We are just home but I still seem to live in that wonderful week – I do hope you were not very tired. I can never hope to hear anything so beautiful (till I have the great pleasure I hope, of hearing it again) as your marvellous Orchestra ....

A few days later Elgar wrote:

> I have been waiting to find a really quiet time to write a proper letter to you to thanks you from my heart for your conducting my music at Covent Garden: now this is Sunday & I should have found time, but – people come to take up my time & now, at ten o'clock the hour at which all good boys should go to bed, I find myself trying to write a sensible letter.
>
> ...
>
> Now, dear friend, I am not going all through the programmes but I must say the variations were marvellously played, I have never heard them sound better & Cockaigne also. ...
>
> Now, once more, thanks, heartfelt & sincere for doing all you did; without you the thing could not have been done at all, & with you it was a great artistic success & your presence gave it a dignity which would otherwise would [sic] have been wanting.

The dedication of the symphony, which was the first rather than the one in E flat that later followed, is mentioned in 1908 shortly before the premiere in Manchester on 3 December:

> 'Many thanks for your letter about the analysis & for the kind interest you take in my work.
>
> I understand that Mr Ernest Newman is the official analyst for your concerts & he has been furnished long ago with rough copies & has been working with them.
>
> For the dedication which between us must be simple & true: I have put
>
> To Hans Richter, Mus. Doc.
>
> True artist & true friend.
>
> I hope you will like this which means everything without long wordy sentences.

There are even references to one of Richter's other legacies to the Hallé – the Pension Fund. In March 1904 Elgar congratulated Richter on having secured the support of Queen Alexandra as patroness: '[I] trust it will lead many others to see the good possible to be done in this way'. There are several references to Elgar's wish to conduct at a Pension Fund concert, in particular at the 1911 concert, which was Richter's final appearance as Hallé Principal Conductor. In a letter dated 2 January that year, Elgar refers to 'my dear friends the members of the Hallé Orchestra'. The following month Richter announced his retirement and Elgar sent him a short letter that remains moving in spite of its simplicity:

> I see in the Telegraph an announcement that gives me a great pain – more than half my musical life goes when you cease to conduct'. The next letter in the sequence is dated 16 March and has the following postscript: 'The proof of the Score of my second Symphony in E flat has come today. I hope you may hear it some day – it was meant for you to like.

It was Elgar himself who conducted the Hallé's first performance of the Second Symphony on 23 Nov 1911 as part of an evening of his own works. It demonstrated that the relationship between the Hallé and the composer went beyond the personal friendship and shows that, whatever discomfort Richter may have felt over his departure, was not communicated to his friend. Richter's successor Michael Balling brought much more new music to the Hallé, including *Falstaff* in 1913. The Hallé musicians worked with Elgar outside Manchester with Richter's involvement with the Birmingham Triennial Festival taking them there regularly. The first item in the archive that I found relating to Elgar was a photograph showing the Hallé at Middlesbrough Town Hall in 1903. It is captioned 'with Elgar' but as he is not on the rostrum! Some years later a call from Middlesbrough Public Library brought to light a programme for this concert.

One of the orchestra's real personalities at this time, Principal Viola Simon Speelman, was also on good terms with Elgar. Speelman took on directing the Hallé's first venture into more popular 'Promenade' concerts in 1905, and also conducted Blackpool's Northern Pier Orchestra. The relationship with the orchestra – and by extension the men who ran it – was close enough that when the First World War broke out and the orchestra was without their permanent conductor (Balling), it was Elgar who stepped in. He conducted the first concert of the 1914–15 season and returned a number of times over the next few years. They were financially straitened times and he accepted expenses only rather than a fee. Unsurprisingly given its associations with the English landscape and patriotism, Elgar's music featured prominently in programming in the war years, as the morale-boosting qualities of music were recognised and utilised. Over the war period Elgar conducted the orchestra in Manchester on three occasions. It was a while before he did again, in that year of his 70th Birthday, referenced at the start of this essay. In 1930 the Hallé, at Hamilton Harty's suggestion, invited Elgar to become the Society's second President, a position he held until he died.[7] He conducted *The Dream of Gerontius* for what was to be his final concert with the Hallé on 26 January 1933. The soloists on this occasion were Muriel Brunskill, John Coates and Roy Henderson.

The week before Elgar died on 23 February 1934, John Barbirolli conducted the Hallé for the third time – in a concert that was entirely devoted to Elgar: *Froissart*, the *Enigma Variations*, Violin Concerto and the *Cockaigne* Overture. Neville Cardus in his review thought that the *Variations* was

> one of the best pieces of conducting of the season. Not a point was missed; the composer's original mingling of masculine and feminine qualities, of the more reflective and the picturesque, sounded more than ever like the greatest music he has ever written...Mr Barbirolli made even the finale dignified and strong; he unfurled the flag of the music masterfully, and for once in a way we were spared a noisy outburst of Jingoism – or perhaps nowadays we should say of Hitlerism. Mr Barbirolli has gifts.... last night's performance of the *Enigma Variations* was a testimony to Mr Barbirolli's love of Elgar and his technical resource; also it was a testimony to the orchestra's ability to read a score.

Cardus also mentioned that the concert was being broadcast, and that the composer was known to be unwell: 'the performance held the attention and must have given a deal of pleasure to the composer, as he listened in miles away on his bed of sickness at Worcester. Let us hope that the audience's applause heartened him and acted better than medicine. The concert proved his genius; we can take pride in the fact that England has produced him'. Elgar had been due to conduct the concert himself. In August of 1933 Barbirolli and a friend visited Elgar at his home in Worcestershire. They were shown round his garden and Elgar talked to them about his music, bestowing an emotional hug on 'JB' as he left and thanking him for liking his music.

The first Hallé concert after Elgar's death was on 1 March 1934. The orchestra was conducted on this occasion by Sir Thomas Beecham (it was during the interregnum after the departure of Sir Hamilton Harty). Elgar's *Elegy for Strings* was played in his memory. It was the start of a new relationship for the orchestra – one that was partly built on a reputation for interpreting English music. When John Barbirolli took up the position of Principal Conductor he once more brought Elgar's music to the fore.

7 Hamilton Harty (1879–1941), Principal Conductor of the Hallé 1920–33.

In all there are 221 entries for JB and pieces by Elgar in the repertoire database over the years 1934–70, bearing in mind these are by and large, just Manchester concerts. Perhaps unsurprisingly, the *Variations* is the most played piece. For me, despite the link to the Symphony, this is the work that represents the relationship between the Orchestra and Elgar. It has featured in many key concerts over the years, including of course the Centenary performance of the First Symphony and in foreign tours, where a point was often made of taking British music overseas. In 1948 when the Hallé went to Austria the report for the British Council (which had funded the tour) commented: 'The *Enigma Variations* in particular aroused astonished and enthusiastic admiration. Austrians spoke of the English Brahms and asked why they not heard Elgar's music before'.

That the Hallé and its conductors have continued to maintain a special relationship with the music of Elgar seems all the more natural and is a legacy which it is to be hoped will continue long into the future. Most memorably, for me, was when 'Nimrod' was included on the joint concert with the BBC Philharmonic Orchestra for the Tsunami victims in January 2005: the massed forces of both orchestras under the baton of Sir Mark Elder being brought to that magically quiet end was spine-tingling and unforgettable.

~ Julian Rushton

The Importance of being Elgar

Neither 'Edward' nor 'Elgar' really works as a reference to Oscar Wilde's most famous play. But the title expresses my angle of approach here: the importance of *being* Elgar; what Elgar *was* – and therefore why what he did remains important.

I became an Elgarian in my teens; the school's LP collection included the symphonies, and for these I developed an abiding passion. In my first undergraduate year, Cambridge University Musical Society performed *The Dream of Gerontius* under David Willcocks in King's College Chapel (I was 2nd clarinet ...). David defied the anti-Elgar prejudice allegedly endemic in the Faculty of Music (stemming from E.J. Dent), as did his colleague Philip Radcliffe, who gave introductory lectures on the work. Later I played bass clarinet for the Cambridge Philharmonic, also in King's: the three great oratorios under Peter Dennison, and the Bach *Fantasia and Fugue* transcription.

After *The Apostles* I met Jerrold Northrop Moore, then at work on his Elgar biography. A year or so earlier, in 1974, the now-defunct monthly periodical *Music and Musicians* honoured the fortieth anniversary of Elgar's death by commissioning my first writing on him, a tribute that elicited a friendly letter from Michael Kennedy. Perhaps that letter sealed my fate; Elgar has been a major preoccupation ever since, despite my engaging in critical and interpretative work in other areas. But that's enough about me ...

* * *

The importance of *being* Elgar: first and foremost, he was *artistically fearless*. This trait is a counterpoint to his many faux-modest pronouncements, in which he disclaimed knowledge of technical matters; and he wrote on his first stab at *The Black Knight* 'Music by Edward Elgar / if he can.' To compose a dramatic cantata, for this then 'provincial musician' (the title of the volume of early diaries), was indeed fearless; in 1889 there was no commission or immediate prospect of performance. Still more original was to make it, in his own words, 'a sort of symphony' – which it is.

With other such ambitious pieces, at least one performance was guaranteed before Elgar began work. But his approach to Festival commissions was no less fearless, especially with *The Dream of Gerontius*. His standing as a (or the) leading English composer of choral works was made by the Festivals: from Worcester via Hanley and Leeds to Birmingham. The Leeds Festival that had declined Elgar's offer of a symphony in 1898 was treated in 1913 to his glorious yet tragic symphonic portrait of Shakespeare's sublime buffoon, Falstaff. Was this perhaps a teasing act of retribution?

Second: his importance was that, if not without struggle, he showed that a 'provincial musician' could become head of the profession, despite being largely self-taught and neither a university graduate nor an alumnus of the Royal Academy of Music. It was important that London performances soon followed his Festival premieres (*King Olaf*, 1897; *Caractacus*, 1899); this in turn must have encouraged Elgar, after composing a new orchestral piece without a commission, to show it to the conductor Hans Richter (who had conducted the first complete *Ring* cycle). The *Variations* ('Enigma') were a success; and if there were occasional setbacks, like the premiere of *Gerontius*, Elgar's confidence surely recovered soon, following this work's success in Germany. The cyclic concept *The Apostles* was no less fearlessly original, and after a performance of *The Kingdom* there is no sense of incompletion.

Third: others such as William Sterndale Bennett, Henry Hugo Pierson, Stanford, and Ethel Smyth all had some kind of reputation in Germany. Elgar's success there has proved more enduring in the long run; and he soon became known across the Atlantic. Today, an international profile of performances (a member of a Madrid orchestra told me how much they loved playing the symphonies) is supplemented by scholarly activity. American scholars have contributed articles and chapters, for instance in Cambridge University Press's *Elgar Studies*. Jürgen Schaarwächter produced the first significant study of that remarkable phenomenon, the British Symphony, which in the last century owed so much to Elgar's example. Two German scholars, Wolfgang-Armin Rittmeier and Florian Csizmadia, are active Elgarian researchers, respectively on his reception in Berlin, and the sources of his highly individual style; and Barbara Mohn, who has published a book in German on 19th-century English oratorios, has now produced a scholarly edition of *The Dream of Gerontius*.

Fourth: Elgar was no doubt patriotic, but his musical pedigree was international. In a recent Zoom talk for the Elgar Society, Florian Csizmadia reminded us of Elgar's eclecticism (a facet mentioned in my 1974 article, but in less detail). In addition to the influences from home (Parry), and from what was once considered the main stream, Austria and Germany (including older composers – Bach, Mozart – and the then recent Wagner and Brahms), Elgar found much to like, and to fertilize his invention, in French music (Berlioz, Gounod, Delibes); and he admired Verdi's *Requiem*. He seems also to have enjoyed Italian opera and the operettas of Gilbert and Sullivan. All this was a counterpoint to weightier influences and opened his ears to brighter colours, longer-spanning melodies, and more pointed rhythms that enliven his work in the greater, as well as the lighter, genres.

* * *

Commissions for *The Apostles* and *The Kingdom* may have prevented Elgar from immediately following the *Variations* with more orchestral works, apart from his string masterpiece *Introduction and Allegro*. In the latter and the First Symphony Elgar turned to unrealised sketches for string quartet, a medium which, like the symphony, was approached with some trepidation by composers after Beethoven (e.g. Schumann and Brahms). One outcome was that Elgar found excellent material for the middle movements of the First Symphony that are *in the 'wrong' keys* for a work in A flat, a daring action that matches the symphony's originality in deployment of themes and orchestration. This achievement was followed up in later orchestral and chamber music, but always in different ways and to different degrees.

The Second Symphony had a shorter gestation, but is no clone of the First: the movement order reverts to tradition, with the slow movement placed second, the middle movements are not conjoined, the *Scherzo* includes a nightmare vision, and the manner in which the symphony's opening 'motto' is recalled at the end is different – in the First a disputed but eventual triumph, in the Second, twilight with shades of a Brahms favourite, the Third Symphony on which Elgar had lectured in Birmingham. The two concertos, also, could hardly be more distinct in design and feeling. The Violin Concerto is modelled, perhaps unconsciously, on Dvořák's Cello Concerto in the same key: a lengthy introduction before the solo entry, a long slow movement, a finale with slow reminiscence before the end. Elgar called the Cello Concerto 'a big piece' but its greatness is not dependent on length; the introduction is given by the soloist, each movement is relatively short, and the reminiscence within the finale is of an altogether different order of intensity. I am of the school of thought which hears in this a parallel to Richard Strauss's lament for a bygone age (*Metamorphosen*), although that came after the World War II.

* * *

There used be identified an 'English [sic] Musical Renaissance', a concept now much criticized, and not only because it implicitly overlooks the Scots (Mackenzie, MacCunn, Wallace). Despite many worthy – if not absolutely outstanding – composers after Purcell (Arne, Boyce, Shield, the Wesleys,

Potter, the Loders, Bennett ...), a revival of British musical self-confidence was attributed to Elgar's generation; he, Mackenzie, Parry, and Stanford were born within a ten-year period (1848–57; Smyth followed in 1858).

Standing on the shoulders of his elders, Elgar possessed a musical vision that reached wider horizons than theirs. His achievement and claim to be considered the best British composer since Purcell, was recognized by the next generation, even if they studied at the RCM (Holst), or Cambridge *and* the RCM (Vaughan Williams). These in turn stimulated others such as Walton, who had to resist being crowned Elgar's successor (two very different symphonies; string concertos; overtures; Coronation music ...). Even Britten, whose greatest achievement is perhaps in the genre Elgar missed out on, opera, and whose music is poles apart from Elgar's, nevertheless conducted *Gerontius* memorably, which could not have been done without admiration and commitment.

Elgar wrote many works that might be considered of lesser importance than those in the challenging genres of oratorio, symphony, concerto, and chamber music. But his shorter orchestral pieces, the part-songs (especially), and the solo songs (not just the masterly *Sea Pictures*) are never just hackwork done for financial reward – even if they were what Novello most willingly rewarded him for. Elgar was always fastidious, even in japes like 'Kindly do not Smoke'. His music for stage and music hall, and his shorter orchestral works, likewise testify to a mastery of musical *expression* as much as technique. This mastery was unmatched even by his most distinguished contemporaries; for his successors, he became the object, not of imitation, but of a thoroughly healthy emulation.

~ Nigel Simeone

For me, it was love at first hearing: my Elgar adventure began with a Prom on 27 July 1970: Vaughan Williams's *Tallis Fantasia*, Walton's Cello Concerto (with Maurice Gendron) and Elgar's First Symphony, played by the BBC SO conducted by Sir Adrian Boult. I was thirteen and went with my music-loving grandfather (as we did to quite a few Proms). The whole concert left a deep impression, but the A flat Symphony knocked me sideways – I was completely smitten by it. By happy chance, the LP transfer of Elgar's own 1930 performance was released around the same time, came as a timely birthday present, and has remained a firm favourite ever since. Soon afterwards, a local church jumble sale yielded the original 78s of Elgar's electric (and electrifying) recording of the Second Symphony and that, too, was a thrilling discovery. I wanted to explore more Elgar and the chance came when choirs drawn from various schools (including mine) came together for *The Dream of Gerontius*. This was another great moment in my early musical education (we performed it in Thaxted Church and in London) and it drew me further into Elgar's world, something that was enhanced by playing the viola in another *Gerontius* a couple of years later at Reading Town Hall, conducted by Maurice Miles and with John Noble as the baritone soloist.

Schoolboy curiosity led to more discoveries: *Falstaff*, *Enigma* and particularly the Cello Concerto which one of my school friends was learning, and for which he needed a rehearsal pianist. Another chance to hear Boult conducting the First Symphony came at the Winter Proms in January 1973, and in the years that followed, I was able to get to Boult performances of both symphonies as well as the concertos and the *Introduction and Allegro*. It was mostly a combination of Elgar's own recordings and Boult's concerts which were my grounding in Elgar, and for that I remain eternally grateful: his music could not have had two more compelling advocates. Alongside them, I also adored Barbirolli's gloriously impassioned recordings of the symphonies – but I only saw him once (a fabulous programme of Britten, Delius and Mahler at the Festival Hall), so never experienced his Elgar live.

I remember enthusing about Elgar (particularly the First Symphony) and Strauss (I'd just seen *Elektra* at Covent Garden, conducted by Rudolf

Kempe) at my university interview early in 1974 and being met with raised eyebrows: did I really think they were any more than 'good second-raters'? I piled a bit of fuel on that particular fire by saying that I'd also fallen for Puccini's *Turandot* too and, above all, for Janáček. Academic suspicions seemed to be allayed when I said that two other favourite works were Mozart's *Figaro* and Wagner's *Meistersinger*. Still, the idea of Elgar being considered a second-tier composer felt like complete nonsense and I probably said so. But my teenage outrage was misplaced: Maurice Aitchison, the person who had asked me those questions, turned out to be a tremendous enthusiast for Elgar and Strauss, and could play large stretches of Puccini by heart; I later had the pleasure of introducing him to some of Janáček's operas. An inspiring teacher and musician, Maurice's infinitely wide musical sympathies were the exception rather than the rule.

It was a wonderful time to be discovering Elgar. During my time as a music student at Manchester in the mid-1970s, I acquired two important recordings thanks to the second-hand bins in Gibbs Bookshop (then in Albert Square). From the first notes of the Prelude, Boult's set of *The Kingdom* was a glorious revelation; and though Barbirolli's *Gerontius* had been around for a few years, and I'd heard it before, it was a thrill to find a copy that I could take home and call my own.

The idea of Elgar as an international figure was brought home to me in 1973 when Bernard Haitink opened a Festival Hall concert with a very exciting performance of *In the South* – the first time I'd heard it. I'd never thought of Elgar as particularly English (any more than Strauss was particularly German) but rather as unmistakably *Elgarian*: a composer of true individuality and enormous stature, and I subsequently learned – unsurprisingly – how much he had been admired by Strauss. It was fascinating to hear other non-British conductors tackling Elgar: I heard live performances of *Enigma* conducted by Eugen Jochum with the LPO (tremendous) and Leonard Bernstein with the BBC SO (notorious), and was particularly struck by Solti's Elgar, both live and on records. Slightly later on, I was lucky to hear outstanding Elgar from Colin Davis with the LSO, and, in 2009, an unforgettable First Symphony from Charles Mackerras and the Philharmonia Orchestra. In his review of that concert, Andrew Clements in *The Guardian* noted that 'this was Elgar very much as a quintessentially European rather than indelibly English composer – as a contemporary and equal of Richard Strauss whose music needs no special pleading or allowances made'. I couldn't agree more. Conductors like Mark Elder and Andrew Davis developed into exceptional Elgarians, and, more recently, Edward Gardner and Martyn Brabbins have shown the same kind of devotion to his music – as have the (unrelated) Kirill Petrenko and Vasily Petrenko, both of whom have given memorable readings of the Second Symphony. In short, Elgar feels as if he's in safe hands – much as I cherish the memory of discovering his music through Boult and Barbirolli.

It's stating the obvious to say that listening to Elgar – and being drawn into his intimate, emotionally complex world – is a musical experience like no other. As a just-about-adequate pianist, I've had the pleasure of playing the Violin Sonata, and as conductor of the University Orchestra at Bangor, I included Elgar in two of my last concerts there in 2003: the Cello Concerto with a brilliant student (Robert Smith, who has gone on to an impressive career as a viola da gamba player), and a memorable *Introduction and Allegro*, given on a summer evening in a small hall with views down to the Menai Strait, the string orchestra made up of students and friends. That stirred the spirit, but then Elgar so often does that: for me, passages in both the symphonies, in *Gerontius* and *The Kingdom*, in the late chamber music and in much else, seem to reach deep into the soul in ways few other composers can, to stimulate a profoundly *personal* response, and to move us far beyond words.

Wilhelm Sinkovicz

Elgar in Vienna

In the 1980s, as a Viennese music critic, I could still cause heads to shake when I wrote after one of the rare performances of *The Dream of Gerontius* that it would be a good thing for the musical city of Vienna to replace every tenth performance of Johannes Brahms' *Ein Deutsches Requiem* with one of Elgar's oratorios. Although this would still not really do justice to the true status of the English master, it would at least represent a slight sign of recognition.

Of course, the Viennese concert organisers did not take this well-meaning advice. Edward Elgar's works still have the status of exotics in the repertoire of the Austrian capital. This is despite the fact that record collectors interested in the late romanticism of the Richard Strauss era naturally own Pierre Monteux's beautiful London Symphony Orchestra recording of the *Enigma Variations.* At best, they only hear live the 'Nimrod' movement as an encore at a performance by a visiting British orchestra.

Yet on the occasion of Sir Edward's 75th birthday in 1932, the musical city of Vienna learnt from detailed newspaper features that the well-known and esteemed George Bernard Shaw had three years earlier already declared Elgar to be the 'greatest contemporary composer'.[1] This will have been met with a shake of the head, just as my call was 40 years ago for *Gerontius* to be performed more often in Vienna. But at least it was favourably acknowledged that, alongside Richard Strauss or the Viennese late Romantics Franz Schmidt, Julius Bittner and Joseph Marx, there were composers elsewhere in the wide world who used traditional, melodious means to stand up to the radical modernism represented in Vienna by Arnold Schoenberg and his students.

What that generation of music lovers perceived as 'modern' could already be gleaned from a review in 1903, when Elgar was praised as the 'most respected modern English composer', who 'throws himself into life' more 'courageously' than many colleagues and in his *Cockaigne* Overture

1 'Feuilleton; Edward Elgar', *Neues Wiener Tagblatt*, 30 May 1932, 2.

makes the 'noise of the big city' sound picturesque. Early Viennese performances of Elgar's works included the *Enigma Variations* (1903), the First Symphony (1909), the Violin Concerto (1912) and *Gerontius*, the first performance of which in the Großer Musikvereinssaal in 1905 was remembered by a reviewer in 1912 with the words: '*The Dream of Gerontius* ... remained in our memory as a beautiful-sounding, perfectly formed work. Even if one could not speak of a lavishly swelling invention, there was still enough of interest, some concise ideas, some things that had the right flow and momentum.'[2]

By contrast, Elgar's second great oratorio, *The Apostles*, made for the critic 'a less favourable impression ... Elgar has certainly created music out of a deeply religious feeling; he has written good, erudite music, but without enlightening inspiration, without a sparkling imagination.'[3] And this despite the fact that the spirituality of Elgar, who – unusually enough for the leading English composer of his time – was a Catholic, had to be somehow familiar to Catholic Vienna.

Be that as it may, the stigma of not being fully mature, of lacking inspiration, resonated in many Viennese comments about Elgar's music over the years and decades. After the first performance of the First Symphony Julius Korngold, the father of the composer Erich Wolfgang Korngold, mocked the harmonic peculiarities of the formal structure, created by 'heterogeneous keys' that had been 'jumbled together.' Nevertheless, the critic recognised 'the Englishness' of Elgar's work, 'more in its basic intellectual character than in its musical substance.'[4] The *Enigma Variations*, which had already been presented in Vienna a few years earlier, was much more to Korngold's liking. Three years later, in 1912, the *Neues Wiener Tagblatt* lauded the Second Symphony as 'the most important new publication of recent times, certainly one of the most interesting.'[5] And the reviewer of the *Wiener Sonn- und Montags-Zeitung* praised the work of a composer 'who also has something to say ... One hears vivid themes that are artfully linked and realised as the work progresses; the form is masterfully handled, nothing is brooding or contrived, but everywhere only organic growth and natural development. None of the four movements offers anything unsettling, but each contains a healthy core, has a genuinely symphonic character and bears witness to the composer's disciplined artistic sense.'[6]

2 *Wiener Zeitung*, 9 April 1912, 4.

3 Ibid.

4 'Feuilleton', *Neue Freie Presse*, 23 January 1909, 3.

5 'Konzerte', *Neues Wiener Tagblatt (Abendausgabe)*, 8 February 1912, 7.

6 'Konzerte', *Wiener Sonn- und Montags-Zeitung*, 5 February 1912, 13.

At least, one might say, that was the time when the Viennese had rarely been friendlier to foreign composers. In the same year, 1912, Korngold showed scepticism after a performance of the Violin Concerto – with none other than Eugene Ysaÿe as the soloist![7] The middle movement revealed Elgar's alleged weaknesses: 'What this fine mind lacks, on close observation, is the deeper art of rhythmic organisation. Hence also breadth without climaxes, and especially in this *Andante* a singing and re-singing of the violin without finding a tune.'[8] Barely ten years later, Josef Reitler commented in the *Neue Freie Presse* on a performance of Elgar's Cello Concerto from a completely 'progressive' perspective, saying that the work suffered 'from the triviality of the invention and a rhythmic monotony extending to the last movement', which 'even some charming effects of instrumentation could not disguise.'[9]

So, Edward Elgar has not had an easy time in Vienna. Nevertheless, the Philharmoniker, Vienna's internationally renowned orchestra, has played during the composer's lifetime, as part of its subscription concert series, *In the South* (1905, under Felix Mottl), the *Enigma Variations* (1905, under Franz Schalk) and, on the occasion of a guest appearance by Adrian Boult in 1933, the *Introduction and Allegro*. After the Second World War, it was John Barbirolli who encouraged the orchestra to dig out the scores of the *Enigma Variations* from its archive. The following year, 1947, the Philharmoniker's concertmaster Wolfgang Schneiderhan was the soloist in a performance of the Violin Concerto (as well as Tchaikovsky's concerto) under Josef Krips. One cannot help but at least consider whether this programming was a tribute to the then Allied occupying forces. After all, it was more than a quarter of a century before Lorin Maazel once again set the *Introduction and Allegro* at the beginning of a Philharmonic subscription concert, Zubin Mehta followed a little later in 1976 with the *Enigma Variations*, Sir Georg Solti with the same only in 1996.

Time and again there have been long Elgar pauses, and it was almost exclusively English conductors who then devoted themselves to the composer with the Vienna Philharmoniker: John Eliot Gardiner, for example, Simon Rattle, Daniel Harding and Roger Norrington, who performed the A flat major Symphony for the first time, during the orchestra's elite matinee cycle in 2002, when the piece was already almost 100 years old!

7 Fritz Kreisler had given the Viennese premiere of the concerto less than three weeks earlier.

8 'Konzert Ysaÿe', *Neue Freie Presse*, 24 February 1912, 10.

9 'Feuilleton', *Neue Freie Presse (Nachmittagblatt)*, 14 November 1921, 2.

I wish I could hear the E flat major symphony played by the Philharmoniker, one of my absolute favourite pieces. Perhaps I should give it a try and suggest replacing every hundredth performance of Brahms's First with Elgar's Second?

❧ Lani Spahr

The Recordings

I've had the distinct pleasure, starting in 2011, of digitally transferring and restoring all the surviving recordings from Sir Edward Elgar's personal record library. Many of these discs had never seen the commercial light of day until the enterprising labels of Music & Arts and SOMM Recordings took an interest in my proposal to issue these rare recordings.

My first project in 2011 was 'Elgar conducts Elgar – The Complete Recordings, 1914–1925' on the Music & Arts label. I had long had a desire to work on these since their first issue on the Pearl label in a decidedly non-interventionist form. With modern cutting-edge tools at my disposal, I was able to eliminate the distracting 'frying sausages' sound that was a prominent feature of recordings from this period, which in many cases can completely obscure the music-making. As I worked on these discs, I had the uncanny feeling of being in the small room with Elgar and his band (several reviewers also mentioned this effect). Given the fact that the technique which was used at the time is considered crude by modern standards, it nevertheless captured something that eludes even the most sophisticated recording technology. How is it that a non-electrical, physical recording method can produce results that are so immediate and life-like?

Elgar was the first important composer to conduct his own works in the recording studio, starting in 1914. The second was Richard Strauss who made his first discs in 1916. These recordings, and Elgar's subsequent electrical recordings from 1926 to 1933, present a unique window into performance practice in the first quarter of the twentieth century.

Here we have direct reproducible evidence of how music was played, and how Elgar wanted his music played, during his lifetime; and the more we immerse ourselves in these recordings the more we sense something missing from our modern recordings and performances. Yes, the orchestras of today are wondrous machines and a marvel of technical facility, but as Elgar said to Beatrice Harrison when recording the Cello Concerto for the second time, (I paraphrase) 'Don't bother the notes Bea, give 'em the spirit!' That, I fear, is what is missing – the spirit. But what spirit? Whose spirit?

During my work on the restoration of the recording sessions for the second recording of the Cello Concerto with Beatrice Harrison (which survive complete, save for one 4-minute take) I spent innumerable hours listening to these discs. When I was finished I was certainly in no hurry to listen to another recording, but when I eventually did I said to myself, 'NO! That's not the way it goes!' Today's hyper-romanticism is a poor substitute for the genuine Elgarian romanticism (a term he would not have used). As fine a recording as the Jacqueline du Pré version on EMI is, it is mystifying to me that it is held up as the finest one available, and one to which all others are compared. I would venture to say that many reviewers (and listeners) are not at all familiar with the Harrison/Elgar version. I would also venture that if they went back and listened to it without knowing who the performers were they would not be very impressed – just because it is so *old* and not at all like what one hears nowadays. In fact it is not possible to *ever* hear playing like that today because the style has been schooled out of today's musicians. Attempts have been made, and continue to be made, to reproduce it, but what we hear are merely modern musicians playing on old instruments. And even if it *could* be reproduced, most people would not want to hear it. One has to have lived in that bygone era to fully understand it, and you could say that, like modern musicians, this sound has been schooled out of modern audiences.

While much of what I have said applies to any recording of this period, what does this have to do with Elgar specifically?

A composer writes what he hears. The same can be said about a conductor – he reproduces what he hears in his mind's ear. Of course I'm talking about proficient professionals. The sound of all the great orchestras was a product of what each conductor heard in his own ear and was able to impress upon the orchestra: Szell/Cleveland, Barbirolli/Hallé, Fürtwangler/Berlin, Munch/Boston, Boult/London, to name a few of the obvious greats.

The recordings that Elgar made give us a window into how he heard his own compositions. Through them we hear what he had in his head even before he put pen to paper. There has been much written about how all the great conductors could change the sound of an orchestra just by their presence on the podium. While not a great conductor, the same can be said about Elgar, since there are accounts of his conducting and the effect he had on his players.

In an interview recorded for the BBC in 1957, Sir Adrian Boult said: 'Elgar as a conductor was a curious paradox. He was not a good conductor, but at the same time he was responsible … for some of the finest performances of his own work that anyone has ever heard'. In the same programme tenor Sir Steuart Wilson talks about the effects Elgar could get in a performance:

'The thing I remember most about him was the kind of feeling that you caught … from his mysterious way of conducting, because technically he was a bad conductor. But emotionally he managed to make everybody give the best performance of their lives … because you felt that magic … in him.'

Magic – that most elusive of qualities in a conductor. It can't be taught – either you have it or you don't. Given the numerous first-hand accounts of his conducting, it is obvious that Elgar had it. These recordings are probably the most intimately revealing testament that Elgar left us. Of course the letters tell us a great deal. But if you read, say, the Windflower letters in which he confided intimately with Alice Stuart Wortley (his *Windflower*) during the composition of the Violin Concerto, without listening to and *learning* his recording with Yehudi Menuhin, you will see only half the man. The same is true, and even more so, if you know only the concerto recording and not the Windflower letters. These letters tell us of Elgar writing his innermost feelings into this concerto. I once was speaking to a violinist who told me she was playing this concerto soon with a well-known American orchestra. I began talking about the significance of these letters and to my astonishment she said she had no idea that anything like this existed. Indeed, I've heard new recordings from famous violinists that sound like they needed to lose the loves of their lives before they can properly plumb the depths of this piece. So I ask, how can anyone play this concerto and not take these letters into account, these letters that tell us so much about Elgar the man?

Musicians who played under Elgar's direction comment on how his nervous manner would affect how he conducted and, consequently, how they played, and how he could change the tenor of a performance with a mere twitch of his expressive left hand. Of course, a recording is not a live performance and, even in the early days of recording, was put together like a patchwork quilt, so that much of the spontaneity of a live performance is lost. However, we can still hear the quick-silver energy in his records that is missing in today's recordings. As brilliant as many of them are, we're missing the 'magic' of the man, the magic that made him who he was. Taken together – his recordings and his letters – we get the most complete picture of the composer that is possible for us today.

6

Other Composers (Recent Essays from The Elgar Society *Journal*)

8. An oval image of Elgar in profile taken by James Bacon & Sons the leading photographic studio in Leeds. Mounted on board signed with an inscription 'To W.H.G. Norton, May 17, 1912'. At the time Elgar's doctor prescribed a course of baths administered by a male nurse called Norton. Alice Elgar's diary for 17 May 1912 includes this passage: '…E finished course of baths. Farewell to Norton. E gave a signed photo to Norton…'.

Walter Parratt (1841–1924)

Relf Clark

I Introduction

Sir Walter Parratt died at 12 The Cloisters, Windsor Castle on 27 March 1924.[1] The following reflections mark the centenary of that event.

The death must have come to Elgar's notice very quickly, for the next day he wrote as follows to Lord Stamfordham, the Private Secretary to George V:

> I see, with the greatest regret, the announcement of the death of my old friend Sir Walter Parratt, Master of the King's Musick.
>
> If there is to be a new appointment may I suggest, without presumption, that I should feel it to be the greatest honour if I might be allowed to hold the position?[2]

The rather unseemly timing of the letter suggests anxiety. Elgar could surely have waited until after the funeral, which took place on 1 April.[3] Why did

1 Information taken from the death certificate. It describes Parratt as 'Master of the King's Musick, / Organist, / Knight' and gives his age as 83. Stanford died two days later. The house occupied by the Organist and Master of the Choristers at St George's is nowadays 23 The Cloisters, which is not 12 The Cloisters renumbered: 12 The Cloisters is the flat beneath Vicars' Hall and today the home of the College archive. I am indebted to Roger Judd, MVO for this information.

2 Moore, J.N., *Edward Elgar* [:] *letters of a lifetime* (Oxford: Clarendon Press, 1990), 381.

3 Tovey, D. and Parratt, G., *Walter Parratt* (London: Oxford University Press, 1941), 137. For a concise account of Parratt's career, with particular reference to his time at Windsor, see Fellowes, E.H., *Organists and Masters of the Choristers of St George's Chapel in Windsor Castle* (Windsor: Oxley and Son (Windsor) Ltd, *c.*1939), 79–86. See also West, J.E., *Cathedral Organists past and present* (London: Novello & Co., 1921), 153 and 167 and Shaw, Watkins, *The Succession of Organists of the Chapel Royal and the Cathedrals of England and Wales from* c.*1538* (Oxford: Clarendon Press, 1991), 350–1 and 384. For an account of the role played by Parratt in the history of the

he not do so? In December 1909 he had had from Gilbert Parker a letter describing him as 'the Master of English Music'.[4] Did that phrase, slightly adjusted, plant a seed in Elgar's mind? Had he toyed with the idea of filling a vacancy that Parratt's death would create? If he had, perhaps he was now fretting over the possibility that someone else would be approached. Elgar was much concerned with status and recognition (with 'the importance of Elgar', in other words). We see that concern at its most unattractive in the episode at the Royal Academy on 3 May 1913,[5] and at its most embarrassing in his attempt to procure a peerage. By 1924, Elgar's admission to the Order of Merit was an event in the foreign country of the pre-war past. Since then, various honours had come his way, but none of them was from the King,[6] and it seems reasonable to assume that succeeding Parratt as Master of the King's Music [7] would provide (for the time being) the reassurance he may well have craved.

It is difficult to know whether the 'if' at the beginning of Elgar's second sentence indicates doubt as to the future of the office or merely a desire not to be thought presumptuous. It has been suggested that fear of abolition was all that motivated him, but from what follows it appears that the possibility had not crossed his mind.[8] Dated 1 April, the reply to his letter came from Sir Frederick Ponsonby, the Keeper of the Privy Purse, and it contained the following sentence:

> It has, however, been contemplated in former years to abolish the post of 'Master of the Music'[9] and I cannot therefore say whether the King will retain this post in the [Royal] Household.

At this point, Elgar seems to have realised that the matter was not entirely straightforward. Not wishing his initial letter to be construed as financially motivated, in a letter dated 2 April he hastened to assure Sir Frederick that

organs of St George's Chapel, see Judd, R.L., *The Organs in Windsor Castle* [:] *their history and development* (Oxford: Positif Press, 2015), 67–85.

4 Moore, J.N., *Elgar and his publishers* [:] *letters of a creative life* (Oxford: Clarendon Press, 1987), 726.

5 See Moore, J.N., *Edward Elgar* [:] *the Windflower letters* (Oxford: Clarendon Press, 1989), 117.

6 See McVeagh, D.M., *Edward Elgar* [:] *his life and music* (London: J.M. Dent & Sons Limited, 1955), 248–9.

7 Geoffrey Parratt pointed out that in all three of his father's warrants of appointment the spelling was 'Music' rather than 'Musick' or 'Musicke', which he regarded as journalistic inventions: Tovey and Parratt, op. cit., 90.

8 Moore, J.N., *Elgar and his publishers*, 838. See also Moore, J.N., *Letters of a lifetime*, 496.

9 Note the spelling 'Music' and see note 7.

he would not have written 'in the first instance' had he not been advised that the post was 'purely honorary'. Turning then to the possibility of abolition, he continued as follows:

> With respect and without wishing to presume in the slightest degree, I desire to urge very strongly that His Majesty the King be advised to retain it, at least for the present ... [because to] ... abolish it at this moment would have a very deterrent effect on the prestige and progress of British music especially abroad.[10]

Elgar's 'prestige and progress' point seems far-fetched. Parratt was no exception to the general rule that in those days the Master of the King's Music tended not to have a particularly high profile. From the year of his initial appointment, 1893, until his death,[11] Parratt divided the majority of his professional time between playing the organ and taking practices at St George's, teaching at the Royal College of Music, and travelling on the Great Western Railway between Paddington and Windsor & Eton Central. For a decade (1908–18) his routines were varied by his duties as Professor of Music at Oxford, but the post did not require residence and could not have interfered very much with the tasks he undertook at Windsor and the RCM. He did not occupy an international stage, and whether musicians abroad knew much about him seems a little doubtful. But Elgar's approach paid off, and on 28 April he was able to tell the Windflower that a letter offering him the post had arrived (at Perryfield) that morning.[12] Parratt's death therefore assisted Elgar in his career. In life, his intentional assistance had been rendered on a number of occasions, and to these we must now turn, but not before giving an outline of Parratt's own career.

II Huddersfield to Windsor and South Kensington

Parratt was born in Huddersfield on 10 February 1841, the son of Thomas Parratt, a professional organist.[13] In 1852, aged only eleven, he became the

10 Moore, J.N., *Letters of a lifetime*, 382. In this letter, Elgar wrote 'Master of the Music', having evidently noted the spelling preferred by Sir Frederick.

11 The appointment was renewed after the accession of Edward VII and again after that of George V.

12 Moore, J.N., *The Windflower letters*, 291. In an earlier letter to the Windflower (16 April) he misrepresented the sequence of events: ibid., 289–90.

13 The date of birth is as given by Tovey and Parratt, op. cit. A certificate appears to be unobtainable, and it may be that Parratt's parents failed through ignorance of the law to register the birth (which occurred only a few years after registration had become a legal obligation).

organist at the church in Armitage Bridge, a nearby village; and later in the same year he went to the choir school of St Peter's Chapel, Palace Street, London, where George Cooper gave him organ lessons. In 1854 he returned to Huddersfield and took up the post of Organist of St Paul's Church. The connection with the Elgar family began in 1861, when he was appointed Organist of the church of St Michael and All Angels, Great Witley, Worcestershire, a post that involved acting as the private organist of the Earl of Dudley; and it was in that capacity that Parratt became acquainted with Elgar's father, William Henry Elgar, who tuned the pianos at Witley Court, the Earl's residence.[14]

Parratt left Great Witley in 1868, and in 1872, after a few years as Organist of Wigan Parish Church, he was appointed Organist – or *Informator Choristarum* – of Magdalen College, Oxford, following John Stainer's translation from there to St Paul's Cathedral, London. In 1882, he succeeded George Elvey as Organist of St George's Chapel, Windsor Castle, and in 1883 he became the first Professor of Organ at the recently opened Royal College of Music. He was knighted in 1892, in 1893 he succeeded William Cusins as Master of the Queen's Music, and he was Professor of Music at Oxford from 1908 (when he succeeded Parry) to 1918 (when he was succeeded by Hugh Allen). He received a number of honorary degrees and was awarded the KCVO.

III 1896–1910

Parratt and Elgar may have become acquainted in the Great Witley years, but Dr Moore felt unable to go further than saying that Elgar 'almost certainly' accompanied his father on his tuning rounds.[15] After leaving Great Witley, Parratt had no obvious reason to be in contact with Elgar, and it seems likely that it was not until the 1890s that they met (or met again, as the case may be). He was certainly present at the Queen's Hall on 3 September 1896, when Elgar rehearsed the Leeds Choral Union in *The Light of Life*, Op. 29,[16] and Kennedy states that a meeting took place on that occasion.[17] Some four months later, in a letter to Novello & Co. dated 9 January 1897, Elgar was

[14] Moore, J.N., *Edward Elgar* [:] *a creative life* (Oxford: Oxford University Press, 1984), 215, 240.

[15] Moore, J.N., *Letters of a lifetime*, 496.

[16] Moore, J.N., *A creative life*, 215. The Leeds Choral Union was one of the ingredients of the choir at the Worcester Festival performance on 8 September 1896.

[17] Kennedy, M., *Portrait of Elgar* (London: Oxford University Press, 1968), 37.

able to claim acquaintance with Parratt,[18] and we have seen that by 1924 he could refer to him as his 'old friend'. Why was Parratt present at that September rehearsal? Was it out of a combination of sentimental regard for the Great Witley days and curiosity about the progress of William Elgar's boy? Was he connected with the Leeds chorus? Whatever the reason, that letter in January 1897 related to the *Imperial March*, Op. 32, which Elgar hoped to dedicate to Queen Victoria. That the work bears no dedication indicates that nothing came of Elgar's approaching Parratt for permission; but some two years later he applied to him for assistance of a similar kind in connection with *Caractacus*, Op.35, and in a letter to Elgar dated 20 July 1899 Parratt agreed to consult Her Majesty.[19] He went on to say not only that he used Elgar's music 'constantly' but also that the Queen herself liked it;[20] and in the same letter Parratt commissioned a work for inclusion in a collection of choral items marking (and to be performed on) Victoria's eightieth birthday, which fell on 24 May 1899. Elgar was summoned to Windsor Castle for this occasion and saw and heard 'Her Most Gracious Majesty'.[21] Later in the same year, Parratt organized a concert at the Royal Albert Institute, Windsor, at which Elgar in the presence of Princess Christian conducted eleven of his own works.[22] For the purpose of this event, Elgar was provided with accommodation in Windsor Castle, a fact he proudly communicated both to his father and to his sister Helen ('Dot').[23] In December 1900, there was correspondence between Elgar and Parratt about the possibility of a setting of Kipling's *Recessional*,[24] but although the latter was enthusiastic ('Please do it, and soon') nothing ensued. However, Queen Victoria died on 22 January 1901, and on 12 March Parratt passed on to Elgar a coronation ode written by A.C. Benson, a master at Eton College, and urged him to

18 Moore, J.N., *Letters of a creative life*, 43.

19 Permission was duly given, and the dedication is as follows: TO / HER MOST GRACIOUS MAJESTY / QUEEN VICTORIA / THIS CANTATA / CARACTACUS / IS BY SPECIAL PERMISSION / DEDICATED / BY HER MAJESTY'S LOYAL AND DEVOTED SERVANT / EDWARD ELGAR.

20 Moore, J.N., *Letters of a lifetime*, 65.

21 Moore, J.N., *A creative life*, 269. The work was *To her, beneath whose steadfast star*, a setting of words by F.W.H. Myers. It formed part of a volume entitled *Choral songs in honour of Her Majesty Queen Victoria* (London: Macmillan, 1899).

22 Ibid., 292. What were they? Dr Moore's 'eleven' is contradicted by Elgar in his letter to his sister Helen ('Dot') dated 20 October 1899, in which he writes 'ten' and underlines the word: see Moore, J.N., *Letters of a lifetime*, 80.

23 Moore, J.N., *Letters of a lifetime*, 80–1.

24 Moore, J.N., *A creative life*, 338.

set it:[25] as amended, it became the text of Elgar's *Coronation Ode*, Op. 44,[26] which included *Land of Hope and Glory*. The coronation having taken place on 9 August 1902, the work was given its first performance on 2 October, as part of the Sheffield Festival;[27] and in the following month Elgar completed a set of five TTBB part-songs, *From the Greek Anthology*, Op. 45,[28] and dedicated it to Parratt, presumably as a gesture of thanks. Perhaps it was in acknowledgement of the dedication that in December 1902 Parratt increased Elgar's exposure to the royal family by taking him to Kensington Palace in order to meet Princess Henry of Battenburg.[29] There then seems to be something of a gap, caused possibly by an absence of royal events requiring music, and perhaps by Elgar's relationship with Edward VII being such that a proxy at Court was no longer required. But on 8 May 1908 Elgar wrote to Parratt from Parker's Hotel, Naples and congratulated him on his appointment as Heather Professor at Oxford.[30] It therefore seems that the friendship was maintained; and a further commission from Parratt came in 1909, for an anthem to be sung at Frogmore on the anniversary of Queen Victoria's death.[31] The result was *They are at rest*, a setting of a text by J.H. Newman; its first performance was given at Windsor on 22 January 1910.[32]

IV Retrospect

Parratt's rise in the world of music is comparable in some ways with that of Elgar. He was born and brought up in the provinces. His father was a musician. His family occupied a relatively low stratum of the middle class. He attended neither a famous school nor a university (but in later years he became a magnet for honorary degrees). However, the combination of outstanding skill as an organist and his affiliation to the Church of England

25 Kennedy, M., *The life of Elgar* (Cambridge: Cambridge University Press, 2004), 84.

26 Moore, J.N., *A creative life*, 347.

27 Kent, C.J., *Edward Elgar* [:] *a guide to research* (New York and London: Garland Publishing, Inc., 1993), 192. See also Bury, D., 'Elgar, the Eton housemaster and the *Coronation Ode*' in Mitchell, K.D., ed., *Cockaigne* [:] *essays on Elgar 'in London town'* (Rickmansworth: Elgar Editions, 2004), 94–137.

28 Although the work was completed on 11 November that year, its first performance took place at the Royal Albert Hall on 25 April 1904: Kennedy, M., *Portrait*, 286. There was much to-ing and fro-ing between Elgar and Jaeger over the proofs, largely it seems because the texts were to appear in both English and German.

29 Moore, J.N., *A creative life*, 378.

30 Tovey and Parratt, op. cit., 112.

31 Moore, J.N., *A creative life*, 557.

32 Kent, C.J., op. cit., 252.

ensured Parratt's apparently smooth transition from the provinces (Huddersfield, Great Witley, Wigan) to a famous university (Oxford) and from there not only to the Royal Household (Windsor) but also to the musical establishment created by the RCM (South Kensington). By 1883, when he was still in his early forties, he seems to have acquired an impregnable position both musically and socially, and he went on to occupy it for the next 40 years. The well-trodden (and not unremunerative) career paths available to Parratt, and to Anglican organists generally, had no immediately obvious equivalents for a Roman Catholic violinist who aspired to be a composer: Elgar remained an obscure figure until the appearance of the various choral works he wrote in the 1890s, and he was 42 when the *Variations on an original theme*, Op. 36 launched his international career. Parratt was an insider, Elgar an outsider. But without the patronage of Frederick Ouseley, whose Wardenship of St Michael's College, Tenbury made him accessible in the Great Witley years, Parratt might have remained an obscure figure.[33] He was aware of, and had himself surmounted, the difficulties that stood in the way of those who lacked a patrician education and well-off parents, and perhaps he regarded Elgar as being in some ways a kindred spirit. It is surely significant that he passed Benson's coronation ode not to his RCM colleague Parry, who might well have made a successful setting of it, but to Elgar.[34] He grasped the importance of Elgar, the fact that he was the rising star; and at this distance his advocacy of the younger man looks like his striking a blow for the class from which they had both emerged, and an equivalent (and perhaps an acknowledgement) of Ouseley's crucial help.

V Coda

Nothing turns on it, but both Elgar and Parratt had a connection with the Pre-Raphaelites. In the Lady Lever Gallery in Port Sunlight, and in the City Museum and Art Gallery in Birmingham, Parratt appears with John Stainer, Varley Roberts, a few dons, and the Magdalen trebles in Holman

33 The important role that Ouseley played in Parratt's career is gone into in Lawford, T., 'Walter Parratt', *Journal of the British Institute of Organ Studies* 29 (2005), 135–161. As far as Parratt was concerned, Great Witley and Tenbury Wells were within walking distance of each other (he was a man of great energy).

34 Parry's ability to write grand occasional music is more than confirmed by *I was glad*, which nowadays receives many more performances than the *Coronation Ode*, the latter having become, in Robert Anderson's words, 'an opulent curiosity': Anderson, R., *Elgar* (London: J.M. Dent, 1993), 193.

Hunt's *May morning on Magdalen Tower.*[35] Elgar's well-known connection is that Alice Stuart Wortley was a daughter of John Everett Millais, who like Holman Hunt was a member of the Brotherhood. Those who seek out memorials to, as well as images of, Elgar's dedicatees may like to know that Parratt's may be found in the floor of the north aisle of the Quire of St George's Chapel, Windsor Castle, near the entrance to the organ-loft (and on the other side of the aisle from the King George VI Memorial Chapel). It reads as follows:

> BENEATH THIS STONE / REST THE ASHES OF / WALTER PARRATT KT. / K.C.V.O. M.A. MVS. DOC., / FOR FORTY TWO YEARS / ORGANIST OF THIS CHAPEL / AND / EMMA / HIS WIFE / 1842–1931[36]

Parratt comes to mind on the quarterly Obit days at St George's, when as a rule one hears his short but moving anthem *The Whirlwind.* Tovey and Parratt give a two-page list of his compositions,[37] but outside Windsor his contribution tends to be limited to a few Anglican chants, the hymn-tune *Obiit,* and *Give rest, O Christ,* a setting of a melody from the Kiev tradition.[38]

35 RC observation. The painting dates from the period 1888–90 (Stainer succeeded Ouseley as Heather Professor in 1889: why Parratt was in Oxford on that occasion does not appear to be known). The Birmingham painting is a smaller version of the very striking one at Port Sunlight. A 1914 portrait of Parratt by J.S. Sargent can be found in the Heckscher Museum of Art, Huntington, NY; it is reproduced in Tovey and Parratt, op. cit. A portrait by William Rothenstein is reproduced by Lawford, op. cit.

36 RC observation. There is another Parratt memorial further along the north aisle: 'In loving memory of / AMY TEMPLE PARRATT / who died within these precincts 18 Sept. 1917. / Dear daughter of / Sir Walter Parratt / organist of this chapel / and Emma his wife. / "Waiting for the morning"'.

37 Tovey and Parratt, op. cit., 168–9.

38 See 301 and 351 in the 'refreshing' edition of *Hymns Ancient & Modern.*

Frederick Delius (1862–1934)

Paul Guinery

Elgar and Delius: Some Common Ground

Elgar and Delius are scarcely reckoned to be kindred spirits. Musical chalk and cheese, they created very different soundscapes. Yet I believe there were more points of contact than either they, or we, might have expected. For a start, both were self-taught, with little or no formal training. True, Delius did at length manage to enrol at Leipzig Conservatoire, parental support grudgingly bestowed only through the persuasive advocacy of Edvard Grieg. Elgar's father, on the other hand, simply couldn't afford the fees. But ironically Delius turned out to be an ungrateful student with a poor attendance record. He soon dropped out; all those academic exercises in writing fugues were not for him. He turned his back and fled to Paris, resigned to bide his time – just as Elgar was having to do, in his case in less exotic Worcester. With hindsight this probably happened for the best, enabling both young men to break away from the long shadow cast by Brahms over his contemporaries and successors, with its short-sighted resistance to Wagnerian chromaticism. Parry and Stanford never avoided speaking with a Brahmsian accent whereas Elgar and Delius certainly did and forged their own styles, instantly recognisable within a bar or so. Leonard Bernstein, when he conducted *Enigma* marvelled at how inimitable Elgar's voice was, whilst still drawing on the basic vocabulary of a late 19th-century language.

Neither Elgar nor Delius had significant imitators or disciples; it's hard to think of any who started out writing 'in the style of Elgar' (let alone Delius). Nor did the two composers make any impression in most European countries. Elgar hardly became a household name in, say, Spain or Italy whilst Delius, despite spending most of his life in France, was totally ignored there. He still is, despite a heartfelt musical tribute to the city of his mis-spent youth in his tone-poem *Paris – Song of a Great City.*

Where both composers did find encouragement and – most importantly – performances, was in pre-war Germany, so much so that 1914 had a traumatic effect on them, both professionally and personally, not to mention practically, in terms of income. Previously their large-scale works, including in Delius's case a couple of operas, were taken up in Germany by sympathetic conductors. Neither man ever hit his stride again after 1919, Delius becoming a chronic invalid, Elgar crushed by personal grief and disillusionment. However, after the compositionally barren 1920s, there came for both a certain late-flowering in the 1930s with Delius able to complete half a dozen or so abandoned works, thanks to Eric Fenby's devoted services, and Elgar embarking on a third symphony. (Interesting to equate this with Rachmaninoff who, after many unproductive years touring as a pianist and conductor, returned to composition and produced three masterpieces, including a third symphony, in half a dozen years before his death in 1943.)

Another point of similarity, it seems to me, is how Delius and Elgar shared a comparably iconoclastic view of musical form. Whenever I accompany Elgar's Violin Sonata I'm struck by how irreverently it deviates from the text-book definition of a sonata, notably in terms of keys and subjects. It is hard to pin it down formally, since it so frequently heads off in totally unexpected directions. Likewise Delius, in his three mature violin sonatas, pays only scant attention to traditional form. He often unveils tantalising scraps and fragments of ideas and then begins to develop and evolve them immediately, too unwilling (or impatient) to wait for the so-called 'development section'. This can be confusing, but as a listener or performer one must simply go with the flow and leave one's expectations behind. But, as with Elgar, it is not a question of mere caprice or formlessness, a charge often levelled by detractors. I am convinced that there is a firm controller in charge, directing from the wings, building a convincing construction. Not haphazard at all but a case of two composers knowing exactly what they are about.

Here's another point of similarity, a regrettable one (I speak as a keyboard player) in that neither composer was drawn to the piano as a solo instrument (joining other reluctant compatriots such as Vaughan Williams, Walton and Britten). Elgar's piano writing, in the Violin Sonata and Piano Quintet, can be quirky, sometimes lying unnaturally under the hand, though it is undeniably very effective. Delius's penchant for writing page after page of thickly spaced, chromatic chords with little change of texture has undoubtedly put pianists off his Cello Sonata, beautiful as it is (just as cellists are deterred by its lack of bars' rest and its severe challenges to intonation). Delius even bizarrely allowed the virtuoso Theodor Szántó to completely rewrite the soloist's part of his Piano Concerto.

It has also struck me how the two composers shared a love of both town and country: Elgar celebrating the bustle and pageantry of London in scores such as *Cockaigne* and *Falstaff* while still relishing his Malvern Hills; Delius, a poet of nature, at his best 'in a summer garden' or listening to spring cuckoos, but also revelling in memories of wild oats sown on the town, as evoked in *Paris* or in the *Idyll.*

I suspect that Delius and Elgar would have been wary of each other as young men, Delius possessing a self-assurance, not to say arrogance, that Elgar would not have found congenial. In any case, they hardly ever met, just occasionally in London and once at the Birmingham Festival of 1912 when Elgar conducted his *Music Makers* which Delius, to put it mildly, didn't care for: 'rowdy and commonplace' was how he dismissed it. Though it's not on record what Elgar thought of Delius's *Sea Drift,* performed on the same occasion, I suspect its yearning poignancy would have greatly appealed to him. But in their final years, they were drawn together when they met at Delius's home in Grez-sur-Loing on the afternoon of 30 May 1933, unaware that it would be for the last time. It was Elgar who'd made the first move, writing to Delius out of concern for his appalling physical incapacity, fascinated that Delius had been enabled to continue composing when all seemed hopeless, through the skill of his amanuensis, Eric Fenby.

They talked music and Elgar brought a gift of new recordings of Sibelius and Hugo Wolf. Delius was on his best behaviour, telling his visitor that he thought there was some 'fine stuff' in the *Introduction and Allegro* and that he admired *Falstaff;* indeed, elsewhere he described it as a magnificent work, rating it as the best of its composer and the product of a 'rich nature', rare praise indeed from Delius who normally disliked any music apart from his own. In turn, Elgar asked to be sent some Delius scores to conduct. They also chatted about books, gardening and Elgar's first trip by aeroplane, from Croydon to Paris, which had induced school-boyish excitement. Delius could grow suddenly tired of visitors and peremptorily dismiss them, but not on this occasion. Indeed, he was disappointed that Elgar had to leave, albeit after several hours (he was over in France to conduct his *Violin Concerto* with young Yehudi Menuhin). They congenially shared a bottle of champagne before parting. Elgar subsequently wrote an effusive account of the meeting for *The Daily Telegraph* whilst Delius later told Fenby that he'd found Elgar genial, unaffected and altogether quite unlike what he'd expected; in short, he liked him very much. Delius's wife Jelka was also won over, especially after Elgar praised her ham sandwiches.

A generous host and an appreciative visitor at a one-off meeting. But what's significant is how this acquaintance was then pursued for several months via their correspondence (Delius though by this stage paralysed, dictated all his letters to Jelka). A month later Elgar had the temerity to request a short work for small orchestra for performance in Worcester.

Delius promised to send the score of his *Song Before Sunrise.* By now both composers were signing their letters 'yours affectionately' and 'your true friend.' The Deliuses listened to a broadcast of Elgar's Cello Concerto and thought it beautiful. One can imagine how the sheer poetry of the slow movement would have moved them deeply.

On Christmas Day 1933, Elgar wrote a long letter to Delius from a nursing home in Worcester where he was being treated for sciatica but was also by then terminally ill with inoperable cancer. Unrealistically, Delius was planning a visit to London in the following spring and a further meeting was spoken of. Elgar touchingly referred to his visit to Grez as a vivid memory and one of highlights of his year. The final piece of correspondence is a letter from Delius in early January 1934 in which he mentions playing gramophone records of the *Nursery Suite,* a new discovery for him and one which he found charming, singling out for praise the first movement 'Aubade' as 'a gem.'

The late flowering friendship between two of England's greatest composers is as remarkable and touching as it is unexpected, especially given the potentially prickly nature of both men. I'm sure that Elgar's admiration for Delius's music – especially what he referred to as the poetic nature of it – was more widespread and heartfelt than any reciprocal appreciation from his new-found friend could ever be. But Delius was never insincere in saying what he thought, and he obviously genuinely admired the *Introduction and Allegro* and *Falstaff,* probably other Elgar masterpieces if he'd come to know them better. True, he was scathing about *Gerontius* but that's hardly surprising given his lifelong, aggressive, atheism.

Both composers had a hard start in their profession, both having to make their own way by unorthodox directions, outside the bounds of the musical establishment. Perhaps it was that above all that finally led them to an instinctive realisation of at least some common ground and to reach out, despite their very different backgrounds and achievements, in such a poignant way.

Ralph Vaughan Williams (1872–1958)

Hugh Cobbe

For many commentators the role of chief torchbearer of English classical music in the twentieth century passed in succession from Edward Elgar (1857–1934) to Ralph Vaughan Williams (1872–1958), and then from Vaughan Williams to Benjamin Britten (1913–1976). The relations between each of these composers can best be described as somewhat distant, which is scarcely surprising given their very different backgrounds and approaches. In October 2022 we will be celebrating the 150th anniversary of the birth of the central figure in this trio, and there is an opportunity to assess recent developments in how Vaughan Williams's music is viewed critically and by the public.

In 2013 Michael Kennedy published an article tracing the rises and falls in the reception of the composer's music.[1] He noted that both Elgar and Vaughan Williams suffered a period of neglect immediately following their deaths. In Vaughan Williams's case this was somewhat paradoxical. He had done much to alleviate the position of German-speaking immigrant musicians before and during the Second World War. However, to some extent it was these very musicians whose influence led the younger generation to compare Vaughan Williams's music unfavourably with the more astringent styles of European avant-garde composers. Even so, Vaughan Williams's flame was by no means entirely extinguished, and performances of the major works never dried up. In 1972, to mark the centenary of his birth, the British Museum mounted an exhibition on his life and music, largely based on the generous donation of a collection of his autograph manuscripts by his widow, Ursula, who was a tireless crusader for her husband's music. Amid a growing awareness of his achievement, by the time of the 50th anniversary of the composer's death in 2008 his stylistic context

1 Michael Kennedy, 'Fluctuations in the response to the music of Ralph Vaughan Williams,' in Alain Frogley and Aidan Thomson, eds, *The Cambridge Companion to Vaughan Williams* (Cambridge: Cambridge University Press, 2013), 275–97.

was perceived within a broader perspective, and his music had attracted ever-increasing interest on the part of musicologists. His preoccupation with folksong (especially evident in his work as music editor of *The English Hymnal* of 1905) had perhaps led to earlier descriptions of his style as 'cow-pat' music and the like but it was by now becoming evident that there were hidden depths.

We have now reached the 150th anniversary of Vaughan Williams's birth and can survey the most recent developments in both the study and general reception of his music. The Vaughan Williams Charitable Trust is a comparatively newly arrived factor on the scene. It was established under the will of Ursula Vaughan Williams to administer Ralph's and Ursula's intellectual property, and to receive the share of the income arising from it which had not already been assigned by them to the RVW Trust, created in 1956 to assist young British composers gain commissions and establish their reputations. The new trust has had the mission to support all aspects of the music of Vaughan Williams, in particular the operas and the publication of hitherto unpublished scores, mostly from his earlier years; the creating of new editions and performing material for the major works, in preparation for the end of copyright protection on 31 December 2028; and the recording of previously unrecorded pieces.[2] Another player in the field has been the Ralph Vaughan Williams Society, founded in 1994 by Stephen Connock, which has done much to foster the widespread appreciation of the composer. The society's *Journal* has become increasingly elaborate, containing articles of insight as well as reviews of performances, while the society's Albion label has created many premiere Vaughan Williams recordings. The society's founder has edited two valuable books: *Toward the Sun Rising*, a collection of personal memories of the composer either recorded directly for the book or culled from other publications; and *The Edge of Beyond*, a detailed study of Vaughan Williams's military career during the First World War. Keith Alldritt has written a biography entitled *Vaughan Williams: Composer, Radical, Patriot – a biography*, while Janet Tennant has written a biography of Ursula Vaughan Williams, *Mistress and Muse: Ursula, the Second Mrs Vaughan Williams*. Most importantly, a new volume on Vaughan Williams by Eric Saylor is to be published in mid-2022 in the Master Musicians series, while two further collections of essays on the composer, *Vaughan Williams in Context* and *Ralph Vaughan Williams and his World*, are due to appear in 2023.[3] Finally, towards the end

[2] A note of the major publications and recordings supported by the trust may be found at https://vwct.org.uk/support/. There are plans to combine both trusts into a new Vaughan Williams Foundation.

[3] The volume by Saylor is published by the Oxford University Press, New York; *Vaughan Williams in Context*, edited by Julian Onderdonk and Ceri Owen, will be

of this anniversary year, a new stained-glass window in Vaughan Williams's memory is to be unveiled in All Saints, Down Ampney, where his father was rector and he himself was born.[4]

Much of the work represented by these recent publications has been supported by two major new resources. First is the extensive collection of papers bequeathed by Ursula Vaughan Williams to the British Library following her death in October 2007. Containing papers of both Ralph and herself, it was arranged and made available as MS Mus 1714 by the end of 2011. Keith Alldritt's biography was an early beneficiary of this. The creation of a further resource arising from Ursula's papers was instigated by her in 1986. This was the formation of a corpus of Vaughan Williams's letters, many of which she had collected either as original letters or as photocopies when preparing the biography of her husband, *R.V.W.*,[5] published in 1964. She continued to approach people she knew had letters from her husband, with the request that they might be made available to the project, and she commissioned the present writer to edit the collection. The first outcome was the publication in 2008 of a volume entitled *Letters of Ralph Vaughan Williams*,[6] which contained some 750 items from a collection that now amounted to some 3,500 in all, chosen to give an all-round picture of the composer, in effect in his own words. The project continued with two new editors so that the letters could be mounted in their entirety as a publicly available database, and this was launched in late 2017 to mark the tenth anniversary of Ursula's death. Since then it has continued to develop, and now amounts to upward of 5,100 letters – its benefit evident in the footnotes to many current articles about Vaughan Williams.[7]

So it is with this background of much increased resource that we have reached the present sesquicentennial milestone. There is no doubt that the whole event, supported in the background by the Vaughan Williams Charitable Trust, is creating an ever more widespread interest in the composer's oeuvre. More than 300 performances have been logged over the anniversary season. Many are of the well-established works such as the symphonies, *Fantasia on a Theme by Thomas Tallis* and *The Lark Ascending*; but

published by the Cambridge University Press; and *Ralph Vaughan Williams and his World*, edited by Byron Adams and Daniel Grimley, will be published by the Chicago University Press.

4 The artist will be Tom Denny, who created memorial windows in Gloucester Cathedral to Ivor Gurney and Gerald Finzi.

5 Ursula Vaughan Williams, *R.V.W.* (London: Oxford University Press, 1964).

6 Hugh Cobbe, ed., *Letters of Ralph Vaughan Williams 1895–1958* (Oxford: Oxford University Press, 2008, revised edition 2010).

7 The database, edited by Katharine Hogg and Colin Coleman, is at http://www.vaughanwilliams.uk/ and letters are quoted by their number prefixed by VWL.

many others are of unfamiliar works, such as the British Youth Opera's production of *Sir John in Love* at Holland Park.

For those who look beyond the immediately popular works which feature year after year in the Classic FM list of public favourites, it is of course the symphonies which form the backbone of the very wide range of works in practically every genre created over a working life of more than 60 years. Michael Kennedy, describing the first symphony, *A Sea Symphony*, commented on the composer's choice of words from Whitman's poems as emphasising the soul's voyage towards the unknown. In a way this is a feature of the whole cycle of nine symphonies, and if there were to be only one achievement from the sesquicentenary it would be to move the public perception of Vaughan Williams's style away from the cosy setting of folksongs by the village green towards his confrontation with the challenges of an unknown future. The last movement of *A London Symphony* echoes this, while the *Pastoral Symphony* is a distillation of memories of wartime experience in the army. The Fourth Symphony is a passionate outburst about the cruelty of life, whether the increasing debility of his wife, Adeline, or the growing threat from Nazi Germany. The Fifth provided solace and comfort to a nation afflicted by the realities of war, while the Sixth in contrast was written amid Britain's post-war austerities and the uncertain outcome of threats presented by the Cold War.

In a sense the Seventh, *Sinfonia Antartica*, reversed the equation, depicting heroism tragically vanquished by an overwhelming destiny, set in the chilling waste of the Antarctic continent. The Eighth Symphony relaxed briefly, bringing pleasure to many with its inclusion of 'all the 'phones and 'spiels known to the composer',[8] and with the fact that it is one of the few works by Vaughan Williams to culminate with an *fff* ending. But if he was clear about this symphony's direction of travel, the same was not true of the last, his Ninth, where he knew that he was heading, in truth, 'toward the unknown region'; and indeed, he so departed just four months after the symphony's first performance. Vaughan Williams's lifelong preoccupation with Bunyan's *The Pilgrim's Progress* is perhaps an indicator of this preoccupation with the journey towards an unknown destination. He used his art as a means to 'look through the magic casements and see what lies beyond'.[9] Perhaps we may learn from the final movement of his Ninth Symphony whether he was finally content with what he thought he saw.

8 As Vaughan Williams wrote in his programme note for the first performance of the symphony.

9 As he wrote to the children of a primary school in Norfolk a month before he died, see VWL3275.

Gustav Holst (1874–1934)

Simon Heffer

Gustav Holst, born in Cheltenham 150 years ago in September, had two handicaps in his career that have helped to prevent him securing the recognition he deserves as one of not just England's, but the world's, greatest composers. The first was his almost pathological resistance to fame or celebrity: although he could be sensitive to criticism – usually when it was applied to a work about which he, as a perfectionist, had doubts – no man blew his own trumpet less than he did, even though few in the profession of music at the time had more to blow one about. He was hopeless – deliberately hopeless, it seems – at promoting his own work, content to compose for its own sake, and content to spread the joy of music through his teaching at both St Paul's Girls' School and Morley College, and in his work in enlisting villagers to the cause of music at Thaxted, where he ran a festival from 1916 until it moved to London due to issues with the vicar, (the 'Red') Canon Conrad Noel, although Host continued to help with the church choir and sometimes play the organ. If he went into the shadows even in his own lifetime, it was partly a self-inflicted wound. However, interest in him started to wane at the end of the 1920s, and with one obvious exception his music seemed to evaporate for twenty or thirty years, before performances became more widespread and recordings began to be made. By the 1970s, aficionados of English music began to realise just what a cultural force Holst had been, and his talent became more extensively recognised.

The second handicap to the development of Holst's reputation as a composer may seem less obvious, and indeed rather ironical: it was the phenomenal success of *The Planets*, which remains the only one of his compositions to have secured fame in every part of the world where western classical music is played. The sensation the work caused after Adrian Boult gave it a first performance six weeks before the Great War ended in 1918 has been extensively documented. With recorded sound in its infancy, four acoustic and electrical recordings were made within eight years of its debut, with the composer conducting all of them. Today, a hundred years later, they retain the power to thrill, not least through the sense of Holst himself helping to make the music we are hearing: whether because of the limited capacity of 78 rpm discs, or because that was precisely how he chose to interpret the music, his tempi are noticeably faster in almost all movements than those of the dozens of conductors who followed him to the recording studios. As such, his own recordings have an authenticity that becomes almost overwhelming, as is the case with the numerous electric recordings Elgar was making at the same period. But the ubiquity and genius of *The Planets* – both are undeniable – create a problem: in an age when intellectual curiosity is so often perceived to be diminishing, and despite the easy availability these days, in various media, of many of Holst's other works, to millions of people he is simply the man who wrote *The Planets*. In the decade after the compact disc became popular no fewer than 26 new recordings of the work were made.

Yet it remains strange that instead of being tempted by the beauty and majesty of that work to listen to the other music that Holst composed, people are content to reach *Neptune* and go no further. One hears of people who react somewhat similarly to Dvořák's *New World* Symphony, which suffered the injury of being used for years in a Hovis commercial; indeed, hearing some classical music recycled for an television advertisement, or in a film or television show, seems to be a signal for the public to wallow in that piece and to act as though the composer had written no other. Perhaps the Coronation last year at last convinced some people, thanks to a superb rendition of *I Was Glad*, that Sir Hubert Parry was not put on this earth solely to write *Jerusalem*. But the way Holst is treated is comparable to people knowing nothing of Elgar apart from the first *Pomp and Circumstance* march; luckily for Elgar, even those with only a casual knowledge of his music know, at least, of the *Enigma Variations* and the Cello Concerto. It is far harder to find, among the wide general audience for *The Planets*, those who know major works such as *The First Choral Symphony* or *At The Boar's Head*.

It is hard to understand why this is. The universal appeal of *The Planets*, recorded and performed in concert halls all over this planet, is built on elements to be found in many of Holst's other works: memorable and original melodies; innovative harmonisation; unconventional time-signatures; reflectiveness; an element of mysticism; a simplicity and clarity of expression; and a timelessness. Despite Holst's grounding, with his friend Vaughan Williams, in English folk song, *The Planets* owes more to his knowledge of the orchestra as a professional musician, and of what each instrument would do. There are elements of other contemporary influences in the work, notably Vaughan Williams's *London Symphony*, and aspects of the two Elgar symphonies then extant. But *The Planets*' appeal is not least that it does not sound as though it is in lock-step with a particular era. Depicting the heavens and not the earth, it summons up ideas of the eternal. Despite Holst's original obsession with Wagner, and the influence of Brahms on him through Parry and Stanford, his teachers at the Royal College of Music, this is a fresh language, inherently English but at the same time modern and innovative. As such, it is as immediately valid today as it was over a century ago.

Yet Holst was susceptible to a wide variety of other influences that take us beyond *The Planets*, and in different ways infuse the rest of his music: and perhaps these appear, superficially, too exotic for some tastes. The most obvious was his fascination with variants of orientalism. At the time he was composing, Britain had an empire in India, held other territories in the Far East and had strong power bases in the Middle East. His daughter, Imogen, dismissed her father's first Indian-influenced opera, *Sita*, as 'good old Wagnerian bawling': indeed, Imogen Holst must bear her share of the blame for her father's low-key posthumous reputation, as she occasionally talked of a coldness, or lack of emotion, in his music that rendered it difficult to be appreciated, however technically impressive it was. Holst's growing interest in the Hindu religion and Indian mysticism led to a group of other works that shared this inspiration: his chamber opera *Savitri*, his choral ode *The Cloud Messenger*, his four groups of *Choral Hymns from the Rig Veda* and one set of Vedic hymns for solo voice and piano. The *Hymns*, according to several critics, show a new departure in Holst's harmonic language, and clear signs of his budding genius as a composer that, within three years, would be deployed in the composition of *The Planets*. However, there is little orientalism in the sound of the music; the inspiration to write it may have stemmed from Holst's interest in the East, but the idiom in which he writes it is entirely, if thinly-disguised, English.

And so it is with two of Holst's greatest and most enduring Eastern-inspired works. His three-movement orchestral suite *Beni Mora* (written in 1908, but first performed in 1912) was the result of a holiday in North Africa that Holst took for reasons of his physical and mental health, which were never strong. He soaked up the local influences, though in the first two movements of the suite any music Holst absorbed in Algiers is, again, shaped in an English musical idiom. However, the third movement is the most categorical example thus far in his career of Holst writing music in a distinctly eastern fashion. He heard an Arab playing an eight-note phrase on a flute while sitting in a street – the 'Street of Ouled Naïls', as the movement is named – and, in a cleverly orchestrated way, it comprises the finale of the suite. Critics have called it an early example of minimalism. Perhaps more pertinently, it shows the composer's vulnerability to his environment: more than twenty years later street sounds would inspire Holst again, in his orchestral masterpiece *Hammersmith.*

In 1915, while writing *The Planets,* Holst wanted to explore Japanese music: but even if there had not been a war on, he lacked the resources to travel half-way around the world to engage with that culture. He was fortunate that the Japanese *Noh* plays were in vogue in London, and one afternoon he went to a West End theatre and sat in the dressing room of a Japanese dancer, Michio Ito, who sang him several Japanese tunes that Holst noted down. The short orchestral work that resulted, the *Japanese Suite* Op. 33, is in six movements; the music has occasional Japanese intonations, but it is, again, an inescapably and profoundly English piece of music. The experience of tramping round rural England collecting folk songs, often with Vaughan Williams, and the influence those songs had on Holst's orchestral style, are absolutely apparent in this work.

Holst wrote an enormous amount of music for voices, too little of which is performed today; the best known are the *Hymn of Jesus* and his *First Choral Symphony,* but he also wrote a comic opera, *The Perfect Fool,* and mostly known from the arrangement Holst made of its exuberant and genial ballet music. The libretto (Holst's own work) was received sniffily by many critics, but it shows a remarkably light touch that reveals some of Holst's own personality in a way different from how his music portrays him: he asked in the score that 'the spirit of high comedy shall be maintained throughout.' He certainly showed astonishing versatility in the decade after *The Planets,* and as such his reputation rose; and not merely in Britain. He was commissioned in 1927 by the New York Symphony Orchestra to write a symphony; but by then he had cut his workload, again because of poor health, and did not feel equal to such a task. Instead, he wrote his short orchestral piece *Egdon Heath,* inspired by the work of Thomas Hardy, and – ironically – first performed a month after Hardy had died.

Holst came to regard *Egdon Heath* as his most perfectly realised work. However, it was taken as further evidence of his coldness, and widely dismissed as unduly bleak. But so, too, are many of Hardy's novels: all the critics were doing was accusing the composer of having made an ideal representation of his subject. Having completed this work, which has been recorded several times and has found a place on the fringes of the repertoire, Holst went on to write what are possibly his finest songs: the twelve Humbert Wolfe settings. Wolfe was a contemporary poet and something of a renaissance man: a senior civil servant, he would die on his 55th birthday in 1940 in bed with his mistress, just as he was about to be appointed a Permanent Secretary. The songs have many of Holst's trademarks: unusual time-signatures, unpredictable progressions of notes, great simplicity, but also an occasional glittering brightness. One or two are songs of exceptional beauty – notably *A Little Music* – but all reflect Holst's intellectually curious interwar world, and an inventiveness and a creativity bursting out of some of its earlier restraints, and quite unlike the musical atmosphere of pre-1914.

Because Holst died suddenly – of heart failure following an operation for a duodenal ulcer in May 1934, just three months after Elgar (who was 17 years his senior) – there was no noticeable diminution of achievement before the end of his life, even though he had seemed to be passing out of fashion. Like Elgar, he left an incomplete symphony, though the *Scherzo* was published posthumously as a separate work. One of his most beloved smaller orchestral pieces, the *Brook Green Suite*, was completed shortly before his death, and the melodic beauty of its first movement suggests a serenity within the composer that was not always apparent in his real life. He had shortly before that spent some time as a lecturer at Harvard, where he had been annoyed by press attention, but had also been plagued by the onset of his ulcer.

For all the glories of his canon of work there is one, beyond *The Planets*, that stands out especially as a demonstration piece of his brilliance as an orchestrator, his ability to experiment radically with melody, and his susceptibility to his surroundings: his Prelude and Scherzo *Hammersmith*, which began in 1930 as a commission by the BBC for wind band, but which the composer quickly orchestrated. It was first performed in that form in November 1931 by Boult and the BBC SO, in the same concert as the first London performance of Walton's *Belshazzar's Feast*, whose Technicolor aspects simply overwhelmed this work of deep, majestic reflectiveness. It was something of an omen: *Hammersmith* then vanished for the best part of 30 years, displaying the indifference to Holst that generally prevailed at the time, even to music that was critically admired: it has only once been done at the Proms, for example, in 1973. Boult recorded it for Lyrita in the late 1960s, which put it back on the cultural map: it is now one of Holst's most admired works. The original version for wind band had to wait until 1954 for its premiere, and that took place in America. It has since become central to the repertoire of military bands.

For all his connection with Thaxted, and the significant periods he spent there, Hammersmith was where Holst had spent much of his working life, and the River Thames, so perfectly represented in its lumbering, relentless passage in the opening and closing section of the work, frames the work exactly. Writing about this late masterpiece, Imogen noted that 'its mood is the outcome of long years of familiarity with the changing crowds and the changing river: those Saturday night crowds, who were always good-natured even when they were being pushed off the pavement into the middle of the traffic ... As for the river, he had known it since he was a student ... In *Hammersmith* the river is the background to the crowd: it is a river that goes on its way unnoticed and unconcerned.'

One imagines Holst walking over the bridge from his house in Barnes and, having left the river behind him, immersing himself in the bustle of the walk through Hammersmith Broadway; the end of the Prelude and the beginning of the Scherzo mark the shift in surroundings, signalled explicitly by a tune on the piccolo that sounds like a butcher's boy whistling as he goes about his errands: it is then taken up with great and transformative force by the orchestra. The composer himself said of Hammersmith that it was 'a district crowded with Cockneys which would be overcrowded if it were not for the everlasting good humour of the people concerned'; and noted 'the background of the river, that was there before the crowd and will be there presumably long after, and which goes on its way largely unnoticed and apparently quite unconcerned.' The American composer Robert Cantrick, who conducted the first performance of the wind band version, said that the work was the expression in music of 'a profound philosophical problem, the paradoxical interplay of the humane and the mystical.' But then a great deal of Gustav Holst's music can be put in that category, and it is not least why this magnificent work, and so many others, deserve deeper consideration, and, in this year and all others, constant celebration.

Norman O'Neill (1875–1934)

ꟹ *Em Marshall-Luck*

Norman O'Neill was born in 1875 into a cultured family; his father was the artist G.B. O'Neill (in whose paintings the young O'Neill occasionally appeared), while his mother came from the Callcott family – a long and distinguished line of musicians, musicologists and composers. His childhood was divided between the family's two homes, in Kensington (once William Makepeace Thackeray's home, in Young Street) and Cranbrook, Kent.

O'Neill studied with Sir Arthur Somervell from the age of fourteen until, on the suggestion of the celebrated violinist Joseph Joachim, he went to study composition at Frankfurt with Professor Iwan Knorr. While there, O'Neill associated with several other immensely talented young composers – Roger Quilter, Balfour Gardiner, Percy Grainger and Cyril Scott. The five students learnt a great deal from each other and were later referred to as the 'Frankfurt gang'.

In Frankfurt, O'Neill also met a very gifted French-Swiss pianist (and pupil of Clara Schumann), Adine Rückert. The couple married in 1899, and in 1903 Adine gave birth to a son, Patrick, and, in 1916, a daughter, Yvonne (to whom Delius was god-father); the family settled at 4 Pembroke Villas, an attractive early-Victorian house in Kensington, to which home they welcomed numerous composers and musicians, including (among many others) Frederick Delius, Gustav Holst, Cyril Scott and Percy Grainger. Although O'Neill later acquired an Elizabethan farmhouse in Surrey, Pembroke Villas remained the couple's main home for the rest of their lives and resonated over the years to much music, joy and laughter.

A few years after her marriage, Adine gave a recital which was attended by Miss Frances Gray, the first High Mistress of St Paul's Girls' School (of which school O'Neill's cousin, Gerald Callcott Horsley, had been the architect). Impressed by her talents, Gray invited Adine to take up the post of head music mistress at the school. Adine – who continued in her post for thirty-four years – was much loved by pupils and fellow teachers alike;

and she rendered a further, tremendous, service to the school when she recommended Gustav Holst to Miss Gray as musical director and choirmaster. Norman O'Neill also went on to be involved with the school, taking over the school orchestra from Holst when the latter took leave to carry out educational work in Salonica during the First World War. O'Neill was highly respected as a teacher, and he held a number of posts over his lifetime, including that of Professor of Harmony and Composition at the Royal Academy of Music.

As well as teaching and conducting, O'Neill spent much time composing a large number of songs as well as ballet, chamber and orchestral works, most importantly the Piano Quintet in E minor, the Overture *In Autumn*, a ballade entitled *Death on the Hills* (which received its premiere at the Proms) and *La Belle Dame sans Merci* for baritone and orchestra, recently recorded on EM Records.

It was, however, for his skill as a composer of incidental music for the theatre that O'Neill was in great demand, writing scores for over fifty plays, including *Hamlet* for the Lyric Theatre, Maeterlinck's *The Blue Bird*, a New York production of *The Merchant of Venice* and for three plays by J. M. Barrie, most notably *Mary Rose*. O'Neill's talents were quickly recognised, and he became known as the foremost incidental music composer of his time; being appointed Musical Director of London's Haymarket Theatre in 1909.

Further to these duties, O'Neill held the prestigious position of Treasurer of the Royal Philharmonic Society and was an adjudicator for the Associated Board. One of Delius's closest friends, he was one of the first to champion Delius's music in this country, and his death, from blood poisoning caused by a collision with a car, pre-dated Delius's by only three months. It was just eleven days before O'Neill's fifty-ninth birthday, in that fateful year of 1934, when the deaths also of Holst and Elgar robbed England of a handful of her very finest composers.

O'Neill's compositions included a few ballets, and a wide range of chamber, choral and orchestral and instrumental music. He was a generous-hearted man with a good sense of humour and produced consistently well-crafted pieces, full of charm and an easy delight; works which perhaps reflected both the English countryside he so deeply loved, and his own warm, charming and sensitive personality.

Arthur Bliss (1891–1975)

Kevin Mitchell

Elgar and Bliss: 'Elgar's music is an enhancement of life'

After leaving the army in early 1919 Arthur Bliss withdrew many of his early works and revived his musical life to make up for lost time – he was 27. In the following years he came to be regarded as an *enfant terrible* and a rebel, with such works as *Madam Noy, Rhapsody, Rout, Conversations* – one movement is called 'In the Tube at Oxford Circus' – and *Mêlée Fantasque.* Years later this was recognised by Britten who, when marking Bliss's 75th birthday wrote: 'In my boyhood you ... were the "avant gardist" of "Rout", "Conversations" and daring possibly apocryphal Parisian exploits. You were almost a myth ... Happy you who can preserve youthful exuberance without youthful immaturity!'.[1] Britten and Pears followed this up with two commissions for the Aldeburgh Festival, in 1969 a choral work *The World is Charged with the Grandeur of God,* a setting of Gerald Manley Hopkins, and a Cello Concerto in 1970: the premiere of the latter was conducted by Britten who never directed anything in which he did not believe.

In an address given at Princeton University in May 1969 Bliss told the students that 'rebellion is a natural ingredient of youth. It is good that each generation is not born a generation of yes-men, or we should have no progress.'[2] Basil Maine described Bliss as a rebel but leavened with 'high spirits, good humour, sense of fun [and] unfailing freshness of mind.'[3] Bliss was strongly influenced by Ravel, Stravinsky and the young French composers such as Darius Milhaud, together with a reverence for the music of Elgar.

1 Britten to Bliss, 4 August 1966: Andrew Burn, 'Bliss's Music 1966-75', in Arthur Bliss, *As I Remember*, revised and enlarged edition (London: Thames Publishing, 1989), 292.

2 Trudy Bliss, 'May 1966–March 1975', in ibid., 277.

3 Basil Maine, *The Best of Me* (London: Hutchinson & Co., 1937), 208. He also noted Bliss's conscientiousness, strength of purpose, sensitiveness and a deep appreciation of the music of some other composers.

Even though his aggressive modernism declined in time, it never wholly disappeared. *Grove* in 1927 noted: 'He avows an inclination to experiment in untrodden ways of sonority and has employed many novel blends of timbre. His music reflects a breezy personality of refreshing vigour and vitality',[4] but by 1935 *Grove* found he was established as Elgar's natural successor.

But is this totally true? He explored genres and musical paths that Elgar did not, composing much music for film, particularly the significant scores for *Things to Come* (1935), *Men of Two Worlds* (1945) and *Christopher Columbus* (1949). Shaw also asked him to compose for a film of *Caesar and Cleopatra.* Bliss composed for television, including the opera *Tobias and the Angel* (1960); his opera *The Olympians* (1949) was written for Covent Garden. He also wrote dramatic and sparkling ballet scores: *Checkmate* (1937), *Miracle in the Gorbals* (1944), *Adam Zero* (1946) and *The Lady of Shalott* (1958). Whilst his *Music for Strings* (1935) is in the tradition of English string writing inherited from Elgar and Vaughan Williams, it is written with Bliss's own voice, especially in its taut, sinewy and athletic string writing: it is regarded by many commentators as one of his masterpieces, worthy to stand alongside the *Introduction and Allegro for Strings* and the *Fantasia on a Theme by Thomas Tallis.*

Bliss maintained his individuality throughout his composing life; when in 1963 he thought he had retired from serious composition his creative imagination refused to be stilled. After 1968 he set off along new paths with energy and produced the song cycle *Angels of the Mind* (1968), the Gerald Manley Hopkins work referred to above (1969), the Cello Concerto (1970), *Triptych* for piano (1970), *Metamorphic Variations* (1972) and *Shield of Faith* (1974) – 'These last works were not soft, ripe or nostalgic: their gusto is astonishing'.[5] A view reinforced by the conductor Vernon Handley: 'Even in late works, his voice remained as individual as ever'.[6]

Bliss inherited Elgar's mantle by becoming Master of the Queen's Music[7] in 1953, and he was well suited to writing fine ceremonial music – even though his march *Welcome the Queen* (1954) follows the mould of the *Pomp and Circumstance* Marches, it is written with a confidence and

4 Edwin Evans, *Grove's Dictionary of Music,* 3rd edition, ed. H.C. Colles, (London: Macmillan, 1927), 391.

5 Giles Easterbrook, liner notes for ASV CD DCA 1128 (2002), which included *Angels of the Mind.*

6 Vernon Handley, *The Full Score,* Spring 1996, 5, quoted in John Sugden, *Sir Arthur Bliss* (Speldhurst: Omnibus Press,1997), 115.

7 Bliss liked to retain the archaic 'k'.

swagger that is entirely Bliss's own. Paul Spicer commented: 'There is, of course, the ghost of Elgar whispering in his ear, but this is pure Bliss.'[8]

Bliss recognized that being a 'romantic' composer in the twentieth century might be seen as an anachronism, but he responded: 'I have often been told that I am a "romantic" composer as though that carried in these days some deprecatory significance. I have not the remotest idea of what is implied by that definition, since the very wish to create is a romantic urge, and music a romantic art *par excellence*.'[9] Peter Pirie found that in his last years Bliss's 'considerable talent remained undimmed … he began as a radical in the early days of the renaissance; and became steadily more conservative as the years went on; but unlike some others, Bliss made a success of it.'[10]

Bliss did forge his own style and has an individual voice which is recognisable: he took what he needed from his contemporaries to write original, dramatic and exciting music, that is a long way from being simply Elgarian. Michael Trend noted: 'From a mix of the traditional and the advanced in music Bliss made a style all his own.'[11] It is too simplistic to state that he regressed into Elgar. And yet he did owe something to Elgar on a personal and musical level which remained lifelong, not least of which was Elgar's pioneering example that an English composer could be an independent, professional creative artist: 'This was to the benefit of future generations of composers such as Ralph Vaughan Williams, Sir William Walton, Sir Arthur Bliss, Sir Arnold Bax and Benjamin Britten, who enjoyed the status, social position and creative space gained for them by Elgar.'[12]

* * *

Bliss was born on 2 August 1891. Elgar was then 34 years old and living in Malvern and it was visits to the West Country as a schoolboy that introduced Bliss to Elgar's music, as he later recalled:

> My father during the summer holidays used to take a house in the country for my brothers and myself … he fixed on Worcestershire, Herefordshire and Gloucestershire as the preferred counties. One of the peaks of these lovely summer holidays was a visit to the Three Choirs Festival. Under Sinclair, Brewer and Atkins, I heard much

8 Paul Spicer, *Sir Arthur Bliss: Standing out from the Crowd* (Marlborough: Robert Hale, 2023), 241.

9 Bliss, op. cit., 108.

10 Peter J. Pirie, *The English Musical Renaissance* (London: Victor Gollancz, 1979), 243.

11 Michael Trend, *The Music Makers [:] The English Musical Renaissance from Elgar to Britten* (London: Weidenfeld & Nicolson, 1985), 164.

12 John Drysdale, *Elgar's Earnings* (Woodbridge: The Boydell Press, 2013), 221.

> great music played at these annual festivals, but none made a greater impression on me than *The Dream of Gerontius.*[13]

In 1905 Bliss went to Rugby School and his musical life there was enriched by a growing love for the music of Elgar: 'I had heard the *Enigma Variations* on several occasions, and in my last year at Rugby I took part in a performance of *Gerontius,* which put the seal on my fervent admiration.'[14] This was in April 1910: Bliss sang in the rehearsals, and at the performance filled in on the piano the parts for which there were not the necessary players. He attended the first performance of the Violin Concerto in November 1910 and that of the Second Symphony in May 1911.

Severn House and the First World War

Bliss was determined to meet Elgar, but it was not easy. A request for an autographed photograph resulted in a chilly printed refusal but in his third year at Pembroke College, Cambridge, he succeeded: through a mutual friend, he was invited to meet the composer at his Hampstead home:

> The Elgars were living at Severn House ... and I received an invitation to tea ... I nervously rang the bell, and wondered what I could possibly say to Elgar that would interest him. Luckily he had his own subject and I was at once put at my ease. *His* subject was *Falstaff,* the Symphonic Study at which he had long been working. After tea in the imposing music-room, he took me into his study, where books on *Henry IV,* essays on Falstaff and histories of the period were strewn about everywhere. Obviously during the composition of this complex work he had been completely absorbed in the study of Shakespeare's world.[15]

In 1957 Bliss recalled that Lady Elgar was very kind with her efforts to put Bliss at ease and also remembered 'hearing Elgar upstairs playing some phrases over and over again on the piano. He soon stopped and came down and there he was, the first time I met him: aloof, shy, speaking to me in his soft Worcestershire voice, and taking me in with his rather curious

13 'Edward Elgar', a talk given in Worcester Guildhall on 5 June 1957, in *Bliss on Music: Selected Writings of Arthur Bliss 1920–1975*, ed. Gregory Roscow (Oxford: Oxford University Press, 1991), 245.

14 Bliss, op. cit., 23.

15 Ibid., 23. Bliss states that this was in 1912, but it was in 1913 that Elgar wrote much of *Falstaff*, completing the score on 5 August 1913.

blinking eyes'.[16] Bliss caused confusion in his autobiography by placing the recollection of the piano phrase being played over and over again to 1917, attributing this to *Le Drapeau Belge*, the piano score of which was published in 1916.[17]

In August 1914, shortly after war was declared, Bliss volunteered and was commissioned into the 13th Royal Fusiliers, sailing for France on 30 July 1915. Just before embarkation he wrote to Elgar on 12 July 1915:

> Now that this battalion is on the eve of departure for France, it does not strike me as absolutely out of place to write and express my real gratitude to you for the many hours of pleasure you have given me through your music.
>
> So many similar effusions have possibly reached you that they have become unbearably boring, but you will not think me impertinent, I know, when I state that 2 lbs. out of the modest 35 that I am allowed to take out with me as necessary kit are taken up by the scores of your variations and second symphony.[18]

In 1913 when Bliss was a student at Cambridge, he completed a String Quartet in A major which had its first performance on 9 June 1914,[19] followed by a private performance at Bliss's home in Holland Park on 7 July 1914,[20] and then at the Aeolian Hall on 25 June 1915. Alice Elgar heard it there on 12 November 1915 and recorded in her diary: 'Liked it very muss [much] & enjoyed Concert very muss', writing on 15 November to Bliss in France:

> I must send a few lines to tell you I had a great pleasure on Friday as I was able to hear your Quartet. I did so wish you could have been present too as it was, at least it seemed to me, beautifully played and was received with much warmth of applause ... I much wished Sir

16 'The Fifteenth Variation: A Portrait of Edward Elgar', broadcast on the BBC on 12 May 1957, transcribed in the *Elgar Society Journal*, Vol. 15, No.3 (2007), 42. In this account, recalled over forty years later, Bliss thought that this first meeting with Elgar took place sometime in the First World War. This was also his recollection in the talk given on 5 June 1957 when he also referred to 'a phrase on the piano being played over and over again'. In a letter to Elgar dated 30 January 1916 Bliss wrote (incorrectly) that a phrase from *Une voix dans le désert* was 'the music you were playing when I first met you' – see below.

17 Bliss. op. cit., 24. *Le Drapeau Belge* premiered on 14 April 1917.

18 Jerrold Northrop Moore, *Edward Elgar: Letters of a Lifetime* (Rickmansworth: Elgar Works, 2012), 328. Later the score of *Falstaff* was sent to France.

19 Sam Ellis: 'Bliss's New England: identity, interdependence and isolation', Bangor University PhD, 1911.

20 Spicer, op. cit., 22.

> Edward could have heard it, but he was engaged that afternoon. The music seemed to me so full of eager life and exhilarating energy and hope, and the writing for the instruments so interesting, and producing delightful effect. I shall hope to hear it again. Sir Edward is very busy and I hope you will hear some wonderful new things some day ... Sir E. does not know I am writing just now or he would send all messages. Your letters interest him greatly.[21]

The concert was given by the Philharmonic String Quartet, Arthur Beckwith, violin, Eugene Goossens, violin, Raymond Jeremy, viola and Cedric Sharp, cello. *The Times* critic noted that this the second London performance of Bliss's Quartet 'was well worth repeating, not because it is music which the hearer has any difficulty in appreciating at a first hearing, but because it is good to repeat a pleasant experience'.[22]

On 30 January 1916 Bliss wrote to Elgar about his experiences in the trenches:

> It has been increasingly brisk at this spot lately, the enemy endeavouring to celebrate the All Highest Day[23] by making it unpleasant for us. So we have had nightly alarms, incipient gas attacks, extra shelling etc. Last night when I was sleeping in bed, I was awakened by the ringing of gongs, the sound coming all down the line – the Germans were gassing one of our divisions several miles off. None came near us, and it was exceedingly annoying being woken up, as it was the third night running – the clash of gongs in the still night is something quite eerie and reminded me of a Chinese Saturday night celebration.[24]

Elgar finished his setting of Emile Cammaerts's *Une voix dans le désert* in mid-July 1915 but it was first performed in London's Shaftesbury Theatre on 29 January 1916: Bliss wished he was in London as he wanted 'very much to see the setting at the Shaftesbury', and stated: 'I remember it was the music you were playing when I first met you'. How could Bliss have known this if he had not yet heard the setting in the theatre? Furthermore, Bliss could

21 Bliss op. cit., 23–4. Bliss's diary records that he wrote to Elgar on 30 September 1915, but the letter is not extant. In November 1915 Elgar was involved in the early stages of writing *The Starlight Express* incidental music. Alice hoped Bliss would soon get leave so he could 'come and see us as soon as possible'.

22 *The Times*, 13 November 1915. The concert included Ravel's Quartet in F and Brahms's Quintet in G. Bliss later withdrew the work, but in 2000 with Trudy Bliss's approval it was recorded by the Maggini Quartet on Naxos 8.557108.

23 The Kaiser's birthday, 27 January.

24 Martin Bird transcription, formerly Elgar Birthplace letter 6387. Now British Library: *Lbl* MS Mus 1843/3/ L6387.

not have heard this music during his first visit to Severn House in 1913. Did he hear it on another unrecorded visit between 1913 and early 1916?

In early spring Bliss earned some rest well behind the lines and returned to England for eight days leave from 7 April. On 14 April he visited Severn House: 'Nice Capn. A. Bliss – Stayed nearly 2 hours, heard gramophone &c. He said "this sort of thing bucks one up tremendously". To leave the next day. May he return all safe & well, I pray – '.[25]

Thereafter Bliss had the 'feeling of being fattened up for the kill', and on 1 July 1916 the Battle of the Somme began; in the first week Elgar sent Bliss a score of *Cockaigne* inscribed with 'Good luck'. This became a cherished possession and when later bound still carried the mud marks of the trenches. Bliss recorded that 'Elgar's handwriting like the shape of his themes was very characteristic: the pen drew incisive strokes, the words rising and falling in sharply angular lines'.[26]

Bliss's luck ran out on the morning of 7 July when launching an attack on La Boiselle; he was wounded in the leg and managed to crawl to a hole for shelter. After over a year in France Bliss was exhausted and even though his wound was slight, he was sent back to England. However, he was soon able to take up Alice's offer to return to Severn House and on 21 July she wrote: 'A. Bliss & Mr. Streatfeild to tea … A. Bliss on crutches but very active and most interesting. He had been in German Dugouts & taken prisoners, very fine … stayed till just after seven'. He and Streatfeild went again on 27 July: 'very delightful time only wanted E – most interesting talk'.[27]

There follows a bizarre letter from Bliss to Herbert Howells written on 26 August 1916 from the Empire Hotel, Buxton, where he was recuperating:

> Elgar is a very curious person. – He combines an intense belief in himself and the sincerity of his emotions with a blind faith that what the hoi polloi think and feel is right. He is a determined believer in expressing the HEART of the PEOPLE – hence – 'for the fallen'. I have never heard or seen it, but from your description I can guess what it portrays. I have seen Elgar in tears over it – and if you consider it as the expression of the man who as a child drove round in the baker's cart to get to grips with and help the poor people of Worcester, I think you can judge it rather more mildly. But still, enough of that. When I see Elgar, I think he is a master; when I sit in my arm chair and peruse his work, I think of him as a charlatan – que faire?[28]

25 Alice Elgar diary, 14 April 1916.

26 Bliss, op. cit., 24.

27 Alice Elgar diary, 21 July and 17 July 1916. Richard Streatfeild (1866–1919), Assistant Keeper in the British Museum's Department of Printed Books (1898–1919).

28 Spicer, op. cit., 40–1.

An odd contemporary view, perhaps engendered by the pain and discomfort following his injury and there is no evidence that Elgar drove round Worcester in a baker's cart as a boy! Paul Spicer commented: 'Interesting reflections from a hot-headed young man, which certainly did not dampen his enthusiasm for his connection with the Elgars – a man in Bliss's position could, and would, benefit greatly from such a friendship.'[29]

Bliss seemingly wanted to strengthen that friendship by apparently wishing at this time to dedicate a violin sonata 'To Lady Elgar', but there is no such dedication on the extant score of the work.[30]

Bliss's younger brother Kennard was killed fighting on the Somme on 28 September 1916. Alice Elgar wrote a letter of condolence to which Bliss replied on 5 October:

> Your letter has been a great source of comfort to me. You and Sir Edward have always been so kind to me, that I find it difficult to thank you, as I wish. My brother was one of the noblest friends I knew – a brilliant musician, a brilliant painter, he would have made his mark. He died a brave death, alone where he would have no one accompany him – a gunner in advance of the infantry that his battery was supporting. I know his battery commander spoke the truth, when he said he had never come across a man so fearless of the dangers of death. I feel comforted that he will have to fight no more, but it is hard that death should have taken the best of our family. Will you convey to Sir Edward my gratitude for his remembrance which I prize so highly.[31]

Bliss later wrote that 'As the years passed I came to realise more and more what a poignant loss to the family Kennard's death had been … he was the most gifted of us all.'[32]

On 17 November Alice met Bliss again: 'A. with Arthur Bliss to the Plum Pudding matinee the immense London Opera House crowded.' This was to raise funds to send out provisions to the forces.

29 Ibid., 41.

30 Letter of 25 September 1916 from Bliss to his father, in ibid., 42.

31 Martin Bird transcription, formerly Elgar Birthplace letter 6388. Now *Lbl* MS Mus 1843/3/L6388.

32 Bliss, op. cit., 45. Francis Kennard Bliss (1892–1916) was killed near Thiepval and is buried at Aveluy Wood Cemetery. Bliss's choral symphony *Morning Heroes* commissioned by the Norwich Festival in 1930, was written as a tribute to his brother and all Bliss's comrades in arms who fell in the Great War: the last movement deals specifically with the Battle of the Somme, using Wilfred Owen's poem 'Spring Offensive' and Robert Nichols's 'Dawn on the Somme'. The orator at Norwich was Basil Maine who in 1933 became Elgar's biographer.

Bliss had the opportunity to hear 'For the Fallen' when it was performed with Agnes Nichols at the Royal Albert Hall on 25 November 1916: 'Most, most beautiful performance of the wonderful music – It seemed more poignant & inspired than ever & at the same time consoling & uplifting ... A & C in loggia with Colvins, Lady Petre & E. Berkley. L. Binyon A. Bliss.'[33] His response to 'For the Fallen' was probably more acute following the death of his brother. Afterwards he wrote to Lady Elgar on 1 December 1916: 'I have been meaning to write to you to tell you how deeply I was moved by the beauty of 'For the Fallen' – a dignified and noble epitaph indeed for those who have died on the Somme and elsewhere. It was good of you to allow me the privilege of listening to it with your party ... With very many thanks for all the kindness you have shown me.'[34]

Bliss had suddenly been called away to Bath so apologised to Lady Elgar that he was unable to hear Elgar's Second Symphony at Queens Hall.[35] He was sent to Prior Park, Bath as an instructor to an officers' cadet battalion. There he met some of Elgar's friends, including Lalla Vandervelde[36] who wished to give a recital to entertain the cadets. Bliss's Commanding Officer agreed to this diversion and the recital 'ended with a performance of Elgar's *Carillon* ...in this I gave what help I could at the piano to support the ringing voice of madame Vandervelde but it was the last frenzied cries of à Berlin, à Berlin that established the evening as a real "diversion".'[37] In February 1917 he was passed as fit for light duties and in April 1917 a medical board in Bath found he was fit for general service.

On 3 May 1917 Alice went to a Russian Exhibition in London 'where she met Arthur Bliss & had tea.'[38] In spite of being fit for general service, Bliss continued to instruct others in military procedure and on 19 September 1917 from a School of Musketry on Hayling Island he wrote to Alice Elgar:

33 Alice Elgar diary, 25 November 1916.

34 Martin Bird transcription, formerly Elgar Birthplace letter 3740. Now *Lbl* MS Mus 1843/3/3740.

35 Elgar conducted part of a Royal Philharmonic Concert on 27 November 1916 in place of an indisposed Landon Ronald. Alice found the first part of the concert, conducted by Thomas Beecham 'rather boring' then condemned 'A detestable audience not worthy of hearing great music' as presumably they did not respond sufficiently warmly to the symphony.

36 Lalla Vandervelde (1870–1965), part-time actress and writer, daughter of Edward Speyer.

37 Bliss. op. cit., 46.

38 Alice Elgar diary, 3 May 1917. The exhibition was at the Grafton Galleries in aid of Anglo-Russian hospitals.

> I write for news of Sir Edward and yourself, if you are not too busy, & for a glimpse of those happy & precious hours that your kindness allowed me to spend at Severn House. It is a somewhat curious and altogether refreshing experience to drink upon them in thought, and I do so here, amid the unending and monotonous preparation for still more war ... The Army life has taken possession of this quiet little island – the one great attraction is the sea – in which I bathe every morning before breakfast – that and the subsequent pipe are the two most comforting things imaginable ... I hope Sir Edward is keeping well and is at work. The last things I heard were the Sea Songs, which I enjoyed enormously, the anticipation of which kept me glued to ... the Coliseum through an otherwise boring programme – they were as salty as the actual thing ... I believe I shall be in town about the end of this month for a weekend. If I could come and see you then, it would be so kind of you.[39]

So, on 2 October 1917 he and Lalla Vandervelde were back at Severn House for tea: 'very pleasant time ... E. seemed to enjoy the evening ... & told stories & we laughed very muss [much]'.[40] He went again on 5 February 1918 – 'very pleasant'.[41]

As the chances of rejoining the remnant of his old regiment were remote, Bliss joined the Grenadier Guards and in September 1918 returned to France, where he was involved in fighting until being gassed in October, only returning to his Battalion in December after the Armistice. He sailed home in February 1919, soon to be back at Severn House.

In February 1919 the Elgars organised a dance for Carice: 'Busy preparing for Carice's Dance ... snowing hard all morning – No coke arrived much worried trying to warm rooms ... Mr. Hogarth Pianist came in good time – Very good – quite different from common dance music. Guests seemed to enjoy themselves immensely'.[42] Alice listed all the guests and there were several from the forces including 'Arthur Bliss Guardsman'. Did the Elgars consider Bliss as a possible suitor for Carice? He had won Alice's favour which was not always easy to attain. Years later Carice told Bliss that 'she remembered me distinctly as the "slim young man in uniform"'.[43] Alice

39 Martin Bird transcription, formerly Elgar Birthplace letter 6386. Now *Lbl* MS Mus 1843/3/L6386. Elgar's four songs *The Fringes of the Fleet*, to poems by Rudyard Kipling and Sir Gilbert Parker were performed at the London Coliseum and elsewhere between June and December 1917.

40 Alice Elgar diary, 2 October 1917.

41 Ibid., 5 February 1918.

42 Ibid., 18 February 1919.

43 'Edward Elgar', talk 5 June 1957, in Roscow, op. cit., 245.

recorded that 'The dance seemed to have been a great success, when A. came down all looked restored already'.[44]

On 2 March Bliss went to the Elgars again when there was 'Quite a crowd for tea', which included Sidney Colvin, Frank Schuster, Lalla Vandervelde, Adrian Boult, E.F. Benson and others – 'Very pleasant'.[45]

Having completed his three chamber works, the Violin Sonata, String Quartet and Piano Quintet were performed privately in the Severn House music room on 7 March by W.H. Reed and colleagues to an invited audience which included Bernard Shaw, Landon Ronald, Rosa Burley, Canon William Gardner and Bliss who recalled that the Violin Sonata was played by Reed with Elgar at the piano. Years later he remembered: 'I had the privilege of turning over the pages of the score for Elgar ... but all I can recall now was a certain embarrassment as to what I ought to say as the sonata ended. Was my disappointment due to the far from brilliant performance [presumably Elgar's] or to the belief that its musical substance had little in common with the genius of his earlier masterpieces? I hope I sat quietly as if absorbed'.[46]

However, at the time he appeared to be impressed by the String Quartet and Piano Quintet, writing a tactful letter to Lady Elgar on 8 March:

> I felt I must write and tell you how greatly I appreciated the honour of being present yesterday. It was a very big occasion for me apart from the performance of the inspired works. It is difficult to speak of them without exaggerated comments – so I won't attempt but the impression they produced on me was of a beauty and dignity that one rarely comes in contact with, and which is kindly rendered and doubly prized. If I could choose from such a feast, I think it would be the middle movement of the string 4te which is Elgar in excelsior and the first movement of the piano quintet. The last is a most individual and amazingly individual work. I cant [sic] cast about in music for a companion. I eagerly await the first performance. I feel assured it will create a profound impression on all music <u>thinking</u> people'.[47]

On 26 April there was a repeat performance of the Quartet, Quintet, and *Romance* from the Sonata, at Frank Schuster's London home before a distinguished audience including Herbert Howells who noted: 'Arthur Bliss

44 Alice Elgar diary, 19 February 1919.

45 Ibid., 2 March 1919.

46 Bliss, op. cit., 24.

47 Martin Bird transcription, formerly Elgar Birthplace letter 10360. Now *Lbl* MS Mus 1843/3/L10360. The first public performance of the Violin Sonata was given at the Aeolian Hall on 21 March 1919 and that of the Quartet and Quintet at the Wigmore Hall on 21 May 1919.

was there, thank God! And I [was] charmed to see him. We sat by one another, smiling simultaneously when anything pleased us, and kicking each other when the vulgarities cropped up. And between the movements he was in a state of holy terror at my remarks (lest these were heard by the devout Elgarians).'[48]

In the summer of 1919 Elgar completed his Cello Concerto and Felix Salmond was the chosen soloist. Bliss attended the second rehearsal and premiere at Queen's Hall on 27 October when Albert Coates went on rehearsing the works he was to conduct, leaving little time for Elgar to take the LSO through his work, thus affecting the evening's performance. This was the last premiere of her husband's work that Alice was to attend as in the following months illness dominated her life, and she died on 7 April 1920. Bliss with Boult and other musicians, was in Amsterdam to see Nikisch conduct and immediately on his return wrote to Elgar:

> It was only this morning on my return from Holland that I leant of your terrible loss. To me she had always remained the very embodiment of all that was kind and gracious, and her death comes as a great blow to one who has been privileged to call her friend. I beg you to accept all my sympathy.[49]

A Colour Symphony

In 1920 the Three Choirs Festival was revived by Ivor Atkins, the Organist of Worcester Cathedral. The 1922 Festival was to be held at Gloucester, and the Cathedral Organist, Herbert Brewer, wished to secure first performances of new works by younger British composers. He sought Elgar's advice, which he was willing to give, and on 16 December 1921 Elgar invited Bliss, Eugene Goossens, John Ireland, Adrian Boult, W.H. Reed and Anthony Bernard to lunch at the Royal Societies Club. Bliss wrote:

> The luncheon went a bit awkwardly with Elgar at his most nervous; then, when the coffee came, he suddenly told us the reason for our being gathered there. He wanted Howells, who was not present, Goossens and myself each to write a new work for the Gloucester Festival of 1922: no limitations on the form of the new works were imposed. Howells complied with *Sine Nominee*, written for soprano

48 Christopher Palmer, *Herbert Howells: A Centenary Celebration* (London: Thames Publishing, 1992), 80–1.

49 Bliss to Elgar, 10 April 1920: Martin Bird transcription, formerly Elgar Birthplace letter 501. Now *Lbl* MS Mus 1843/3/L501.

and tenor soloists, mixed chorus and orchestra; Goossens with a work called *Silence* for chorus and orchestra, and I wrote a symphony to be called the *Colour Symphony.*[50]

Following the lunch Elgar reported to Brewer:

> I could see Arthur Bliss and Eugene Goossens only yesterday. I hope you worded your announcement, if made, just as I telegraphed. They both 'hope to furnish a new work' – Goossens choral, for the Cathedral, and Bliss orchestral. This last might be either for the Cathedral or the concert-room. Both work *short.* This is as far as we could get, but the boys are pleased and it would be a first-class thing for the festivals to get in new blood and away from the heavy dullness of the – well, you know. Whatever they do has some vitality and grip about it'.[51]

Shortly after Elgar wrote to Brewer about the Festival programmes:

> I think the scheme looks well now. I only regret the appearance of my own name so often. I think Bliss had better be for the Cathedral (if possible). These young men will do something good I feel sure and their presence in the Cathedral will do much, apart from vivid interest in their compositions, to attract people, and do away with the remnant of the notion that everything must be a sort of Ch. of E. propaganda.[52]

Bliss acknowledged the invitation by writing to Elgar:

> I thought I should write and wish you the best of health and happiness for 1922, and also to thank you so much for giving me the chance to write a work for the Gloucester Festival. It is a great opportunity, and I look on it as one more proof of your generosity to us younger musicians.
>
> I do not think you realise what a fine and rare encouragement your presence is, when, as you did at luncheon the other day you gave the lead to younger composers. It is such a unique thing, this broadminded generosity … that I hope you will be long spared to make the music of Englishmen pre-eminent.[53]

He admitted that he needed a 'trouvaille' or a 'donnée' to commence writing as he found it easier to write 'dramatic' music rather than 'pure' music:

50 Bliss, op. cit., 71. As John Ireland was at the lunch, why was he also not invited to write a work for the Festival?

51 Elgar to Brewer, 17 December 1921, in Basil Maine, *Elgar His Life and Works*, Book I (Bath: Cedric Chivers Ltd, 1973), 237.

52 Elgar to Brewer, December 1921, in ibid., 237–8.

53 Bliss to Elgar, 26 December 1921: Martin Bird transcription, formerly Elgar Birthplace letter 10366. Now *Lbl* MS Mus 1843/3/L10366.

> So for weeks I sat before a blank sheet of manuscript paper trying to make up my mind what shape, what character this new work should have. And then one day, looking over a friend's library, I picked up a book on heraldry and started reading about the symbolic meanings associated with the primary colours. At once I saw the possibility of so characterising the four movements of a symphony, that each should express a colour as I personally perceived it.[54]

At first Bliss called it a 'Symphony in B', but Percy Scholes argued that the idea of colour had inspired the work. Bliss re-named it *A Colour Symphony* with the subtitles to the movements of Purple, Red, Blue and Green. Bliss did much preliminary work at Vaughan Williams's home, 13 Cheyne Walk in Chelsea. RVW worked on the top floor, his brother-in-law R.O. Morris had his study on the floor below and Bliss worked in a room on the ground floor, occasionally hearing slow-moving chords from RVW's piano: 'I loved working there in such a sympathetic and creative atmosphere'.[55] Simon Heffer has cogently argued that the recent war permeated the work. Bliss used the words 'Death' the colour of mourning when describing the Purple movement, 'Courage' for Red, 'Loyalty and Melancholy' for Blue and 'Victory' for Green, even though it is a life-affirming work.[56]

The first performance of the symphony was in Gloucester Cathedral on 7 September 1922, but Bliss was disappointed. Rehearsals were restricted and there was little time for the London Symphony Orchestra to learn the work – amazingly, just before the performance several players had to be removed from the large orchestra as there was insufficient room for them on the platform with a chorus which was required for other works in the programme. Despite this, critical opinion was favourable with *The Times* stating 'that a razor-edge mind is at work ... Probably the work was not altogether performed to the satisfaction of Bliss ... but it is worthwhile to add that the orchestration all came out with extraordinary clearness. There was no difficulty in following the detail in even the more complex passages'.[57] Samuel Langford considered Bliss 'far and away the cleverest writer among the English composers of our time'.[58] However the *Annals* of the Festival subsequently concluded that the works of Bliss and Goossens 'contained such terribly harsh progressions and positively ugly idioms of the ultra modern school' and doubted that their music was 'suitable to the

54 Bliss, op. cit., 71.

55 Ibid., 74.

56 Simon Heffer, 'Why *A Colour Symphony* is pure Bliss', *The Daily Telegraph*, 26 January 2016.

57 Bliss, op. cit., 74.

58 *The Manchester Guardian*, 8 September 1922.

solemn and mysterious atmosphere of religious exaltation' reserved for the Cathedral. Their work was for the secular concert hall.[59]

Elgar apparently found the work disconcertingly modern, but according to Eugene Goossens Elgar 'immensely admired Bliss's vivid symphony. After the concert we ate an enormous roast-beef lunch at the New Inn, and with Arthur Bliss and Willie Reed … spent the afternoon walking in open country along the banks of the Severn. Elgar not only outwalked us all, but completely out-matched us in matters of local history and topography.'[60] Elgar thought highly enough of the work to attend its first London performance on 5 December 1922, conducted by Adrian Boult, the work's dedicatee, with the student orchestra of the Royal College of Music.

A number of influences contributed to the symphony written, according to Herbert Howells, when Bliss was 'in the heyday of his volcanic Anglo-Americanism.'[61] Whilst some of the melodies are rather Elgarian, there are moments of dissonance and the influence of *Les Six* and Stravinsky (especially in the 'Red' *Scherzo*) is apparent. For Paul Spicer it is 'one of the great twentieth-century British symphonies, and there is considerable competition.'[62]

Pastoral: 'Lie strewn the white flocks'

Early in 1923 Bliss and his father travelled to America, where on 1 June 1925 he married Trudy Hoffman. Shortly afterwards Bliss and his new wife returned to England and therefore did not see Elgar for several years. In his autobiography Bliss recalled that Elgar 'was really a shy and proud man given to great extremes of emotion. He could laugh uproariously or weep: he had a biting tongue, which on one occasion hurt me much.'[63] It is not known when this took place, but an estrangement occurred which lasted until 1928 when Bliss attended a concert at Queen's Hall which included a

59 C. Lee Williams, H. Godwin Chance and T. Hannam-Clark, *Annals of the Three Choirs of Gloucester, Hereford and Worcester and the Charity connected with it* (Gloucester: The Three Choirs Festival Association, 1931), 86.

60 Eugene Goossens, *Overture and Beginners* (London: Methuen, 1951), 193–4.

61 Herbert Howells, 'Memories from the Twentieth Century', ed., Barry Still, in *Two Hundred and Fifty Years of the Three Choirs Festival* (Gloucester: The Three Choirs Festival Association, 1977), 23.

62 Spicer, op. cit., 75.

63 Bliss, op. cit., 25.

rare performance of *Falstaff*, writing afterwards to Elgar who replied on 8 November 1928:[64]

> Your letter gave me great pleasure and satisfaction and I am obliged to you for writing it.
>
> I do not refer to the concert now but to what you say about our friendship: this I valued and shall value again if you will allow me to do so.
>
> Frankly, I was greatly disappointed with the way you progressed from years ago. There was so much 'press' of a type I dislike and newspaper nonsense. I can easily believe you were responsible for little or none of this but it rankled a great deal because I had great hopes for you: I had affection. It will seem vulgar to you if I add that commercially you have (I believe or was led to believe) no concern with the success of your works – an unfortunate side of our art which we penniless people have always with us, and try to ignore. I hoped you were going to give us something very great in quite modern music, the progress of which is very dear to me; and then you seemed to become a mere 'paragraphist'. I am probably wrong and trust I was.
>
> Now I have written at greater length than you would like but my reason (not excuse) must be that you are one of the very few artists in whom I took an interest, to use the word again, affectionate interest.[65]

The letter is interesting in that it perpetuates the myth that Elgar was impecunious[66] and even though it is couched as an apology, it shows a harshness in its use of the word 'paragraphist' against a man who had a secure financial background and had studied at Cambridge University and the RCM both, at that time, bastions of anti-Elgarian sentiment. Michael Kennedy concluded that the coolness was an 'example of Elgar's jealousy of the artistic and financial success of a younger man'.[67] It is questionable to what

64 On 1 November 1928 Elgar and Carice went to a Philharmonic concert conducted by Sir Landon Ronald and heard Bach's Brandenburg Concerto in G, William Wallace's *Villon*, Nichols Medtner's Piano Concerto No. 2 in C minor and after the interval Elgar's *Falstaff*. Carice recorded: 'Lan conducted *Falstaff* magnificently'.

65 Bliss, op. cit., 94. Spicer thought the word 'paragraphist' was insulting and the letter frank yet wounding, Spicer, op, cit., 79.

66 See Drysdale, op. cit., for an analysis of Elgar's finances. However, in early life Elgar's finances were not secure as Bliss recalled in a speech given in June 1971: 'I remember so well Elgar telling me rather bitterly of his struggles in his early years due to lack of means, and indeed, at the start of this century any young man or young woman who aspired to be a composer without a private income was regarded as mad or suicidal'. In Roscow, op. cit., 275.

67 Michael Kennedy, *Portrait of Elgar*, 3rd edition (Oxford: Oxford University Press, 1987), 296.

extent he was really concerned about the work of the younger men such as Bliss and Bax for as Kennedy stated, despite Elgar's above claim: 'The truth is that ... he was not very interested in the work of his contemporaries and juniors.'[68]

Be that as it may, the friendship with Elgar revived and Bliss dedicated his next work to him. *Pastoral: 'Lie strewn the white flocks'* was conceived by Bliss on a visit to Sicily in the spring of 1928. It was at Syracuse, where he sought the site of the classical fountain of Arethusa, with a copy of the *Idylls* of Theocritus in his pocket, that he found the theme for this choral work, and assembled an anthology of poems representing a Sicilian day from dawn to dusk. The anthology format was one he was to use in later works such as *Morning Heroes* and *The Beatitudes*. After a brief orchestral introduction, Ben Jonson's 'The Shepherd's Holiday' honours Pan, followed by John Fletcher's 'A Hymn to Pan,' who appears and dances a stately *Sarabande*; the fifth section tells the story of Pan and Echo. Two poems by Robert Nichols form the next two parts, and to verses from Theocritus men's voices sing a lusty prayer to Demeter. A short orchestral introduction introduces the finale, and as dusk falls love and slumber are celebrated by Robert Nichols and John Fletcher.

Bliss wrote the work for a small City of London choir conducted by Harold Brooke who was a director of Novello and Co. Previously Bliss had no connection with a single publisher and their printing of *Pastoral* forged a 'close alliance' which lasted until Bliss's death in 1975. Brooke had also known Elgar, Novello being Elgar's principal publisher. *Pastoral* has been described 'as an astonishingly original masterpiece – nothing like it had appeared before from any composer.'[69]

Having received Elgar's letter Bliss wrote to him on 31 January 1929:

> I have just finished my first extended choral work, being a pastoral to the words of Theocritus, Ben Jonson, Fletcher and Robert Nichols. Would you do me the honour of accepting this and allowing the dedication to stand in your name? I would wish you to regard it as a partial return for what in many ways I owe to you.
>
> I have read and re-read your letter to me and thank you for it. I delayed an answer until I might have something to offer in return.[70]

[68] Ibid., 295.

[69] Robert Matthew-Walker, 'The Songs of Arthur Bliss,' *The Arthur Bliss Society Journal*, Vol. 22, No. 2 (2024), 11.

[70] Martin Bird transcription, formerly Elgar Birthplace letter 1299. Now *Lbl* MS Mus 1843/3/L1299.

Elgar replied on 1 February: 'I accept, with grateful feelings, the honour of the dedication of your new choral work: may it flourish exceedingly'.[71] When the work was broadcast, he wrote again on 9 May:

> Under conditions far from good I listened to the performance of the *Pastoral* you kindly dedicated to me: the transmission or reception (I know nothing of the workings of the BBC with its aerial sprites) was not good. But I could judge that your work is on a *large* and *fine* scale, and I like it *exceedingly*. The Pan sections suited me best but that is only a first hearing notion. Some of it naturally puzzled me, but I am none the less sympathetic: thank you![72]

It is no surprise that the Pan sections suited Elgar, as Pan was depicted in the ballet score *The Sanguine Fan* which he wrote in 1917 – the role of Pan was danced by Gerald du Maurier. Bliss replied to Elgar on 15 May 1929: 'Your appreciative letter gave me great joy. I quite realise that I have but started – and late too in pursuit of a glimpsed beauty – but I can assure you there will be no turning back into softer and more fashionable paths'.[73] This was certainly the case with his later music, particularly his film score for *Things to Come* (1935) and his ballet *Checkmate* (1937).

Another letter from Elgar followed on 24 June 1929: 'Very many thanks for the 'Pastoral' you so kindly dedicate to me: I wish I could be at the performance but I have been and still am a prisoner for cold & this cold has kept me from acknowledging your very distinguished 'present' to me: I highly appreciate your kindness'.[74]

On 30 January 1930 Elgar conducted *In the South*, the Violin Concerto and the First Symphony at a Philharmonic Concert at Queen's Hall and afterwards he and Carice had a merry supper with Bliss and his wife at Oddenino's restaurant.[75]

Following Elgar's death in February 1934 an appeal was launched in 1935 to maintain the Elgar Birthplace cottage at Broadheath following its purchase by the Mayor, Aldermen and Citizens of the County of the City of Worcester for £400, and Bliss contributed to this fund. After the war Bliss became a Trustee of the Elgar Birthplace and was the Chairman for a

71 Bliss, op. cit., 95.

72 Ibid.

73 Moore, op. cit., 471.

74 Bliss archive: Music Department, Cambridge University Library. The words are slightly ungrammatical, but this appears to be what Elgar wrote. I am grateful to Chris Bennett for his assistance in deciphering Elgar's handwritten text.

75 Carice Elgar diary, 30 January 1930. Oddenino's restaurant was at 54–62 Regent Street.

number of years,[76] standing down in 1960. In that September he attended the Three Choirs Festival in Worcester to conduct his *Music for Strings*, where there was also a first performance (from the tower of the Cathedral) of Bliss's arrangement for brass of three Bach Chorales from the *St John Passion*. He was following in Elgar's footsteps, as in 1911 Elgar had arranged chorales from Bach's *St Matthew Passion* which were played from the tower of Worcester Cathedral. Bliss was also present as Master of the Queen's Music when a Memorial Stone was unveiled to Elgar in Westminster Abbey in June 1972.[77]

Recordings of Elgar

Bliss recorded some of his own compositions, but he never benefited from a friendship with a regular record producer such as Elgar had enjoyed with Fred Gaisberg, or Britten with John Culshaw. Nevertheless, he did record some music by other composers, including Elgar, and on 17 March 1957 at Walthamstow Assembly Hall he set down the five *Pomp and Circumstance* Marches for RCA. In his Worcester talk, Bliss set out his approach to recording them: 'I have recently been recording the five *Pomp and Circumstance* Marches. Now, a march is a comparatively humble form of music, but a detailed study of *these* five very different marches gives a remarkable insight into what Elgar can do in the manipulation of sound.'[78] It was an inspired choice to have a former guardsman conduct these military marches for, when reviewed in *The Gramophone* in April 1959, Trevor Harvey was very positive. Oddly numbers 4 and 5 were transposed on the disc so that it was book-ended by the most popular marches:

> I am astonished again at what good listening the *Pomp and Circumstance* marches make, heard right through at one go for their range is remarkable ... This change of order frames the set with the two most popular Hope-and-Gloryish ones and makes a most effective point by setting Nos. 3 and 5 next to each other, the sheer jauntiness of No. 5 sounding really delightful after the restless agitation of No. 3 (which is surely a minor masterpiece in itself). All this is most successful.

76 See Andrew Neill, *'It is the only wish I've got': The Story of the Elgar Birthplace* (Lower Broadheath: Elgar Foundation Enterprises Ltd, 2006), 29–30.

77 A further bizarre connection with Elgar became apparent when Bliss received a mysterious document from the Clemens Society, appointing him a Knight of King Arthur's Round Table, in succession to Edward Elgar. Bliss was never able to ascertain what duties this entailed! Bliss, op. cit., 238.

78 'Edward Elgar', in Roscow, op. cit., 246.

> As conductor, Sir Arthur gets consistently lively performances and good playing from the L.S.O. Here and there one could imagine a more acutely pointed style – for example, in one or two of the middle section – but in general, all is very well. And that is true, too, of the recording. You will be surprised that five marches heard straight through, could provide such varied mood and good listening.[79]

When reissued in 1970 it was noted that 'The record dates from the early days of stereo ... but the sound is still fresh and spacious with quite good stereo. Bliss gives excellent performances'[80]; and in 1975 this was still the case: 'Despite the age of the recording the sound still comes fresh and spacious with excellent playing.'[81] A year later, Ivan March found it 'the best set of the *Pomp and Circumstance* Marches currently before the public. Sir Arthur Bliss conducts the LSO in vigorously characterized performances and the bright slightly pithy sound recording suits his direct manner admirably.'[82] In 1979 the marches were coupled with Monteux's excellent *Variations*, and again: 'Sir Arthur Bliss gives entirely idiomatic and lively performances of the complete *Pomp and Circumstance* Marches.'[83] On 29 November 1967 Bliss recorded the *Cockaigne* overture in Kingsway Hall for Readers Digest: when it was issued for the Silver Jubilee in 1977 the reviewer found that Bliss's *Cockaigne* 'is an outstanding delight.'[84]

Conclusion

In 'The Fifteenth Variation' Bliss summed up his view of Elgar, who, he considered, 'was a man of inspired musical personality. He wrote because he was compelled to do so. It wasn't a mental activity. It was something that welled out of him and he had, of course, the mastery to express what he felt. I thought he was a man of great imagination.' Regarding his personality he did not see him as a typical countryman, nor was he at his best when 'dressed up in a magnificence of robes and orders; that's just one small part of him.'[85]

Bliss returned to this in his autobiography: 'I have always thought the popular image of Elgar, in his last decade, as a typical country squire or

79 Trevor Harvey, in *The Gramophone*, Vol. 36, No. 431 (April 1959), 513.
80 Wiliam A. Chislett, in *The Gramophone*, Vol. 48, No. 570 (November 1970), 859.
81 *The Gramophone*, Vol. 53, No. 629 (October 1975), 703.
82 Ivan March, in *The Gramophone*, Vol. 54, No. 637 (June 1976).
83 *The Gramophone*, Vol. 57, No. 674 (July 1979), 199.
84 William A. Chislett, in *The Gramophone*, Vol. 55, No. 650 (July 1977), 226.
85 'The Fifteenth Variation,' op. cit., 43.

retired colonel, wholly ridiculous … That he liked being photographed with a couple of dogs and a shooting stick, or that he overemphasized his interest in racing probably arose from his need for a decoy to lure the inquisitive away from private preserves, I have known many artists, especially British ones, employ a similar stratagem.'[86] As Bliss, particularly in his latter years, projected a military persona, was this also a decoy?

In his talk at Worcester in 1957 Bliss outlined the three main impressions that Elgar's music made on him. The first was his mastery of the sound he wanted: 'His orchestral scores are wonderful examples of consummate craftsmanship. No wonder orchestral players, whether string, woodwind, brass, or percussion, delight to play them. Each is given passages to play which seem to be a personal compliment to the player.'

His second impression was Elgar's originality as his musical phrases were very much his own: 'They are like personal gestures, so much so that … we have had to coin the word 'Elgarian' to describe them. The conviction that a very marked individual is speaking to us is all the more pronounced when we remember that his vocabulary was the one generally in use in the Europe of his day … *yet*, what he says is his own.'

Third, was Elgar's delight in the inexhaustible vitality of nature and life: 'He may have written at the head of his Second Symphony "Rarely, rarely comest thou, Spirit of Delight". But this is surely regret that he could not grasp more of the beauty of life he apprehended in everything around him. His music abounds in vitality, and is continually leaping forward, moving swiftly like a mountain torrent, or like the Severn when the tidal wave sweeps up it.'

Bliss concluded his talk with these fine words:

> The predominant effect of Elgar's music is an enhancement of life. That is why I give thanks for the appearance in England of this great composer; that is why I rejoice to celebrate his genius … and that is why I believe that, after a fine performance of his music, we emerge better, stronger, and more sensitive human beings.[87]

In the radio portrait, when asked of his view of Elgar he replied: 'I think he was a very sensitive, highly imaginative, often harassed human being and whenever I hear the slow movement from the First Symphony I see the man – especially do I see a clear-cut image of him in the final bars.'[88]

86 Bliss, op. cit., 25.

87 Roscow, op. cit., 246–7. This was also Bliss's musical philosophy as he told Vernon Handley in 1974: 'I do demand enhancement of life.' Extract from the Granada documentary quoted in Trudy Bliss, 'May 1966–March 1975', in Bliss, op. cit., 286.

88 'The Fifteenth Variation', op. cit., 43.

I acknowledge and thank Paul Chennell for his assistance in providing material from the database compiled by Martin Bird and himself. I thank Margaret Jones, curator of the Bliss Archive held in the Music Department, Cambridge University Library and Chris Bennett, formerly of the Elgar Birthplace Museum. Also, I thank my colleagues in the Elgar Society, Andrew Dalton, David Morris, Andrew Neill and John Norris.

Benjamin Britten (1913–1976)

Andrew Neill

BB and EE

On 2 October 1930 the sixteen-year-old Edward Benjamin Britten wrote in his diary: 'Go to Queen's Hall & prom. Elgar 2nd Symphony, (dreadful, nobilmente sempre) – I come out after 3rd movement – so bored. He (Elgar) conducts – ovation beforehand!!!!!!!!!!'.[1] In this way Britten records his vividly negative experience of hearing Elgar's E flat Symphony, during which he also had the privilege of hearing and seeing the composer conduct; an experience that seems to have left no impression on an impressionable young mind. This article demonstrates how the strongly-held feelings of youth can change and how one great artist can develop and begin to show a grudging respect for the work of another whose music he once despised.

Three and a half years after that visit to The Queen's Hall in London, the BBC broadcast the first performance of *A Boy Was Born* by the twenty-year-old Britten on 23 February 1934.[2] *A Boy Was Born* consists of fifteenth- and sixteenth-century poems set in the 'form of a theme and six variations', the exception being the setting of Christina Rossetti's 'In the Bleak Midwinter', in which Britten 'reveals himself as a true genius instead of (merely!) a remarkable talent'.[3] Of all the great composers born in the twentieth century, few matched Britten's natural ability, which was akin to that of Mozart or Korngold in its early brilliance and promise.[4] The contrast with Elgar's self-taught progression as a composer could not be greater and

1 John Evans, ed., *Journeying Boy: Diaries of the Young Benjamin Britten 1928–1938* (London: Faber and Faber, 2009). The concert included two songs by Vaughan Williams and Ireland's piano concerto (which Britten liked).

2 Britten was born on 22 November 1913.The Queen's Hall was destroyed in a bombing raid on 10 May 1941.

3 David Matthews, *Britten* (London: Haus Publishing Ltd, 2013), 29.

4 No doubt Britten would have loathed being mentioned in the same sentence as Korngold.

this broadcast, on the day of Elgar's death, was a coincidence of more than passing significance. In 1963 the musicologist Hans Keller, who admired Elgar, said of Britten: 'I personally would not hesitate to call Britten the greatest composer alive.'[5] In comparison it is likely only a few critics would have said the same of Elgar during his lifetime, although Hans Richter's tribute before the first London rehearsal of Elgar's A Flat Symphony on 6 December 1908 – 'Gentlemen, let us now rehearse the greatest symphony of modern times, written by the greatest modern composer, and not only in this country' – is praise at its most generous. However, that to Britten, from an Austrian *émigré*, really is exceptional particularly as Keller's views were expressed at a time when Shostakovich and Stravinsky were still very much alive.

In his 1932 diary Britten recorded hearing Elgar's music twice; once in April when he says: 'Elgar I didn't like' but before Christmas he noted: 'Listen to wireless inc. Elgar's Falstaff which contains some v. fine stuff – also some … !!!.'[6] Like Elgar, Britten was not an 'easy' character but created a circle of devoted friends who protected him and, as W H Auden noted, 'you will always be surrounded by people who adore you, nurse you and praise everything you do.'[7] This can be unhealthy and, a partial consequence of this adulation, was the legion of 'Britten's corpses' including Eric Crozier, Sir Charles Mackerras, Robert Tear and Sophie Wyss. It might be said that Sir Adrian Boult became an Elgar 'corpse', albeit a temporary one. However, at least Elgar had the grace to patch up their relationship after what he perceived was a slight to his music. Britten's contempt for the music of other composers is also well-known. He described Victor Hely-Hutchinson's *Carol Symphony* as 'utter bilge'[8] and although many who worked with Britten recall his sense of humour, he failed to see beyond Vaughan Williams's ironic observation on his own Fourth Symphony. Having been impressed by the symphony, Britten was horrified by the composer's comment, 'If that's modern music, all I can say is I don't like it.' He had already made up his mind about most of the older composer's music describing Vaughan Williams's *Benedicite* as 'music that repulses me.'[9]

5 John Bridcut, *Britten* (London: Faber and Faber, 2010), 18.

6 Evans, ed., *Diary*, 11 December 1932.

7 Henry Boys (1910–1992), the dedicatee of the composer's Violin Concerto from 1939 and first cousin of the author's mother, remained a devoted friend of the composer until his death in 1976. Boys worked with Robert Duncan on the vocal score of *The Rape of Lucretia* and as Britten's repetiteur at Glyndebourne.

8 Donald Mitchell, ed. *Letters from a Life: The Selected Letters and Diaries of Benjamin Britten 1913–1976* (London: Faber and Faber, 1991), 133.

9 Matthews, *Britten*, 29 (from an unpublished letter).

In their biographies of Britten, John Bridcut and Michael Kennedy draw on a number of parallels between Britten and Elgar all of which seem plausible: they were both ignored before being taken up by the establishment and their music praised (even over-praised) by non-British musicians and musicologists. Both could be very sensitive about any implied criticism of their music and were happiest when at home in the countryside of their birth. They were outsiders, too: Elgar because of his class and religion and Britten because of his homosexuality. John Bridcut shows how Britten mellowed towards the music of Elgar at the end of his life and, clearly encouraged by Peter Pears to consider *The Dream of Gerontius*, looked at the music through the eyes and ears of experience.[10] However, there were clear divergences.

Michael Tippett, in his inspired broadcast tribute on the day of Britten's death, said that the triumph of *Peter Grimes* meant for Britten that 'he was now willing in himself, and, indeed, determined to be, within the twentieth century, a professional opera composer. That in itself is an extraordinarily difficult thing to do; and one of the achievements for which he will always be remembered in musical history books is that, in fact, he actually *did* it.'[11]

Elgar, too, more or less, managed to become a self-supporting composer on his own terms. Furthermore, Britten the opera composer had set himself on a very different course to Elgar, who worked towards the composition of a symphony for most of the preceding thirty years.

On 2 June 1967 (110 years after Elgar's birth) the Queen opened the Maltings Concert Hall in Snape. At 3.15 pm the inaugural concert began with Britten's brilliant arrangement of The National Anthem, followed by his Overture *The Building of the House*, Delius's *Summer Night on the River*, Holst's *St Paul's Suite* and concluded with Handel's *Ode for St Cecilia's Day*. The following year (on 18–19 December) in the now renowned acoustic of the Maltings, Britten made his celebrated recording for Decca with the English Chamber Orchestra: 'Britten conducts English Music for Strings.' A view of the Maltings adorned the cover of the sleeve and the performance of the *Introduction & Allegro* remains one of the finest recorded.[12]

Britten's early comments on the music of Elgar show the length of the journey he travelled to consider performing and recording his predecessor's music. In his early twenties Britten developed increasingly left-wing views and, after attending a Prom in 1935, 'he commented on Elgar's First

10 In a conversation with John Bridcut on 2 September 2021 we agreed on how alike, in certain areas, Britten and Elgar were.

11 Michael Kennedy, *Britten* (London: J.M. Dent & Sons Ltd, 1981), 117.

12 The disc (SXL 6405) also included Frank Bridge's *Sir Roger de Coverley*, Britten's *Simple Symphony*, Delius's *Two Aquarelles* and the Purcell *Chacony*.

Symphony: "I swear that only in Imperialistic England could such a work be tolerated"'.[13] In 1931 he had listened briefly to a broadcast of Elgar, '1 min of Elgar Symphony 2 but can stand no more'. Earlier he had written to his parents after attending a Promenade Concert: 'The concert was very nice (Prom at QH). We came out at half time, and I wasn't very sorry because the seats were very hard ... the second part was all Elgar'.[14]

On 6 May 1931 Britten heard the BBC Symphony Orchestra perform under the direction of Sir Adrian Boult in London's Queen's Hall. The young Britten's criticisms not only demonstrate his ability with words but also lay bare his prejudices:

> Euryanthe ov. beastly bit of music, mauled about by Boult (2nd subject more than 2ce as slow as 1st sub.). Bad slips on part of orch. V. Williams Tallis Fantasia, V. beautiful (wonderfully scored), but over long. well played. Cortot in Saint-Saëns 4th Con, very wonderfully playing in spite of many wrong notes, which one didn't mind. Encored, playing (marvellously heavenly [sic]) a Chopin Waltz (C# min). Mahler's Lieder eines fahrenden Gesellen (Maria Olszewska, wonderful singing). Lovely little pieces, exquisitely scored - a lesson to all the Elgars & Strausses in the world. Enigma Variations, a terrible contrast to these little wonders. I listened with an open mind but cannot say that I was less annoyed by them, than usual. Of course there must be alot [sic] in them, but that type of sonorous orchestration (especially in Var. V, IX, XII, (which seem exactly alike to me) cloys very soon. Of course there are lovely moments (Dorabella is good, but is spoilt by trite ending =Var. XIII is very effective=. On the whole I think Ysobel's the best) but Oh! No X1V!! The orchestra played their exacting, but effective parts very well & Adrian Boult was a sympathetic conductor, I suppose. I suppose it is my fault, and there is something lacking in me, that I am absolutely incapable of enjoying Elgar, for more than 2 minutes.[15]

As Michael Kennedy and others have pointed out, Britten was ahead of his time in appreciating Mahler's music and had already purchased a score of the Mahler song-cycle, *Lieder eines fahrenden Gesellen.* In November 1931 he again attended another BBC concert when Elgar's *Introduction and Allegro* was performed: 'nice spots but terrible –"Toselli's Serenata"'. The concert was one more conducted by Boult, whom Britten judged to be a

[13] Humphrey Carpenter, *Benjamin Britten: A Biography* (London: Faber and Faber, 1992), 68–9.

[14] Donald Mitchell and Philip Reed, eds, *Letters from a Life, selected letters and diaries of Benjamin Britten 1923–39* (London: Faber and Faber, 1991), 24 September 1930.

[15] Mitchell and Reed, eds, *Diary*, 6 May 1931.

'terrible execrable conductor'.[16] It should be noted that Frank Bridge, Britten's teacher, also wanted the job as the first conductor of the newly formed BBC Symphony Orchestra.[17] Britten did not ignore Elgar's music; he just did not like it and to be fair he tried: 'After dinner I listened to prom on radio. Delius's marvellously beautiful tho' meandering and too long Song of the High Hills, completely dwarfs the rest of the anaemic programme … Elgar's typical Sea Pictures …'[18] 'Listened to Elgar concert after dinner. The Intro and All. makes some nice sounds, but the form seems so unsatisfactory … so does most of the Enigma Var. and all of the Second Sym.'[19]

In the summer of 1934 Britten noted: 'Listen to Toni Brosa and [Ivan] Phillipowsky give a rather stiff perf. of Elgar's violin Sonata … how I wish I could like this music. Of course, it is beautifully done but says nothing that Franck & Brahms haven't said before – not that I even want the latter.'[20] Elgar and Brahms coincided on the programme when Britten attended one of Toscanini's renowned concerts with the BBC Symphony Orchestra: 'To Queen's Hall for BBC Orch under Toscanini. Rather unfortunate programme, as two works are anathema to me – Brahms 4th and Enigma Var. of Elgar.'[21] In August 1937 Britten arrived as an international composer when the Boyd Neel Orchestra performed the premiere, in Salzburg, of his *Frank Bridge Variations*. The review in the *Salzburger Volksblatt*[22] began: '*English Music* played by a quite dazzling English string orchestra.' The review thanked the Austrian Ambassador in London for suggesting the concert which 'began with a Chaconne by Purcell and then played two Aquarelles by Delius and a concert piece by Elgar [the Introduction and Allegro] and a quite splendid series of Variations on a Theme by Frank Bridge of Benjamin Britten.'

Michael Kennedy once wrote of Britten as a great 'hater'[23] and, of course, Elgar had his dislikes too, but these were hardly as strong as 'hating', with the possible exception of the emotion he directed at Stanford. Before he was 30 years old Britten had commented on the score of Strauss's *Der Rosenkavalier*: 'I am impatient to see how the old magician makes his effects! There's a hell of a lot I can learn from him!'[24] However, in 1971 he referred to *Der*

16 Mitchell and Reed, eds, *Diary*, 4 November 1931.
17 Michael Kennedy, 'Trading Insults', *The Spectator*, 8 January 2013.
18 Mitchell and Reed, eds, *Diary*, 20 September 1932.
19 Mitchell and Reed, eds, *Diary*, 7 December 1932.
20 Mitchell and Reed, eds, *Diary*, 11 June 1934.
21 Mitchell and Reed, eds, *Diary*, 31 May 1935.
22 Edition of 28 August 1937.
23 Kennedy, 'Trading Insults'.
24 Bridcut, *Britten*, 39.

Rosenkavalier as 'that loathsome opera, which makes me almost physically sick to hear it'.[25] We all change as we age, and Britten and Elgar were no exceptions. In 1962 Britten confided in Peter Pears, referring to a proposed programme of British Music and Art in Leningrad and Moscow: 'It is a curse about Russia and those concerts ... they could have been fun – but now it all seems so mediocre & pointless. What a first concert – Elgar (well, not so bad, I suppose), Fricker, Bliss and VW. I'm jolly well going to get hold of those programmes and see if I can't think of something a bit brighter'.[26] In 1967 he wrote to Sir William Glock (then Controller of Music at the BBC) concerning a proposed visit of the BBC Symphony Orchestra to the Aldeburgh Festival: 'Colin D(avis) will be taking charge of the orchestra that week & one would like to think of a programme of works which he likes and which we normally wouldn't do ourselves here: something like Elgar (In the South, I like particularly)'.[27]

In March 1968 Pears was in Canterbury for the filming, by the BBC, of *The Dream of Gerontius* conducted by Sir Adrian Boult. Britten wrote to Pears: 'This is to bring my love to Canterbury, and to wish you lots of good things for your Gerontius – I'll be thinking of you and that ought to help, plus Adrian's conducting! ... remember to keep your eyes closed reverently!'[28] In May 1969 Pears sang Gerontius in Norwich prompting Britten to write to Myfanwy Piper: 'Peter did an absolute knockout Gerontius on Saturday in Norwich'.[29] A day later he wrote to the conductor of the performance, Philip Ledger: 'I wanted to tell you how impressed I was by your Gerontius. I think you did a most efficient and musical job, and to move one, as you did me, under those circumstances, was amazing'.[30]

The success of his recording of music for strings had clearly inspired him and it is believed that he even suggested making another disc which would have included Delius's *On Hearing the First Cuckoo in Spring* and the Vaughan Williams *Tallis Fantasia*. Furthermore, Britten's youthful criticisms of Elgar's orchestration seemed to have been forgotten and, it is difficult to imagine that with his own ability as an orchestrator, he did not

25 Kennedy, 'Trading Insults'.

26 Philip Reed and Mervyn Cooke, eds, *Letters from a Life: The Selected Letters of Benjamin Britten 1913–1976, Vol. 5* (London: Faber & Faber, 2010), 20 October 1962.

27 Reed and Cooke, eds, *Letters*, 20 June 1967.

28 Reed and Cooke, eds., *Letters*, 26–29 March 1968. The performance, made by the BBC, is available on DVD (ICAD 5140). Dame Janet Baker and John Shirley-Quirk were the other soloists, and the London Philharmonic Choir and Orchestra were conducted by Sir Adrian Boult.

29 Reed and Cooke, eds, *Letters*, 14 May 1969.

30 Reed and Cooke, eds, *Letters*, 15 May 1969. (Quoted as a footnote.)

come to admire Elgar's orchestrating skills too. Had Elgar lived to study the scores of the *Frank Bridge Variations* and *The Young Person's Guide* it is not difficult to imagine him lost in equal admiration.

Before his death, Britten bought a set of recordings of Elgar conducting his own music, *Images of Elgar*, issued by EMI in 1972.[31] At the Britten Pears Arts Archive in Aldeburgh I examined the scores relating to Elgar's music that are archived there including a vocal score of *The Dream of Gerontius*. On the inside if the title page is inscribed the signature 'E B Britten' with the date 1925. It is not known whether this was a gift or a purchase, but it is clear that Britten was familiar with Elgar's music at the age of eleven or twelve. The score is annotated in pencil by Britten but was also used by Sir Peter Pears, for the tenor part is heavily marked in his hand in coloured ink. Britten's full score of *The Dream of Gerontius* is marked up by Britten in pencil (as conductor) and reflects the seriousness with which he took the performance and recording. There is no conductor's score of *The Spirit of England*, only a vocal score of 'For the Fallen'. There are no markings of significance by Britten, and the cover has the initials 'BB' on the top right-hand corner. It is possible that Britten might have used this score for his intended performance but, bearing in mind his fastidiousness, this seems unlikely.

* * *

In 1931 Britten said that the *Introduction and Allegro* had 'nice spots' but was 'terrible' and, after seeing Toscanini conduct it, was 'not for me'. But a few days later he bought the score, just at the time he was starting his own orchestral piece for strings, *Variations on a Theme of Frank Bridge*. Perhaps he wanted to learn how another 'old magician' made his effects and maybe he had come round to them when, by 1969 he wrote of the novelty of Elgar's 'subtle sonorities, contrasting and combining the quartet and orchestra'?[32] Even though Britten in his youth, declared that he was 'absolutely incapable of enjoying Elgar for more than two minutes' he had 'come a long way' by the time he conducted *The Dream of Gerontius* for the first time in June 1971 for the Aldeburgh Festival and, in one or two instances, allegedly decided to 'improve' Elgar's orchestration.[33]

31 The set included a copy of Jerrold Northrop Moore's *Elgar: A Life in photographs*.

32 Bridcut, *Britten*, 118.

33 When I examined Britten's score, I could detect no obvious alterations to Elgar's orchestration in the time available. A more detailed study may reveal some minor changes. One passage that has often puzzled listeners is Britten's phrasing of the semi-chorus passage (Cue 64) beginning 'Noe from the waters in a saving home'. Britten had entered no markings to suggest why this should be phrased in a different

Inevitably, opinions differ but it is generally considered that Britten produced one of the more 'interesting' and perceptive recordings of the work. Edward Greenfield, in his review for *The Guardian,* felt that, despite his preference for Dame Janet Baker in the Barbirolli recording, he recommended the new issue because of its better sound, the other soloists and Britten's conducting. The recording took place in the Maltings on 19-24 July 1971 with soloists Peter Pears, Yvonne Minton and John Shirley-Quirk and the Choir of King's College Chapel, Cambridge, the London Symphony Chorus and Orchestra. Arthur Oldham (1926–2003) as chorus master of the LSO Chorus worked on the recording. He had been one of Britten's few private pupils and in his autobiography wrote of a visit to The Red House to discuss the preparations for the recording:

> I asked (Britten) why he had chosen to record this particular work since, when I had been working with him as his pupil (in the 1940s), he had expressed considerable distaste for Elgar's music. 'Well you know', he told me 'I've been looking at the score again, and if you strip off all the encrustations which have accumulated over the years' – (he was no doubt referring to the Barbirolli 'tradition' which had become the norm for performances of Gerontius) – 'there is really a very good piece underneath.'[34]

Britten wrote to Donald and Kathleen Mitchell, saying: 'Think of me ploughing through Gerontius next week ...'[35] and later sent copies of the recording to both Clifford Curzon and Sir William Walton – the latter replying: 'It has almost overcome my antipathy to it. At any rate my protestant hackles didn't quite rise as they usually do when I listen to this work.'[36] Michael Kennedy wrote of the recording:

> Those present at the sessions recall that Britten was 'far fussier about Gerontius than he ever was about one of his own works' and made nine 'takes' of the prelude to Part 1 (which he referred to as 'Act 1') before he was satisfied. Certain remarks of his at the rehearsals have been preserved. Thus, in the Demon's chorus: 'Make it sulky' and 'laugh as if it were the oldest joke you've ever heard'; in the stretto on the chorus 'Praise to the Holiest': 'if you feel in your bones that you can't stop it getting faster, you know we're making the accelerando just right'; at 'Novissima hora est': 'make it sound like a long forgotten

way to any other performance. One of the glories of the Britten recording is his use of the Choir of King's College Cambridge as the semi-chorus.

34 Arthur Oldham, *Living with Voices* (London: Thames Publishing, 2000), 30.

35 Reed and Cooke, eds, *Letters*, 18 July 1971.

36 Reed and Cooke, eds, *Letters*, 7 August 1972. (Quoted as a footnote.)

lullaby'; to the cellos during 'sanctus fortis': 'Don't dig into the strings; glide over it, it'll be too heavy otherwise'.[37]

This was the same man who, as a youth, could not bear listening to Elgar's music but now he had admitted to 'liking' *In the South* and was taking the recording of *Gerontius* very seriously and enjoying himself. Given another twenty years of life who knows where Britten's great musical intelligence would have taken him. Britten's note on 'For the Fallen' written for a performance he had intended to conduct shows he understood what Elgar was trying to say but fate, or rather fire, intervened and The Maltings was destroyed a week earlier on 8 June 1969. Fate also intervened when Britten died – too young - aged 63 on 4 December 1976.

The respective journeys of Elgar and Britten to greatness could not be more different and few of their compositions have much in common, but they set alight British music in the first two decades of the twentieth century and for the years after World War Two. It might be argued that between them they composed the two most important British works of the century. Elgar's A Flat Symphony demonstrated that, at last, the country had a composer who could produce a great symphony and, likewise, in *Peter Grimes*, Britten did the same for opera.

I am grateful to Dr Nicholas Clark the Librarian and Judith Ratcliffe, Archivist of Britten Pears Arts, for making available Britten's scores when I visited The Red House and its Archive in October 2021. Dr. Clark was also most helpful with some later comments. Andrew Dalton also provided assistance and advice. I thank him as well as Britten's biographer, John Bridcut, for his wider advice.

Britten on Elgar

The story of Britten's relationship with Elgar's music is also about a 'what if': Britten's non-conducting of Elgar's 'For the Fallen', not through any change of mind or prejudice but because of the burning of The Maltings in Snape. His intention to perform this, in the 1960s then a rarely performed work, shows that Britten's journey had been a remarkable one. His programme notes for the performance scheduled for The Maltings on Sunday 15 June 1969 are reproduced below. With the destruction of the Maltings a week earlier, the concert took place in the faithful Blythburgh Church. Britten conducted the *Introduction and Allegro for Strings* but 'For the Fallen' was

37 Kennedy, *Britten*, 102.

dropped in favour of Holst's *Fugal Concerto* with Richard Adeney, flute, and Peter Graeme, oboe. The English Chamber Orchestra was conducted by Imogen Holst. After the interval Haydn's Mass in B flat, *Harmoniemesse*, was conducted by Philip Ledger with Heather Harper (who would have sung the solo part in 'For the Fallen'), Janet Baker, Kenneth Bowen and Anthony Williams.

'For the Fallen' remains one of the few masterpieces to be composed about war during wartime, something I believe Britten understood. There is no correspondence in the Britten Pears Arts Archive explaining the change of work for Holy Trinity, Blythburgh: it may be possible to detect the influence of Imogen Holst, but this would only be conjecture. The concert was scheduled for broadcast by the BBC and would have been one of the first broadcasts of 'For the Fallen' since the end of World War Two. For those who had never heard the work its cancellation was, to say the least, disappointing.

Introduction and Allegro for Strings *Op. 47*
for quartet and orchestra

First performed in the Queen's Hall, London, on 8th March 1905, this work was dedicated to Professor S. S. Sanford, of Yale, at which University Elgar was made an Honorary Doctor of Music in June of that year. The Introduction is fragmentary, with much foreshadowing of the thematic material of the Allegro–the 'nobilmente' second theme, the ambling first theme with its rising fifths and sixths, but principally the haunting melody of the work-supposedly a folk-melody, which Elgar heard sung in the Welsh mountains, characterised by a repeated falling third. There had been many great works for strings before this: one thinks of Purcell's Chacony, the third Brandenburg, Handel, Mozart, Tchaikovsky and Grieg, but all these subtle sonorities, contrasting and combining the quartet and orchestra, and, above all, the brilliant Kreutzer-like scales and arpeggios, were something new.

For the Fallen (The Spirit of England No. 3)
for soprano solo, chorus and orchestra

It is not surprising that the war of 1914–18 produced from the red-hot patriot Elgar many immediately inspiring works: Carillon, Polonia, Le Drapeau Belge, *and* The Spirit of England *(The Fourth of August, To Women, For the Fallen). In the rather different atmosphere of today some of these works have lost their immediacy, but 'For the Fallen' has always seemed to me to have in its opening bars a personal tenderness and grief, in the grotesque march an agony of distortion, and in the final sequences a ring of genuine splendour. It was first performed in Leeds on 3rd May 1916, and in London the following week at a series of concerts in aid of the Red Cross, during which week* The Dream of Gerontius *was performed daily.*

B.B.

9. A photograph of Elgar from the London studio of Ernest Walter Histed. The studio was also well known as the exclusive photographer of the Order of Merit recipients, including Elgar who is wearing his OM decoration.

Biographical Notes on the Contributors

JANET BAKER

One of the greatest singers of the twentieth century, Dame Janet Baker is renowned for her operatic portrayals, lieder and art song recitals and performances in oratorio and on the concert platform. Many of her recordings remain indispensable, notably many of her operatic roles and song cycles such as those by Mahler and Wagner, also of the music of Elgar: *The Dream of Gerontius, Sea Pictures* and *The Music Makers.* Dame Janet formed a close musical relationship with the composer Benjamin Britten and he composed the cantata *Phaedra* for her. She also premiered the role of Kate Julian in his opera *Owen Wingrave.*

Born in Yorkshire, she moved to London in 1953 and made her debut at Glyndebourne three years later before embracing many of Handel's operatic roles, notably the title role in English National Opera's *Julius Caesar.* At Glyndebourne she sang in Cavalli's *La Calisto,* Dido (Purcell), Lucretia (Britten) and Penelope in Monteverdi's *Il ritorno d'Ulisse in Patria.* Other roles for which she became renowned were Dorabella in *Cosi fan Tutte,* Hermia in Britten's *A Midsummer Night's Dream,* Charlotte in Massenet's *Werther,* Queen Mary in Donizetti's *Maria Stuarda* and Orfeo in Gluck's *Orfeo ed Euridice.*

Dame Janet has been honoured around the world, and in the UK was appointed a Dame in 1976 and a Companion of Honour in 1993. Widowed in 2019 when her husband and manager, Keith Shelley, died Dame Janet remains active and interested in musical activities which she attends when possible. Dame Janet is a Vice-President of The Elgar Society

(On being asked to supply a biography for this volume Dame Janet said 'why don't you write it?'. This we are honoured to attempt, realising that to condense Dame Janet's life into just a few words is almost impossible. Graciously, she approved the above.)

MARTYN BRABBINS

Martyn Brabbins studied composition in London and conducting with Ilya Musin in Leningrad, subsequently winning first prize at the 1988 Leeds Conductors' Competition which launched his international career.

He was Associate Principal Conductor of the BBC Scottish Symphony Orchestra 1994–2005, Principal Guest Conductor of the Royal Flemish Philharmonic 2009–2015, Chief Conductor of the Nagoya Philharmonic 2012–2016 and Artistic Director of the Cheltenham International Festival of Music 2005–2007. He is Prince Consort Professor of Conducting at the Royal College of Music, Visiting Professor at the Royal Scottish Conservatoire and Artistic Advisor to the Huddersfield Choral Society.

He has enjoyed a busy opera career since his early days at the Kirov and more recently at La Scala, the Bayerische Staatsoper and regularly in Lyon, Amsterdam, Frankfurt and Antwerp. He opened English National Opera's 23/24 season with David Alden's production of *Peter Grimes* in what turned out to be his swansong, as well as a musical highpoint of his seven year tenure. In the 24/25 season he conducted *The Makropoulos Case* for Scottish Opera and *Mazeppa* for Grange Park Opera.

His discography ranges from Romantic to contemporary repertoire, with over 60 recordings for Hyperion Records alone, notably of Elgar, Walton and Tippett. He has received three Gramophone Awards, the Concerto Award with viola soloist Tim Ridout for Elgar and Bloch with the BBC Symphony (Harmonia Mundi). He also won the Cannes Opera Award for Korngold's *Die Kathrin* with the BBC Concert Orchestra (CPO), and the Grand Prix du Disque for Jonathan Harvey's *Wagner Dream*.

Martyn Brabbins was recently appointed Chief Conductor of the Malmö Symphony and of the Symphony Orchestra of India, both starting in the 2025/26 season. He has conducted many of the world's finest orchestras including the Radio Sinfonieorchester Berlin, Lahti Symphony Orchestra, Royal Concertgebouw, San Francisco Symphony, DSO Berlin and Tokyo Metropolitan Symphony, as well as most of the leading UK orchestras.

He has recorded nearly 150 CDs, including prize-winning discs of operas by Korngold, Birtwistle and Harvey. In 2023 he received the RPS Conductor Award for his 'colossal' contribution to UK musical life. Martyn Brabbins is a Vice-President of The Elgar Society.

JOHN BRIDCUT

John Bridcut's performance-documentary *Elgar: The Man Behind The Mask* won a BAFTA award for sound and won the Best Documentary award at the Golden Prague TV Festival. His other composer films, featuring Britten, Vaughan Williams, Delius, Parry and most recently Tippett, have been well-received. He has also made documentaries about Rostropovich, Karajan, Haitink, Sir Colin Davis, Jonas Kaufmann and Dame Janet Baker.

DAVID BRIGGS

David Briggs is an internationally renowned organist whose performances are acclaimed for their musicality, virtuosity, and ability to excite and engage audiences of all ages. Consistently ranked as one of the finest organists of his generation, David's extensive repertoire spans five centuries. He has also become one of the foremost organ transcribers of symphonic works, thereby giving listeners the opportunity to experience the organ in a new way. He has transcribed orchestral compositions by Schubert, Tchaikovsky, Elgar, Bruckner, Ravel, and Bach as well as Mahler's Second, Third, Fourth, Fifth, Sixth, and Eighth symphonies.

At the age of 17, David obtained his FRCO (Fellow of the Royal College of Organists) diploma, winning the Silver Medal of the Worshipful Company of Musicians. From 1981 to 1984 he was Organ Scholar at King's College, Cambridge University, during which time he studied with Jean Langlais in Paris. The first British winner of the Tournemire Prize at the St Albans International Improvisation Competition, he also won the first prize in the International Improvisation Competition at Paisley. Subsequently David held positions at Hereford, Truro, and Gloucester Cathedrals.

Deeply committed to ensuring organ music remains relevant and vibrant, David enjoys giving pre-concert lectures and demonstrations that help make organ music more broadly accessible. He teaches performance at Cambridge University, frequently serves on international organ competition juries, and gives master classes at colleges and conservatories across the US and Europe.

David performs more than 50 concerts a year and is also a prolific composer and his works range from full scale oratorios to works for solo instruments. He is currently Artist-in-Residence at the Cathedral of St John the Divine in New York City.

ADRIAN BROWN

Adrian Brown comes from a distinguished line of Sir Adrian Boult's most gifted pupils, studying intensively with him for some years after graduating from the Royal Academy of Music. Sir Adrian wrote: 'He has always impressed me as a musician of exceptional attainments who has all the right gifts and ideas to make him a first-class conductor'. Adrian remains the only British conductor to have reached the finals of the Karajan Conductors' Competition: the Berlin Philharmonic was the first professional orchestra he conducted.

In 1992 Adrian was engaged to conduct one of the world's great orchestras, the St Petersburg Philharmonic. In 1998 Sir Roger Norrington recommended him to conduct the Camerata Salzburg. Adrian has also conducted many leading British orchestras including the City of Birmingham, the BBC and BBC Scottish Symphony Orchestras, and the London Sinfonietta. He is a great proponent of contemporary music and has given several first performances.

Working with young musicians has been an area where Adrian has made an invaluable contribution to British musical life, as well as abroad. Between 1972 Adrian and 2013 he was Music Director of Stoneleigh Youth Orchestra, his tenure honoured with a Celebratory Concert in Cadogan Hall in March 2013. He has frequently conducted both the National Youth Orchestra (working with Sir Colin Davis and Norrington) and the National Youth Wind Orchestra. He regularly runs courses for young musicians, coaches young conductors, and was given the Novello Award for Youth Orchestras at the 1989 Edinburgh Festival. Adrian was one of a hundred musicians presented with a prestigious Classic FM Award at their Tenth Birthday Honours Celebration in June 2002. In 2013 he was awarded the Making Music NFMS Lady Hilary Groves Prize for services to Community Music.

Adrian is particularly highly regarded for his interpretations of Berlioz and Elgar. In December 2017 he was presented with the Berlioz International Society Medal and, coinciding with his 70th birthday in October 2019, he was awarded the Elgar Medal. Adrian founded his own orchestra, the Elgar Sinfonia, in 2018: it has gone from strength to strength, including performing Elgar's *Falstaff* in June 2021 and, in October 2021, celebrating the London Branch of the Elgar Society's 50th anniversary with *Sea Pictures*, *Polonia*, and the *Crown of India* in the presence of Dame Janet Baker. The Sinfonia recently performed a cycle of the Elgar Symphonies *The Black Knight* and the Bliss Piano Concerto.

DAVID CAIRNS

David Cairns was chief music critic of *The Sunday Times* and the *Spectator*. He has been Distinguished Visiting Professor at the University of California, a visiting scholar at the Getty Centre in Santa Monica and a visiting fellow of Merton College, Oxford. His two-volume biography of Berlioz has established itself as the definitive work on the subject and won the Whitbread Biography Award, the Samuel Johnson Prize for Non-Fiction and the Royal Philharmonic Society Prize. He was co-founder of the Chelsea Opera Group and is founder-conductor of the Thorington Players. His most recent book is *Mozart and his Operas* (Penguin/Allen Lane).

RELF CLARK

After tuition with Sidney Campbell at St George's Chapel, Windsor Castle, Relf Clark won an exhibition to Oxford, where he studied with Robert Sherlaw Johnson and F.W. Sternfeld and assisted at the University Church; and while still an undergraduate he became a prize-winning Fellow of the Royal College of Organists. He completed his musical education at London University, where he read musicology, and at Reading University, where he was taught by David Sanger and gained both a distinction in performance studies and a PhD.

Dr Clark writes and lectures on music and has contributed to *The Oxford Dictionary of National Biography*, *The New Grove Dictionary of Music and Musicians*, and musical periodicals of various kinds. From 1990 to 2005 he was on the council of the British Institute of Organ Studies and for seven of those years was the BIOS publications officer. He is an honorary life member of the Elgar Society; his publications include four volumes of Elgar-related essays; and he featured in the Durham University DVD about Elgar's Sonata for Organ, Op. 28. He composes for the organ and has given recitals in many parts of the UK.

In 1982, Relf Clark qualified as a solicitor. Having spent a decade with Costain Group plc, in 1993 he returned to private practice, and from 1998 until 2017, when he retired, he was with a City of London law firm. His clients there included the Royal Society of Musicians of Great Britain, of which he is now an honorary life member.

HUGH COBBE

Hugh Cobbe studied classics at Trinity College Dublin and joined the Department of Manuscripts in the British Museum in 1967. While there he was especially concerned with music manuscripts and in particular worked on the Elgar, Vaughan Williams and Holst collections. He was Head of Music at the British Library from 1985 until January 2002 and then held the post of Head of British Collections until his retirement from the British Library in November 2002. He was President of the Royal Musical Association 2002–2005, a Trustee of the Britten-Pears Foundation 1987–2003, Chairman of the Gerald Coke Handel Foundation 1996–2013 and Trustee of the Elgar Society Edition 2001–2007. He was appointed OBE in the New Year's Honours 2003. He was Chairman of the RVW Trust 2008–2022, of the National Folk Music Fund 2008–2023 and Director of The Vaughan Williams Charitable Trust 2008–2022. He is a trustee of the Vaughan Williams Foundation and Vice-President of the Ralph Vaughan Williams Society. His edition of the letters of Ralph Vaughan Williams was published by OUP in 2008 with a paperback edition published in 2010.

NEVILLE CREED

Neville Creed was director of the Bournemouth Symphony Chorus 1987–2003 and Artistic Director of the London Philharmonic Choir from 1994. He has announced his retirement at the end of the 2024/25 season. He has worked with some of the world's leading conductors, notably with Vladimir Jurowski and Edward Gardner for the London Philharmonic Orchestra. He has directed the choir in over 500 performances and led the choir in Tippett's *The Midsummer Marriage* with the London Philharmonic Orchestra under Principal Conductor Edward Gardner to critical acclaim and a Gramophone award.

FLORIAN CSIZMADIA

Florian Csizmadia studied conducting and piano in Dresden and musicology at the University of Hamburg, where he earned his doctorate with a study on Elgar's choral works. After 10 years as chorus master and staff conductor of the Hamburg State Opera, he embarked on a full-time career as an orchestral conductor in 2012. Since 2017 he has been Music Director of the Philharmonisches Orchester Vorpommern in the Hanseatic cities of Stralsund and Greifswald. He is particularly interested in promoting British music in Germany and regularly performs Elgar's orchestral works.

ANDREW DALTON

On graduating from the University of London in 1969 with a degree in philosophy, Andrew Dalton joined the Classical Department of the Decca Record Company in its Advertising Department and subsequently worked in marketing and promotion. As Classical Promotions Manager for both Decca and Philips Classics, he worked with numerous internationally acclaimed classical artists, including Luciano Pavarotti, Dame Joan Sutherland, Dame Kiri te Kanawa and Sir Georg Solti. He inherited a love of 1930s dance band music from his father, and was honoured to work with Dame Vera Lynn, leading to the discovery of several rare recordings in her personal collection which he arranged to be transferred to CD. He has also worked in concert promotion and managed over fifty classical concerts at all the major London concert venues. As a Friend of Pushkin House, he is a passionate advocate for Russian culture and has given talks to musical and literary societies on Pushkin and other aspects of Russian music and literature. He lives in East London with his wife, two children and three grandchildren. Andrew Dalton has been a member of the Elgar Society for thirty years, during which time he has served on both its Council and the Committee of its London Branch.

HILARY DAVAN WETTON

Hilary Davan Wetton, a prize-winning student of Sir Adrian Boult, is closely identified with 20th-century British music. He has had extended relationships as Musical Director with the Guildford Choral Society, the City of London Choir and the Holst Singers, as well as conducting most of the London Orchestras. He has also been presenter of Classic FM's *Masterclass*, Artistic Director of the Military Wives Choirs and Founder Conductor of the Milton Keynes Orchestra, with which he recorded several neglected symphonies by 19th-century British composers.

Hilary worked extensively with young musicians. He was Director of Music at St Paul's Girls School from 1978 to 1993 and at Tonbridge School from 1993 to 2006. Conductor of the Edinburgh Youth Orchestra, the Birmingham Schools' Symphony Orchestra and the Orchestra of the Royal Birmingham Conservatoire, he appeared on many occasions with the National Children's Orchestra. He was a Professor of Conducting at the Guildhall School of Music and Drama and Senior Music Associate of Somerville College, Oxford.

His discography includes award-winning recordings of Holst's *Planets* with the LPO, Beethoven's *Glorreiche Augenblick* with the CLC and the RPO and Holst's *Evening Watch* with the Holst Singers. His 1993 recording of Holst's *Choral Symphony* was awarded the *Diapason D'Or*. *Flowers of the Field* (Naxos), was released on Remembrance Day 2014 and went straight to the top of the specialist Classical Chart. Hilary's book, *Reflections on Conducting*, is published by Queens Temple Publications. Musical Opinion described it as 'Quite simply the best book on conducting I have encountered.'

NEAL DAVIES

Neal Davies is a British bass-baritone. Recent engagements include performances of Bach's *St. John Passion* with Music of the Baroque and Jane Glover, *Yeomen of the Guard* (Sergeant) and Don Alfonso *Cosi fan tutte* for the English National Opera, and Papageno in the Welsh National Opera's production of *The Magic Flute*.

24/25 included concerts of Berlioz's *L'Enfance du Christ* at the Festival Berlioz with Paul McCreesh and the NFM Wroclaw Philharmonic. Neal will also join Bernard Labadie and the Kansas City Symphony for Mozart's *Requiem Mass in D minor*, make a *Messiah* concert tour with The English Concert and Harry Bickett, sing Elgar's *The Dream of Gerontius* with Ryan Wigglesworth and the BBC Scottish Symphony Orchestra, and join Jonathan Cohen and the Rotterdam Philharmonic Orchestra for Bach's *St*

Matthew Passion. Neal will also sing Dr Bartolo in a forthcoming English National Opera's production of *The Marriage of Figaro*.

Notable collaborations include concerts with the Oslo Philharmonic Orchestra under Mariss Jansons, BBC Symphony Orchestra under Pierre Boulez, The Cleveland and Philharmonia orchestras under Christoph von Dohnányi, Chamber Orchestra of Europe under Nikolaus Harnoncourt, Orchestra of the Age of Enlightenment under Frans Brüggen, English Concert with Harry Bicket, Gabrieli Consort under Paul McCreesh, Hallé Orchestra with Sir Mark Elder, Concerto Köln under Ivor Bolton, Scottish Chamber Orchestra with Adam Fischer, Bergen Philharmonic Orchestra with Edward Gardner, Deutsches Symphonie Orchester Berlin with David Zinman, Melbourne Symphony Orchestra with Sir Andrew Davis, and the London Symphony and Vienna Philharmonic Orchestras under Daniel Harding. He has been a regular guest of the Edinburgh Festival and BBC Proms.

Neal Davies studied at King's College, London, and the Royal Academy of Music, and won the Lieder Prize at the 1991 Cardiff Singer of the World Competition.

JEREMY DIBBLE

Fellow of the Royal School of Church Music and Guild of Church Musicians, Emeritus Professor of Music at Durham University and a specialist on British and Irish music of the nineteenth and twentieth centuries, Jeremy Dibble is the author of monographs on Parry (1992), Stanford (2002), Stainer (2007), Esposito (2010), Hamilton Harty (2013) and *The Music of Frederick Delius: Style, Form and Ethos* (2021). The musical editor of the *Canterbury Dictionary of Hymnology* (2013) and the joint editor (with Julian Horton) of *British Musical Criticism and Intellectual Thought 1850–1950* (2018), he has recently authored a revised and expanded edition of his book *Charles Villiers Stanford: Man and Musician* (2024) which has been recently been re-published for the composer's centenary. He has also contributed articles and chapters to various publications on Sterndale Bennett, Elgar, Frank Bridge and Vaughan Williams as well as the British symphonic poem. Although he has devoted much time to music in nineteenth-century Britain and Ireland, and this continues with the *Cambridge Companion to Charles Villiers Stanford* and a book on Charles Wood for his centenary in 2026, he is also now working more in the twentieth century, which includes studies of music by Samuel Coleridge-Taylor, Thomas Pitfield and William Alwyn. He has also worked closely in the capacity of editor and consultant with many commercial recording companies such as Chandos, Hyperion, Regent, Signum, Delphian and Naxos and edited the scores of Stanford's

The Veiled Prophet and *The Critic* when they were performed at Wexford in 2019 and 2024 respectively. He is currently President of the Stanford Society and an Honorary President of the Association of English Speakers and Singers.

SCOTT DICKINSON

Scott Dickinson was appointed Principal Viola of the Philharmonia Orchestra in 2024. He was born in Glasgow and studied in Manchester, London and Salzburg, where he won the 1996 Mozarteum Concerto Competition. This led to the first performances in Salzburg of the Walton Viola Concerto.

He has appeared with Karen Cargill, Ivry Gitlis, Steven Isserlis, the Brodsky, Chilingirian, Elias, Maxwell, Navarra and Royal Quartets, regularly with the Hebrides, Nash, Wigmore Soloists and Red Note Ensembles and as guest principal viola with numerous orchestras including the Australian Chamber Orchestra, BBC Symphony Orchestra, Chamber Orchestra of Europe, Frankfurt Radio Symphony, London Philharmonic, London Symphony, Mahler Chamber Orchestra, Philharmonia, Scottish Chamber Orchestra, Sinfonia of London, Swedish Radio Symphony, the John Wilson Orchestra, Tonhalle-Orchester Zürich and the World Orchestra for Peace.

For five years he was a member of the Leopold String Trio, performing worldwide (including Carnegie Hall, New York, Musikverein, Vienna, on CD and frequently at the Wigmore Hall, London) and from 2002 he was principal viola of the BBC SSO, with which he has also regularly appeared as soloist, including performances of Mozart's Sinfonia Concertante to celebrate Donald Runnicles's 60th birthday and *Jubilus* by Jonathan Harvey on CD which was nominated for a Gramophone award. Recent projects include an acclaimed solo video for Hebrides Ensemble's 'Inner Hebrides' series and a number of commissions of duos – for two violas with his BBC SSO desk partner Andrew Berridge and for flute and viola with his wife Susan Frank. Scott loves people, words and wildernesses and is passionate about the benefits of music in all areas of society. He teaches at the Royal Conservatoire of Scotland and is an Artistic Advisor to the Tunnell Trust for Young Musicians.

THOMAS EISNER

Thomas Eisner spent five years in Denmark as a member pf the Aarhus Symphony Orchestra before returning to Britain and joining the First Violin section of the London Philharmonic Orchestra.

He has performed as soloist in Mozart's *Sinfonia Concertante* (with the Aarhus Symphony Orchestra) and his recording of Bartok's violin duet Sorrow with Philippe Graffin was hailed as pick of the albums in *The Independent.* He has played with the Bavarian State Opera, and in 2022 performed *Lohengrin, Tristan, Das Rheingold* and *Siegfried* at the Bayreuth Festival.

In recent years Thomas has taken a lead in encouraging more people from different cultural backgrounds to attend LPO concerts. Alongside this he has demonstrated a keen interest in fundraising and has enjoyed transforming interested enthusiasts into patrons. Recently, he was a delegate at the conference of The Association of British Orchestras.

Languages and travel are his passions, and Thomas enjoys touring with the Orchestra. In 2008 he visited Palestine, where he played in schools and refugee camps. He is a member of the Athenæum and has always found it intriguing that his grandfather played cards with Richard Strauss – and wishes he could have been there!

EDWARD GARDNER

Edward Gardner is Principal Conductor of the London Philharmonic Orchestra and Music Director of The Norwegian Opera and Ballet. He additionally serves as Honorary Conductor of the Bergen Philharmonic Orchestra, following his tenure as Chief Conductor from 2015 to 2024.

Edward opened his inaugural season as Music Director of The Norwegian Opera and Ballet with concert performances of Wagner's *The Flying Dutchman* and Mahler's Symphony No. 2 *'Resurrection'.* He then conducted two fully staged operas, Verdi's *La Traviata* and Janáček's *The Cunning Little Vixen,* following earlier productions of Bartók's *Bluebeard's Castle,* Zemlinsky's *A Florentine Tragedy* and Verdi's *Un ballo in Maschera.*

During his fourth season with the LPO, Edward conducted nine concerts at the Royal Festival Hall as well as a US tour culminating at Carnegie Hall, and in major European cities including Vienna, Frankfurt and Hamburg. Highlights of their London season included Strauss's *Alpine Symphony,* Ravel and Rachmaninov double bills and several world premieres, closing with Mahler's Symphony No. 8, *'Symphony of a Thousand'.*

Edward has an extensive discography with Chandos. His many recordings with the Bergen Philharmonic feature Brahms, Sibelius, Nielsen, Grieg, Bartók, Schoenberg and Britten, their recording of *Peter Grimes* winning the 2021 *Gramophone* Award for best recording. Their recording of Janáček's *Glagolitic Mass* received a Grammy nomination and his recording of Tippett *The Midsummer Marriage* for LPO Live received the Gramophone Opera Award in 2023. During 2025, the LPO celebrated the 20th anniversary of its record label with recordings conducted by Edward. Releases included his acclaimed performance of Elgar's *The Dream of Gerontius.*

A passionate supporter of young talent, Edward founded the Hallé Youth Orchestra in 2002 and regularly conducts the National Youth Orchestra of Great Britain. He has a close relationship with the Juilliard School of Music, and with the Royal Academy of Music which appointed him its inaugural Sir Charles Mackerras Conducting Chair in 2014. Edward Gardner is a Vice-President of the Elgar Society.

RONALD GRAMES

Ronald Grames is an American Music Critic and Trustee of The Ralph Vaughan Williams Society.

ANDREW GREEN

Andrew Green has presented many hundreds of live and recorded BBC programmes for Radio 3, Radio 4 and the World Service. Music and history have been his main areas of interest. As a music journalist, Andrew has written for a long string of magazines and national newspapers. British music has been a significant (but not obsessive!) area of interest. He has written, broadcast and lectured widely on the life and work of Ralph Vaughan Williams and is a trustee of the RVW Society. His interest in Elgar goes back to teenage years and has broadened and deepened over the years.

Andrew is also a longstanding senior research fellow in oral history at the University of Hertfordshire, where he has overseen memories projects on a wide range of subjects. Most recently he has masterminded the harvesting of recollections of choristers who sang at the 1953 Coronation and also of former members of the choir at King's College, Cambridge with memories of legendary organist Boris Ord.

DANIEL GRIMLEY

Daniel M. Grimley is the Head of Humanities and Professor of Music at the University of Oxford, where he is also a Fellow of Merton College. His research concerns music, landscape, and cultural geography, especially in the Nordic region (Grieg, Sibelius, Stenhammar, Carl Nielsen) and England (Elgar, Delius, and Vaughan Williams). He has published four monographs, most recently *Delius and the Sound of Place* (Cambridge University Press, 2018) and *Sibelius: Life, Music, Silence* (Reaktion, 2021), and edited five further volumes. His published work on Elgar includes essays for *Elgar and His World* (edited by Byron Adams) and *Elgar Studies* (edited by J.P.E. Harper Scott and Julian Rushton) and in 2004, he co-edited with Julian Rushton the *Cambridge Companion to Elgar*. In 2011 he was Scholar-in-Residence at the Bard Festival, *Sibelius and his World*, and returned in 2023 for *Vaughan Williams and his World*. He is a musical advisor to the Delius Trust.

PAUL GUINERY

Paul Guinery studied piano at the Royal College of Music, gaining an ARCM and winning the Accompanist's Prize (adjudicated by Gerald Moore); he was also a répétiteur for the RCM Opera School. He subsequently took a degree in modern languages at Oxford. Paul performs regularly, either as a piano soloist or in chamber music. He has just recorded his third CD of light-music piano solos, to be released in May on EM Records.

A former vice-chairman of the Delius Society, Paul was commissioned to record the CD *Delius and his Circle.* He is the co-author, with Lyndon Jenkins, of a photographic study of visitors to Delius's home in France; and, with Martin Lee-Browne, of *Delius and his Music,* in which he broke new ground in offering detailed analyses of the composer's complete works. He is currently Chairman of the Delius Trust.

For many years Paul was a staff announcer and presenter for the BBC, working latterly for Radio 3. He is still on the air as a newsreader.

SIMON HEFFER

Simon Heffer is Professor of Modern British History at the University of Buckingham. He is also a columnist for the *Daily* and *Sunday Telegraphs* and the author of numerous history books, the most recent of which is *Sing As We Go: Britain Between the Wars.* He is also the author of a biography of Ralph Vaughan Williams.

TOM HIGGINS

Particularly noted for his 'stylish' and 'attentive' conducting, Tom Higgins has regularly appeared with leading British orchestras. After commencing his career as an oboist with the English National Opera Orchestra, he studied conducting with James Lockhart, Music Director of the Kassel Opera House in Germany. Among his first engagements was a four-year association with London's Opera Holland Park where he conducted the Royal Philharmonic Orchestra. His diverse repertoire includes more than fifty operas, ranging from Mozart's *The Magic Flute* to Menotti's *The Consul.*

Recognised for his promotion of the composer Robert Stolz, he was awarded a Diploma of Honour by the *International Robert Stolz Society of Vienna.* He made his German debut conducting the New Year's Day Concert in 2003 with Dresden's Staatsoperetten Orchestra and later directed a series of concerts in the Berlin district of Charlottenberg. His discography includes the world-premiere recording with the Hanover Band of Sir Arthur Sullivan's last completed work for the stage, *The Rose of Persia,* released through the BBC Music Magazine. As a SOMM label artist he has recorded many Elgar rarities including a highly acclaimed revival of *The*

Fringes of the Fleet with Roderick Williams. His latest CD is entitled *Elgar and His Peers.*

A published author, he has written extensively about the late Sir Charles Mackerras. He also assisted Mackerras in the reconstruction of Sullivan's Cello Concerto. His most recent conducting appointment is Music Director of the Guards Association Band at Chelsea.

STEPHEN HOUGH

Named by *The Economist* as one of 'Twenty Living Polymaths', Sir Stephen Hough combines a distinguished career as a pianist with those of composer and writer. He was the first classical performer to be given a MacArthur Fellowship and was awarded a Knighthood for Services to Music in the Queen's Birthday Honours 2022.

He has performed extensively in recital and with most of the world's major orchestras, and his catalogue of around 70 albums has garnered four Grammy nominations, eight Gramophone Awards and France's Diapason d'Or de l'Année. As a composer he has been commissioned by Westminster Abbey, Westminster Cathedral, Wigmore Hall, BBC Sounds, the Gilmore Foundation, Chamber Music Society of Lincoln Center, members of the Berlin Philharmonic amongst others. He wrote the commissioned work for the 2022 Van Cliburn International Piano Competition, performed by all 30 competitors, and his String Quartet No.1 *Les Six Rencontres,* commissioned for the Takács Quartet, was recorded for Hyperion Records. His music is published by Josef Weinberger Ltd.

As an author, Hough's memoir *Enough: Scenes from Childhood* was published by Faber & Faber in Spring 2023. It follows his 2019 collection of essays for Faber, *Rough Ideas: Reflections on Music and More* – a Royal Philharmonic Society Award-winner and a *Financial Times* Book of the Year – as well as his first novel, *The Final Retreat* (Sylph Editions, 2018). He has also been published by *The New York Times, The Daily Telegraph, The Times,* and *The Guardian.* Hough is an Honorary Bencher of the Middle Temple, an Honorary Member of the Royal Philharmonic Society, and is an Honorary Fellow of Girton College, Cambridge.

ANDREW KEENER

Andrew Keener was bitten by the bug from Broadheath as a twelve-year-old when discovering a seven-inch EP among his parents' record collection of the first two movements of the *Serenade for Strings* and *Bavarian Dances* (LSO/Lawrance Collingwood). From his days as a pupil at Barry Boys' Comprehensive School, a music graduate from Edinburgh University, then a brief spell as a freelance critic for *The Guardian, Gramophone,*

Hi-fi News and other magazines, he has for the past forty-odd years been an independent recording producer, fortunate to have worked with many Elgarians in the studio, including Daniel Barenboim, Sir Andrew Davis, Sir Mark Elder, Vernon Handley, Andrew Litton, Sir Charles Mackerras and Leonard Slatkin.

KATE KENNEDY

Kate Kennedy is Weinrebe Director of the Oxford Centre for Life-Writing, General Manager of the Museum of Music History, and a Research Fellow at Wolfson College, Oxford. She is the author of multiple publications on twentieth century British music and literature, including, as editor: *The Silent Morning: Culture and the Armistice 1918*, *Literary Britten*, *Lives of Houses*; and, as author: *Dweller in Shadows – A Life of Ivor Gurney*, and *Cello – A Journey Through Silence to Sound.* She is a Fellow of the Royal Historical Society and regular broadcaster on British music for BBC Radio 3.

CHRISTOPHER KENT

Christopher Kent studied at Manchester University and at King's College, London, where he completed a doctoral dissertation on Elgar's sketches; he was a Reading University lecturer from 1980 to 2002, when he retired. He co-edited several of the early volumes of the Elgar Complete Edition and over the years has contributed to a number of scholarly publications about the composer. The first edition of his Elgar research guide was published in 1993, a second edition received the C.B. Oldman Prize, and he completed the work for a third edition before his death. An organist, Dr Kent performed in Britain and abroad, served as Secretary of the British Institute of Organ Studies, and made many contributions to organ scholarship. He was a member of the Association of Independent Organ Advisers and a Fellow of the Royal College of Organists. Dr Kent was awarded the British Empire Medal in the 2024 New Year's Honours 'for services to Music and Musicology'. He died, aged 75, on 22 December 2024.

TASMIN LITTLE

After a career spanning more than 30 years giving concerts around the world, violinist Tasmin Little retired from the concert platform in 2021 to devote her time to broadcasting, writing, teaching and mentoring. During her career as an international concerto soloist, recitalist and chamber musician she performed in some of the world's most prestigious venues, including Carnegie Hall, Musikverein, Concertgebouw, Philharmonie Berlin, Vienna Konzerthaus, South Bank Centre, Barbican Centre,

Royal Albert Hall, Wigmore Hall, Lincoln Center and Suntory Hall. She has released numerous albums to critical acclaim, also winning the Critics Choice Award at the Classic BRIT Awards in 2011 for her recording of Elgar's Violin Concerto with Sir Andrew Davis and the Royal Scottish National Orchestra. She has received multiple other awards, as well as a CBE for Services to Music in 2023.

Renowned for her gifts of communication and presentation, on and off the platform, during the early 1990s she pioneered verbal introductions during performance from the stage to audiences, and in 2008 her ground-breaking project 'The Naked Violin' drew a global audience of half a million in a few weeks and resulted in *The Southbank Show* – the longest-running Arts show on British television – dedicating a full hour's programme to following the project as she toured. She has appeared on and made many television and radio programmes; in February 2021, her three-week series for BBC Radio 3, 'Journeys with my Violin' was widely lauded and was 'Pick of the Week' in *The Times*. In January 2023, she was commissioned by Radio 3 to make eight programmes, which were aired later in the year. Tasmin Little is a Vice-President of The Elgar Society.

ANDREW LITTON

Andrew Litton, Music Director of New York City Ballet since 2015, is also the former Principal Guest Conductor of the Singapore Symphony, Conductor Laureate of Britain's Bournemouth Symphony and Music Director Laureate of Norway's Bergen Philharmonic. Under Litton's leadership the Bergen Philharmonic gained international recognition through extensive recording and touring. Norway's King Harald V knighted Litton with the Norwegian Royal Order of Merit. Other honours include Yale's Sanford Medal, the Elgar Society Medal, and an honorary Doctorate from the University of Bournemouth.

Litton was Principal Conductor of the Bournemouth Symphony from 1988 to 1994 and Music Director of the Dallas Symphony from 1994 to 2006. During his twelve years in Dallas, he led the orchestra on three major European tours, and appeared four times at Carnegie Hall. Litton's discography boasts over 135 recordings.

An avid opera conductor with a keen theatrical sense, Litton has led major opera companies such as the Metropolitan Opera, The Royal Opera Covent Garden, Opera Australia and Deutsche Oper Berlin. In Norway, he was key to founding the Bergen National Opera, where he led numerous acclaimed performances.

An accomplished pianist, Litton performs as a soloist, conducting from the keyboard. He is also an acknowledged expert on and performer of Gershwin's music and serves as Advisor to the University of Michigan Gershwin Archives.

JULIAN LLOYD-WEBBER

Julian Lloyd Webber is one of the leading musicians of our time. He has played with the world's greatest orchestras in the world's most famous concert halls and has performed and recorded with musical legends including Yehudi Menuhin, Georg Solti, Lorin Maazel, Neville Marriner, Andrew Davis, Mark Elder and Stephane Grappelli. His recording of Elgar's Cello Concerto conducted by Menuhin won a Brit-Award for Best British Classical Recording and was chosen by both BBC Radio 3's *Record Review* and *BBC Music Magazine* as the finest ever version. Julian has also inspired more than fifty new works for cello from composers as varied as Malcolm Arnold, Joaquín Rodrigo, Andrew Lloyd Webber, James MacMillan, Philip Glass and Eric Whitacre.

As the founder of the British Government's *In Harmony* music programme Julian continues to promote personal and community development in some of England's most deprived areas. In 2014 Julian was forced to retire from playing due to a neck injury which reduced the power of his bowing arm. In July 2015 he was appointed Principal of Birmingham Conservatoire. During his five-year tenure he oversaw the move to a new £57 million building and, in September 2017, the Conservatoire was awarded Royal status by Her Majesty Queen Elizabeth II.

Julian is married to fellow cellist Jiaxin Cheng. A lifelong Leyton Orient supporter, he was the London Underground's first official busker and the only classical musician to perform at the Closing Ceremony of Olympics 2012. He is a former President and now Vice-President of the Elgar Society.

BERNARD LONGLEY

On 8 December 2012 Bernard Longley was installed as the ninth Roman Catholic Archbishop of Birmingham. He was born in Manchester in 1955 and educated at the Xaverian College, Manchester, The Royal Northern College of Music, New College, Oxford (MA) and St John's Seminary, Wonersh.

He was ordained priest in 1981 and then: Assistant Priest, St Joseph's, Epsom, 1982–85; English College, Rome, 1985–87; Theology Tutor, St John's Seminary, Wonersh, 1987–96; Surrey Chairman, Diocesan Committee for Christian Unity, 1991–96; Catholic Bishops' Conference National Ecumenical Officer, 1996–2003; Moderator, Steering Committee, Churches Together in Britain and Ireland, 1999–2003 and Assistant General Secretary, 2000–03; Auxiliary Bishop of Westminster 2003–09; Titular Bishop of

Zarna, 2003–09; Co-chair, Anglican Roman Catholic International Commission (ARCIC), 2012–; Member, Pontifical Council for Promoting the New Evangelisation, 2011–22; Co-chair, English Anglican-Roman Catholic Committee, 2011–17; Chair, Commission for Overseas Seminaries, 2012–23; Chair, Bishops' Conference Department for Dialogue and Unity, 2014–.

JAMES MacMILLAN

Knighted in 2015, James MacMillan is the pre-eminent Scottish composer of his generation. He first attracted attention with the acclaimed BBC Proms premiere of *The Confession of Isobel Gowdie* (1990). His percussion concerto *Veni, Veni Emmanuel* (1992) has received over 500 performances worldwide by orchestras including London Symphony Orchestra, Royal Concertgebouw Orchestra, New York and Los Angeles Philharmonics and Cleveland Orchestra. Other major works include the cantata *Seven Last Words from the Cross* (1993), *Quickening* (1998) for soloists, children's choir, mixed choir and orchestra, the operas *Inès de Castro* (2001) and *The Sacrifice* (2005–06), *St John Passion* (2007), *St Luke Passion* (2013) and Symphony No. 5: *'Le grand Inconnu'* (2018).

He was featured composer at Edinburgh Festival (1993, 2019), Southbank Centre (1997), BBC's Barbican Composer Weekend (2005) and Grafenegg Festival (2012). His interpreters include soloists Evelyn Glennie, Colin Currie, Jean-Yves Thibaudet and Vadim Repin, conductors Leonard Slatkin, Sir Andrew Davis, Marin Alsop and Sir Donald Runnicles, choreographer Christopher Wheeldon and stage director Katie Mitchell. His recordings can be found on BMG/RCA Red Seal, BIS, Chandos, Naxos, Hyperion, Coro, Linn, LPO and Challenge Classics.

Recent highlights include MacMillan's *Stabat Mater* for The Sixteen streamed from the Sistine Chapel and premieres of the 40-voice motet *Vidi aquam*, *Christmas Oratorio* streamed in 2021 by NTR Dutch Radio from the Concertgebouw in Amsterdam and recorded by the London Philharmonic Orchestra and Choir, and the anthem *Who Shall Separate Us?* commissioned for the funeral of HM Queen Elizabeth II in 2022. The annual Cumnock Tryst festival was founded by the composer in 2014 in his childhood town in Scotland.

NEIL MANTLE

Neil Mantle was born in Essex in 1951 but has lived for most of his life in Edinburgh. He began conducting at the age of fifteen when he formed a chamber orchestra of around twenty players. Neil studied horn at The Royal Academy of Music and subsequently at The Royal Conservatoire of Scotland. He pursued a successful career as a freelance player working chiefly with the RSNO, SCO and Scottish Opera and is still very active as a recitalist with his pianist wife Gillian with whom he also performs chamber music.

In 1970 Neil founded Scottish Sinfonia, a full-sized symphony orchestra of ninety players and has remained its conductor, directing the orchestra in around 250 concerts. Elgar's music has always been a high priority giving, over the years, over 50 performances of his music.

Neil has also had extensive experience in the choral field, having held appointments with the Edinburgh Bach Choir, Dundee Choral Union and Malcolm Sargent Cancer Fund Choir . Neil was an examiner to the Associated Board of the Royal Schools of Music from 1989 to 2022 where, in addition to activities in the UK, he made extended foreign tours to Malaysia, Singapore and Ghana.

The RAM awarded Neil an honour accorded to past students who have achieved distinction in their chosen field. He received an MBE in the 2008 Queen's Honours List for services to music in Scotland and in 2023 the Elgar Society Medal in recognition of his promotion of the music of Elgar in Scotland. Neil is also an elected member of The Royal Society of Musicians.

EM MARSHALL-LUCK

Em Marshall-Luck was educated at St Paul's Girls' School and read Greats at Brasenose College, Oxford. During her teens she worked for the specialist music publishers, Thames Publishing, and became heavily involved in various British composer societies, including the Association of English Singers and Speakers, the Peter Warlock Society and the Elgar Society. Later, she cherished holding the position of Chairman of the Ralph Vaughan Williams Society (of which she had been a Founder member) for many years.

In 2002 Em established the English Music Festival, which she has run ever since, along with the Festival's recording and publishing arms, EM Records and EM Publishing. In 2011, Robert Hale published her hardback book, *Composers in the Landscape,* which sets the lives of British composers in the context of the landscapes that brought them joy and inspiration.

Em has written extensively over the years, mainly on the topics of music, food, wine and travel; more recently she has appeared as narrator on recordings and in concerts, including with the BBC Concert Orchestra in a disc of Holst's music (EMRCD090). She can be regularly heard on BBC Radio 4, talking about British composers, as well as having appeared on Classic FM, BBC4 and BBC Radio 3.

RUPERT MARSHALL-LUCK

Hailed by *BBC Music Magazine* for his 'handsome tone and laser-like tuning', and acclaimed by audiences and critics alike for the verve, commitment and intelligence of his performances, Rupert Marshall-Luck appears as soloist and recitalist at major festivals and venues throughout the UK as well as in France, Germany, the Netherlands, the Republic of Ireland, South Africa, Sweden, Switzerland and the USA. His extensive discography includes many World Premiere recordings as well as conspectuses of the complete music for violin and piano of Herbert Howells and C. Hubert H. Parry; and his solo performances have been frequently broadcast on BBC Radio 3, ABC Classic FM (Australia), RTÉ (Ireland), SABC (South Africa), Radio Suisse Romande (Switzerland) and in Canada, France, New Zealand and the USA.

His recordings have attracted glowing critical acclaim from the international musical press, including *BBC Music Magazine, Classica, Fanfare, Gramophone, MusicWeb International* and *The Strad.* As well as his busy schedule as a soloist and chamber musician, Rupert is active as a writer and speaker on the performing aspects of music, and he has presented lecture-recitals, seminars and masterclasses at major universities and conservatoires throughout the UK and overseas. His radio broadcasts include several appearances on BBC Radio 3's *In Tune* and a programme for Radio 4's series *Tales from the Stave.* He is currently working on a series of scholarly-critical editions for G. Henle Verlag of Munich which together will comprise the complete violin music of Elgar.

ROBERT MATTHEW-WALKER

Robert Matthew-Walker, born in London in 1939, studied at Goldsmiths College, University of London, and London College of Music before undertaking military service. He studied composition privately with Darius Milhaud in Paris, and joined CBS Records in 1970, as head of their classical department in London, later becoming Director of Marketing and serving as Director of Masterworks Marketing, Europe, in Paris. In 1975, he joined RCA Records in London, where he launched James Galway's solo career.

Matthew-Walker founded several classical labels – Phoenix Records, Trax Records and AVM Classics – and has produced over 160 albums. He won the Grand Prix du Disque of the Academie Charles Cros in 1980 for his recording of Brian Ferneyhough's *Sonatas for String Quartet* by the Berne Quartet. He appeared with the rapper Adamski on a dance single, *Kraktali Daze.*

Matthew-Walker was publisher of the Seven Arts Group magazines and edited *Music and Musicians* from 1984 to 1988. He wrote and presented a

History of Classical Recording for BBC Radio in 1988, and was owner and publisher of Alfred Legnick & Co Ltd from 1988 to 1991. He was appointed editor of *Musical Opinion* and of *The Organ* in 2009. He has composed six symphonies, *Symphonic Variations* for Orchestra (1955 – premiered in Romania in 2016), concertos for flute, oboe, bassoon, horn, violin and viola, eight string quartets and various violin and piano sonatas. His *Concertante on a Theme of Paganini* for piano and double string orchestra was premiered by Mark Bebbington (who has recorded much of Matthew-Walker's music) and the RPO in 2021. His interest in rock music is shown in *Days To Remember, Three Pieces for Rock Band* (1966) and *Meditation on the Death of Elvis Presley* – blues for solo clarinet (1980). He has published thirty-two books and also edits the Grieg Society of Great Britain annual journal.

COLIN MATTHEWS

Colin Matthews was born in London in 1946. He studied at the Universities of Nottingham and Sussex, and subsequently worked as assistant to Benjamin Britten, and with Imogen Holst. He collaborated with Deryck Cooke from 1963 until 1975 on the performing version of Mahler's Tenth Symphony. He was Associate Composer with the London Symphony Orchestra from 1992-9 and with the Hallé from 2001-10. Over four decades his music has ranged from solo piano music through six string quartets, many ensemble and orchestral works, and an opera..

He is Founder and Executive Producer of NMC Recordings, Administrator of the Holst Foundation and President and Music Advisor of Britten-Pears Arts. With Oliver Knussen he set up the Aldeburgh Composition Course in 1992, and has been composition director of the LSO's Panufnik Scheme since 2005. He holds honorary posts with several universities and is Prince Consort Professor of Composition at the Royal College of Music.

DAVID MATTHEWS

David Matthews was born in London in 1943 and started composing at the age of sixteen. He was mainly self-taught, though he studied privately with Anthony Milner and was greatly helped by Nicholas Maw and Peter Sculthorpe. He also learned much from being an assistant to Benjamin Britten in the late 1960s. His extensive output includes eleven symphonies, five symphonic poems, nine concertos, eighteen string quartets, and much other instrumental, chamber, and vocal music. His music is frequently broadcast, and a large number of his works are available on CD. Many of his pieces are inspired by the natural world, by paintings and literary texts, and by collaborations with instrumentalist friends.

David has also written books on Tippett and Britten, and has worked extensively as an arranger. His 9th Symphony was the second to be composed in Kenneth Woods's project to commission nine British Symphonies. His latest orchestral CD, *A Vision of the Sea*, including that symphonic poem and the 8th Symphony, with the BBC Philharmonic under Jac van Steen, was released on Signum Classics in 2021, and his 10th Symphony was premiered in 2022 by the same forces. Last year his 17th Quartet was premiered at the Aldeburgh Festival, and his opera *Anna*, to a libretto by the late Sir Roger Scruton, was given a concert performance at The Grange, Hampshire. He is currently writing a violin concerto for Anthony Marwood. www.david-matthews.co.uk

STEWART MCILWHAM

Born in Glasgow in 1965 Stewart Mcilwham started playing the flute and piccolo at the age of eight. Initially studying with his father (who was a member of the BBC Scottish Symphony Orchestra as well as a composer and noted Highland bagpiper) he entered the Douglas Academy Music School in its inaugural year in 1979. While there he studied with John Wiggins before further study in London at the Guildhall under Peter Lloyd and Edward Beckett.

While still studying at the Guildhall he was offered the position of principal piccolo with the BBC Philharmonic in Manchester, a chair he held from 1985 to 1990. He subsequently joined the Royal Philharmonic Orchestra before moving to the London Philharmonic (LPO) in 1997 also as principal piccolo, a position he still holds. He gave the world premiere of Sir Peter Maxwell-Davies's Piccolo Concerto with the RPO under the composer's direction in 1997 and the British premiere of Erikki Sven Tuur's *Solastalgia* for piccolo and orchestra with the LPO and Marin Alsop in 2019. Stewart was a founder member of the National Youth Orchestra (NYO) of Scotland as well as a member of the NYO GB and the European Community Youth Orchestra. He was also twice a finalist in the Shell/LSO music scholarship, in 1981 and 1985.

Stewart served as a member of Board of Directors of the LPO from 2003 to 2022, serving as Vice-Chairman from 2005 to 2012 and LPO President from 2012 to 2019.

DIANA McVEAGH

The late Diana McVeagh studied at the Royal College of Music. She wrote as an occasional critic for *The Times*, was assistant editor of *The Musical Times*, was on the Royal Musical Association Council and was on the executive committee of the 1980 *New Grove*. Her interests ranged from Josquin to Birtwistle, but she wrote mostly about English romantics. She was the author of *Elgar: His Life and Music* (Dent, 1955), *Elgar: The Music Maker* (Boydell, 2007) and the highly acclaimed *Gerald Finzi: His Life and Music* (Boydell, 2005). She edited the equally acclaimed *Gerald Finzi's Letters 1915–1956* (Boydell, 2021) and contributed to the *New Grove* (1980, 2001) and the *Dictionary of National Biography* (2004). Diana McVeagh was a Vice-President of The Elgar Society. She died on 2 July 2025 aged 98.

KEVIN MITCHELL

Kevin Mitchell, a solicitor, is CEO of the All Saints Educational Trust, a charity in the City of London that supports teachers of Religious Education, Home Economics, Food, Nutrition and Textiles. He has been a member of the Elgar Society for over 50 years, has served on the Council, been Vice-Chairman of the London Branch and a Director of Elgar Enterprises. Currently he is one of the editors of the *Elgar Society Journal* and in 2004 edited *Cockaigne*, being lectures given to the London Branch over the years. In 2022 he jointly edited with David Morris *A Pilgrim in Cockaigne*, being a selection of additional lectures and a celebration of the Branch's 50th anniversary. Kevin also contributes articles for the Society's *Journal.*

CHRISTOPHER MORLEY

Christopher Morley was born and educated in Brighton, and it was a visit as a schoolboy to a rehearsal at Glyndebourne of Mozart's *Idomeneo* in 1964 which made him realise that he had to have a life in music. In 1966 he was admitted to the Music Department of the University of Birmingham on an Open Entrance Scholarship, under the inspiring Professorship of Anthony Lewis.

Upon graduating with Honours in 1969 he took up a career as a schoolteacher, serving as Head of Music in various local schools. In the same year he was invited to write his first review for the *Birmingham Post,* and in 1988 he was appointed Chief Music Critic to the newspaper. He resigned from the post in 2024, but still contributes, as well as writing for *Musical Opinion* and *Opera* and editing *Midlands Music Reviews.* Also in 1988 Christopher Morley began teaching at Birmingham School of Music, lecturing in music history, performance practice and theory. He was awarded an Honorary Fellowship in 2002, and retired in 2010. As a result of a commission from Julian Lloyd Webber, then Principal of the now Royal Birmingham Conservatoire, he published a history of the institution in December 2017. During the course of his reviewing, he has accepted invitations from all over Europe, as well as from Russia and Japan, where he was invited in 2017 to assess the country's symphony orchestras with a western critic's ears. Christopher loves cricket and Brighton and Hove Albion, but cannot escape the tyranny of his beloved cat, Poppy.

DAVID MORRIS

David Morris is a retired director of a firm of chartered surveyors. He joined the Elgar Society about 40 years ago and has spent 25 of these as, successively, Treasurer, Membership Secretary and Vice-Chairman – he is currently Honorary Secretary. A member of the editorial team for the Elgar Society *Journal* and an honorary life member of the Society, he is an experienced choral singer and church music director. He is currently a member of a secular Oxford Choir, of which he is also a trustee and treasurer, and is a deputy churchwarden for his local church, also a member of Synod.

ALICE NEARY

Alice enjoys a varied performing career as a chamber musician, soloist and orchestral player and is much in demand as a guest principal cellist. She is delighted to have recently joined the London Haydn Quartet. Familiar to listeners of Radio 3, festival performances include BBC Proms chamber series, Bath International, Marlboro Festival, Santa Fe, AWE New Zealand and Lofoten. Recent concerto performances include Strauss's *Don Quixote* and Honegger and Cheryl Frances-Hoade concertos with BBC NOW.

Alice was a member of the Gould Piano Trio from 2001 to 2018. Highlights include the complete piano trios of Beethoven, Schubert and Dvořák at the Wigmore Hall, commissioning new works from Sir James MacMillan and Mark Simpson, regular US tours and over 25 CD releases.

Alice has appeared as guest cellist with numerous groups including the Nash Ensemble, Academy of St Martins Chamber Ensemble, Ensemble 360 and the Endellion, Elias, Sacconi and Heath Quartets. She collaborates with pianists Viv McLean, Jâms Coleman and Benjamin Frith. Regular visits to IMS at Prussia Cove, Marlboro Festival and Wye Valley Chamber Music Festival provide ongoing inspiration. From 2017 to 2024 she was principal cellist of BBC National Orchestra of Wales and has made recent appearances as guest principal cello with the orchestra of the Royal Opera House, Philharmonia, Academy of St Martin's and BBC Symphony Orchestra.

Alice studied with Ralph Kirshbaum at the RNCM and, as a Fulbright scholar, with Timothy Eddy at Stonybrook, USA. Alice has been tutor in cello at the RNCM and RCM and now teaches at RWCMD where she was awarded a Fellowship in 2015. She and her husband, David Adams, founded the Penarth Chamber Music Festival in 2014. Alice plays a cello by Alessandro Gagliano cello of 1710.

ANDREW NEILL

Andrew Neill, a retired businessman, was Chairman of the Elgar Society (1992–2008) and a founder trustee of The Joyce and Michael Kennedy Award for the Singing of Strauss. He is a member of the Advisory Council of the London Philharmonic Orchestra and, in 2024, was honoured to accept an invitation to become President of The Elgar Sinfonia of London. His early musical enthusiasms were stimulated by a first cousin of his mother, Henry Boys, dedicatee of the composer's Violin Concerto. Andrew is also the author of numerous articles, programme and recording notes and essays on Elgar and Richard Strauss. He is the author of the official history of the Elgar Birthplace, *'It's the only wish I've got'* (2006). Andrew Neill is a Vice-President of The Elgar Society and recipient of the Society's medal.

DAVID OWEN NORRIS

David Owen Norris is a pianist, composer and broadcaster. He won prizes in international competitions in Geneva, Leeds and Sydney; and since his appointment to the prestigious Gilmore Artist Award has performed all across the world, with concerto appearances in the BBC Proms, concert tours of Europe, Australia and North America, including performances at Sydney Opera House, the Kennedy Centre, Lincoln Centre, Ravinia Festival Chicago, the South Bank Centre etc., and a discography of 60 commercial CDs including his own Piano Concerto with the BBC Concert Orchestra and his oratorio *Prayerbook*. His other compositions include a symphony, the oratorio *Turning Points*, and the multi-media tribute to the passing seasons, *HengeMusic*. He recently gave the premiere of his Piano Sonata.

His *Chord of the Week* programmes on BBC2 television were a popular feature of the Proms for six years. His *Perfect Pianists* has been shown fourteen times so far on BBC4 television, where he has also contributed to programmes on Handel, Parry, Vaughan Williams, Tippett, Mendelssohn and Elgar. His first TV presentation, *The Real Thing?* from 1990, was hailed by the *Daily Telegraph* as 'the most literate and probing programme on music for many years', and his most recent *Chord of the Week* was reviewed by the *Observer* as 'the most consistently intelligent three minutes you'll watch on this or any other television this year'. The Beethoven 9 app, for which he wrote the book and the analyses, won the Best Music App Award.

His many radio presentations have included the frequently repeated *Playlist* series on BBC Radio 4 and *In Tune* and *The Works* on Radio 3, where he recently made his 36th appearance on *Building a Library*. Recordings recently released include Mozart on fortepiano for Hyperion, featured in the *New York Times*, the complete Chamber Music of Grace Williams, which was a *Guardian* CD of the Week, and the complete songs of Sir Arthur Sullivan on Chandos.

ANTONIO PAPPANO

One of today's most sought-after conductors, acclaimed for his charismatic leadership and inspirational performances in both symphonic and operatic repertoire, Sir Antonio Pappano is Chief Conductor of the London Symphony Orchestra and was Music Director of the Royal Opera House Covent Garden from 2002 until 2024. He is Music Director Emeritus of the Orchestra dell'Accademia Nazionale di Santa Cecilia in Rome, having served as Music Director from 2005 to 2023. Pappano was appointed Music Director of Oslo's Den Norske Opera in 1990, and from 1992 to 2002 served as Music Director of the Théâtre Royal de la Monnaie in Brussels. From 1997 to 1999 he was Principal Guest Conductor of the Israel Philharmonic Orchestra.

Pappano is in demand as an opera conductor at the highest international level, including with the Metropolitan Opera New York, the State Operas of Vienna and Berlin, the Bayreuth and Salzburg Festivals, Lyric Opera of Chicago and the Teatro alla Scala, and has appeared as a guest conductor with many of the world's most prestigious orchestras, including the Berlin and Vienna Philharmonic Orchestras, the Staatskapelle Dresden, the Gewandhausorchester Leipzig, the Bavarian Radio, the Czech Philharmonic Orchestra, the Orchestre de Paris and the Royal Concertgebouw Orchestra, as well as the New York Philharmonic Orchestra, Chicago and Boston Symphonies and the Philadelphia and Cleveland Orchestras. He maintains a particularly strong relationship with the Chamber Orchestra of Europe.

Highlights of the 2024/25 season and beyond include return visits to Boston Symphony, the Chamber Orchestra of Europe, the Royal Concertgebouw Orchestra, the Gewandhausorchester Leipzig and a new production of *Die Walküre* at the Royal Opera House. In his first season as Chief Conductor of the London Symphony, Pappano took the orchestra on a wide-ranging tour to the USA, including Carnegie Hall, Japan, Korea, China and across major European capitals and festivals. This collaboration also includes flagship concerts at London's Barbican Centre with concertante performances of Puccini's *La rondine* and Strauss's opera *Salome*, and symphonic repertoire including Mahler's and Walton's first symphonies, Holst's *Planets*, Strauss's *Ein Heldenleben*, Tippett's *A Child Of Our Time*, Elgar's *The Dream of Gerontius* and Vaughan Williams's first and ninth symphonies in the continuation of Pappano's Vaughan Williams recording cycle for LSO Live. Pappano was knighted in 2022.

ADRIAN PARTINGTON

Adrian Partington has been Director of Music at Gloucester Cathedral since January 2008. During his years there, he has introduced girl choristers to the Cathedral Choir, has taken the choir to sing overseas several times and has made a number of CDs, most recently a disc of music by the international clarinettist Emma Johnson. In May 2019, he took the choristers to sing with the Berlin Philharmonic at the Philharmonie in Berlin

He has also been Conductor of the BBC National Chorus of Wales since 1999. Since then he has conducted or prepared that chorus for well over a hundred broadcast concerts (including over forty BBC Proms). The chorus has made about twenty CDs, two of which have been nominated for Grammy awards. Adrian has recently conducted the BBCNOW and NCW in three CDs, including Grace Williams's masterpiece, the *Missa Cambrensis*, in January 2024. He has directed five Gloucester Three Choirs Festivals, in which he has conducted the Philharmonia, the Royal Philharmonic Orchestra and BBCNOW in many of the great choral-orchestral classics by Beethoven, Berlioz, Elgar and Mahler, as well as symphonies and concertos and much contemporary music.

Adrian was educated at the Royal College of Music and King's College Cambridge, where he was the Organ Scholar. He is still active as an organist, having recently played in Hungary, Japan and Russia (before the war). He has made a dozen solo CDs, and been the soloist at the BBC Proms, in 2018.

JOHN QUINN

John Quinn was born in Yorkshire and has been involved in amateur music-making for most of his life. In 1986 he moved to Gloucester – in the heart of Three Choirs Festival territory – at which point he took up choral singing seriously. One of the choirs with which he sings, Philomusica of Gloucestershire and Worcestershire, was awarded the Elgar Society's Certificate of Merit in 2016 to recognise the choir's significant advocacy of Elgar's music. Since 2001, John has been a regular contributor or reviews of recordings to the website MusicWeb International and of concert reviews to the sister site, Seen and Heard International.

ARTHUR REYNOLDS

Arthur Reynolds is a financial advisor who divides his time between the United States and the United Kingdom, where he writes and lectures on the life and works of Edward Elgar. A lifelong rescuer of Elgarian artifacts, Arthur owns what is believed to be the largest accumulation of 'Elgariana' in private hands. Arthur holds degrees from Columbia University, Cambridge

University and New York University's Graduate Business School. He is also Chairman of the North American Branch of the Elgar Society.

WOLFGANG-ARMIN RITTMEIER

Wolfgang-Armin Rittmeier was born in 1974 in Hildesheim, Germany. He is an alumnus of Braunschweig Technical University, where he studied German and English language and literature. After teaching for some time at the Department of German Literature in Braunschweig, he took up work in adult education. He has been a Deputy Managing Director of a large adult learning organisation since 2019.

In 2014 he started www.edwardelgar.de, the first (and only) website in German on Elgar and his music. In 2015 he was awarded the Elgar Society's Certificate of Merit. In the same year he founded the Elgar-Freundeskreis Deutschland (The Friends of Elgar in Germany), which is an affiliate of the Elgar Society.

Wolfgang also works as a music critic, is a regular speaker on music and presents pre-concert talks throughout Germany.

ELEANOR ROBERTS

Eleanor Roberts is Deputy Director of Development and Archivist of the Hallé Concerts Society.

DONALD RUNNICLES

Donald Runnicles attended George Heriot's School and George Watson's College in his native Edinburgh before reading music at the university there, after which he embarked on postgraduate studies at St John's College, Cambridge, and the London Opera Centre where he learned the craft of repetiteur. This was followed by an assistant conductorship in the National Theatre of Mannheim and a music directorship in Freiberg. There he 'breathed the air, this Wagnerian air. It was life changing.' His career as music director of San Francisco Opera from 1992 to 2008 was notable for his performances of the operas of Richard Strauss and Wagner's *Ring* cycle (more than one of his student contemporaries recalls his blithely accomplished realisations of Wagner's scores at an upright piano during his Edinburgh undergraduate days), repertoire with which he continued to impress audiences and critics during his years from 2001 to 2024 at Deutsche Oper, Berlin. From 2009 to 2016 he was chief conductor of the BBC Scottish Symphony Orchestra (of which he is now the much-revered conductor emeritus), is currently music director of the Grand Teton Summer Music Festival in Jackson Hole, Wyoming, and was principal guest conductor of the Atlanta Symphony for more than two decades, a post he now holds with the Sydney Symphony Orchestra. He is currently principal conductor of the Dresden Philharmonic. Runnicles holds honorary doctorates from the University of Edinburgh and Glasgow's Royal Scottish Academy of Music and is an Honorary Fellow of the Royal Society of Edinburgh. He was knighted in 2020.

JULIAN RUSHTON

Julian Rushton studied music at Cambridge and for his doctorate at Oxford, supervised by J.A. Westrup. He taught at the Universities of East Anglia and Cambridge before being appointed to the West Riding Chair of Music at the University of Leeds (1982); he is now Emeritus Professor following his retirement (2005). He was President of the Royal Musical Association (1994–9) and Chairman of the Editorial Committee of *Musica Britannica* (1993–2019). He has published extensively on Gluck, Mozart, Berlioz and Elgar, including the volume on Mozart in the series *The Master Musicians.* He is joint editor of the *Cambridge Companion to Elgar* (with Daniel M. Grimley) and Cambridge University Press's *Elgar Studies* (with J.P.E. Harper-Scott). A paper on *Caractacus* is included in *Music and Performance Culture in Nineteenth-Century Britain: Essays in Honour of Nicholas Temperley*. He edited the *Elgar Society Journal* (2006–10), to which he continues to contribute. For the Elgar Complete Edition he edited *Music for String Orchestra* (2011) and *Solo Songs with Orchestra* (2012). In 2023 he was honoured by his appointment as a Vice-President of the Elgar Society.

ROBERT SAXTON

Robert Saxton was born in London in 1953. He won the Gaudeamus International Composers Prize in Holland at the age of twenty-one and, from 1985 to 1986 was Fulbright Arts Fellow at Princeton, USA. He is Emeritus Professor at Oxford University, Hon Fellow St Catharine's College Cambridge, Senior Research Fellow at the RAM (London) and Composer-in-Association at the Purcell School for Young Musicians.

He has written works for the BBC (TV, Proms and radio), LSO, LPO, ECO, ESO, London Sinfonietta, Nash Ensemble, Arditti, Kreutzer and Chilingirian String Quartets, St Paul Chamber Orchestra (USA), Opera North, Aldeburgh, Cheltenham, City of London, Three Choirs, Presteigne and Lichfield festivals, Susan Bradshaw and Richard Rodney Bennett, Jonathan Clinch, Clare Hammond, Teresa Cahill, Leon Fleisher, Tasmin Little, Steven Isserlis, Mstislav Rostropovich and Roderick Williams. Robert Saxton is married to the soprano Teresa Cahill.

NIGEL SIMEONE

Nigel Simeone (b. 1956) is a writer and broadcaster and a regular contributor to Radio 3's *Record Review* with a very wide range of musical enthusiasms. His books include *Ralph Vaughan Williams and Adrian Boult* (2022), *The Janáček Compendium* (2019), *Charles Mackerras* (2015, co-author), *The Leonard Bernstein Letters* (2013), *Messiaen* (2008, co-author), and *Janáček's Works* (1997, co-author). His book *Edward Elgar and Adrian Boult* was published in 2025. In 2024 he was awarded the Janáček Foundation Memorial Medal in Brno and his latest book is a study of Janáček's *Sinfonietta.*

WILHELM SINKOVICZ

Dr Wilhelm Sinkovicz, musicologist, journalist and broadcaster, has, since 1984, been chief music critic of *Die Presse* (formerly *Neue Freie Presse*), the leading Austrian daily newspaper.

LEONARD SLATKIN

Internationally acclaimed conductor Leonard Slatkin is Music Director Laureate of the Detroit Symphony Orchestra (DSO), Directeur Musical Honoraire of the Orchestre National de Lyon (ONL), Conductor Laureate of the St. Louis Symphony Orchestra (SLSO), Principal Guest Conductor of the Orquesta Filarmónica de Gran Canaria, and Artistic Consultant to the Las Vegas Philharmonic. He maintains a rigorous schedule of guest conducting and is active as a composer, author, and educator.

To celebrate his 80th birthday, he is returning to orchestras he led as Music Director, including the DSO, ONL, SLSO, and National Symphony Orchestra (Washington, DC). Additional 2024–25 highlights include the New York Philharmonic, Nashville Symphony, North Carolina Symphony, Manhattan School of Music Symphony Orchestra, Eastman Philharmonia, National Symphony Orchestra (Ireland), Tokyo Metropolitan Symphony Orchestra, Osaka Philharmonic, Hiroshima Symphony Orchestra, Kristiansand Symfoniorkester, Jersusalem Symphony, and Opera Theatre of St. Louis. Moreover, his composition *Schubertiade: An Orchestral Fantasy* and his arrangement of Scarlatti keyboard sonatas are receiving world premieres this season.

Slatkin has received six Grammy awards and 35 nominations. Naxos recently reissued Vox audiophile editions of his SLSO recordings featuring the works of Gershwin, Rachmaninov, and Prokofiev. Other Naxos recordings include *Slatkin Conducts Slatkin* – a compilation of pieces written by generations of his family – as well as works by Saint-Saëns, Ravel, Berlioz, Copland, Borzova, McTee, and Williams.

A recipient of the National Medal of Arts, Slatkin also holds the rank of Chevalier in the French Legion of Honor. He has been awarded the Prix Charbonnier from the Federation of Alliances Françaises, Austria's Decoration of Honor in Silver, and the League of American Orchestras' Gold Baton. He received the ASCAP Deems Taylor Special Recognition Award for his debut book, *Conducting Business* (2012), which was followed by *Leading Tones* (2017) and *Classical Crossroads: The Path Forward for Music in the 21st Century* (2021). His latest books are *Eight Symphonic Masterworks of the Twentieth Century* (Rowman & Littlefield, spring 2024) and *Eight Symphonic Masterworks of the Nineteenth Century* (fall 2024), comprising essays that supplement the score-study process. Leonard Slatkin is a Vice-President of The Elgar Society

LANI SPAHR

Audio restoration engineer, producer, annotator, and lecturer Lani Spahr has garnered critical praise from *Gramophone*, BBC Radio 3, *BBC Music Magazine*, *Fanfare*, *The Sunday Times*, MusicWeb International, and many others. In 2020, he was awarded an Honorary Membership of the Elgar Society for his work on the recorded legacy of Sir Edward Elgar. His work can be heard on SOMM Recordings, Music & Arts, West Hill Radio Archive, Naxos, Boston Records, and Oboe Classics. Formerly a period instrument oboist in the US, he was a member of Boston Baroque and the Handel and Haydn Society Orchestra of Boston. In addition, he has appeared with many of North America's leading period instrument orchestras, including Tafelmusik, Philharmonia Baroque, Tempesta di Mare, Apollo's Fire, Washington Bach Consort, Boston Early Music Festival Orchestra, and many others.

Also a modern oboist, he was the principal oboist of the Colorado Springs Symphony Orchestra, the Colorado Opera Festival, the American Chamber Winds, and the Maine Chamber Ensemble and made his European solo debut in 1999 playing John McCabe's Oboe Concerto with the Hitchin Symphony Orchestra in England. He has recorded for Telarc, Linn, Koch, Naxos, Vox, Music Masters, L'Oiseau-Lyre, and Musica Omnia.

ANDREW STAPLES

Andrew Staples is one of the most sought after tenors being equally at home in the concert hall as on the opera stage. He recorded the tenor part in Daniel Barenboim's performance of *The Dream of Gerontius* (stepping in at the last moment) and *The Spirit of England* with Sir Andrew Davis.

RICHARD STRIVENS

Richard Strivens is a musician, researcher and singing teacher. He has recently published *The Singer's Handbook*, co-written with Andrew Heggie, and is a vocal coach for the Hallé Choir. He also teaches singing at Manchester and Oxford Universities. With Nina Whiteman, he founded and co-directs Manchester Contemporary Youth Opera. His PhD research into the bass and baritone operatic roles of Richard Strauss is supervised by Prof. Sarah Hibberd at Bristol University.

DAVID TEMPLE

Under the direction of David Temple for 41 years, Crouch End Festival Chorus is now one of the world's leading symphonic choirs. His eclectic tastes have shaped the enormously varied work of the choir, making Crouch End Festival Chorus a beacon of excellence and versatility.

David's recording of Bach's *St John Passion* (in English) with CEFC for Chandos Records has been received with glowing reviews. In 2020, his recording of Britten's *St Nicolas* and *A Ceremony of Carols* was released by Signum Records. David and CEFC released Elgar's *The Kingdom* in May 2025.

David's highlights with Crouch End Festival Chorus include Mahler's Eighth Symphony to a sell-out Royal Festival Hall and John Adams's *Harmonium* at the Barbican in the presence of the composer. David has also prepared the choir for concerts with Ennio Morricone, Andrea Bocelli, Hans Zimmer, Danny Elfman, James Newton Howard and MUSE.

David has been Musical Director of the Hertfordshire Chorus since 2000. David's commissions with Hertfordshire Chorus include Will Todd's *Mass in Blue*, which has received well over 600 performances all over the world. In early 2025 he directed a recording of the music of Elgar and Parry which included Elgar's *From the Bavarian Highlands*.

David Temple was awarded the MBE in the 2018 New Year's Honours for services to music.

CHRISTIAN TETZLAFF

Christian Tetzlaff is one of the most sought-after violinists and most exciting musicians on the classical music scene. Concerts with him often become an existential experience for the interpreter and audience alike, old familiar works suddenly appear in a completely new light. In addition, he frequently turns his attention to forgotten masterpieces such as Joseph Joachim's Violin Concerto or the Violin Concerto No. 22 by Giovanni Battista Viotti, a contemporary of Mozart and Beethoven. To broaden his repertoire, he also commits himself to substantial new works, such as Jörg

Wildmann's Violin Concerto, which he premiered in 2013. With devotion he cultivates an unusually extensive repertoire and performs approximately 100 concerts every year.

In the 2023/24 season, Christian Tetzlaff appeared with the world's foremost orchestras. In Europe, he performed with the Norwegian Radio Orchestra, Symphonieorchester des Bayerischen Rundfunks and the Orchestre de chambre de Paris and Orchestre National de France, among others. He also appeared on stage with the most renowned English ensembles: with Philharmonia Orchestra Tetzlaff gave performances in Grafenegg and Hamburg's Elbphilharmonie, and with BBC Symphony Orchestra he appeared at the BBC Proms. He returned to the Chamber Orchestra of Europe, undertook two tours to Korea and Europe with the London Philharmonic Orchestra and recorded Thomas Adès's Violin Concerto with BBC Philharmonic. In the US, he returned to the Cincinnati Symphony Orchestra and Los Angeles Chamber Orchestra.

WILLIAM VANN

A multiple prize-winning and critically acclaimed choral, orchestral and opera conductor and song accompanist, William Vann is particularly renowned for his revival performances and recordings of vocal and choral music by British composers, including Edward Elgar. Born in Bedford, he was a Chorister at King's College, Cambridge and a Music Scholar at Bedford School. He subsequently read Law and took up a Choral Scholarship at Gonville and Caius College, Cambridge, where he was taught the piano by Peter Uppard, and studied piano accompaniment at the Royal Academy of Music with Malcolm Martineau and Colin Stone.

His extensive discography includes over twenty-five recordings for Albion, Champs Hill, Chandos, Delphian, Etcetera, Navona and SOMM with artists including Mary Bevan, Dame Sarah Connolly, Sarah Fox, Jack Liebeck, Nicky Spence, Kitty Whately, Roderick Williams, Britten Sinfonia and the London Mozart Players. His world premiere recording of Hubert Parry's *Prometheus Unbound* was awarded Gramophone Recording of the Month in October 2023 and subsequently shortlisted for a 2024 Gramophone Award.

He is an Associate of the RAM, a Trustee of the Ralph Vaughan Williams Society and Director of Music at the Royal Hospital, Chelsea. In 2024 he took up the role of Chorus Master at The Grange Festival, where he returns in 2025 for productions of *La Traviata* and *Die Fledermaus.*

IAN VENABLES

Ian Venables studied composition with Richard Arnell at Trinity College of Music, London and later with John Joubert, Andrew Downes and John Mayer at the Royal Birmingham Conservatoire. Described as 'Britain's greatest living composer of art song' (*Musical Opinion*) and 'a song composer as fine as Finzi and Gurney' (*BBC Music Magazine*), Venables has written over eighty works in this genre, including eleven song-cycles. Beyond the world of art-song he has written many chamber works that include a Piano Quintet Op. 27 and a String Quartet Op. 32, as well as smaller pieces for solo instruments and piano. His most recent large-scale choral work is a *Requiem*, which has been recorded by both Gloucester Cathedral Choir and Merton College Choir, Oxford, the latter in an orchestral version. Venables is President of the Arthur Bliss Society, a Vice-President of the Gloucester Music Society, Chairman of the Ivor Gurney Society and an Honorary Fellow of Exeter University. His music is published by Novello (Wise Music Group) and has been recorded on the Regent, SOMM, Signum, Naxos, Delphian and Albion labels.

RODERICK WILLLIAMS

Roderick Williams is one of the most sought after baritones of his generation with a wide repertoire spanning baroque to contemporary music. He enjoys relationships with all the major UK and European Opera Houses and performs regularly with leading conductors and orchestras throughout the UK, Europe, North America and Australia. Festival appearances include the BBC Proms, Edinburgh, Cheltenham, Aldeburgh and Melbourne.

As a recitalist he is in demand around the world and appears regularly at venues including the Wigmore Hall, Concertgebouw and Musikverein and at song festivals including Leeds Lieder, Oxford International Song and Ludlow English Song.

Roderick Williams was awarded an OBE in June 2017 and was Artist in Residence with the Royal Liverpool Philharmonic Orchestra from 2020 to 2022, Artist in Residence at the 2023 Aldeburgh Festival and Singer in Residence at Music in the Round. He was one of the featured soloists at the coronation of King Charles III in 2023. As a composer he has had works premiered at Wigmore Hall, the Barbican, the Purcell Room and on national radio. In 2016 he won Best Choral Composition at the British Composer Awards and from 2022/23 he holds the position of Composer in Association of the BBC Singers.

DEBBIE WISEMAN

One of the UK's most successful female music ambassadors, Debbie Wiseman is in demand as a composer and conductor. Her 200-plus film and television credits include *Wolf Hall, Wilde, Warriors, Judge John Deed, Tom & Viv, To Olivia, The Undeclared War* and *Father Brown.*

Her albums *Wolf Hall* (2015), *The Glorious Garden* (2018), *The Music of Kings and Queens* (2021, celebrating the 95th birthday of Queen Elizabeth II) and *Signature* (2023) all reached no. 1 in the UK Classical Chart. Debbie is Classic FM's Composer in Residence. She was voted the most popular living composer in Classic FM's Hall of Fame 2022. In October 2014, Debbie was Kirsty Young's guest on *Desert Island Discs.*

Debbie was one of 11 composers chosen to compose music for the Queen's Diamond Jubilee Pageant in 2012 and composed the Overture and Finale music for the Queen's 90th Birthday Celebration in 2016. In the 2018 Queen's Birthday Honours List, Debbie was awarded the OBE for services to music. She was the official composer and musical director of the Platinum Jubilee Celebration at Windsor in May 2022.

CATHERINE WYN-ROGERS

Catherine Wyn-Rogers has had a varied and international career as a mezzo-soprano since leaving the Royal College of Music. At first she worked mostly in oratorio and concert and then opera became a significant part of her professional life. She has appeared with all the major British opera companies, and overseas engagements have included working at La Scala, the Metropolitan, Paris Opéra, Madrid Teatro Real, and most frequently at the Staatsoper in Munich. She has been a soloist many times for the BBC Proms, including the Last Night in 1995. Conductors she has worked with include Bernard Haitink, Zubin Mehta, Sir Andrew Davis, Sir David Willcocks, Sir Charles Mackerras, Sir Mark Elder and Edward Gardner – she has been much associated with the works of Elgar in concert throughout her career as well as Handel's oratorios, most particularly with Harry Christophers and The Sixteen.

Benjamin Britten's operas have also figured largely in her repertoire, for example in *Peter Grimes* and the *Rape of Lucretia* (Bianca for ENO and Glyndebourne) and in many productions, most recently for Deborah Warner and Melly Still. She has also now made her maiden flight as Queen of the Fairies in *Iolanthe* for ENO. Catherine is a voice professor at the Royal Academy of Music and was made Hon RAM in 2018.

10. While Elgar was in Gloucester for the 1922 Three Choirs Festival he sat for the photographer Richard Hall, who produced four portraits of which this is one (see frontispiece).

Index

www.ingramcontent.com/pod-product-compliance
Lightning Source LLC
LaVergne TN
LVHW020503100826
845148LV00003B/690

* 9 7 8 1 8 3 7 6 5 3 5 2 2 *